STOWE

STOWE

The History of a Public School
1923–1989

BRIAN REES

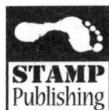

STAMP
Publishing

First published 2008
by Stamp Publishing
26 Colwell Road, London SE22 8QP

Typeset in Palatino by Colset Pte. Ltd., Singapore and by Richard Cook

Printed and bound in the UK by CPI Mackays, Chatham ME5 8TD

British Library Cataloguing in Publication Data
A catalogue record for this book is available from the British Library

ISBN 978-0-9544879-2-8

To the memory of Julia,
a Headmaster's Wife for all seasons

CONTENTS

PREFACE – 2008

This History of Stowe School was originally commissioned by the governing body for publication in 1991 to mark the Seventieth Anniversary (in 1993) of the School's Foundation. The point at which the narrative concludes is, in fact, 1989. Just before its appearance, publication was postponed and then, after a long interval and several years of uncertainty, cancelled. I am grateful to the present Governors and their Chairman, Christopher Honeyman Brown, for allowing me to publish the book on my own initiative, making it clear that all the views and judgements expressed in it are my own and not those of the School authorities.

The years from 1989 onwards must be material for future writers, either in the Centenary Year 2023 or another significant date, as it would be too unwieldy a task to try and attach further chapters written at a different time and pace from the original. Some of the final pages of Chapter 15 must, therefore, read rather strangely to present readers, but I have not rewritten or altered them. The years between 1923 and the 1990s do form a self-sufficient narrative. The efforts to establish a new Public School, and the extraordinary talents of J.F. Roxburgh in creating a unique educational institution, were followed by a major crisis, as well as problems that affected all schools in the Sixties and their aftermath. The stalwart labours of Bob Drayson to steer the school back into the march of progress and the commitment of Christopher Turner to 'Godliness and Good Learning' returned Stowe to its present position of one of the leading independent schools of the present day.

A further expression of thanks should be given to Roger Hudson and Kate Chenevix Trench, both then at John Murray, the original publishers, who gave immense help over the preparation of the original text. Many thanks also for all the work done on the present edition by my son Philip Rees (of Stamp Publishing), Anne Owen and Richard Cook.

PREFACE – 1991

The governing body of Stowe was keen that this History should be written by someone who did not have a lengthy acquaintance with or received opinions about the school, and that it should not be simply an enlarged version of a prospectus. They have made available without restriction all the archives and this book is based very largely upon their minutes, those of the finance committees, masters' meetings, tutors' committees and headmasters' reports, as well as the correspondence contained in the files of masters and Old Stoics. As a result there is an emphasis on those matters which preoccupied the school community from day to day; sometimes the problems and difficulties must seem to outweigh those familiar catalogues of success which everywhere form the staple of Speech Day addresses. Yet it is from these experiences that Stowe has derived its resilience and energy, has avoided those periods of complacency which affect many public schools and come to terms stage by stage with the needs and demands of the present.

Stowe was born in the age of the typewriter and the records are voluminous. In more recent years the paperwork generated by university admissions procedures, fuller student reports and the greater desire for contact with parents and Old Stoics have multiplied the filing cabinets in the ducal basements exceedingly. As we were aiming at the school's Seventieth Anniversary rather than its Centenary I have had to be selective. Long experience of school magazines has induced a certain suspicion of the encomiums found in official ones and a certain scepticism towards the cries of oppression which rise from student ephemerals. But thanks must be accorded to their many editors and contributors who have made this task so much easier and more entertaining.

There already exists an authoritative biography of J.F.Roxburgh by Noel Annan (assisted by Patrick Hunter) and, with no wish to challenge its conclusions, I have consciously tried to avoid a repetition of material and shown him rather in relation to events as they arose, reaching at the end a picture which I hope is not dissimilar. For general guidance I also owe a debt to Alasdair Macdonald's two Histories of the school.

The readiness of Stoics to enter into competitive events, local, national and even international, springs from the records from the outset. These range from the early successes of the O.T.C. in summer camp competitions (at a time when many contingents affected flippancy) down to modern contests such as the BBC's 'Young Scientist of the Year'. As a result of condensing the original typescript to bring it into manageable proportions there may be some who feel that the laurels have been unfairly distributed and I must ask the indulgence of those Old Stoics whose achievements have been pruned by economy or oversight. The aim has been to give a broad picture of immense diversity.

The tolerant friendliness for which Stowe is famed has been evident in discussion, correspondence, much of it lengthy, and hospitality. My thanks are due in particular to the headmaster, to Christopher Turner, Bob Drayson, Donald Crichton-Miller and the late Eric Reynolds; to former masters: Patrick Hunter, George Clarke, Muir Temple, Roger Rawcliffe, the Reverend 'Jos' Nicholl, Robin Totton, Joe Bain, Andrew Vinen, David Donaldson and Colin James (Bishop of Winchester); to present members of the Common Room: Charles Macdonald (second master), Jonathan Kreeger (housemaster of Temple), Chris Atkinson, James Larcombe (for permission to use the Grafton Annals), Andrew Rudolf, Michael Bevington (author of an invaluable guide to the house), Lionel Weston, Peter Farquar, Dr David James, Timothy Stunt, Tony Meredith (compiler of the Chatham Register 1925–85), David Barr (Community Service), Dr C.R. Brown, A. Waterworth and most particularly Brian Stephan, now Librarian who produced the MS of the Gilling-Lax History of Stowe and the recollections of Hugh Heckstall-Smith along with many other sources. Present masters will, I am sure, recognize that sweeping generalizations about their roles become harder as the present-day draws nearer and neither the General Certificate of Secondary Education nor the National Curriculum (in so far as it is adopted) are great friends to eccentricity or anecdote.

I have been greatly helped by a large number of Old Stoics including: Colonel Andrew Croft D.S.O., O.B.E., Sir David

Croom-Johnson, Lord Annan O.B.E., Lord Boyd-Carpenter P.C., D.L., Toby Robertson O.B.E., Julian Budden, Stephen Dodgson, Lord Quinton, Sir Hugh Dundas C.B.E., D.S.O., D.F.C., Nicholas Horden, Mrs R.A. Carnegie, Sir Nicholas Lyell Q.C., M.P. (Attorney General), Kenneth Henderson, John Buchanan M.B.E., D.L., A. Farnell-Watson, Lieutenant-Colonel I.C.S. Munro, Colin Graham, P.B. Lucas C.B.E., D.S.O., D.F.C., J.R. Kayll D.S.O., D.F.C., O.B.E., M. Colston, J.D. Thurn, P.D. Ward, A.G. Howland-Jackson, Sir Brooks Richards K.C.M.G., D.S.C., F.T. Gardiner D.F.C., Surgeon-Captain C.J.P. Pearson F.R.C.S., J.V. Bartlett C.B.E., Dr P. Wintersgill, R.R.G. Close-Smith, Professor R.A. Oliver, G.P. Allsebrook, Dr I.A. Roxburgh, T.L. Dewhurst M.C., Dr A.F. Weaver, Major-General Fergus Ling C.B., C.B.E., D.S.O., I. Earle, E.M. Arnold, M.E. Harding, J.W.A. Downing, George Melly, P.M. Ward, Reverend C. Lawson-Tancred, W.J.H. Graaf von Limburg, Ms Lilias Daly (Sister), J.W.A. Downing, R.A. Andrews, Reverend R.C.D. Brow, R.N. Harding, Major-General D.G. Levis C.B., O.B.E., D.L., Peter Lewis, E.B. Foster-Moore M.C., Major J.P. Robertson, J.W. Myers, (and the organizer of the 1940 Charity Fête whose name I have inadvertently obliterated!).

Mr Edward Judge sent a graphic account of the rescue of Eric Reynolds from the mountains of Skye and for further help on the Reynolds years I am indebted to: Mrs J. McRory, Archivist of Rugby School, Professor Cameron Watt, Will Inge, and Simon Francis. Martin Marriott, headmaster of Canford School, and Michael Rathbone's History of Canford School have assisted with details of the Reverend Percy Warrington's 'Empire' as has Dr R.G. Edrich of Wrekin College, and Mr A.J.B. Mussell, Archivist of the Legal and General. My daughter-in-law, Deborah Lawrenson, from a vantage point in Fleet Street was able to supply details of what was mysteriously wrapped up in various minutes as 'The Vandervell Case'. I must thank the staff of the Imperial War Museum and Canon Ian Savile of the Church Pastoral Aid Society, legatee of the Martyrs' Memorial Trust. At a crucial moment the bound editions of the *Buckingham Advertiser* went up in flames in a fire at the Public Library. Work on restoration and micro-filming of assorted copies was speedily accomplished thanks to Julian Hunt of the County Library (Local Studies). The Buckingham Town Library staff have been unfailingly helpful.

The smooth administrative path of the History owes a great deal to Paul Whitfield O.S., former Governor, and to Captain Peter Northey of Allied Schools. I have been very conscious of the encouragement received from many friends especially Dr David Newsome, former Master of Wellington College, Kenneth Rose, and Robin Macnaughten, former headmaster of Sherborne School. Stowe's present headmaster and Mrs Nichols, even in the midst of their busy schedules, have found time to share much of the interest and entertainment afforded by the whole enterprise as well as the cheerful atmosphere and hospitality of Kinloss. The clarity and condition of the records bear witness to the excellence of the headmaster's secretarial staff and the pleasure of working in such a picturesque environment, at a desk which looks out on a vista to the Corinthian Arch, brings to mind constantly how much is owed to the generations past and present who have created and now maintain such an impressive setting.

Brian Rees
Flore 1991

N

OBELISK

BRIDGE

BOURBON TOWER →

BOURBON FIELDS

GRECIAN VALLEY

HA-HA

HA-HA

COBHAM MONUMENT

TEMPLE OF CONCORD AND VICTORY

QUEEN'S TEMPLE

SPORTS PAVILION

GEORGE I

GYMNASIUM

WALPOLE COURT

SEASONS' FOUNTAIN

GOTHIC TEMPLE

CHAPEL COURT

GRENVILLE COLUMN

COOK'S MONUMENT

CHAPEL

SHOP

CHURCH

SHELL BRIDGE

NELSON'S WALK

CHATHAM HOUSE

HEADMASTER'S HOUSE

TEMPLE OF ANCIENT VIRTUE

TEMPLE OF BRITISH WORTHIES

PALLADIAN BRIDGE

LYTTELTON HOUSE

DORIC ARCH

TENNIS COURTS

ROTONDO

CONGREVE MONUMENT

LAKE

BOYCOTT PAVILIONS

GURNET'S WALK

OCTAGON

PEBBLE ALCOVE

QUEEN CAROLINE'S MONUMENT

CASCADE

TEMPLE OF FRIENDSHIP

OXFORD BRIDGE AND LODGE

(ROAD TO BUCKINGHAM AND BRACKLEY)

HA-HA

SAILING CLUB

ELEVEN-ACRE LAKE

LAKE PAVILIONS

HERMITAGE

BATHING PLACE

HA-HA

(DRIVE CLOSED)

TEMPLE OF VENUS

STOWE

SCALE

YARDS 0   440   880

CORINTHIAN ARCH

1

The Setting

The Temple and Grenville families, the original lordly occupants of Stowe, sought all the appurtenances of power as eagerly as power itself. When the Marquis of Chandos, the heir to Stowe, went to Aylesbury for the formalities of his election as a Member of Parliament during the Reform Bill crises of the 1830s, he displayed his political sympathies by sweeping into the town in a fleet of carriages, with postilions and outriders, like some visiting Tsar. Their chief dwelling mirrored their importance in successive administrations and when principle or pique drove them into political exile or disgrace, they would enlarge and embellish it as a signal of their return. Enriched by marriage to a succession of heiresses and by the fruits of office, during the eighteenth century they indulged in massive schemes of rebuilding sustained by the conviction that long years of domestic inconvenience would be recompensed by national authority and recognition.

Yet Stowe became more than a great house in a splendid park. The remorseless dynasty used it to impose rather than to follow fashion. In the aftermath of the civil disturbances of the seventeenth century they created a Classical paradise, a recreation in three dimensions of the scenes painted by Poussin, Claude and Dughet. Religion with its enervating enthusiasm was excluded and replaced by the more gracious ideals of Arcadian contentment. Armies of gardeners and workmen toiled to exalt the valleys and lower the hills; geometrical patterns of avenues, water courses and startling structures erased the rough landscape of the old rural setting. Later, when the Romantic view of nature began to stir men's thoughts, they destroyed their own creations in the same grandiose spirit as they had laid them out. Lakes and canals were released from their strict shapes, an artificial air of ruin was spread over what had been expensively erected.

It was inevitable that the illusion of omnipotence should dissolve. The creative spirit gave way to the collecting instinct: the later Grenvilles amassed books, treasures, royal guests, heraldic bearings and surnames. The last male scion of the ducal line was christened Richard Plantagenet Campbell Temple Nugent Brydges Chandos Grenville. When the extension of the franchise caused the close-knit family alliances which had dominated politics to give way to broader party alignments, the Grenville influence could not be maintained, even by the most profligate electioneering. The eventual outcome was a descent to poverty and unavailing attempts to keep house and estate together.

For the future history of Stowe the period of decline was as important as the period of splendour. The house escaped further conversion or hideous additions and remained throughout those busy and interfering Victorian decades an example of Palladian architecture at its highest. The effect of this upon the growth and development of Stowe School was of immense importance. Once the mansion was selected as the home of a new educational establishment it could never be a small experimental venture or a minor institution. Its ambitions had to match its surroundings and its appeal was to a clientele which did not affect to despise the outward vestiges of worldly success. Any governing body which succeeds to a dukedom is likely to find much in the inheritance to relish. The grounds of Stowe offered ample opportunities for sport and field pursuits. There was scope for training the artistic eye and settings ideal for outdoor theatre. Dignified staterooms were available for dining, assembling and the library. The chance to enjoy the more restrained pleasures of an eighteenth-century grandee seemed likely to attract an interesting staff. Urban centres of temptation were far off, curtained by hill and forest.

There were inherent dangers of course, which would present challenges during the school's history. The massive social changes of modern times were harder to understand from Stowe's sequestered glades. There was a danger that the inhabitants might feel that they were taking part in some pageant of the *ancien régime*. There were missing some of the elements which time and tradition had woven into the life of many great schools. The powerful religious and puritanical forces of Victorian days, the seriousness and the centrality of Chapel, were on the whole concepts alien to the Grenville mind. The free-thinking Lord Cobham hid the distasteful sight of Stowe Church behind thick planting which none of his successors thought fit to remove. The great South Front proclaimed the grandeur of the pre-Christian era as eloquently as the opening pages of Gibbon.

But on balance all this might be said to have brought benefits. Stowe looked out on the world. It was not built around cloisters and closed courts reminiscent of the monastic foundations. New species in its groves and plantations reflected the conquests of Chatham and the spread of empire. If there were no royal saints or bewhiskered divines looking down from portraits upon more modern generations, in the grounds there were temples to Friendship, Victory and the Ancient Virtues and, deeper than these in meaning, homage paid to natural beauty and those pagan intuitions which are older than history itself.

In Tudor times it was fashionable for the younger sons of wealthy sheep-farmers to engage in the wool trade and then return to invest their profits in land. Peter Temple, younger son of a family in Witney, Oxfordshire, followed such a course, acquiring the lease of Stowe, a manor which had belonged to the Church since Norman times, and its adjoining villages. As a sign that the Temple family had entered the ranks of the landed gentry he educated his son John at Lincoln's Inn in order to fit him for the duties of Justice of the Peace and Sheriff. Thomas Temple of the next generation benefited from the distribution of honours made by King James I and at a cost of £1095 joined the new order of Baronets, 35th on the precedence lists. He, too, had been to the Inns of Court, had been a Member of Parliament and High Sheriff in Buckinghamshire as well as Oxfordshire and Warwickshire. He had a large family, quarrelsome and litigious. His son, Sir Peter, who inherited the baronetcy in 1637, was party to a lawsuit with his daughter which lasted throughout the Civil War with a ferocity peculiarly its own. His second wife was Christine Leveson, a descendant of the Brookes of Cobham Hall in Kent. It was through her that the Cobham title, closely associated with Stowe, came into the family. Sir Peter's appointment as High Sheriff of the county proved an uncomfortable post. He was obliged to collect the Ship Money tax for the Council of King Charles I and may be accounted especially unfortunate in having John Hampden on the proposed list of contributors. Hampden's bust was later to grace the grounds among those in the Temple of 'Worthies', but he cannot have been a popular figure at Stowe in the time of Sir Peter, who fell into arrears and was held responsible by the Council for the shortfall. Either because of this treatment or because his gentry neighbours in the county were hostile to the King, he identified with the opposition in the Short and Long Parliaments and, when the Civil War began, commanded a regiment of horse in the Parliamentary Army. It proved a costly exercise. Bankruptcy ensued and at his death in 1653 creditors seized his property and the administration was granted to trustees.

His son, Sir Richard, succeeded to this dismal inheritance at the age of nineteen. He enjoyed some favour with Cromwell but as one whose ancestors had held shrievalties he could not stomach the rule of the Major-Generals. His political activities were always tortuous. Although he was too young to have been a Member of Parliament when Colonel Pride excluded those who opposed the rule of the Army in 1648, he managed to secure a place at Westminster along with the genuine survivors of Pride's Purge. Having greatly magnified the extent of his royalism in the recent past, he was permitted to attend Charles II at his Coronation and became a Knight of the Bath. To secure his election as MP for Buckingham he supplied the timber required to build a new Town Hall and was henceforward known as Sir 'Timber' Temple. The Town Hall, unfortunately, could only be built once. In subsequent contests it was the local ale-houses which profited from his methods of canvassing. His scepticism over the alleged Popish Plot cost him his seat in 1679 and, to recover it, even greater quantities of ale had to be poured down ardent protestant throats. Unlucky in his search for high office in government he nevertheless amassed sufficient capital through his marriage with an heiress, Mary Knapp of Oxford, to build a mansion at Stowe to replace the existing Elizabethan building. The farm lands were pushed further from the house and replaced by gently descending ornamental gardens.

The fourth baronet, also Sir Richard, was the first to enjoy national fame. His army career, most of it spent with Marlborough in the Netherlands and Germany, was distinguished. By 1710 he had reached the rank of Lieutenant-General. He placed his confidence in the Hanoverian Succession and was duly rewarded. King George I, whose statue has made him the British monarch most familiar to Stoics, if not to the rest of the world, sent Temple to Vienna to announce his succession to the Emperor and raised him to the peerage as Baron Cobham. In 1719 he led an expedition to Spain and wreaked some destruction upon the town of Vigo, but it was the last of his military ventures. As Sir Robert Walpole became the country's foremost statesman and pursued more peaceful policies, Cobham retired to the country and set about the reconstruction of his residence. It was the turn of the local environment to be disciplined. Stowe village was razed and the inhabitants moved to Dadford so that Lord Cobham's plans could proceed.

Cobham had married the daughter of a brewer in Southwark. Her wealth assisted him in his scheme to enlarge the simple rectangular structure he had inherited. The Ionic portico was raised on the North Front, the dormer windows of the third storey masked by a parapet and two large additional blocks built to east and west. In a later phase two pavilions were joined to the centre block by substantial galleries. To cater for the large establishment and for numerous guests, a dairy and stables were built and enclosed by semi-circular walls which followed the lines of the present colonnades. Guests included poets and writers such as Pope and Congreve who enthused on the growing wonders of house and gardens. Mrs Montagu, a bluestocking, who had a circle of wit and learning of her own, referred mordantly to Cobham's gatherings of men of letters and aspiring young politicians: 'It was frequented by chiefs out of War and statesmen out of place and celebrated by Poets, so the Mob supposed it was the favourite and chosen place of Virtue and Witt; alas! the Patriots went thither because they were angry and the Witts because they were hungry and the Master administered abundantly to the passions of the one and the appetites of the other.'

The design of the gardens seized Cobham's imagination even more than the house. Before the eighteenth century, English gardens, walled and sheltered, had a defensive quality. Now from the Dutch was borrowed the idea of introducing stretches of water as part of the landscape and from the French the use of the geometric line to point to the grandeur of the chatelain. English

adaptations of French ideas had a certain jollity which the gardens
of Versailles lacked. Sir John Vanbrugh, playwright and architect,
employed his talents as a dramatist to enhance his landscapes.
Surprises and sudden new vistas confronted the beholder, as twists
and turns in a plot might arrest the attention of the audience at a
play. One feature that is thought to have originated in France – the
substitution of ditches to replace walls as a means of protection –
became the new way to link the formal garden with meadow or
parkland. These cattle-proof trenches were known as ha-has to
denote the surprise strollers felt when coming unexpectedly upon
them. On the eastern side of the grounds William Kent softened
further the patterns imposed by mathematical forms. He used
water, no longer in circular basins and straight cascades, but in
meandering streams and irregular pools. Art was employed to
enhance rather than replace the shapes of nature, the grouping of
trees and the shadows of hills.

Few Englishmen had visited Greece at this time and the imagination dwelt upon vistas peopled by lovelorn shepherds and
decorated with temples and sculptures of the deities. The notion of
constructing temples to the gods was an irresistible exploitation of
the family name. Vanbrugh, Kent and Gibbs all contributed
edifices mostly in a neo-classical style and sometimes with didactic
purposes: the Temple of Ancient Virtue, for example, was matched
by a Temple of Modern Virtue, intended from the outset to be a
calamitous ruin and so a comment on the age of Walpole. Satire
set in stone cannot fail to be heavy and the mirth of Cobham's more
frequent guests must have lacked spontaneity.

He died in 1749. Alexander Pope had earlier assumed that his last
words would be a Prayer for his country. 'Oh Save my Country,
Heaven' was the phrase foretold and inscribed on the column Lord
Cobham had erected to himself. His actual demise, as related by
Hannah More in her memoirs was more prosaic: 'In his last
moments not being able to carry a glass of jelly to his mouth he was
in such a passion, feeling his own weakness, that he threw jelly,
glass and all into Lady Chatham's face and expired.' There are
many places of great beauty which owe their origins to hard men
and Stowe is no exception. Cobham was a bold man. In younger
days, even when he knew that his death would devolve Stowe
upon an unloved cousin, he sought out danger in battle. He
remembered old comrades. The Boycott Pavilions were intended

for a retired campaigner, though he died before they were ready for occupation. He knew a great deal more about the world than many around him. Later in the century, Lord Shelburne left a portrait which rings true: 'I have always understood him to have been an officer bred in the Queen's time, licentious, factious, and no speaker, but who passed his whole time in clapping young men on the back, keeping house with good economy and saying things at his table which nobody else would say in a private room; with a good degree of shrewdness, however, in his conversation as well as his conduct.'

His title passed to his second sister, Hester (the elder had put herself out of court by marrying a clergyman), and hence into the Grenville family. It was Hester who transmitted the Temple ambitions and talents into what had hitherto been a dynasty of unassertive country squires from Wotton near Aylesbury. Within a fortnight of his uncle's death and with a haste that shocked even that hardened veteran of political jobbery, the Duke of Newcastle, her eldest son, Richard, pressed for her to be given the rank of Countess. The Duke acquiesced but, to the unconcealed anger of the family would not bestow the territorial title of Countess of Buckingham. She became Countess Temple and Richard succeeded her as Earl Temple in 1752. She had five sons who had all been sent into Parliament as soon as they were of age. Other relatives were grouped around them and William Pitt the Elder, who married their sister, Hester, was a notable if wayward, adherent. There was nothing unusual in members of the landed class seeking to control the destiny of a country in which they had such great stakes. The Grenvilles were exceptional only in their close family ties – breaches of which were visited with ostracism and malice – and the birth rate which replenished their ranks. 'Within the space of fifty years,' declared Macaulay, 'three First Lords of the Treasury, three Secretaries of State, two Keepers of the Privy Seal and four First Lords of the Admiralty were appointed from among the sons and grandsons of the Countess Temple.' To this list could be added the Pitts and more distant dependents.

Wealth was sought as eagerly as the territorial title which had first eluded them. The profits of the places and posts they disposed of in office were enormous. Even infant members of the family were put forward for sinecures. Other dynasties rested occasionally in their pursuit of gain. The Grenvilles seemed to be constantly acquisitive and were often mightily hated. Lord Rosebery long afterwards described them as a 'political Company of Jesus' (Jesuits) and said of their effect upon politics: 'It is a singular story; there is nothing like it in the History of England; it resembles rather the persistent annals of the hive.'

Earl Temple's expectations had enabled him to marry Ann Chambers, daughter of a wealthy London merchant. They were ill-matched physically, she being short and he tall and ungainly (in satires he was referred to as 'Squire Gawky') but it was a happy union. Both shared a broad sense of humour and men from the local villages were summoned to regale Lady Temple with earthy tales and gossip. By contrast, the Earl's political life was marked by storms and ill-temper. As he controlled the Parliamentary votes which supported Pitt during the Seven Years War, King George II was forced to grant him the Garter, though on grounds of personal dislike he mightily wished to withhold it. At the investiture the King is said to have flung the Garter ribbon at its recipient in a rage. Political exile came to him as it had done to his uncle and he too used it to reconstruct what was now a veritable palace. When minor alterations failed to give a pleasing unity to the South Front he ordered a complete rebuilding of the whole façade. The design was a composite achievement based upon the ideas of Borra, his principal architect, Adam, from whom a design was obtained, Lord Camelford, a relative who had assisted with the plans for the Corinthian Arch, and Temple himself. The importance of the central block was emphasised by its extension and by the great portico. The pediment was to have been crowned by a statue of King William III in a triumphal chariot but the plan was abandoned. The tradition of sacrificing comfort to grandeur was instituted. The ceilings of the principal rooms were raised to accommodate large windows, thereby depriving the upper storey of both light and outlook. The façade was the dominant feature, the interior was governed by its forms and, as the staterooms swelled in numbers and dimensions, the occupants were gradually driven into small and ill-assorted suites without southern aspects. The house became the architectural climax to a vista, like the follies and temples in the park. To the north the two splendid colonnades were added. These diminished the uncomfortable impression of bulk which was now evident and made the whole edifice appear to lie comfortably and securely on the terrain.

The Earl also gave his attention to the gardens. The South Front demanded a wide and uncluttered approach, so the main sweep up to the Corinthian Arch was cleared and the avenue of trees south of the parterre felled. Elsewhere there was a further softening of the lines and patterns of former years. A Doric Arch was built to honour Princess Amelia, daughter of George II, and to frame a view across the valley known as the Elysian Fields. Horace Walpole, after whom Walpole House is named, was a frequent visitor and is fortunate to be thus honoured as he repaid the hospitality with unkind comment.

There was a gentler side to Temple. His only daughter died in infancy but he was generous and affectionate towards his nephew and heir, George Grenville, son of George III's minister of that name who attempted to tax the American colonies, and towards his bride, Lady Mary Nugent, whose name has also been given more recently to a girls' House. He would have liked to have had the couple with him at Stowe but decided regretfully that life with an elderly widower would dampen their high spirits too greatly. He was driving in the Stowe Ridings when he was thrown from his carriage and died as a result of the fall.

George Grenville, the second Earl, was the eldest of seven children. It is an interesting comment upon the continuity of British political life that his youngest sister was the grandmother of Mr Gladstone. Through his wife he inherited a fortune and the title of Earl Nugent in the Irish Peerage. He played an important role in the manoeuvring by which the coalition government of Charles James Fox and Lord North was brought down, for it was through Temple that George III made known his opposition to the government's India Bill and his disposition to refuse honours to anyone who supported it. For acting as the channel of these tidings Temple was rewarded with the Marquisate of Buckingham, the territorial title long coveted, though not the Dukedom which his uncle had sought to wrest from Pitt. The Marquis was not a learned man (he considered George III the wisest sovereign since Alfred) but he was a great collector of books. As Eton schoolboys he and his brother, Tom, had thrown their books into the Thames during one of the riots frequent in public schools at the time, yet both were to become passionate bibliophiles. In 1803 he began a collection of manuscripts and a special library was designed by Sir John Soane to house them. It was in a neo-Gothic style, certain details being copied from the Henry VII Chapel at Westminster. The manuscripts went eventually to the British Museum but the room remains as the headmaster's study, one of the most elegant and impressive in the land.

During the Napoleonic Wars Stowe was visited by the exiled Bourbon Princes. The chief interest of the future Louis XVIII was food, but the remote and unwieldy kitchens defeated even the French chefs who travelled in his train. The Prince Regent paid two visits. Critics opined that the quest for a dukedom lay behind the invitations. In 1805 the Prince was accompanied by his brother the Duke of Clarence, who stayed in the suite named after him. This was the year of Trafalgar and Austerlitz, when Europe was being torn apart, but there was no austerity evident at Stowe. Ten thousand people gathered to watch the entertainments and fireworks. The Prince led off the dancing at the ball given in his honour but succeeded in spraining his knee after a few stately paces and retired.

The elder son of the Marquis, also Richard, represented the county in Parliament from the age of twenty-one until he succeeded to the Lords. While barely thirty he was made Deputy President of the Board of Trade, Joint Paymaster-General and a Privy Councillor by his uncle who was Head of the Ministry at the time. In 1813, when the government authorized the local militia to serve abroad, he raised a battalion to join Wellington who had been a great favourite of his father. He arrived in France to learn that Napoleon had abdicated and his own services were not required, but he turned his visit to commodity by bringing back large quantities of claret, scarce since the outbreak of the wars, to the cellars of Stowe. In 1796 he had married the daughter and heiress of the last Duke of Chandos and had the names of Brydges and Chandos added to his own. There is not space to recount the history of this preposterous family but it may be noted that the Second Duke of Chandos had married Lady Mary Bruce, who thus contributed a very acceptable and traditional house name to the Stowe School Lists. She also brought the Barony of Kinloss, after which the headmaster's house is named and, as she was descended from the younger sister of Henry VIII (Mary, Duchess of Suffolk), this rather tenuous link allowed Plantagenet to be added to the family surnames, which now extended like one of the estate's great avenues.

The last Duchess of Chandos had a penchant for practical jokes but unfortunately her brand of humour put an end to the ducal line, for she pulled aside her husband's chair as he was about to sit down and he died from the fall. She, poor lady, lost her reason as a result of this mishap but the vacancy which it occasioned added weight to the Grenville case for promotion and the Second Marquis enjoyed the triumph which had eluded his forbears: in 1822 he attained the dukedom, part of the price paid by the government of Lord Liverpool which required the votes of the Grenvillites when changing course in the post-war period. Ironically, the moment which saw the capture of the commanding heights of society marked the beginning of the family's rapid decline. The new Duke of Buckingham and Chandos had many talents but he was corpulent, afflicted with gout and melancholia. Thwarted in his wish to be Governor-General of India, he spent long months sailing on his yacht in the Mediterranean, buying pieces of art and merchandise which were despatched to the silent halls at Stowe. Eventually he returned to become Steward of the Household to William IV. He was flattered by this Court appointment and was an active perspiring figure on ceremonial occasions.

The second Duke hastened on the advance of ruin. He achieved some fame through the 'Chandos Clause' in the Great Reform Bill of 1832, which included in the franchise the £50 tenants over whom the landed magnates like himself still had some sway. His own election campaigns were some of the most ostentatious ever witnessed. Receptions were held for countless gentry and mock naval battles fought on the lakes. He succeeded to the dukedom in 1839 but continued to encumber the estate with debt. The visit of the young Queen Victoria and Prince Albert in 1845 was marked by a further enlarging of the staterooms while the family was pushed ever deeper into far recesses. The bailiffs were already in evidence, though it is said that they sportingly agreed to wear footmens' livery during the junketings. Two years later, more conventionally attired, they took possession of the property. The Duke had invested heavily in land which lost value after the Repeal of the Corn Laws. He alienated the Court, which he had so expensively entertained, by the publication of family papers. Though these were edited with some discretion and sound comment, the impression was given that they revealed scandals in high places during previous reigns, and he was excluded from the Garter ceremonies (he attended but was not invited to dine) which accompanied the visit of Napoleon III of France to Windsor. He was divorced by his wife, Lady Mary Campbell, and quarrelled with his blameless and hard-working son. He died in 1861 in the Great Western Hotel, Paddington. Even that resting-place was chosen as an insult to his son, who was Chairman of the London and North Western Company. Yet he had a claim on posterity for having recognized the talents of the young Disraeli and assisted him on the road towards imperial visions. Old retainers on the estate whispered a macabre tale that a few of their number had, one dark night, been summoned by the Duke, who appeared from nowhere, to descend with lighted torches to the vaults where the coffin of a dead Duchess had been ripped open and the jewels snatched from her corpse, the witnesses being sworn to secrecy.

The third Duke lived a useful life of public service. As Governor of Madras he won high praise for his efforts during two great famines. He paid off a proportion of the family debts, though the family never regained its commanding position in social and political life. He had no male heirs. On his death titles went to other branches of the Grenville and Lyttelton families and only the Barony of Kinloss was left to his eldest daughter.

For a time Stowe was leased to the Comte de Paris, claimant to the French throne. So many French visitors came to pay court that Buckingham Station had the essential notices up in both languages. When the school opened and the old servant families provided recruits for the domestic staff, it was remarked upon by sharp intelligences in the Common Room that several seemed to have the pronounced features of the Bourbons: certainly the Count was a popular figure in the town where he spent freely. At his death, in 1894, he lay in state in the Marble Hall but his son did not renew the lease of the house.

The First World War increased the costs of maintenance beyond anything that Lady Kinloss could afford. Her eldest son, Captain Richard Morgan-Grenville, was twice Mentioned in Despatches for gallantry. Private Butler of the Rifle Brigade gave an account of his death in 1915 leading his platoon against the German lines to assist a beleaguered detachment:

He was, as usual, full of life and determination. We leapt over the first trench which was filled with dead and wounded Germans and it was when we were going to the second trench that both officers were killed. Captain Morgan-Grenville was hit in the head by a bullet and died immediately. I cannot tell you how we felt seeing him lying dead there. There was not a man in the platoon who would not have given his own life for their beloved Captain. A deep grave was dug in the wood close by and his body reverently placed in it. We also placed a mound over and round it for protection and erected a wooden cross at its head with the name 'Captain Morgan-Grenville' and the date of his death.

The dynasty ended in what seemed to be the eternal theatre of European war, not far from other blood-soaked fields where Cobham had won his spurs. The brother who succeeded as Master of Kinloss was in Holy Orders and had no resources to revive the estate. The farms were sold off piecemeal. Nature invaded the ornamental grounds. The home of the family, once the richest in the land, became a gloomy mausoleum, the gilded salons silent and the monumental fabric a source of despair.

2

The Founders

As revolution and economic chaos swept over large areas of post-war Europe, there emerged in Britain a peculiarly local problem that would not even have been comprehended across the Channel: entry to the public schools. Beneath the soil of Northern France, among the hosts of casualties, lay thousands of ex-public-school officers. Of the fathers among them many had not even seen their sons and certainly had had no opportunity to plan their education. The survivors had snatched periods of leave that were too short and precious to be spent in travelling from school to school.

The systematic entering of sons on admission lists had been disrupted, and other factors added to the sudden demand for places. The population of Great Britain had increased vastly during the previous century but no major public school had been founded for around sixty years. A new class of professional people had arisen who thought that, with sacrifice, a superior education for their children could be within their grasp. Many reflected that, in the coming years, the spread of popular democracy would make competition harder. Pressure on the renowned schools was great and many parents discovered to their dismay that their Alma Mater was unable to extend a welcoming arm in their direction. They could have chosen less famous establishments but the gap in prestige between major and minor schools was a profound one.[1]

[1] 'I say, you cast your net pretty wide, don't you?' said the seventh Duke of Wellington loftily, as late as the 1970s, as he mounted the staircase of the Public Schools' Club in Piccadilly with Frank Fisher, Chairman of the Headmasters' Conference, and observed the numerous heraldic shields of dozens of minor institutions.

The ancient grammar schools could not readily assist. Many, as a result of the 1902 Education Act, enjoyed a strong local and competitive entry and, set in cities, they lacked the space for certain of the sacrosanct sports.

As a result, the major schools in 1919–20 had long waiting lists. Headmasters of preparatory schools, accustomed to unlocking closed doors with a few magic words, came under intense pressure. Boys of high ability could still obtain entry but the old-style testimonial, which could extol little but a likeable character, no longer served as a guaranteed visa for acceptance.

Fortunately, these men had a means of sharing their troubles. In 1893, a small number had formed an association on the model of the Headmasters' Conference. By 1920, it was established and incorporated as the Independent Association of Preparatory Schools, had a membership of 600 and was divided into twelve branches. The Secretary of the influential London branch was Edward Henry Montauban, headmaster of The Hall, Hampstead. He was a creative man who enjoyed the setting up of schools. He had had to build up numbers at The Hall as his predecessor had taken away almost half the strength to his new establishment. Montauban added a pre-prep school and a girls' school, Selwyn House, where he taught carpentry, and constructed with his own hands a pool in which he taught swimming. He was imaginative and well ahead of his time; he extended entrance to the physically and even the mentally handicapped, encouraging them to participate in as many activities as possible. He periodically made attempts to move out some of his pupils to a boarding establishment at a house in Caversham, Reading. It was Montauban who first conceived the idea of establishing a new public school which, from the first, would be in the top rank and display sufficient distinction to satisfy the educational and social aspirations of the most demanding parents.

He promoted this novel plan energetically through the London branch of the I.A.P.S. and among his own parents. It was significant for the history of Stowe that the early discussions on the character of a new foundation took place in Hampstead where, one assumes, the shade of Dr Arnold did not rise above criticism. From the beginning there was a firm belief that a new school could shed the spartan harshness and the subservience to tradition which marked so many of the older places. There were many sceptics who thought that the financial problems of the day would render

Montauban's scheme impossible but, such was his enthusiasm that in December 1920, he persuaded the Council of the I.A.P.S. to establish a committee to examine the practicalities; within months his inspiration had become a crusade.

Most importantly he found a place that would house a school of the quality he had in mind. In the summer of 1921, the Master of Kinloss and his mother ordered the last of the great sales at Stowe and the mansion itself was put under the auctioneer's hammer. Four thousand lots were advertised in a catalogue of 230 pages. Montauban took a party of friends down for a pre-sale inspection. They picnicked in the State Dining Room (noting that the table was more or less the length of a cricket pitch) and departed with a firm conviction that they had found the ideal premises and the challenge they had sought.

For three weeks the sale proceeded amid great excitement. Buyers of statues struggled through the undergrowth to locate their purchases, a local alderman slipped in the Marble Salon and crashed into a glass case of *objets d'art*. It was rumoured that 'rings' of dealers met in the pubs of Brackley. The mansion and 1400 acres were due for disposal on 4 July. Montauban had received promises to the extent of £3000 and, thus fortified, he took his place in a crowd of about 200 ranged in seats across the lawn. Many were obviously bidders for farms and outlying properties and he calculated, his mind swimming with figures, that he could bid up to £30,000 if the property should be offered as a whole. He would have 10 per cent for the deposit and might have looked for £15,000 from the sale of farmland. He would be left with £12,000 still to find for completion of sale, but he decided to take the risk. In his later years he was still able to recall the beating of his heart as the auctioneer went through the preliminary exhortation. This ended with the words: 'I have been offered £50,000 for the property as a whole. Any advance on that?' Visions of mounting tension as the bidding rose were swept away. 'Gone', declared the auctioneer. 'The purchaser is Mr Harry Shaw.'

Harry Shaw was a man of mystery. A native of Newcastle and an engineer concerned at one time with projects in Afghanistan, he had been employed during the war at the Ministry of Munitions though he also conducted business from his homes in Wilton Place and an estate near Newbury. When the press reported this to be of 2000 acres he replied with some irritation that it was nearer three times the size. In August 1921, he was vehemently attacked in the *Morning Post* by the Duke of Northumberland as the channel through which baronetcies were being offered for the sum of £40,000. At one time he asserted that he hoped to persuade his rich friends to give Stowe to the nation, though nothing definite was ever settled and there were rumours that, until the house was re-sold, his purchase was never completed. Montauban did not intend that his plan should be set aside without a struggle. He made contact with Shaw and was invited to spend an evening at Newbury where, amid a degree of luxury he found overwhelming, he persuaded the tycoon to make an offer of Stowe to the I.A.P.S. committee. Mr Shaw would give the house and 28 acres as a gift, if the I.A.P.S. could speedily find £200,000 for conversion and endowment, plus £25,000 for the necessary equipment.

Within a few weeks Montauban had prepared a scheme by which, in return for rights of nomination, I.A.P.S. schools would make gifts ranging from £50 to £150. He took and furnished Brookfield, a house in Buckingham, from which he could conduct headmasters and prospective parents over the property. The Croom-Johnsons, parents at The Hall, were invited to one such foray. David Croom-Johnson, one of the sons, remembered the white-bearded caretaker, Mr North, leading the party through 'secret' doors in the tapestries and down to the solitary bathroom, a subterranean cell of slate, installed for the Comte de Paris.

By December 1921, a report on suitability for school use had been prepared by an architect, Maxwell Ayrton. It revealed many problems: the North Front and the roofs needed much repair, battered and missing trees made the avenues unsightly, the Grecian Valley was overrun by black-and-white Belgian hares and the single bathroom had the additional handicap of needing to be filled by hand. The sole water supply came from drainage on the copper roof of the Oval Hall. Despite all these and many other hazards he considered that the building could be adapted for 150 boys and staff and that, as numbers increased and funds became available, purpose-built teaching rooms would release space for larger numbers of boarders.

Such was the impetus of the project that, even in the precious days of rest between Christmas and New Year, the Preparatory Schools met in a special conference to appoint a further committee to push the plan forward. Support came from another quarter on the last day of 1921 when a report from committee on the teaching of Classics stressed the need nationally for more institutions based upon the principles of the great schools where classical learning was honoured and dominated the timetable.

There arose at the same time a strong tide of opposition. On 17 January 1922, *The Times*, in a leading article, made the project a matter of public contention. It claimed to voice a national concern because a public school education was inevitably 'the ambition of the wealthiest and most influential portion of the community'. It stressed the high costs: 'If it is destined only to struggle for existence, it will not provide the type of education expected from it and it will be in consequence a waste of money and energy. If, on the other hand, it succeeds, it would be equally regrettable if it succeeded at the expense of similar schools already in existence: for in that case its foundation would be otiose and equally a source of unjustifiable expense.' *The Times* pointed to the elaborate needs of a new school, which were different from the hugger-mugger classes and primitive conditions of previous centuries. It averred that several smaller schools did have difficulty in filling places; it raised the spectre of ever-rising fees and pleaded for the development of small schools which might then take on a new character, as Rugby and Shrewsbury had done. Its apprehensive conclusion hinted that, if the venture failed, the whole public school system, already subject to periodic attacks, would be brought into ridicule (the system, of course, which provided the bulk of the paper's readership – the amount of space devoted in *The Times* to house football matches, Speech Days and addresses conventional to the point of petrifaction was very great). 'To this extent, therefore, a real public interest lies in the proposal to turn Stowe into a public school; for money is money wherever it is and to whomsoever it belongs, and a mistaken use of it by private persons for a laudable public purpose would be more than a private error of judgement: it would be, in a true sense, a public loss.'

The Hall parent, Mrs Croom-Johnson, replied on the following day. She challenged the author to find a place for a boy of nine at any of the major schools. She accepted that money was scarce but praised the instinct which motivated the professional classes who made sacrifices in the interests of their children's education. She pointed out correctly that money despatched to existing minor schools would not have to go just into facilities and equipment but into accommodation since it was the shortage of actual places which had produced the crisis and this could be remedied more easily in a new setting than an old one. Furthermore, she foresaw that, in the hands of an imaginative headmaster, Stowe might establish certain traditions which would be better than those stifling the progress of even some of the greatest of the old foundations. 'It may lack some of the things that they possess; on the other hand there is a great chance that starting unhampered it may provide some of the things that they lack; and it is largely for this reason that the project has been greeted with so much enthusiasm in private from so many quarters.'

Montauban was meanwhile canvassing his Association and he organized a public meeting in Hampstead Town Hall, presided over by the Mayor, to draw up a formal proposal which was cast in the parlance of the time. Stowe, he declared would not be a 'private, sectarian or a fad school' and his scheme for nomination by headmasters would prevent it from becoming 'the refuge of rotters, rejects, or the superannuated'. The I.A.P.S. he said, did not seek to run a school but to launch one: 'To do this is, I maintain, our business, seeing that the thing is wanted and that nobody else will take the initial step.' He suggested an Appeal and, as headmasters of the time had not, as they have done since, joined the ranks of the Mendicant Orders, he tactfully offered some help: 'In case there are some headmasters who dislike the idea of themselves making an Appeal, the Sub-Committee have prepared a quantity of leaflets (specimen enclosed) which might perhaps be used for the purpose.' In April 1922, he gathered together a 'Provisional Committee for Stowe' consisting of parents, I.A.P.S. personnel, the headmasters of Westminster, Oundle, Charterhouse, and Dr A.A. David, Bishop of St Edmundsbury and Ipswich, who had been headmaster of Clifton and Rugby. Mr, later the Hon. Mr Justice Croom-Johnson K.C., MP, was Chairman.

Before this august body could meet, its intentions again came under attack in *The Times*. Dr Edward Lyttelton commanded notice, not only as a former headmaster of Eton (and a cricketing hero – the only man to score a century against Australia in the tour of 1878) but as a member of the family so closely associated with Stowe's past. He considered that the exercise might well prove 'a flagitious waste'. Assuming that the financial situation nationally would continue at a low ebb, the country would be left with one major school too many. Other schools shorn of the valuable 'marginal boys' would be forced to run at a loss, resulting in 'less efficiency, prolonged anxiety, failure among boys of belief in their respective schools (a most serious matter) and waste of staff, equipment and premises'. Edward had the Lyttelton gift of phrase. Remarking that the unostentatious expansion of cathedral schools would 'not catch the popular imagination so well as the more dazzling re-creation of the Stowe mansion', he suggested a board might be set up to look at his plan for expanding smaller establishments 'to be formed of half-a-dozen patriots who understand education – if there are as many'.

Montauban, in his reply, pointed to the presence of distinguished headmasters on his committee, reflected that the assumption of ever-increasing poverty in the nation would dampen the very spirit needful for prosperity and called for support from philanthropists whose hearts might be stirred by seeing a bold plan encompassed about by enemies. 'Can we expect to turn out men of enterprise and courage if the schools of England are to be afraid of a new competitor, and if no new venture is to be attempted unless success is guaranteed beforehand?'

The *Times* debate expanded in all directions. Some headmasters took the opportunity to put their own schools forward as candidates for extra endowments. Others wrote in to say that their own academies were thriving but they knew that others were not. A statement that Old Etonians experienced no problems with last-minute entries constrained Dr Alington, the headmaster, to warn readers that a certain amount of foresight was still desirable. Eventually the correspondence veered off tangentially into a long tussle over the question of school food and culminated in a massive advertisement by the manufacturers of Virol, a patent health food, addressed to parents who considered that their children might be under-nourished.

Throughout the war of words the provisional committee continued to meet with Montauban as Secretary. It was agreed that there was no purpose for which the building was suitable except as a school. An opening with one hundred pupils was envisaged. Yet the task of raising funds was hampered by continuing doubts over matters such as the curriculum and the likely ethos of the new establishment. Questions over which code of football would be followed appeared above the horizon (Donald Crichton-Miller, later headmaster, recalled that, as a schoolboy, he had been horrified to hear rumours that Stowe might embrace Association Football). Mr Harry Shaw was unable to wait while delicate issues such as the role of the Classics were discussed. In the summer of 1921 he had granted a two-month reprieve – insofar as he had now taken no action for several months, he had shown benevolence. But he could not wait for ever and in July 1922, he put the property back on the market once again. The *Daily Telegraph* of 11 July reported the collapse of Montauban's hopes. The times were hard and, although one gentleman from the City had shown an interest in founding a second Oundle and then demurred, no other serious benefactors had been found. 'Various schemes for its use', said the *Telegraph* '– there was for a time the hope of starting a new public school there – have fallen through and, while it is a matter for regret, it is reasonable to suppose that "the fair majestic paradise of Stowe" will shortly share the fate that has befallen so many of England's stately homes – complete dismantlement.' Montauban told the press in September that all negotiations had fallen through and there were no plans to purchase. Fresh catalogues were printed. It was clear that everything that could be carried away would be stripped from the fabric. The sale was advertised for 11 October 1922. It was a matter of days before the demolition men moved in and began their irreversible work.

Then, like the trumpet call in *Fidelio*, or the bugles of the U.S. 7th Cavalry as it thunders to the rescue across the plains, came the possibility of an eleventh-hour reprieve. Where the distinguished headmasters and the provisional committee had failed, an almost unknown West Country clergyman took command of the situation. The Reverend Percy Warrington, Vicar of Monkton Combe near Bath, happened to meet a parishioner who told him that Stowe was for sale. He replied that that must be a mistake as he was reliably informed that the Preparatory Schools were buying it. The parishioner persisted, adding that the house seemed likely to fall into the hands of the breakers and that his information came from that morning's *Times*. Warrington asked the time. It was 6 p.m. The village mail left at 7 p.m. and carried with it a letter from the vicar offering to buy Stowe and turn it into a public school. Four days later he was standing in the North Hall and, within a few days of his visit, a plan to acquire the house had been evolved.

The story of Percy Warrington is one of the sagas of British education. He was the greatest founder of schools this century; twelve were created or re-created under his aegis in addition to St Peter's Hall, an Oxford college. Yet for many years a silence hung over his participation in their foundation. He was the son of a Derbyshire tenant-farmer and as a lad of fifteen left school and started working on the land. His abilities impressed a local clergyman who enabled him to gain admittance to Hatfield College, Durham. At the age of twenty he was fired by a vision of a strong Protestant evangelical movement that would drive back the Anglo-Catholic advances in parishes and, through the High-Church Woodard Corporation, in schools. While still under thirty he acquired the living of Monkton Combe, which he held for forty-three years. In 1934 he told a reporter from *The Times* that he had travelled 50,000 miles a year for over a decade, had provided direct employment for over 1,000 people and indirect employment for an infinitely greater number.

There already existed a body which shared his aims, the Church of England Trust, founded before the First World War. He became Secretary and greatly extended its activities under the name of the Martyrs' Memorial Trust, which invoked memories of the fires of Smithfield and those who had died for the Protestant faith. Warrington, who possessed ferocious energy and enormous confidence, set to work to emulate Anglo-Catholic traditions: the buying up of advowsons and the founding of schools and seminaries. Although a ruthless and none-too-scrupulous man, he acted upon impulse rather than calculation. His decision to acquire Stowe was taken within the hour. He turned aside to see Canford while on his way to view another possible venue. He heard of Westonbirt purely because he was late for a wedding and chanced to meet an acquaintance who told him it was on the market. Wellington School in Shropshire was brought to his attention by a clerical friend in the area. It was the first province of his empire, a proprietary school owned by a businessman, Sir John Bayley. Warrington busily arranged a series of mortgages without consulting his trustees and turned it into Wrekin College. 'If I had had a committee to dog my steps you may take it from me that there would have been no Stowe, Canford or Westonbirt today,' he once declared. 'I did the work, got the schools going and formed the committees afterwards.'

In the *Evening Standard* of 29 September 1922 two weeks before the sale was due, Sir Archibald Boyd-Carpenter MP confirmed that Stowe House had been purchased by a committee of which he was a member and that it was the intention to found a new public school 'on the lines of Eton and Harrow'. The price was said to be £30,000. Stowe had not been a rewarding speculation for Mr Shaw, a point symbolized by the early death of his prized racehorse, 'Stowe, son of Cicero', shortly after the school was founded. But there were still items that could be torn out and sold off. Lord Gisborough, Chairman of the Martyrs' Memorial Trust, wrote to *The Times* calling on men of goodwill to buy some of the remaining treasures and present them to the new school, thereby earning for themselves the honorary title of 'Founder'. Lord Gisborough had served in the Afghan and South African Wars and, for a time, in Parliament. He owed his title less to his own political skills than to those of his brother Walter Long, and his large estates in North Yorkshire to a fortunate bequest from a maternal uncle and a change of name. He was the first Chairman of Stowe Council, faint yet pursuing in the wake of Warrington's financial manoeuvres.

A Mr Lytton, otherwise unknown, sought to be a Founder by purchasing the reliefs of *Darius and Alexander* by Christophe Veyrier and *Caractacus and Claudius* by Thomas Banks which remain in the Entrance Hall. Warrington himself, against bidding opposition, bought the *Battle of Bosworth*, a late sixteenth-century relief by an unknown hand originally at Castle Hedingham, which for some curious reason had greatly appealed to King Edward VII, for 420 guineas. (It had cost Shaw 1000 guineas in the previous sale.) Shaw personally made a gift of the panelling in the private chapel; the leaden lions were knocked down to Blackpool Corporation. Clough Williams-Ellis, architect and Welsh landowner, had the foresight to buy the Grand Avenue linking Stowe to Buckingham for £1,425, which might otherwise have been taken for building land. The *Observer* expressed the hope that local landowners would soon relieve him of this burden. There were no funds available for any further acquisitions.

Stowe had, in fact, been bought on resources made available from Wrekin College, which was a sound property already in operation as a school. The college had the right to nominate six members to the Council and to be permanently in a majority of two. In 1925 Canford gained the right to nominate six members. In effect this meant that the Martyrs' Memorial Trust governed the school. Montauban was included in the Council and Bishop David, soon to be translated to Liverpool, who had served on the Preparatory Schools committee.

Various pronouncements came forth in the following weeks concerning the nature of the new establishment. There would be space for 500 pupils though it would begin with half that number. The fees would be less than Eton or Harrow (over £250 p.a.) or Rugby (£200 p.a.) and probably somewhere between £150 and £200. The wicked old system of housemasters buying their houses and then profiting from them would be eschewed and this would open the doors to housemasters of wider abilities. The headmaster would have the power to choose his own staff, a luxury by no means universal at the time. In January 1923, a company was formed to 'establish schools in accordance with the Protestant principles of the Church of England, for boys of classes above those ordinarily attending public elementary schools'. The social, if not the religious, distinction was reinforced by an edict warning that all future trespassers in the grounds would be prosecuted. Warrington, simultaneously involved in setting up Canford, informed the press that applications were 'pouring in'.

It was important to raise income quickly and events moved swiftly. In December 1922, it had been announced that Mr J.F. Roxburgh, a housemaster at Lancing College, had been appointed as headmaster-elect. At a Speech Day in 1928 Sir Charles King-Harman, Vice-Chairman, recalled that of fifty candidates twenty-six had been seriously considered and referred to the five 'finalists': a Fellow of Balliol, two Rugby masters and an applicant from Tonbridge (as well as Roxburgh). Lancing was the flagship of the High-Church Woodard Corporation, whose machinations Warrington was out to destroy. The Council deliberated for four hours. It was said that Warrington endeavoured to mobilize the votes of the absent members to prevent Roxburgh's appointment but King-Harman, a forceful Victorian who had governed Sierra Leone and Cyprus in his time, brought down his pro-consular weight on Roxburgh's behalf; he was supported by Sir Archibald Boyd-Carpenter. A correspondent wrote to the *Buckingham Advertiser* of the chosen candidate: 'He has a good presence and great charm of manner and is an accomplished speaker. Not being himself an athlete (beyond being a mild average golfer) he encourages athletics in his boys. His house is reputed to hold most of the cups at Lancing.'

The tradition of married clergy has hugely affected social life in Protestant countries. John Fergusson Roxburgh was descended from the Manse. His grandfather had departed from the main body of the Scottish Church in 1843 with the severe group known as the 'Wee Frees'. John's father worked for some years in commerce in South America but had re-settled in England before his second son was born. In 1901, the boy followed his elder brother, Archie, to Charterhouse. His house, Lockites, continues, though the gloomy barrack-block in which it was housed has gone. To grow up in an evidently imperfect school is a good form of training for a future headmaster and Charterhouse under Dr Gerald Rendall had many imperfections. We can see in Roxburgh's conception of a headmaster's role a reaction to them. Rendall was a university don, learned, conscientious, and a good administrator, but he had little experience of the young. He mounted the words of Marcus Aurelius, in Greek, 'Live always on the mountain tops', over his fireplace and, as one of his successors remarked, 'he lived there a great deal more than most of us'. Boys toiling over classical impositions on sunny summer afternoons were wont to be congratulated for their preference for study over sport as he passed dreamily by. He is said to have begun an address to a Godalming Working Men's Guild with the words, 'When you come to open your Euripides . . .' Discipline was ineffective. Ability at games, at which Roxburgh – tall and uncoordinated – did not excel, determined status within the school hierarchy and the 'bloods' enforced a harsh regime of pointless regulation on the everyday traffic of school life. The strongest housemasters ruled independent palatinates and the differences in the quality of life enjoyed in different houses was marked.

Many years later, to a Stowe parent who feared that Cobham under D.I. Brown might be too 'gamesy' a house, Roxburgh wrote that several unathletic boys had thrived there and added, 'I was always hopeless at games myself and was in a very athletic sort of school.' When the ex-Stowe master, J.T. Hankinson, published some successful books on sports coaching he congratulated him with the words: 'Everything I hear from you and of you makes me think how foolish it is of anybody to become a schoolmaster who is not good at games. This is a deficiency which has handicapped me from the start.' Roxburgh was never hostile towards the games fraternity. On the contrary, he cultivated a persona which was to draw from star schoolboy games players the admiration which had been witheld in the important years of his youth.

One other experience must have impressed him. As a very junior boy he would have witnessed the triumphant visit to Charterhouse of Baden-Powell to lay the foundation stone of the South African Cloisters, a memorial to those Carthusians who had died in the Boer War, and heard his message:

> Every beholder of it cannot but remember what his duty should be in every walk of life – I am not talking only of soldiers now, but of every walk of life – It should be his aim and ambition to forget himself in benefiting others, to try and help them in every way as he goes through life. The highest principle you can follow is the great Christian principle of sacrificing yourself for others.

Charterhouse had some exceptionally able teachers. T.E. Page, into whose orbit Roxburgh moved, was one of the great classical scholars of his time and was able also to impart a love of the well-turned phrase and the *mot juste*. Roxburgh gained several prizes for English Literature, which it was ever his policy to make the corner-stone of the Stowe curriculum. He won an exhibition in Classics to Trinity College, Cambridge, and, since he found there a freedom from conformity of dress and opinion which he had not enjoyed at school, the college unlocked a great tide of institutional loyalty which he would have begrudged Charterhouse. He guided large numbers of pupils there and at the time of his retirement in 1949, Stoics constituted almost one tenth of Trinity's large under-graduate population.

There must have been much at Cambridge to lure him into seeking permanent residence. The Scottish work ethic, however, was strong in him. His father had died when he was still at Charter-house and there were family reasons for seeking employment in the world beyond. He gained a First, though not one of the highest listings, and gave an indication of the strength of his ambitions by enrolling at the Sorbonne for one year to add Modern Languages to the qualifications he already possessed. He did remarkably well in the French Language and Literature papers for the 'Licence-ès-Lettres' and came second in the French Essay, a *tour de force* for a foreigner.

The formative process did not end at the Sorbonne: Lancing College, where he secured his first appointment, proved to be an excellent setting for the nurture of his teaching talents. After a difficult period around the turn of the century, Lancing was showing evidence of a renaissance. H.T. Bowlby, the headmaster, an Old Carthusian himself, and previously an Eton housemaster, wanted to improve the academic record and appointed four Firsts at the start of his time in office. Stimulating teaching was encouraged and Roxburgh's sometimes flamboyant methods were not suppressed. At Eton, Harrow or Rugby his preoccupation with dress, his mannerisms and impulsive generosity – trips to the theatre and restaurants – would have inflamed powerful barons among the senior staff and he would have been either crushed or ousted. Lancing was not too large a stage or too traditional an institution to diminish his individuality. Bowlby thought sufficiently highly of him to make him tutor in his own house and, as numbers in the school rose, he was chosen as housemaster of Sanderson's, one of the newer houses.

This was in 1915. By then the war had begun to take its toll and Roxburgh did not escape its tragic consequences. His younger brother, Bob, was killed at the Battle of Jutland and, not for the last time, he began to read the names of his pupils in the casualty lists. In 1917, as restrictions on recruiting were lifted, he was accepted for service despite a suspected heart ailment. He served with the Signal Corps of the Royal Engineers. When Field Marshal Viscount Plumer came to Stowe to give the prizes in 1930 Roxburgh recalled that he had once been 'an unregarded subaltern' in Plumer's Second Army, though according to 'Fritz' Clifford, his second master, he had a story to tell about being given the task of finding a headquarters for his General and earning high favour by locating an extremely comfortable château with the aid of his fluent French. He took part in the last Allied advance, was Mentioned in Despatches by Haig and recommended for the Military Cross. When George Barclay O.S. was posted as missing over France in the Second World War Roxburgh wrote to his housemaster, Playford, 'I have rather poignant memories of Hazebrouk and Cassel dating from 1917–18.' In 1943, reviewing Leonard Cheshire's *Bomber Pilot*, he added, 'Men who have risked their lives together and shared intense emotions have ever afterwards a unique relation to each other.'

These experiences deepened his conviction that the public schools had an inescapable duty to produce the leaders and thinkers who would shape a new order. It is difficult today to recapture the spirit of reconstruction which inspired oratory on the platforms and in the pulpits of Britain in the 1920s, urging that the huge sacrifice of life should be honoured by greater seriousness in society. Roxburgh's editorials in the *Stoic* and his sermons returned constantly to the theme. The fact that the vision failed and that even greater evils led to conflict and destruction once again, underscored the grief which personal loss occasioned in the 1940s.

The suggestion that he should apply for Stowe would appear to have come from Amabel Williams-Ellis, literary editor of the *Spectator*, to which Roxburgh contributed some classical reviews. Her husband had a personal and professional interest in the rehabilitation of Stowe. Tonbridge, it was believed, had also demonstrated an interest in approaching Roxburgh, but he later told Clifford that the challenge of a new school and the creation of a new ethos in education was much the greater attraction.

In March 1923, the Montaubans gave a celebratory dinner in London. Ninety guests assembled to meet Lord Gisborough and the newly appointed headmaster. Roxburgh wrote rather apologetically to Warrington afterwards to confess that his speech had been 'rather disjointed', but this was needlessly modest. Declaring that he had been recently reading a Life of Percival, the headmaster of Rugby, who had previously 'made Clifton into a little Rugby', he stated that Stowe would have its own character and would not be a replica of any other school, however noble and revered. He himself was a Carthusian and a loyal one but Stowe was not going to be a 'Little Charterhouse' or a 'Little Lancing'; it was going to be a little Stowe and very shortly it was going to be a big Stowe.

He was certainly not short of advice, he said. One hundred and forty-four preparatory and public school headmasters had vouchsafed their views on the way in which he should go! Nevertheless, though the school would listen to the wisdom of experience it must forge its own path. 'No one could be absolutely contented with public-school education as it was. Had we learnt to preserve the freshness, the eagerness, the curiosity, the unclipped imagination of childhood such as they were when boys were sent to school?

And, secondly, had we learnt how to harness and use for good all those new powers which were released in a boy at the budding of his manhood? All public schoolmasters of the old schools as well as of the new must admit that those problems still awaited solution.' His speech placed great emphasis on the effects that Stowe's beauty would have on the residents but, given the period in which he spoke, when a majority of headmasters were in orders and many like Alington of Eton and Norwood of Marlborough and Harrow wrote copiously on the centrality of Chapel and worship, the absence of even conventional references to such matters is striking, especially as the language in which he spoke of the Stowe inheritance was that of the aesthetes Walter Pater and John Addington Symonds. It was an unusual spokesman for a new public school who refrained from implying that spiritual fare would be plentiful. The omission was also at variance with Warrington's very purposes, which Roxburgh might have wished to under-emphasise but could scarcely ignore. In 1934, writing to a parent who had been converted to Catholicism and was concerned with Warrington's public Protestant rancour, Roxburgh wrote,

> It is quite true that a proportion of the men who were concerned in the founding of Stowe were and are extreme Protestants. This was quite unknown to me when I accepted the appointment and I did not discover it until shortly before the School actually opened. You may suppose that the question of whether I should continue to serve these men or let down the new school was a difficult one to answer . . . The idea that any young creature should be taught to hate any honest man or woman is quite intolerable to me. We have kept hatred and bigotry out of the school for eleven years and they will not make their way into it now.

It seems strange that one who was so closely bound up with Lancing College should not have heard of the Martyrs' Memorial Trust and its intentions, although Warrington was only at the outset of his programme, or that Roxburgh should not have been closely questioned on his religious affiliations. At all events he placed his confidence squarely behind the determining affects of Stowe's contrived 'natural' beauties, the philosophy of the enlightenment rather than nineteenth-century religion. A few weeks before the school opened, after saying in a press interview

that Science would be prominent and that English would follow
the recent recommendations of a committee headed by Sir Henry
Newbolt which wished to see culture diffused nationally through
language as in France, he returned to the aesthetic theme: 'I have
always found in my own teaching that boys respond much more
quickly to beautiful surroundings than they are usually given credit
for. And, even if they do not feel continual enthusiasm about the
beauties amidst which they live they form unconsciously a standard of judgement which enables them ever afterwards to recognise
and dislike what is ugly.' Having scotched a 'ludicrous' rumour that
a large number of boys were going to be imported from a northern
grammar school he said that it had been intended to start with
eighty pupils but the pressure had been so great 'that we have compelled the architect, at the point of a bayonet as it were, to give us
more accommodation'.

Bowlby generously released him from Lancing within days of his
new appointment. Many years later, writing to H.W. Heckstall-
Smith, a master who had left Stowe for the headmastership of
Ludlow Grammar School and found two pupils wished to follow
him, Roxburgh wrote: 'My mind naturally goes back to my own
departure from Lancing. I arranged with my Headmaster a fortnight before the end of term to take three of my own House with
me to be Prefects at Stowe and from that time to the end of term
I was constantly refusing applications from both boys and parents
(I remember one whole dormitory of twenty which made a determined attack on me).'

He acquired an office at 74 Eccleston Square. Warrington paid
for a secretary, typewriter and filing cabinet, and thus equipped,
he began a long series of interviews with prospective masters and
parents. Before the opening of the school in May he had collected
over 500 pupils registered for every term until 1934 except two.
Clough Williams-Ellis was appointed architect and charged with
the rescue and conversion of the house. His problems were urgent
and manifold. The approach roads had to be repaired before lorries
could reach the building and supplies and equipment came in a
hired pony and trap until Roxburgh arranged the purchase of a
second-hand car with Warrington's permission. Fencing was battered and broken and Farmer Davies's cows roamed the incipient
cricket pitches on which Captain G.J.V.Weigall, whom Roxburgh
had extolled as 'the finest coach in the country', was shortly to

practise his craft. At a higher level, ideas put forward by the Council failed to bear fruit. A reception at the Mansion House failed to establish an endowment fund; a plan for a railway link from Buckingham to Stowe proved stillborn; an imperialist scheme mooted by Leo Amery to associate Stowe with universities in the empire did not attract funds. Undeterred, the pioneers pressed forward; the stocks of prospectuses were soon exhausted; groups of parents were ushered round the staterooms, Roxburgh switching on the lights to illuminate the magnificence and the bursar following closely behind to turn them off. It was announced that two houses would be ready to open in May 1923.

Montauban's part in the development of the enterprise was complete. Warrington, traversing the country in his chauffeur-driven limousine, was not given to power-sharing and he alone appeared to have the gift for raising mortgages and providing a flow of funds. He was a difficult collaborator. Sir John Bayley removed his wife's coffin from Wrekin College because of his dislike of the prevailing powers. Montauban, in turn, soon became suspicious of Warrington's financial ventures and his lack of charity in matters of religion. Yet it was Montauban who had seen the growth of the initial idea of a new school, born in discussion with two or three parents, into the plan firmly centred upon Stowe. He had combatted a great deal of Establishment criticism, elicited a reprieve from the demolition squads, and given credence to the notion that the time was ripe for some adventurous changes in educational traditions. Lord Gisborough, in his speech at the London dinner, had mentioned the sadly denuded shelves in the Library. Possibly bearing in mind the importance which Roxburgh accorded English Literature in the curriculum, Montauban's Hampstead parents provided by subscription some hundreds of finely printed volumes of the English classics, which he in turn could present to the School. In each there was a plate which recorded that it was Edward Henry Montauban M.A. 'who first imagined a School at Stowe and became a member of its original Governing Body'.

3

The Early Years

On Friday 11 May 1923, Ian Clarke, assistant master, set off to London to accompany the 4.15 from Euston to which two special carriages had been attached; at Bletchley these were slipped and coupled to the Banbury train. In addition to Stowe's first pupils the Montaubans were aboard, as were a number of parents. A small crowd had gathered at Buckingham station to gaze upon the first arrivals, some already wearing their straw hats, green bands for Temple House and red for Bruce. A uniform had not been stipulated for the journey. One father wrote a fortnight earlier concerning his thirteen-year-old son: 'As nothing is said in the Prospectus about headgear, I suppose the ordinary bowler will be the correct thing to arrive in.' A cavalcade of buses, cars and lorries carrying luggage passed through the town and along the Grand Avenue, which was resplendent with spring foliage; a Union Jack floated from the Corinthian Arch after a long absence.

None of the first 'ninety-nine' were ever to forget their arrival at the North Front, floodlit by the setting sun. Half-way up the steps was an immaculate figure wearing spats, who held out his hand to each in greeting: 'Good evening, my name is Roxburgh.' A few paces away stood Warrington, in clerical attire and gaiters, and Montauban, who later had Warrington cut off the edge of the photographic record. The headmaster's cool self-possession gave no hint of the triumphs of improvisation which had enabled the school to open on the appointed date, triumphs not always repeated. The second term had to be postponed for four days and the Autumn Term the following year was delayed for a week owing to slow progress with the plumbing.

The boys tumbled into the long-deserted apartments. Five senior pupils had been recruited as prefects. Dudley Wilson, head of school for the first four terms, Andrew Croft who succeeded him, and Harold Robinson, had been trusted members of Sanderson's, Roxburgh's house at Lancing. Gordon Bowie came from Eastbourne with a master, Ivor Cross and the Hon. Godfrey Butler, son of the Countess of Carrick, a neighbour of Williams-Ellis at Portmeirion, came from a small private school in Switzerland. The prefects shepherded the remainder to their dormitories and desks. The State Drawing Room became the Temple house room and the Great Bedchamber fulfilled the same function for Bruce. The private chapel was used for services and, on the first night of term, a preponderantly treble chorus hymned the opening of Stowe with 'Through the Night of Doubt and Sorrow'. At the first assemblies in the Oval Hall the 'ninety-nine' were heavily outnumbered by the figures on the Valdre frieze. Reception rooms along the South Front became temporary classrooms: 'The ceiling is an education in itself, if all else fails', said the first issue of the *Stoic*, possibly thinking of *The Revels of Sardanapalus* and other decorative panels. Visitors to the headmaster waited in the Gothic Library under the 719 armorial bearings of the Grenvilles.

On the first evening there was no hot water for baths but to those who were used to the regimes of preparatory schools this did not seem a cruel deprivation and Roxburgh's apologies appeared unnecessarily profuse. 'The Butler's Pantry was large enough to hold four billiard tables but had only two wretched sinks', wrote Williams-Ellis later. In former times the boiler was said to have consumed one ton of coal per day. The old pipe that used to run beer from the brewery to the cellars now carried the oil to feed the boilers below the western wing which supplied 60 baths, 120 wash basins and dozens of radiators. In June, Roxburgh had to write to a prospective master regretting his inability to offer hospitality as 'my guest rooms are still being used as the plumbers' workshops'. Thirty-five miles of piping and similar lengths of electrical wiring wound their way around the building. The first bursar, a Mr Millner, left swiftly to join a religious order. The first 'dame', an Eton title bestowed on the chatelaine, also left after one term. She was a lady of good family fond of introducing recollections of her travels abroad. A frequent opening, 'When I was in Egypt . . .', became one of the first catch-phrases of the community, not least because the lavatory area was sited around the Egyptian Hall. Egypt acquired a metonymical status as a result. Attempts to establish a workable team comprising bursar, housekeeper, matrons, steward and butler were to vex the authorities for many years.

The dark corridor which ran the length of the ground floor came to be known as 'Plug Street'. Corresponding much later with one of the 'ninety-nine', Roxburgh said that he thought the word derived from the First World War and Ploegsteert, a place on the Western Front where unwanted equipment was sent, as the boys' trunks were stored there in termtime.

As there was no one with the vast experience of a term or two to spread cynicism and disenchantment, every experience had novelty and excitement. The first issue of the *Stoic* reported that on six consecutive days during the summer sixty names had been registered. 'This would, if continued, result in 3650 entries a year.' (In fact 1000 names were put down in the first twelve months.) A wireless installation belonging to G. Buckley was described as being 'in daily touch with most of the European Capitals'. At the suggestion of Harold Robinson, one of the prefects, a zoo was set up on the present site of Walpole House. Ferrets, pigeons and rabbits were reared and Roxburgh had to promise his Governers that any rabbits caught by ferrets would be handed in to the kitchens. Presentations were made, including a laughing jackass from Australia and a pair of Japanese ducks. Sir Auckland Geddes presented a bear, but it soon outgrew its attractive cubhood and had the melancholy distinction of pole position on the roll of expulsions.

In an effort to recapture some eighteenth-century grace, five peacocks strutted on the lawn, waking all and sundry as the four cocks serenaded the hen at dawn. E.D. O'Brien of Chandos House, one of the first leading scholars, pelted them with a consignment of eggs from home. Heckstall-Smith, a master who had been promised some fresh eggs for breakfast, responded with a couplet suitably in the style of Pope:

> Here in the dawn, ere Chandos showed a leg
> Swift the loud peacock dodged th'avenging egg.

A primitive golf course ran from the South Front to the Octagon Lake and up to the Gothic Temple, though the grass was so long that it was possible to lose the ball even on the greens. Song and piano recitals, mostly by the masters, sprang up on Sunday evenings. 'It is believed', said the *Stoic*, 'that even a piano version of the 'Capriccio Espagnol' or the 'New World' Symphony may do something to broaden a boy's musical sympathies, while it is not thought reprehensible to include Edward German's 'Henry VIII Dances' and other works in a lighter vein.' The modern house-master, bombarded with megawatt decibels, must sigh with nostalgia for such idyllic days. It was thought that, given time, 'tunes from the B Minor Mass will oust "Yes, we have no bananas" from the halls and passages of Stowe'. There were paper-chases, country-dancing classes on Saturday evenings and on Wednesdays the Choral Society met to sing Rounds, with some help from the staff. Rapidly increasing numbers added to the feeling of enthusiasm. A *Stoic* correspondent imagined the sort of school which might exist in 1938, with 583 students, a railway station in the Gothic Temple, news of cricket victories over Eton and Harrow, 313 boys learning musical instruments and massed choirs and orchestra performing works by Stowe composers.

Masters too, had the jollity of a small pioneering fraternity. Two were caught red-handed by a constable crossing fields that were closed owing to foot-and-mouth disease. Both burst volubly into French and passed themselves off as lost and bewildered tourists. An account of meetings of the Gilbert and Sullivan Society gives a picture of the house-party atmosphere which prevailed:

> A play is read completely through at each sitting and the more attractive tunes are played on the piano at appropriate places: some members read their songs in the rhythm of Sullivan's music, the more enterprising, while confessedly having no pretensions to good voices, cast self-consciousness to the winds and sing them. The standard of reading is not at present high: cues are constantly missed, mispronunciations occur and occasionally members' tongues become twisted . . . But all this will improve.

Two more boarding houses, Grenville and Chandos, opened in September 1923, and numbers rose to 208. Cobham opened in January 1924, with fifteen boys, and gradually increased its numbers. In 1925 the first purpose-built house, Chatham (with a third storey added to the original plans), swelled the lists, and Grafton in 1926 brought the school roll to 452. 'Since the end of our first term', wrote Roxburgh to the Governors, 'the School has grown at an average rate of 35.3 boys per term. It is hoped that henceforth it will grow only in efficiency.' He dealt with all entries himself and the balancing of numbers was a difficult task. In 1925 he felt unable to give guaranteed places to many applicants with the result that more than half withdrew and less good candidates gained admittance. For September 1926, he took names more freely and was left with the prospect of thirty surplus pupils for a school already uncomfortably overcrowded. The Governors encouraged inflated lists as the revenues bolstered a very uncertain financial situation. Roxburgh, too, was aware how quickly demand could melt away. Though his public speeches were buoyant, in private he displayed a healthy realism. In 1926 he wrote: 'It may be wise to remember that the reputation of so young a School must still be a fragile thing and that (apart from the possibility of a real misfortune) a moment may come when as much will be said in criticism of the School – and with as little reason – as is now said in its favour, by those who know least and talk most about Public Schools. The influence of such chatter upon a school's forward entries is unhappily great.' In 1927 he was concerned that the post-war boom in entries was evaporating. 'There is no doubt', he informed the Council, 'that a lean period is coming for all Public Schools – probably from about 1930–32. The Preparatory Schools are now beginning to find out that the birth-rate fell considerably, especially in the officer class, during the years 1916–18.' As a result of his dislike of failing applicants, numbers in 1927 rose to 463 and six Bruce boys had to sleep in classrooms.

Stowe lists were maintained not only by his persistent tact with parents, even the most exasperating, but by the succession of major social events. At the annual Sports Days the prizes were distributed by ladies of title and the guest lists, given to the press, included the humblest with the grandest names. Special trains brought guests to the major events. In his first term a large gathering was invited to witness the presentation of a Japanese samurai sword by Sir Owen Seaman, editor of *Punch*, on behalf of the Agenda Club, a public-spirited body, which sought to bring to the social problems of peacetime the sense of national unity which had prevailed in the

First War. During the years of the Anglo-Japanese alliance at the turn of the century the British public had been fed by the Foreign Office with stories of similarities between the two nations and these had included comparisons between the samurai code and the code of honour at the public schools. The impression had persisted and the Agenda Club had removed the weapon from the South Kensington Museum. 'As a work of supreme art it was in its right place but as a symbol of loyalty and a stimulus to high patriotic endeavour it was thoroughly wasted there.' It was the work of a great craftsman of the eighth century, called Yatsutsuna, who had perfected forging to a degree where his blades were capable of cutting iron bars. The hilt was bound in deerskin called iris leather as it was exposed to the smoke of burnt irises for colouring. The scabbard was of sharkskin, off which blood flows easily. It was pointed out to the audience that the samurai also carried short swords to cut off their opponents' hands. Books on civic service accompanied the gift, and Sir Owen's speech was kindly and humane. He urged the Stoics not to be guilty of petty cruelties and to continue discussion of their work into leisure hours. Calling upon them to play their part nationally, he concluded, 'It is unbelievable that the evils of our age – poverty, unemployment, certain forms of disease and, in particular, the evils that give childhood no chance – are incapable of correction if only the youth and heart's blood of England are resolved that some cure should be found.'

It was symptomatic of the feeling that Stowe had aroused that this sinister implement, which must have been through a few necks in its time, was thought likely to propel the young listeners towards a programme of reform that reads like a Labour Party manifesto. Yet the theme of leadership was strongly urged upon the generations. In his first editorial for the *Stoic* Roxburgh wrote of the beauty of the surroundings and 'the stimulus which it gives to all honourable ambitions'. Referring to the special character of Stowe he declared, 'The important question for us is this – shall we be able to preserve that character when we are getting used to our surroundings and beginning to lose our youth? The right answer to that question is that we mean never to get used to our surroundings and never to lose our youth.' The new foundation would be characterized as far as possible by liberty: 'Liberty always involves a risk – that is why the best kind of man values it so highly . . . the only really safe life is life in prison. But the best, if not the safest way of keeping a community free from wrong and folly is to teach its members to prefer right and sense.' Life at Stowe was not gentle – the Charterhouse tradition of daily compulsory P.T. for all boys was followed, and certain housemasters such as Ivor Cross did not disdain mass beatings for unruly behaviour. But compared with other schools there was much less in the way of hierarchical rules of dress, which could provide agonies for new boys or the permanently absent-minded. The headmaster permitted with reluctance a certain amount of fagging, which was termed 'officing' and, when he could, he ensured that this was confined to general tidiness of the house rooms and studies. There were many opportunities to roam the grounds and countryside. He established agreement over matters he considered important almost imperceptibly. It was acknowledged that, if he picked up more than three pieces of litter on his shooting stick in the day, a half-holiday would be forfeit.

In 1924, the question of the Grand Avenue led to the first of Stowe's many royal visits. Williams-Ellis had preserved the Avenue from the predatory hands of timber merchants at the 1922 sale, but he could not afford to retain it, and the school could not afford to purchase. An article in *The Times*, in October 1923, criticized the lack of public spirit in Buckinghamshire and provoked a correspondence. The Royal Horticultural Society made an appeal for the preservation of what were described as 'hundreds upon hundreds of these kings of the forest' and the bursar of New College, Oxford, which held the Manor of Tingewick and could inhibit the cutting of timber, entered the fray. An anonymous Old Etonian suggested to Hugh Macnaghten, Vice-Provost of Eton, that it would be a 'graceful act' if the Avenue could be preserved and presented to the new school as a gift. The price sought was £1750 and Macnaghten proposed that Old Etonians or their families might raise this sum: 'First, Eton, one of the oldest and not the least famous of our public schools will have held out a hand of welcome to the youngest of them and secondly a noble avenue, one of the glories of the country for which lately 1157 Old Etonians gave their lives will have been saved, a possession for ever, an inspiration for the living and a living memorial of the dead.' He wrote subsequently to the press to say that Queen Mary, 'the mother and sister of Etonians (Prince Henry of Gloucester and the Earl of Athlone) wished to contribute as did Prince Henry.' The Queen and Princess May had visited

Stowe in the time of Lady Kinloss. The funds were forthcoming. Old Harrovians who wished to participate were tactfully pointed towards other worthy objects and Roxburgh assured enquirers that forestry was a matter of special interest at the school and planting and maintenance would be carried out. One hundred and sixty of the donors remained anonymous but were thanked handsomely through the columns of *The Times* by the head prefect Dudley Wilson, over whose shoulder the headmaster may have leant. 'If their kindness really results in a concordia with Eton, as Mr Macnaghten hopes, that will matter more to us, who are actually members of the School and to those who will come after us than it does to anyone else and also it will be our business more than anyone else's to live up to it.' The threatened fate of the Avenue had turned into a blessing. Stowe, which as yet in reality had few resources and with difficulty was establishing minimum academic standards, had established a 'special affinity', which made many of its older rivals seem prosaic.

Once again the special trains chugged from Euston to bring guests to the handing over of the title deeds by Prince Arthur of Connaught, grandson of Queen Victoria, recently Governor-General of South Africa and an Old Etonian. He drove down the Avenue with Eton ribbons streaming from his car, although his chauffeur inadvertently turned left at Chackmore into the mêlée of vehicles belonging to parents and sightseers and had to be redirected on to the intended route through the Corinthian Arch. At the ceremony rain gradually filled the loudspeakers and Roxburgh's speech had to be curtailed. Macnaghten spoke eloquently on the important role which trees played in the Bible and added from under his umbrella that the guests could sympathize with Jonah sheltering under his gourd. The *Buckingham Advertiser* reported admiringly, 'The Prince, soldier as he is, sat unperturbed through the rain, which came down torrentially.' A number of cricketing and fencing fixtures with Eton followed. Perhaps somewhere, under Elysian elms, Earl Temple and George III forgot their differences and inclined graciously towards one another. An unusual, almost mystical, aspect to the whole story which seemed to be noticed only in the *Advertiser* was that the axis of the Avenue, if continued, ran almost directly through Eton College and Windsor Castle.

Behind these grand events work proceeded slowly on the provision of basic requirements. There were already five houses in operation when Warrington proposed, subject to funds, to provide a proper sanatorium, a wooden gymnasium, two masters' houses for three bachelors each and two teaching blocks, each with four classrooms. A Science area was created in an extension of the former Orangery (the *Stoic* proudly described the Chemistry laboratory as being better equipped than the corresponding premises at Cambridge), but the new classrooms were not completed until several weeks of term had passed. Lessons had often to be given in house rooms and, on occasion, in places such as the squash courts. The majority of the Council had little knowledge of schools or school planning. Throughout the 1920s, thanks to Roxburgh's tact and Warrington's admiration for his professionalism, relations between the two men were fairly harmonious. By contrast, Warrington regarded the Council as his whipping boys. Early in 1924 Roxburgh stressed the urgency of the sanatorium. A cottage in the grounds had to be used for isolation cases of measles, an unoccupied dormitory in Cobham for victims of influenza. Warrington agreed. 'Your letters are never any trouble to me, so please don't hesitate to make your wishes known.' Of the Council he wrote:

> I very much hope the Bishop of Warrington will not be present. I should not be surprised if he opposed practically everything, requiring to see the very last shilling in his hands before he sanctions the laying of a brick. Some of these episcopal gentlemen who preach about Faith wouldn't trust their God for sixpence. [He told Roxburgh to present the matter forcibly.] Don't forget to knock into the Council's silly heads that if they put up a Sanatorium they will get one third of its cost back within the first year by releasing accommodation which will be used for boys.

He focused his wrath especially upon the Earl of Leitrim. 'The only contribution this brainy member of the aristocracy made to the debate was to wave his arms and say, "There should be more meetings, that's what I say".' He added that the only communication he had had from the Earl was a request for fees for meetings at which he never opened his mouth, 'and I declined to pay them'. There were storms when Lords Gisborough and Leitrim wished to raise money through the City rather than the Church of England Trust. Warrington accused the Chairman of 'an outrageous and untruthful statement', which had influenced the Dean of Bristol and others, and threatened to expose their perfidy in *The Times*, quoting a comment about himself from one of his parishioners: 'When you get over he, you've only got one more to git over and that be the Devil hisself'. By the time that the presence of 320 boys in the school made the sanatorium imperative, the delays in sanctioning the gymnasium were causing concern. A parent had offered £500 if the Governors would find the remaining costs. Progress was slow but during 1924 a structure which would house the school for worship, gymnastics and entertainment appeared. Sir Oswald Stoll, the impresario, presented some cinema equipment.

By the summer of 1924 it was clear that, even with the most ingenious use of space, a new house would be required. Warrington, much engrossed in acquiring a girls' school in Harrogate, wondered whether selected parents might pay a year's fees in advance. Roxburgh was not in favour: 'There are two kinds of parents whose boys come here – those that are very keen to send them and those who have to be persuaded. The first kind is as a rule not the desirable kind and not the kind that has money. The second is the kind that we need most and the kind that I spend my days in pursuing.' Rightly he explained that he would be enslaved into accepting the sons of those who paid in advance and that the publicity would harm the school's credit in the country. Warrington, who nearly always accepted Roxburgh's views on public relations, turned instead to the Norwich Union Insurance Society. He thought that the plans of Williams-Ellis both for the new house and the masters' houses were unworthy, declared for a more Palladian style and remarked that they were building for posterity. He thought that the Norwich would be helpful, 'as they were tremendously impressed by the entries'. Montauban had written to him to say that the school should cease expansion with 350 pupils and avoid further expense. 'This', said Warrington, 'is most unbusinesslike and typical of our friend. I do not wonder that his scheme fell through.' Despite the risks and the near-catastrophe to come, Warrington was correct. With numbers frozen at 350 (and with the coming Depression and the Second World War it is unlikely they would ever have risen), Stowe would have remained a lesser school. Roxburgh, beset by applications, assured Warrington that he would press hard at the Council for a new house. 'If it does not come through I shall have to go off to New Zealand or stand the chance of being shot by an infuriated parent.'

In order to clear more space in the main building, plans for the new house were enlarged to accommodate masters or servants in a third storey, and provide music practice rooms. In the changes, modes of access were overlooked and the first masters to have rooms on the west wing had to climb up to their studies on ladders. The rift between Montauban and Warrington deepened over the Norwich loan. According to Montauban, a certain Alderman Neal had received £7500 for arranging the loan and would be receiving an annual percentage, 'the price Stowe would have to pay . . . as a token of his friendship with Mr Warrington'. Warrington said that these were private arrangements between Neal and the insurance society. He pointed out that the Norwich Union had four times rejected Stowe's application before Neal's intervention and accused Montauban of trying to unsettle the headmaster by sharing the accounts with him. Despite the efforts of Dr David, Bishop of Liverpool, King-Harman and Pearman-Smith (a solicitor) carried an amendment in the Council explicitly condemning Montauban, who resigned a few months later. He came to Sports Day in 1929, but his role in the history of Stowe was virtually ended. Roxburgh admitted his worries about the high interest rates privately to Warrington, but affirmed that he could not possibly take more boys. Parents were already beginning to complain about the over-crowding. Warrington, in turn, lamented bitterly clerical opposition to the loan. 'How bitterly, intensely bitterly I regret bringing Stowe into being I cannot say. If I had my time over again nothing in this world would induce me to do this work again'. From time to time he resigned but seems to have been prevailed upon to remain.

It had been decided to call the new house 'Gisborough' but, with some temerity and 'knowing that Lord Gisborough likes frankness', Roxburgh had pressed for another eighteenth-century title, 'Chatham', and suggested that the Chairman's name should be reserved for the Assembly Hall when it was finally erected. Chatham opened in 1925 with forty-nine boys, including twenty-two from other houses, and 'Pop' Earle as housemaster. His place in Bruce was taken by F.T. Arnold. Even with the additional building too many boys were pressed into the space and planning errors became apparent. Seventy-two had to use changing-room space suitable for thirty-five. When Ivor Cross took over Chatham in 1931 he did not mince his words. 'The wearing of other people's change [games clothes] is beyond anything I have come across in our worst periods in the main building. In fact the changing-room conditions are a real aid to demoralisation and mobbism. Earle tells me that skin diseases usually start in Chatham. I have no doubt they do!'

Chatham was soon over seventy strong and it was clear that the school was not so much growing as exploding. It must be remembered that the mid-1920s were not good times for fee increases. When such an increase was put to the Council as a solution to the problem of borrowing, W.B. Hards, who came from the Ministry of Education, opposed the idea and pointed to the difficulties facing fathers in the professions. Yet the only alternative was to add to the school population. As the three classrooms in the Old Stable area to the east of the main building had been unfavourably commented upon by the first inspection of His Majesty's Inspectors of Schools in 1925, it was decided that these would go into yet another new house. The plan demanded considerable reorganization. Two floors would be added to each wing and one to the centre of the stable block. There would be a general extension and exchange of dormitory spaces in the main building. The two largest houses, Bruce and Temple (seventy-nine and seventy-three respectively), could then be reduced. It was pointed out that the seventh house would add £5000 to the revenue. Warrington found £3000 belonging to the mortgages already issued by the Norwich. He resisted cuts in the design which would have eliminated the boys' studies and reduced the masters' accommodation.

Yet the building was far from ready when it opened in September 1926. Roxburgh had wanted to call it 'Nelson' but could find no connection between Stowe and the Admiral. It was named 'Grafton' after the hunt which met occasionally in the grounds. (In the early days a party of geographers doing some field work near to the Gothic Temple were scattered in all directions by the Grafton in full cry. The Prince of Wales hunted with the Grafton but this did not prevent the Council, when it discovered that alcohol had been served at the Stowe Meets, from forbidding the practice. The school's alternative magazine, the *Epicurean*, published a cartoon of hunting squires looking mournfully into their orange juice.) Some parents found it dark and airless; windows were ill-fitting and boys sleeping on the south side were liable to be drenched during rain storms. There was some feeling that it was housed in what was clearly a servants' area rather than the *piano nobile* in the mansion. It was in time a popular house but the myth persisted that the degree of 'politesse' displayed during tea with Roxburgh in some way determined the allocation of boys to it. The presence of the future Duke of Wellington in Grafton should have demolished the theory.

Very slowly the most pressing needs of the school were met. The completion of a small hostel for masters meant that they no longer needed to reside at a distance in Montauban's house, Brookfield. The levelling of the grounds proceeded, but in 1927 only half the boys could play cricket at any given time, and there was only one pitch which the school could afford to keep free from football in the winter. There were, however, fives courts in use and Mr Miall of Tunbridge Wells, a parent, presented three squash courts, one of which served temporarily as the formroom of Upper IVB with an oil stove in the corner. A tank for the teaching of swimming was set up though the Inspectors noted that it was too close to the maids' rooms and suggested canvas screens, even though bathing suits were worn. Four lengths had to be achieved in the tank in order to qualify for swimming in the lake. Here a raft was constructed (at the point from which the Comte de Paris used to take his dip), knocked together from pieces of wood thrown out by the workmen, bearing motifs such as LARDER DOOR etc. Warrington, however bristly he might be on certain issues, was extremely sound on questions of safety and ordered the most thorough dredging and clearing of the swimming area. The future Marquis De Amodio, as early as 1923, had read a paper on fencing and illustrated certain fencing techniques, arousing sufficient interest to found a club. Quick to expand any activity which did not require lavish premises and might shed lustre, Roxburgh immediately presented two épées and found the club some accommodation.[1] Generous gifts were

---

[1] Many distinctions were won by Stowe's first groups of fencers. H.D.H. Bartlett was Public School Foils Champion. There were three Internationals: N.G. Winton, M.F. Villiers-Stuart, and D.P. Choyce. In 1933 J. (later Sir Joseph) Cheyne was Public School Foil and Sabre Champion, and J. Mansfield Champion Epée. N.C. McLintock was the English Universities Foil Champion. In 1927 Philip Charlot, son of 'Charlot's Revues', broke two épées in three fights during a win over Westminster.

made to the Library: the Governors gave two hundred books including a full set of the *Encyclopaedia Britannica*. Another parent, Mr Bertram, presented some rare and valuable works as well as a telescope for the observatory on the roof. Unfortunately this last item was mistaken for a roll of linoleum and put into storage for a considerable time.

It is the staff, however, which is the most vital ingredient of any school and we must turn to the appointments of the men who helped to set Stowe upon its course. It was necessarily a young and eclectic group for it was not easy to attract men from relatively well-paid senior posts in other establishments. The future of Stowe was far from assured, there was no provision for married men whatsoever and the in-house quarters were so unwelcoming that some of the younger masters preferred to camp out in the temples. In making his selection Roxburgh seems to have tried to strike a balance between solid, not to say stolid, men and the mercurially unorthodox. This was to lead to some sharp divisions within the small community, which were accentuated by the headmaster's ability to make several masters feel that they had a unique place in his esteem.

The first housemaster of Bruce was the Reverend Ernest Earle, son of one of Thring's housemasters at Uppingham and head boy of Marlborough in his day. He had previously been headmaster of Bilton Grange Preparatory School and was therefore accustomed to the young age-group to which he was assigned. After seventeen years at Bilton he had taken a sabbatical year in Australia and felt the need for a change. He was a keen rider to hounds and was said to enjoy the sport twice a week. After a hunting accident he had his bedroom window at Bilton enlarged so that the boys could wave to him during his convalescence. He was an hospitable and kindly man who contributed humorous articles to the *Epicurean* and played Bridge in the evenings, habitually selecting the young Boyd-Carpenter, who had had some home training, as his partner. His Edwardian breakfasts on Sundays and his Saturday evenings of readings and cocoa were to became nostalgic memories for the boys of Bruce and Chatham.

Ivor Cross, first housemaster of Temple, was very different. He had been a pupil at Lancing and then taught at Eastbourne. He was a stern man with many talents. His hearing had been affected in an anti-aircraft battery during the war and this handicapped a musical career which had earlier gained him a choral exhibition to Cambridge. But he sang solo parts in the Buckingham Music Festivals and Stoics remembered his resounding performances of 'The Trumpet Shall Sound' from the organ loft in Chapel. He was gifted as a draughtsman and produced the first issues of the *Stoic* and designed the hymnbook cover. Immensely serious, he took to heart Roxburgh's every word on the moral force with which Stowe should imbue its pupils. At the end of his first term he wrote to the latter: 'Our tradition is our attitude to life and I believe it is perceptible already after a bare term . . . I believe that by moulding Stowe nearer to the heart's desire . . . your heart's desire which I guess is pretty nearly mine . . .' A year later he continued: 'I am trying not to think of Stowe for a fortnight but I'd like to bear testimony to the superlative way in which you conduct it.' Not many headmasters receive letters from their assistants signed 'With Love'. He was keen to teach Civics and played a major part in establishing a branch of the League of Nations Union at the school. He was easily hurt and could be unsympathetic to the follies of youth. Roxburgh had to guide him through difficulties when his stubborn rectitude led to clashes with parents.

T.W.G. Acland, first housemaster of Cobham, was a brilliant chemist with a First from Cambridge, who had worked in munitions during the First War, and later on explosives in industry for Brunner-Mond. He was a stickler for punctuality. A boy half a minute late was given 200 lines. Because his system was one of reflex actions a boy who never turned up at all usually escaped punishment and Acland himself quite often forgot his classes. The same brittle methods applied to the house which, on the surface, ran with precision. He believed in early bed and unbroken sleep and regularly departed for slumber at 10 p.m. His house quickly grasped the situation; good conduct and order prevailed until 10.05 p.m. and thereafter liberty was unconfined. Early repose brought early rising and the punctual appearances of 'Cheerful Charlie' for breakfast at 7.45, full of heartiness and back-slapping, added twenty minutes to the breakfast hour of his colleagues. He left in 1930 to be headmaster of Norwich School where his business-world methods included an exchange of bells and buttons by his study door. When Roxburgh heard of the suicide of another ex-master, he wrote to a colleague, 'One should always fear for people who are always in a hurry. They're fleeing from something which will catch them in the end. I hope Acland has become less efficient.'

Alfred Fremantle, first of the Modern Linguists, was by contrast a likeable but impossible eccentric. Scion of a stalwart naval family and rumoured by the boys to be proficient in twelve languages, his efforts to reduce English inhibitions over language-speaking led to clamour and tumult. The singing of French and German songs in the gymnasium involved certain party pieces where he took off his shoes revealing large holes in his socks at which there was the customary hilarity. 'With more brilliant pupils or in a different age he might have been a brilliant success', wrote Roxburgh to a potential employer. He left in 1927 but in 1946 suddenly contacted Roxburgh to announce that he had re-married his divorced wife and to return £1 borrowed fifteen years before. The service tradition returned in his son, Oscar, who died gallantly in Italy in 1944.

The first head of Science, J.F. Whitaker, was one of the most interesting appointments. In the 'Recollections' about his colleagues (unpublished) by Heckstall-Smith, he is portrayed as flippant over marking and in conflict with Ernest Earle over the periodic form orders. In truth he had come to detest the competitive system whereby he had ground his way from poor circumstances to an exhibition at Emmanuel College, Cambridge. He was engaged to design the laboratories but was not fitted to run a department and seems to have come to Stowe believing it to be a more experimental school than it was. A devout Quaker, he was an early advocate of 'child-centred learning' and wrote copiously to Roxburgh criticizing the school's subservience to exams when it was clear that his days were numbered. He was opposed to the identification of Stowe with a governing class: 'The servants . . . live a life apart from the rest of us. Speech and other Public Days look like days for the ostentation of wealth. The OTC, which I know in many ways gives an excellent training – and the connection of the School with the Navy and Air Force – seems to me utterly at variance with the Indwelling Spirit.' On leaving Stowe he crossed Siberia to teach English in Japan, returned to burden Roxburgh like many departed colleagues with a seemingly endless correspondence in search of employment, set up a coaching establishment which inevitably failed as, on principle, he would not coach for examinations, and finally benefited from the wartime shortage of masters which enabled him to find a post. In 1958 he founded the Stowe Middle School Prizes to be awarded on 'subject interest' rather than marks.

Two masters who were to contribute most richly to the early growth of Stowe were Ian Clarke and Major Richard Haworth. Clarke became housemaster of Grenville when it opened in the second term. His father was a distinguished Scottish educationist and his mother belonged to the Andersons of Inverugie who, generation after generation, produced notable figures in learning and administration. He won an Oxford Rugby Blue and a Half Blue for athletics. Although three times wounded in the war he proved to be a brilliant Rugby coach. During his housemastership Grenville won the house Rugby Cup (presented by Warrington) for seven successive years. He had intended to take up a career in forestry and was reputed to know all the trees in Stowe Park, often advising on plantations. His tight tartan trousers, worn on O.T.C. parades, and his bowler hat for the Varsity Match, were familiar emblems. He had a good tenor voice heard in 'The Road to Mandalay' and other such songs and when, after marriage, he moved to the new Walpole House, the Walpole Glee Club and Walpole concerts were the popular offspring of these talents.

Major Haworth arrived in September 1923 to launch Chandos. An Old Carthusian, he had narrowly missed a V.C. but won the D.S.O. at Gallipoli. Roxburgh would like to have had him as bursar, but when this post was filled by the Council he offered Haworth, who was on the staff at Sandhurst, command of the O.T.C., some general teaching and a House. 'It would be delightful to get you to share the struggles and triumphs (if there are any) of Stowe.' Andrew Croft, a prefect in Temple, where he found the treatment given to the new boys rather oppressive, was invited to dine with Roxburgh and Haworth alone. The discussions over champagne, served in Venetian glasses, went well and Croft was invited to be head boy of Chandos. Haworth provided the style of discipline based upon goodwill and friendship which Andrew Croft had known under Roxburgh at Lancing. 'The Major' was not a scholar but Roxburgh promised that his programme would not be exacting: 'The essential facts are that everybody in the School, except for 6 or 7 . . . are 14 years old or younger, that with the exception of the Middle Fifth all . . . are remarkably stupid, that everyone will do Geography for one period only.' A few days later the academic challenge was further diluted: 'I ought to warn you that the Geography arrangements . . . had to be cancelled when we discovered how extremely low the standard of the boys was.

The books designed for them were very much too difficult and had to be got rid of.'

The first application to establish an Officers' Training Corps at Stowe had been rejected by the War Office. 'As I rather think that the Stafford Green who signs the letter is the Stafford Green who married my Housemaster's daughter, Winnie, I think he ought to have done us better', said Roxburgh in a letter urging Haworth to put the case in Whitehall in person. Permission gained, the Major created a contingent that was quickly recognized as one of the best in the country and one of Stowe's immediate successes.[2] At camp competitions it regularly defeated older and more famous schools and internal competitions for drill and efficiency were keenly contested. Rollo Spencer, head of school in 1936, in order that Grafton boots should be perfect for drill competition, polished thirty pairs himself. Roxburgh, very much the pragmatic schoolmaster as well as reformer, appreciated the distinction brought by the O.T.C. and it was Haworth himself who had to dissuade him from extending recruitment to the very youngest boys. Nor was the O.T.C. in any way like the Cadet Forces of modern times with their imaginative adventure training exercises: there was a great deal of drill and marching. Hampered by the lack of a parade ground and, in early days, by the shortage of senior N.C.Os which meant very large squads, the Corps served as a useful source of exhaustion to balance the hours of leisure. Sergeant-Major Elliott, who came in 1924 and gave instruction in boxing and P.T., had been an R.S.M. in the Coldstream Guards and sparring partner to some of the country's champion boxers.

Hugh Heckstall-Smith also arrived in the second term. A gifted physicist, who also won praise from the Inspectors for his English teaching, he presided over musical evenings at which, to the concern of Ivor Cross, Wagner was played on the gramophone. He was one of the few masters with the temerity to tease 'J.F.' as Roxburgh was universally known. He helped with the casting at the Play-Reading Society:

J.F. persisted that he wanted a SMALL part but as he was a good reader and tended to raise the general level by example and competition he got good parts. He continued to protest with

[2] Neil Blair won the Sword of Honour at Sandhurst in 1930, C.S. Madden in 1934.

well-feigned sincerity until we [H-S and Toby O'Brien] decided he should have a small part, just to 'larn' him. We found a play of Galsworthy's containing a 'Voice from the Crowd' which only spoke one line: 'Step dahn then and I'll step up'. J.F. said this alright, but for the first and last time he was quite snappy about everyone's reading instead of expressing criticism by veiling his compliments in the style of which he was a master. Honour was satisfied and from then on J.F. accepted good parts without a fuss.

He recalled that Roxburgh's very rare lapses included the uncompleted notice in the masters' dining room: 'The Bishop of X will be dedicating the − on Thursday at − p.m. I hope as many Masters as possible will make it convenient to be present at this innocent little ceremony.' The Reverend E.F. Habershon, the first Chaplain, wrote in 1963 to cheer up the then headmaster, Donald Crichton-Miller who had been accused of being undiplomatic: 'J.F. once came into my room, threw himself into an arm-chair and said "Heckstall has just said to me: "Trouble about you is you are too damned diplomatic".' Heckstall left to be headmaster of Ludlow Grammar School, having kept his marriage secret for a term, but he kept up his correspondence with J.F. In 1941 Roxburgh wrote gloomily urging Heckstall to pursue farming experiments, in which he was interested. 'There are plenty of people who can be Head-masters . . . any competent clerk is equal to the job.' Heckstall retorted that when Stowe came to choose the next headmaster J.F. would take a lively interest and would certainly not subscribe to the idea that 'any competent clerk' could follow him. He took a lively interest in educational theory and worked for a time with Kurt Hahn at Gordonstoun. He recommended various works on the mind and the unconscious to his former boss: 'If you want to increase your power to dominate the staff at a Masters' Meeting, read the first three chapters of Freud's *Group Psychology and the Analysis of the Ego.*'

Habershon was an Old Harrovian. He is said to have chosen Harrow in preference to Eton as an aunt lived near and could give him tea. He was a vigorous parson, time-keeper at boxing matches and mystifyingly described by his colleague 'Fritz' Clifford, in his scattered reminiscences, as looking like Richard Coeur-de-Lion. With his own hands he built the cricket scoring box, henceforward known as 'The Habernacle'. (By the same token a sugar-sifter he presented to the Common Room was always known as 'The Haberdasher'.) His marriage, difficulties with housing, and above all disapproval of the Protestant bigotry of the Council drove him to Gresham's, Holt in 1931 although he had been marked out for Walpole House, if it had been completed on schedule. After the Second World War, enquiring about a country living, he asked if it were in the hands of 'a certain Trust . . . If it is, I myself should feel that the particular kind of pitch with which the Trust deals cannot be touched without defilement.'

Others in the group which founded the Common Room included F.T. Arnold, senior English master. In 1925 when Earle left Bruce to take over Chatham, Arnold succeeded him, but within two years he left to follow in the footsteps of his great-uncle Matthew Arnold, as a Schools' Inspector. Dr Philip Browne, first Director of Music, took the same course. He was probably unique among Music Directors in that, having gained a classical scholarship from Winchester to Oxford, he used to set the Latin prose papers in Stowe's scholarship exams. He was a fair cricketer, too, but had his own eccentricities and once took a taxi fifty miles to Bradfield to play the timpani for a fellow director. He had a habit of playing patience between courses in restaurants and, at his club, where he disliked the bread, he would hand out rolls to his guests from a paper bag. He could do little choral work until he had more broken voices and as almost all the school were beginners on their instruments the scope for concerts was limited. But he was a popular figure in Buckingham as conductor and accompanist. In 1958 Arnold wrote to the headmaster,

If next Saturday, which is, I believe, Old Stoic Day, two elderly strangers are seen wandering about, they will probably be Philip Browne and myself renewing distant memories. We shall, of course, be there as pre-historic members of the Staff and not as H.M.I.s but as we are what we are I am writing to let you know of our intention which I hope you will not think presumptuous.

Considering the low salary scales, the lack of proper housing and the other discomforts the first generation of masters contained a high proportion who gave virtually all their lives to Stowe. Edward Hart Dyke (Modern Languages) and C.W.G. Ratcliffe (Mathematics) came in January 1924. Hart Dyke had been a boy at

Tonbridge, served with the Royal West Kent Regiment and was an exhibitioner of Queens' College, Cambridge. He came from a strict military family where prayers were held each day. Roxburgh first heard of him through friends in Belgium whose son he had tutored. 'Dear Mr Hart Dyke,' ran a letter, 'Thank you for these testimonials which I have read with interest. I cannot help thinking that you are a very rash man to send originals through the post to busy headmasters! I am returning them at once in case by any misfortune they should be mislaid or lost . . .' He was a quiet, self-effacing member of staff, in early days a useful spin-bowler in the Masters' XI and a thrusting three-quarter in Rugby sides. Save for one occasion when characteristically he failed to realize that he had priority at the surgery and complained about having to wait 'in a queue of house-maids', he does not appear in thirty-four years to have troubled any headmaster about anything. Eric Reynolds declared that he had never known a more loyal or trustworthy colleague.

Ratcliffe, 'Ratters', from Trinity College, Dublin, was a type of which almost every common room in England before the Second World War had a representative, caustic and quotable, a taskmaster who would be sought out by penitent examinees apparently doomed to failure. Stories accumulated around him such as the conversation with a somewhat similar bachelor of strong views, Bertie Miles:

'And what are you doing this afternoon Mr Ratcliffe?'
'I am minding my own business Mr Miles.'

He had a habit of walking with one arm behind him. One Stoic following him down Plug Street, greatly daring, as Ratcliffe was the sternest of disciplinarians, for a bet placed a coin in the outstretched palm. Doomsday did not break, the fingers closed around the coin and the gowned figure stalked onwards. Like many such crusty characters he was privately most generous, helping to maintain his sisters, and donating towards the Stowe Boys' Club.

W.E. Capel Cure, an ex-pupil of Roxburgh's from Lancing, arrived from Trinity College in the autumn of 1924. He was a first-class cricketer and wicket-keeper and a man of many talents who could write songs and sketches, some of which reached the professional stage, as well as contributing fourth leaders to *The Times*. He took a great interest in the gardens and would collect up leaves from the trees which had been imported from many continents, bring them into class and explain their origins.

A.G. ('Wilfred') Archer, Patrick Hunter and the Reverend Humphrey Playford came in September 1925. Archer had a First in Mathematics and had been in the Sherborne Cricket XI. The rooms in Chatham for the new arrivals were not ready. 'We can accept your furniture in the early part of September,' wrote Roxburgh to Archer, 'but if you send it earlier than that, it would have to be stacked under the open sky.' Some masters began their days at Stowe in the White Hart Hotel, Buckingham. Having sought advice on discipline Archer received the following:

> I am quite certain that the first essential is to assume in your mind as well as your manner that there will be no trouble. The sort of fellow who starts with threats and lines and drills as if he was in terror of not being taken seriously enough is foredoomed to fail. If you start on the assumption that you and the boys are all there to get on with the business together in a quiet and orderly fashion, the boys will respond at once to your attitude.

In 1927, still very junior, Archer asked permission – with some hesitation – to see his brother off on a liner via Cherbourg. Roxburgh replied, 'My experiences of getting off Atlantic liners at Cherbourg have not been entirely happy, but perhaps you will be luckier than I was. Please arrange not to be carried on to America.' He was always very accommodating about such requests. 'I hope you will arrange to miss as much work here as will enable you to do the trip in reasonable comfort.'

Archer was a Maths Tutor for many years and gave intense scrutiny to the marks of his candidates in the Woolwich Army and the university entrance examinations. He took over the Scout Troop from Robert Hole, the first woodwork and handicraft master, who eventually left to become a full-time Sea Scout instructor. Patrick Hunter came from Winchester and Magdalene College, Cambridge where he won a Half Blue for athletics. For many years he had been in the same house at Winchester as Philip Browne and he was a distinguished classic who was to play a very full part in the life of Stowe, as senior tutor and second master as well as an authority on all matters of administrative detail.

The Reverend Humphrey Playford (St Paul's and Jesus, Cambridge) was in total contrast. He came from a dynasty of oarsmen, was in the University Boat in 1920–2 and the Leander Crew which won the Grand Challenge Cup in 1925. In its own way the Cambridge Tripos proved an even greater challenge and having taken Orders, he stayed on at Jesus, coaching crews and serving as assistant chaplain until, as Eric Reynolds put it, Cambridge designed a pass degree which he could pass. Although he was not a scholar he was no fool and when, in 1930, another headmaster asked if he could approach him, Roxburgh wrote: 'H.B. Playford is quite first-class. If you take him away from me I shall go for you with a revolver . . .' He succeeded to Bruce House as early as 1929, held the position of housemaster for longer than any other in Stowe's history and gave to Bruce something of a select and patrician air. Rival housemasters muttered that the less or least distinguished pupils ran away and certainly one or two did, chased along the Buckinghamshire lanes by Humphrey in his Lancia. He was a law unto himself. When the masters' food fell below standard he would dine in Buckingham. On impulse he would whisk boys off to sporting events. He once drove three boys in their first fortnight to Cambridge to see the great Don Bradman bat, only to discover that he had been bowled for nought before their arrival. At the start of the Second World War he bought up all the paperbacks he could find in Cambridge, fearing that the art of reading might be imperilled by shortage of books. Demonstrating the long fire chute in 1934 he ended up in the sanatorium, being of large build. Incident and argument constantly attended his progress but he had a good rapport with the senior members of his house.

The most daring appointment was that of Martin McLaughlin as head of History. Claiming descent from the O'Melaghlins, Kings of Meath in the Dark Ages, he supported the Fenians and the Easter Rising. He was oblivious of ordinary constraints and saved himself postage by writing O.H.M.S. across all his mail. His technique for teaching was to make the most outrageous assertions which obliged his pupils to engage in research to show how unsound his views were. The results were phenomenal. Of Stowe's first twenty-four university awards half were in History, and Roxburgh added £50 to McLaughin's salary by way of appreciation. He was not less successful in the Fencing Club which enjoyed many triumphs. Some of these were assisted by his wholly partisan methods of judging.

The first housemaster of Grafton was P.B. Freeman who had been a friend of Roxburgh's at Trinity and had house tutoring experience at Sherborne and Loretto. He was thirty-nine and imported, as other masters were thought to be too young for the office. The appointment was not one of Roxburgh's most successful. David Niven and Neil Blair, two of his seniors, would invade his quarters to mark the whisky bottle and note how the tide had receded. Prayers were conducted from the bannisters and other places of communication between his apartments and the house. Yet he infused a good house spirit and started the Grafton records which noted the details of every success and every game and team appearance from those first days. The picture that David Niven gives in his autobiographical accounts of his schooldays leaves out his own continuous involvement in all the house teams where, a triton among minnows, he had the task of leading the new boys against much older and heavier teams. Freeman left without explanation after three years and was replaced by Robert Timberlake who had a First in Classics and taught the top forms. Timberlake left for Rugby in 1932, as he wished to get married and accommodation for married men at Stowe did not exist. He subsequently became headmaster of the Royal Grammar School, Lancaster, but returned to draw on his reminiscences of the first years of Stowe at the Roxburgh Centenary Dinner in 1989.

Another keen rowing man was Alfred Clifford, known always as 'Fritz' because of his close-cropped hair. He was recommended strongly by the Dean of St Catharine's, Cambridge, where he was a leading man in the college and Captain of the Boat Club. He came from comparatively humble circumstances in East London, attended Alleyn's School and held a commission in a Territorial regiment in a depressed area of Camberwell. He gave a good account of Roxburgh's interview:

At Finmere Station old French, Gardener/Chauffeur, met me with a salute and 'For Stowe, Sir'. A bow-legged little man, he looked his best in brown uniform and gaiters. The road to Stowe was still gated and every so often, as a smart drill, he stopped the old black Crossley and fixed the gate with a short piece of stick which had to be retrieved: so our journey was a little stately . . . Before long a door in the glass enclosed bookshelves opened and I saw J.F.R. for the first time. He was impressive,

because tall and young with a mobile face and engaging smile.
I passed through and entered his immaculate and attractive
study. We sat down. He helped himself to a silver-tipped
cigarette and then remembered his manners and offered me a
smoke with apologies: he had lost himself in thought.

Clifford had carefully worn his Toc H Tie and Roxburgh noted
this with approbation. Fifty-six years later Clifford's impressions of
the youthful headmaster remained vivid: 'Stowe gravel takes its
toll of shoes so he had those Phillips rubber soles and heels screwed
on which made them clumsy . . . Double-breasted suits, pencils,
spectacles that folded, gave him plenty to do with his hands: he was
essentially mobile like the Latin races. He had been to the
Sorbonne.'
Clifford was an effective disciplinarian whose bright blue eyes
could quell disturbances dozens of yards away. When the young
George Melly left Stowe for the Navy without handing back every
item of his Corps equipment Clifford's epistles on the subject left
him with no doubts that a row of braided admirals would be ordering him shortly to walk the plank. Clifford became head of Modern
Languages, O.T.C. commander, housemaster, second master and,
for a brief period, acting headmaster. He gave to Stowe an
inexhaustible energy and great loyalty, both qualities under rather
erratic control.
Charles Spencer was an enthusiastic member of the English
Department. If a passage or a line seized his imagination he would
plunge into a nearby formroom and declaim it, calling for reaction
and comment. He had the unenviable task of marking all the Upper
School essays once a term as part of Roxburgh's plan to make
English the central plank in the curriculum. He stayed only for a
few years and left in 1932.
The achievements of these pioneers can be appreciated only if all
the hazards and setbacks are recorded. It was later to be the
received opinion that Roxburgh was broken by the casualties and
losses of the Second World War. There is truth in this, but the
nervous and physical strains that he had to carry were there from
the start despite the ease with which he appeared to deal with
awkward situations.
Recurring illnesses were a constant problem. The grounds were
luxuriant and noxious. The close age range of the pupils meant that

infection spread widely and the crowding in dormitories and studies compounded the dangers. Term after term Roxburgh reported to the Governors plagues of influenza, or schoolboy ailments complicated by persistent streptococcal infection. In February 1926 a boy died as the result of a mosquito bite and blood poisoning and later in the year 200 went down with German Measles. In the Easter Term of 1927, 150 boys, 4 masters, 4 matrons, 10 menservants and 7 maids suffered influenza, most of them seriously, and there were 15 cases of pneumonia, one fatal. In summer there were plagues of horse-flies and septic bites.[3] The lakes were treated with paraffin and some of the undergrowth over damp ground was cleared. The O.T.C contigent going to camp was reduced to twenty and School Certificate papers had to be taken in the sanatorium. Many of the drains were re-laid, but 1928 saw little improvement. In his report Roxburgh expressed alarm. Having said that all schools experienced mass illness occasionally he continued: 'The continual illness to which boys who come here appear to be subject, besides causing great expense and great loss of working time is beginning seriously to affect the school's reputation. A distinguished surgeon in London, both of whose sons have suffered mastoid abscesses tells me that we are now widely believed to suffer some endemic infection such as resulted some years ago in the abandoning of Osborne Naval College'. In cold weather it took four hours from the lighting of the furnaces to achieve a reasonable temperature. Bitter draughts swept through the long corridors and many windows and doors were ill-fitting. In 1929, Dr Pemberton, the first school doctor, died as a result of overwork during the winter plague and the streptococcal infection. Four prefects acted as pall-bearers and the O.T.C. formed a Guard of Honour at his funeral. Despite investigations by the Ministry of Health the cause of the outbreaks, which continued into the 1930s, was never fully ascertained. Eventually, less overcrowding, a wider age range and the end of constant building, which stirred up dust and dirt everywhere, lessened the rapid spreading of illness, but the unsuspected hazards of both building and grounds took a heavy toll in the first eight years. The lines in an ecstatic

[3] On his strolls through the park Roxburgh was in the habit of carrying an elegant silver handled fly-swatter. 'Even the flies at Stowe are snobs', he exclaimed to a wondering group of visitors.

poem printed in the local paper when the school first arrived in Buckingham: 'From these splendid ruins, / Shall blossom forth the flower of English youth', did not seriously underpraise the buildings.

Dismay arose also from a survey of the intellectual landscape. Many of the first generation of Stoics did, in fact, go on to carve out for themselves careers of great achievement in many different fields. The picture that presented itself to Roxburgh in the 1920s did not incline him to optimism. There was always a leaven of bright students, but the first admissions contained many boys who had failed or were likely to fail elsewhere. In 1926 he reported, 'The lower part of the School is still populated almost entirely by backward boys, but every term some of the worst move on and there are now only two forms the inhabitants of which are quite beyond hope.' This last group he was wont to refer to as 'the ancient monoliths'. As late as 1931, having already promised a place to a boy who did badly in Common Entrance, he wrote to the father, 'He will have to go into the bottom form (the most miserable fate that can befall any boy here) and he is extremely unlikely ever to get out of it'. He was encouraged by a report prepared by an inspecting team in 1925, led by A.W. Pickard-Cambridge of Balliol College, Oxford, although they noted short-comings with which he was all too familiar: 'I heard a number of lessons in which some boys did not get a turn at all owing to the slowness of those who did', said the Inspector, who added that prepared work in Latin showed that 'some of the boys prepared it badly and made wild shots; others were perhaps scarcely capable of studying the language at all.' They had praise for Acland and Heckstall-Smith and the evident interest in Science. Pickard-Cambridge, who was to become guide, philosopher and friend to Stowe, concluded his survey, 'It has been a great pleasure to inspect a School which has made so energetic and promising a beginning. I hope that it will continue to make educational experiments freely as it has every opportunity of doing and I have no doubt that, when it is completed by the growth of the sixth form, it will in due course take its place in the full sense among the great English Public Schools.'

The sixth form did, slowly, make its appearance. In 1924, only five of the twenty entrants for School Certificate gained the required number of passes but in 1926 twenty out of twenty eight were successful. Of the forty-eight leavers in July 1926, Roxburgh wrote, 'Their departure, which was not in every case regrettable, has lowered the average age of the School while raising its intellectual standard.' In the following year there were six successes in the Oxford and Cambridge entrance examinations though he informed the Council that, of the three failures at Oxford Responsions, 'two were quite unfitted for University and were only sent in to convince their parents of the fact'. In the winter of 1927 there came the first three open awards, followed swiftly by a fourth at Easter.

Financial worries were ever-present. It was not just new buildings and equipment which proved expensive. The long-neglected premises needed minor repairs constantly, the charges for which mounted up and horrified Warrington when they arrived in bulk. Both Wrekin and Canford had, in different ways, taken over existing schools and existing stock and Warrington could not comprehend why the expenses for Stowe outran those elsewhere in his empire. He denounced Mr Beebee, third bursar in two years, for his failure to guard the Council's interests. Although he shared an interest in pig-breeding with Mr Beebee and the bursar was a strict Sabbatarian, noted in Buckingham for wearing a frock-coat on Sundays, Warrington accused him of fondness for 'pub-trotting', of discourtesy to servants (a point on which Warrington felt strongly) and indifference to the standard of the food.[4] Roxburgh had to request that masters received their salary cheques before they left on holiday as he frequently had to lend them money himself. He paid his secretary, Lucas, out of his own pocket, purchased part of the Oxford Lodge approach from Farmer Davies as it made an inroad into the property and personally guaranteed part of the cost of constructing Grafton. He also generously suggested that his own salary should not rise with the school numbers indefinitely but be fixed at a reasonable level. Even so he had to contend with the effects of the economy drives which the Council enjoined, and the resulting interference in many school matters.

The stationery on which he conducted his vast correspondence came under suspicion and he was told that its quality would have

---

[4] The bursar was described in those days of classical learning as 'Eumoeus, ille noster' after the swineherd of Odysseus. His pigs were kept by the Temple of Venus and won many prizes.

to be approved by the bursar. When a local resident, Lady June Charlton, opened a tea-room which provided refreshments for boys on half-holidays and for visiting parents, the Council ordered that it should be placed out of bounds as sweets and ice-creams were bad for health. Lady June's husband was a Flying Officer and had arranged some displays of aircraft and flying at the school. Roxburgh fought a rearguard action and it was agreed that 'no cakes of more than moderate richness' would be served, but eventually the Council won. In 1928 Warrington reported that he had visited the school the day before and found that electric fires and toasters were being used in some rooms contrary to the instructions of the economy committee. He ordered the resident engineer to remove the offending plugs. He heard that masters sometimes paid the waiters to bring food to their rooms so that they could dine alone. It was ordained that any servant taking tips from a master should be dismissed on the spot.

One must be fair to Warrington. He was anxious that building standards should be high and inveighed against the Council cuts which had made the sanatorium such a poor structure. He deplored the replacement of the waiters by lower-paid apprentices as soon as they were trained ('I am afraid that we shall have a continuous succession of grubby young boys').[5] When the resurfacing of the Grand Avenue threatened a rise in the rates in Buckingham he agreed to a grant to keep relations between town and gown amicable. He found the funds to enable Roxburgh to subsidize many worthwhile activities. Nor is it difficult to sympathize with him over the famous incident when he ordered bars to be put up on some of the dormitory windows during a surprise visit. The Governors were responsible for safety and an employee reported cavortings on the roof at night. Besides, it is hard not to be won over by his account of the servant's protestation: '"Me 'art is nearly always in me mouth". So to keep 'is 'art in the right place I at once ordered bars to be put across the windows.' His forays into Stowe generally produced repercussions. On a March day in 1926, three boys fooling around fell into the lake. They hung their trousers up

---

[5] In the Autumn Term 1929, a houseboy of $17\frac{1}{2}$ was convicted of a string of thefts which ranged from Ivor Cross's bicycle to 'a catapult valued at 2s/6d'. Other articles were returned to their owners but the Chairman of the Magistrates observed that the catapult could not be returned 'as it was by law the property of the Government'.

to dry and then walked straight into the view of a party of ladies which the vicar was leading around the grounds. They were sternly reported for indecency and Roxburgh had to explain that Stowe did not resemble the court of Caligula.

It was in matters of religion that Warrington was implacable. In 1927 he informed his local MP that he would rather have his 'right hand severed at the wrist' than use it to vote for that gentleman again after the debates over the Prayer Book revision. Early in 1925 the headmaster received, via the *Spectator*, for which he sometimes wrote, a furtive letter from the rector of Caversham, who suspected that the Church of Rome was infiltrating propagandists into certain well-known schools, including Stowe. It transpired that a recent appointment, a Mr C.W. Phillips, had been 'perverted' to Rome many years before, when an Anglican curate in Oxford. He had been a loyal Chapel attender at Stowe and both Roxburgh and Habershon were convinced of his sincerity. Roxburgh blamed himself for not having made enquiries about the master's religious background before appointment. Despite assurances the Ayatollah of Caversham refused to be satisfied and informed Warrington. Phillips offered his resignation and the Council accepted it. He was not a young man and despite Roxburgh's help had difficulty in finding further employment.

Roxburgh was a great shock-absorber and all these difficulties were not permitted to lessen the normal growth of public school life. In 1926, E.R. Avory began the long predominance of Stowe in the world of tennis by winning the Junior Lawn Tennis Championship of Great Britain. The first Challenge Cup came to Stowe when D.E.C. Trench won the Mile in the Public Schools Championships in 1930. He was described in the press as a 'big and not too graceful runner', but he burst through at the close of the penultimate lap and snatched victory from the leaders. Chatham, the youngest house, with a very junior side, won the cricket house final in 1926 which was so drawn-out that, in those far-off days when examination results were of less importance, several half-holidays had to be granted to get it finished. Sir Oswald Stoll had presented the cinema projector because he believed that 'the future of the British Cinema depends upon the supply of educated men as producers and the Public Schools are the sources from which they should be drawn.' Performances were compulsory. The first was a war film, *Ypres*, the second a Western, *Covered Wagon*, accompanied by six volunteers on the piano, at the climax of which the cowboy hero reached the end of the trail in Oregon to the strains of César Franck. In these days of simpler tastes the 'love interest' in films merely induced boredom and it was customary to speed up the projectors and marry the couple off as soon as possible. The first house music competition was judged by Mr (later Sir) Adrian Boult. One house had a very good pianist but no other performers. The pianist produced an arrangement of Rachmaninov's C Sharp Minor Prelude for trombone and piano, hoping that the effect of the piano part would distract the judge's attention from the fact that the trombone had only three notes to play, even though these recurred frequently. The boy suborned to play the trombone was unable to grasp musical notation and, though he appeared to have a normal score on his stand, he had in reality a series of instructions: '8 inches out, 18 further inches out, wait a bit etc'. As the item approached the crowds swelled and, after wondering for a moment at the universal mania for Rachmaninov, the famous Boult composure gave way. It was not the only eccentricity in these early competitions: a quartet from Chatham of violin, saxophone, fife and piano played the Love Duet from Act I of *Madam Butterfly*. The tests included a unison song for 'not less than 35 voices' with attention paid to 'enunciation, phrasing and unanimity'. 'Mere loudness', said the rubric, 'will avail nothing.'

The XII Club was founded by McLaughlin for political and historical discussion; a fourteen-compartment railway carriage was acquired for the Wireless Club; the programme of the Classical Society, which included papers on 'The Ovidian Pentameter' and 'The Pre-Socratic Philosophers', showed that age and learning were advancing. Rex Whistler, whose brother, Laurence was a pupil, designed the membership card of the Vitruvian Society dedicated to the study of architecture. Using coloured chalks he created ravishing murals on the blackboards of deserted classrooms which eventually had to make way for Algebra and French verbs. Roxburgh was elected to the Headmasters' Conference in 1926. His comment to the headmaster of St Bee's indicates that he was not dazzled by the honour. 'I thought H.M.C. one of the dullest affairs I had ever been at. You got away early and you were wise, for the second day was even worse than the first. What dull dogs we Ushers all are.'

He himself entered into a contest with Dr Cyril Norwood,

now at Harrow, on the subject of Common Entrance. Norwood believed that the examination had a narrowing effect on young minds and harboured suspicions that in small preparatory schools burdened with mortgages the owners sometimes surreptitiously guided the candidates over the hurdles. Roxburgh, though in practice he often ignored the marks in favour of his knowledge of parents and schools, liked to have a prepared line of retreat and wrote to *The Times* in his best style:

> I find it hard enough to tell a father that his son is rejected because he did not get enough marks in Mathematics; it would be much more unpleasant to explain that I did not like the look of him or thought him stupid in conversation. What is more, if a boy fails in an examination he may sometimes be offered a second try. But if he has failed at interview, to offer a second try could imply that he might look more intelligent by artificial light or talk better sense on Thursdays than Tuesdays.

Men with less gravitas than Norwood might have been depth-charged out of the water by this, but the headmaster of Harrow replied by suggesting that Roxburgh could be guilty of steering the C.E. results to a desired conclusion and that his interview notes might run as follows: 'Mr and Mrs X called. Father pompous. Mother vulgar, uses lipstick; say boy is highly strung; can be led, not driven. See the boy gets nought in mathematics.'[6]

A Debating Society had been inaugurated as early as 1924 and at its first meeting the young Boyd-Carpenter spoke in the Conservative cause against the Liberal, Ivor Cross. David Niven defended the freedom of the cinema from censorship, following a ban on the film *Dawn*, the story of Nurse Cavell, supposedly to propitiate

---

[6] In the thousands of interview notes which exist at Stowe there is a rich mine for research. Roxburgh: 'Mother fair and fluffy', 'Mother stone deaf and wears wondrous hats', 'Father (divorced but friendly) is the distinguished discoverer of Dinosaur eggs in Mongolia', 'The boy as described by them is a wonderful athlete and has the character of a saint and a hero'. Reynolds: 'Father unlikely to be found in the stud-book', 'Lucas took them round and patted the black curly head of the small boy again and again'. Crichton-Miller: 'Boy, adopted out of the blue, looks like the father (pretty surly)', 'I said he would have high priority on the chance list and when they began saying he was growing out of his prep school and couldn't conveniently be postponed, I said firmly that CONVENIENCE didn't come into it and they dried up.' Drayson: 'This family all seem to be the same shape!' 'Nice old-fashioned Colonel. Cricket and Character. What does work matter?'

German opinion. There were Swiss camp trips: 'The outward journey was uneventful except for the temporary but alarming loss of Niven and Griffin at Boulogne. The next day they arrived safely at Bale(sic), cheerful but exhausted.' (*Stoic*)

In the major team games grounds had to be levelled and physiques strengthened before the full fixture lists could be established. Cricket began on the second day, 12 May 1923, but was interrupted by a thunderstorm. The first coach, Captain Weigall, had been a well-known player in his day but was past his prime. His two golden rules were: 'Don't cut until you have made 87' and 'Don't eat pie for lunch'. His successor, Arthur Newman, from Wiltshire, was an excellent coach and Capel Cure introduced some rigorous training. The team practised positioning for every bowler, and for both left and right-handed batsmen, so little time was lost in matches, and he hurled the ball in fielding sessions with legendary force. By the third season, in 1925, the Stoics were playing several Second XIs. J.F. gave a cricket bat to both the boys who first scored centuries. Summoned to the Gothic Library they were told to go to the school shop and choose a bat at his expense. One, Charles Pearson, scored another century a few days later on an excellent batting wicket at Charterhouse against the Second XI. A further summons came: 'My dear fellow, congratulations. You have doubled my obligation to you. You won't want another bat so get yourself a tennis racket.' At the end of the same week he scored 130 in a house match and waited for the call, anticipating a set of golf clubs. The third century was never mentioned but when he left, in 1927, a silver tankard arrived at the sick bay where he was confined, with all three dates engraved.

The ease with which the world's leading sportsmen can be viewed on television, added to the heightened importance of the examination season, has removed some of the excitement that surrounded school contests in the past. Even before senior sides arrived at Stowe surges of school spirit had made themselves evident. Describing an Under-16 cricket match against Wellington College in 1925 the *Stoic*'s powers of reporting failed: 'No written words could adequately give a description of the last few minutes of play, so with the preface that the match was to stop at 6.45 I will set down a bare statement of the facts:

6.30. The Umpires declare the match over, not having understood the arrangement, but play is resumed on the request of the Wellington Captain. Score: Wellington 135 for 7, Stowe 189 for 9 declared.

6.35. Cowell bowls Affleck Graves with a ball which just hits the top of the middle and leg stump. 140 for 8.

6.37. Moore tries a short run to Griffin at cover and has his wicket thrown down. 140 for 9.

6.43. Lefeuvre hits the ball slowly to Pearson at extra cover and calls for a run. Pearson on picking up on the run throws his wicket down. All out.

In 1927 the Cricket XI played a First XI from Radley but the match was drawn owing to rain. Pitches still had to be shared with the Rugby games and campaigns waged against the rabbits, which thronged the cricket areas but left the golf course clothed in luxuriant grass. Other First XI fixtures followed and there were two-day matches against Westminster, where Howland-Jackson on one occasion scored 204 not out.

At the end of the first year Roxburgh reported on the progress of Rugby to the Council: 'The experiment of setting our smallest boys to play neighbouring Preparatory Schools merely resulted in the massacre of our opponents and when a very "minor" Public School sent its Second XV to meet our First the result was happily similar. This, of course, proves nothing, but the boys clearly show promise and if any school has a better Rugby coach than Mr Clarke it is very fortunate.' One famous preparatory school which at least provided some opposition, had a secret weapon in the headmaster's daughter. Ousted from the XV because other schools objected to her rough play, she stood on the touch line making comments of such ferocity that the Stowe players, thinking she might come on to the pitch, misjudged their kicks.

Second XV Colours appeared in 1924 and in the following season the school First XV were wearing the familiar blue-and-gold shirts and white shorts, meeting other first teams in 1926.[7] After a

---

[7] The first full-sized goal-post to be set up on the North Front was hailed with the lines from *Paradise Lost*:

> . . . to equal which the tallest pine
> Hewn on Norwegian hills to be the mast
> Of some great admiral were but a wand

victory over the Radley Colts in 1924 the Captain asked Roxburgh for a half-holiday in celebration, to be rebuffed with the urbane reply: 'My dear fellow, we will always win matches at Stowe. You and your colleagues have only done what you are supposed to do. Certainly not.'

Other attributes of a public school – a school song, a London mission, an Old Boy Society and an imposing Chapel – came rapidly in these early days. The school song was an ambition of Lord Gisborough, who approached Rudyard Kipling for some verses without success. Eventually the Dean of Bristol, a genial Governor who enjoyed putting on shorts and having pillow-fights in the dormitories and who later became Bishop of Ripon, obliged. Henry Ley, Precentor of Eton, and several Directors of Music were asked to adjudicate on the tunes though the ultimate choice, by a Mr Brent Smith, failed to win adherents. The *Advertiser* reported that it was sung with great gusto at Speech Day in 1930 but it did not survive longer. A Boys Club founded in 1927 in London on the site of a public house called the Pineapple was more enduring. During the General Strike the previous year the Wireless Club relayed bulletins from a loudspeaker on the South Front. Roxburgh contributed an article to the *Spectator* in which the public schools were described as 'guilty of almost complete failure to educate their boys for the leadership of the nation'.

The *Stoic* reprinted and called for comment on an article in the *St Martin's Review* by 'An Anonymous Schoolmaster' which may have been by Heckstall-Smith or even Ivor Cross:

> There have long been 'Two Nations' in the country. But it is only since May 1926 that so many people on both sides have known each other not only for foreigners but enemies. During those disastrous days one half of us saw organised selfishness riding triumphantly in cars and buses and lorries through the forces that were fighting to get us justice and a decent life; the other half saw organised selfishness trying to rob us of our lawful inheritance and destroy all the culture and beauty that the toil of centuries had built up.

While helping to establish the Paddington Club Heckstall-Smith wrote, 'If one walks round these streets and looks at the boys one's first feeling is of rage against a system which removes such good people from school when they are fourteen and puts most of them not into a skilled trade, where self respect is possible but into fatal blind-alley jobs which must inevitably blight their good qualities and create bad ones'. Habershon was a strong supporter of the Pineapple as was Clifford, who knew a great deal about working-class conditions in London. In the Christ Church area of Marylebone and Paddington the death rate for children was 113 per thousand, as against 72 per thousand in other parts of London. In the immediate surroundings of the club it was even higher. Sir Douglas Hogg, MP for the local constituency, helped to launch the scheme and expressed the hope that those who joined would learn 'discipline, unselfishness, honour and love of country'. Boys were invited in from the streets to play billiards and by 1928 membership had risen to over fifty. One room was set aside as a chapel, for the old Mission concept died hard. Lower IVB, fired with enthusiasm, dramatized *A Christmas Carol* and acted it at the club. Parties from Stowe made visits. Paul Trippe described one of these in the Grafton Records:

> Played draughts and billiards, then a run to the Zoo and back while others did gym. Changeover, next run for second party was Regent's Park. Blair, on account of his running vest was nicknamed 'the ruddy wasp' by a spectator who yelled the name after him. Many rude remarks and constant jeering; running along London streets in change at nine o'clock at night was a new experience for us and everyone thoroughly enjoyed it. Down to the gym for community singing. 'Ginger' giving a little jazz on the piano. Pineappleites went home 10.10 (proper time 9.30). Billiards and bed!

'The Stowe Show', playlets and musical items, was given annually for some years at London theatres to raise income for the club. The *Times* critic commenting on A.P. Herbert's *Two Gentlemen of Soho* said, 'There were moments when one fell under the awful impression that Mr Anthony Marr was trying to capture the magnificently rotund delivery of his Headmaster.'(This was an error. It was a future High Commissioner in Canada, Sir Peter Hayman, who was the guilty party.)

There were return visits with games of football and cricket though the countryside did not exercise inescapable charm. 'It is an interesting sidelight on the mind of the London boy', said the *Stoic*, rather bemused, 'that the whole party walked the six miles to

Buckingham and back to visit the cinema on Saturday night and walking is not a popular pastime.' Camps were held and a Pineapple Hut erected with boy labour near to Lord Cobham's statue. Clifford later recalled how the Stoics, including the future England Rugby Captain, Bernard Gadney, John Lilley, Steve Taylor, (the future Lord Taylor), Arty Pearce and others, 'slaved as scullions from gunfire tea at 5.30 a.m. for the kitchen staff, to get a smouldering log fire blazing for making porridge and frying eggs and bacon, or sausage and mash, for hungry visitors.' The food allowance was 1s/6d per day, the rate for feeding Stowe boys, and nothing was wasted: left-over boiled rice went into the porridge, 'as they have never since allowed me to forget'.

On 23 December 1927 the first Old Stoic Dinner was held in London. There was some debate over the colour of the Old Stoic tie. Some felt that the original silver and blue design was too closely akin to the Fascist Party colours and the supporter of a rival design declared, 'I can imagine nothing more annoying than to be assaulted by a gentleman of Communistic leanings because he has mistaken the nature of your neck-wear'.

The old private chapel in the main building was soon too small to hold the school. Services were held in a variety of places: the gymnasium, Assembly, and even on the South Front steps. There was pressure from parents for a new chapel and some pledges of support were made if the project could be completed in a specified time. Several designs were considered by the Governors and eventually Sir Robert Lorimer, a Stowe parent, was entrusted with the task. The building was to be large enough to hold 800 people and the interior was to be 150 feet long and 40 feet high. The design had certain similarities with St Paul's Outside the Walls, most beautiful of Rome's basilicas. The interior roof was of unusual form, finished in timber and with deeply coffered panels. Following the practice in many Italian churches, where columns from classical buildings had been incorporated, pillars from the Temple of Concord and Victory were removed to create arcades. 'The first pillar to be removed from Concord left for the Chapel site at 3 p.m. on July 15th. It reached its destination eight minutes later.'This is believed to be a record for an Ionic Column', declared the *Stoic*.

Work began two days after the visit of H.M.Queen Mary to lay the foundation stone. It was a stirring occasion on a glorious summer day with the band of the Irish Guards playing and a huge throng of visitors, though it began anxiously. Owing to some error in the presentations in Buckingham, Her Majesty was not in the most serene of tempers when she arrived. She waved away the first two courses of lunch and as protocol forbade anyone else to start, the guests looked dismally at the empty space between the cutlery for some time. Eventually she called for a drink and Roxburgh poured out as large a whisky as he thought could decently be offered. A thaw then became manifest and the meal was summoned back. The rest of the day proved less fraught and so regal was her bearing that, according to Eric Reynolds, the boys decided that she would be the only possible consort for Roxburgh. A copy of *The Times*, the school lists and a set of coins dated 1927 were placed in a casket made of lead from the roof of the Temple of Bacchus, which was demolished to make room for the new building, and placed in the cavity beneath the foundation stone. At the garden party which followed, two housemaids watching from an upstairs window decided to put on their best clothes and in their words, 'have a good tuck in'. They were spotted by the Temple House matron and told to report on the following morning. Expecting to be dismissed, they were congratulated on their initiative. 'She knew how to keep staff', was the comment of the Old Stoic to whom they related the story many years later.

The Chapel was itself a remarkable testimony to the ambition of a four-year-old school, but it weighed heavily on the finances. The estimates rose from £40,000 to £50,000; much of the panelling from the old chapel used for the chancel proved to be veneer or in poor condition; the organ and the proposed stalls had to match the design in size and dignity. A small levy on the bills of new entrants added to the monies available, but it was necessary to postpone other desirable projects such as the workshops. At one moment Pearman-Smith, a Governor, had to advance £4,000 of his own money so that the masters could be paid. But the Chapel brought about the good of fortune of establishing links with the Legal and General Assurance Company. Warrington had already negotiated loans to Westonbirt and Canford and £15,000 to the Wrekin Company to enable Wrekin to advance more money to Stowe. The levy was bringing in £698 per term, but it was deemed possible to borrow up to £30,000 from Legal and General to complete the Chapel and certain classrooms. Parnells, the builders, also agreed to accept payments spread over three years. Before they began their work a huge tree on the site had to be felled while the entire school hung on the retaining ropes. It was reported that the Chapel organ would produce a 'volume of sound which would have a radius of more than a mile'.

The Chapel was opened on 11 July 1929, by Prince George, who drove his $4\frac{1}{2}$ litre Bentley saloon himself, handing over to the chauffeur just before his arrival. A spate of disputes over matters such as the cross on the altar had arisen with the building and Warrington was not the most extreme. 'I do not think I have ever sat through a more unpleasant half hour than the one for which the General (Adair) was responsible yesterday', wrote the normally emollient Roxburgh. 'We shall probably have a worse scene still on the 26th March and heaven knows what sort of an East End we shall be urged to have. Happily I know you may be counted upon to insist on what is right and reasonable.' Alternatives such as a Crusader's Sword or a Maltese Cross carved in the woodwork were mooted though at the time of the opening neither had been adopted. Happily, an idea of Roxburgh's that the school might commission a reproduction of the Watts *Sir Galahad* in Eton College Chapel for the East End came to nothing. *The Supper at Emmaus* was by Meredith Williams. Above the Ionic columns were plaques illustrating the Benedicite. The opening hymn at the service was 'Round the Lord in Glory Seated'. Prince George read from the Bible used at the Coronation of King George III, which had been presented to the school, and the Bishop of Ripon preached the sermon. There were 2,000 guests present but at the end of the proceedings the Prince through some misunderstanding asked for a day's holiday. Royal visits usually brought a much longer period of freedom and a silence fell upon the multitude. Once again Roxburgh saved the situation and called out after the departing Bentley, 'And we'll add three days to that Your Royal Highness.' So the royal party left to loud acclamations.

At Speech Day, 1930, Roxburgh declared it the 'Festival of a Thousand'. There were over 500 in the school and around 450 Old Stoics. There were Old Boys in Argentina, Australia, Canada, Ceylon, Columbia, France, Germany, India, Kenya, South Africa and Spain. Five held regular commissions in the Army, two in the Navy, five in the R.A.F. There were sixty Old Stoics at Cambridge, fifteen at Oxford. In the two previous years there had been six open awards and this year there were seven including the first Balliol scholarship won by K.S. Toms. John Boyd-Carpenter had just been elected as President of the Oxford Union, soon to be followed in that office by Toby O'Brien. Replying to the criticism that there had been too many Generals as guests of honour at Speech Days J.F. affirmed his belief that 'a great soldier is rarely a great militarist'. Field Marshal Plumer, in his address, warmed to the theme and stressed that 'at the present time there was happily no prospect of anything like a Great War.'

4

The Thirties

Seen retrospectively through the veils of social revolution and war, the pre-war period appears in some ways to have been a time of happiness never easily to be recaptured. The Depression, with which the decade opened, did not have an immediate effect upon numbers. On Speech Day, 1931, observing that the school was 496 strong when it should have been 450, Roxburgh declared: 'They say that the slump and the birth-rate are going to empty the Public Schools. I wish I saw some sign of their doing so in our lists. If I did, I should feel there might be some use in Mr Snowden [the Labour Chancellor] after all.' But in reality there were many anxieties. It was not uncommon for boys to spend only four or even three years at boarding school because of the costs, which multiplied the work of registration and career advice. The Depression of 1930–31 also helped to bring about the disasters which encompassed Warrington and gave rise to the birth of Allied Schools, a process which was not achieved without moments of worry and despair. A letter from 'The Major' to Roxburgh which is undated although it undoubtedly comes at the end of an Autumn Term in the early 1930s, begins: 'I looked in yesterday before I left but you were out. I just wanted to express my sympathy with you in your weariness of mind, and my hope that you were going to get away from Stowe as soon and for as long as possible. Shyness and the dislike of "butting in" on another's private affairs have kept me from saying anything before this but I have been most awfully sorry for you.' A mother, who had chosen Stowe because she thought that Eton might give her son expensive tastes, wrote

apropos of the 1931 Confirmation Service, 'I don't suppose there
has ever been a time when it is more difficult for the young to steer
a straight course, or find stepping stones that don't submerge
amidst present day so called broadmindedness.' The international
situation cast dark shadows and was the theme of many confusing
and contradictory lectures. Yet, overall, enterprise and distinction
marked the advance of the school year by year and it seemed to be
fulfilling many of the hopeful prophecies made at its outset.

Numbers rose to over 550. In September 1933 some of the new
classrooms had to be used as dormitories and bathrooms. Hill
House in Buckingham sheltered a dozen boys though as Roxburgh
stated, 'The arrangement . . . was never satisfactory and was
acutely displeasing to the parents concerned'. In Chatham, beds
stood in the middle of the dormitories and those around the walls
were closer together than the three feet stipulated by the Ministry
of Health. Some balance was maintained by the number of young
leavers, as many parents wished their sons to have the experience
of a public school rather than the full course, and examinations
were of less importance. 'It is a symptom partly of "parental
poverty" and partly of the restlessness of the new generation which
is so impatient to get away from books to work – even though
there is not enough work to go round', wrote Roxburgh in 1934.
Walpole House was delayed, not only because of financial worries
but because of construction difficulties. The Grecian Valley had
originally been formed by removing thousands of tons of earth and
depositing them at the eastern end of the mansion. The foundations
therefore had to plunge below this soft earth and go twenty feet
deeper than expected. Married quarters were available and when
the house opened in 1934 Ian Clarke, who had conducted the
customary secret courtship, concealed even from 'The Major',
moved in taking with him a large number of boys from Grenville.
Yet even with the addition of an eighth house Cobham was still over
full at eighty-one, as was Bruce at seventy-six. Grafton required
more studies but these could only be made from a classroom currently used as a dormitory.

By the end of the decade the Upper School had grown to around
200 out of the total. It was divided into nine 'Sides': first the
Classical which generally numbered about a dozen, many potential
scholarship candidates; second, the Modern Linguists numbering
around thirty and very varied in ability. There were about twenty

Historians who developed a strong *esprit de corps* and had success in university awards. The Maths and Science Sides followed with some sharing of programmes, and a separate Medical Side of about thirty boys combining Biologists and intending doctors taking their first M.B. before leaving school. The Geography, Economics and General Side, usually a large body of around thirty, had been intended originally for the older Certificate takers who had only a few terms left. Under the guidance of H.V.G. Kinvig, who had a First in Geography, the Side devoped from its utilitarian beginnings and entered boys for university Geography courses. Thus in time a further Side had to be created to absorb those who were genuinely unfitted for specialization.

On this was imposed a tutorial system to cater for the needs of university entrance and professional exams, and at the same time to introduce methods of work that would follow in university years. Tutors were also expected to encourage their boys in the Art School and other activities. The career of tutor became an avenue different from that of housemastering and tutorial salaries were made comparable with those of housemasters. The system, which fairly frankly followed an Eton model, did provide a strong addition to the pastoral care and gave prestige to the academic work. It was expensive in manpower, as the tutors tended to organize the minority subjects and the general studies of their pupils independently. It was also in certain respects divisive. In the late 1920s the Croom-Johnson parents had taken Roxburgh severely to task, with long memoranda which were well argued, for failing to establish a homogeneous intellectual élite which could outshine the more traditional sporting power bases. Patrick Hunter, senior tutor, thought however that tutors helped to produce a large number of boys who, even if not scholars, were 'interesting conversationalists, good critics of what they read and what they meet with'.

The second wave of staff appointments, the men who had to work this system in which private personality had as great a part to play as driving force in the classroom – quite a different art – was no less interesting than the first. McLaughlin left in 1933, another entrant into the Inspectorate for which he was totally unsuited. He had just published *Newest Europe* on the post-Versailles political scene and it gives a taste of the flashes that enlivened his teaching: 'Intellectually, Russia looks to the American policy of mass production and it is as unlikely to turn out exceptional men as Mr Henry Ford is to build a Rolls by error in his popular line of cars.'

A year later the History Side came under the care of W.L. McElwee, who made a huge contribution to the liveliness of academic life at Stowe though, in the tradition of historians, it was individualistic. Sedbergh, Christ Church, research under Namier and a period in Vienna had fitted him to be an eloquent and prolific historian as well as a gifted teacher. He had collaborated with the young A.J.P. Taylor on a translation of Friedjung's *Struggle for Supremacy in Europe* and published a Life of the Emperor Charles V. His wife, Patience, had known Roxburgh at Lancing: 'It must be twelve years . . . since you . . . walked about our garden on stilts', she wrote, conjuring up an unlikely image, and telling Roxburgh that 'Bill' would give up all thoughts of a university job if Stowe offered an appointment. 'It would be wonderful for me to anchor in a School again.' In 1939 Henry Marten, Vice-Provost of Eton, wrote about McElwee in connection with some historical research. In his reply Roxburgh stated: 'I regard him as one of the two or three best teachers I have had here in these sixteen years . . . I sincerely hope that you are not going to lure McElwee away from me. I could ill afford to lose him in peacetime and it would be a disaster to lose him now.' McElwee did in fact leave for a period of war service and won the Military Cross in Normandy.

Charles Spencer, senior English tutor, was as hard to replace as McLaughlin. In 1931 he produced *Comus*, making full use of the terrain around the Temple of British Worthies with entrances across the water. A Literary Society, under his aegis, heard papers by John Masefield, Edith Sitwell, Walter de la Mare, and Ronald Knox, a galaxy probably unequalled by any other school. Even Bernard Shaw vouchsafed a written refusal as opposed to the customary printed card. Spencer was also a fine cricket and Rugby player who continally lamented the hours he spent at the billiards table. High aspirations alternated with periods of depression. 'I am fed up with myself because I teach without knowing anything, without knowing how to teach, without knowing anything about the minds of the boys I teach, without knowing anything about the world, so as to know what ought to be taught.' He left for a teacher training college, spent some time in the U.S.A., enjoyed his first experiences in the Royal Marines but committed suicide in 1941.

Roxburgh wrote: 'Clarke provided strength, wisdom and rectitude; Spencer fire, delight and imagination.'

He was succeeded by the equally complex Terence Hanbury White, known always as 'Tim', and later to the world at large as the author of *The Sword in the Stone*, whose arrival soon produced a mild crisis. He had published two youthful novels under a pseudonym, James Aston, which was revealed when a boy called James Ashton received correspondence by mistake. Neither book would raise an eyebrow today but, when White's identity was discovered, although he protested that he had mentioned 'some literary wild oats' when appointed and that he had endeavoured to portray immorality as 'boring', Roxburgh had to placate some stern parents. 'The book is utterly abominable and it filled me with disgust,' he wrote 'but Mr White himself is a fine type of man . . . a very healthy, manly and satisfactory person, devoted among other things to riding and hunting, whereas the book reads like the work of a degenerate.' Another parent had nobly forced himself to read the book from cover to cover in the public interest: 'Although I was told it was a filthy book I felt it my duty to wade through it last night for the reason of its alleged authorship. I regard it as the most putrid bit of beastliness I have ever seen or heard of.' He dismissed the author as 'a depraved specimen of human garbage'.[1]

White's sturdy sporting persona – he would rush out of school on a Saturday, remove his grey flannels to reveal hunting breeches and, leaping into his car, head for the Grafton Meet – extended to his teaching which was stylish and turbulent. He cultivated authentic writing and denounced affectation. His energy was displayed as a producer of *Miracle at Verdun*, which contained thirteen scenes and involved a cast of ninety on the stage of the gymnasium which measured 30 feet by 20 feet. The housemasters decided at a subsequent meeting to pass a resolution that 'in view of the immense expenditure of time and energy involved in the production of *Miracle at Verdun* and the complete dislocation of ordinary life, no production on that scale should be allowed again.' He established a Motion Picture Society to make a film of life at Stowe and both his novel, *Mistress Masham's Repose*, and the more autobiographical, *England Have My Bones*, contain

[1] *The Times* in T.H. White's obituary described *They Winter Abroad* as 'a brilliant novel in a genre he did not repeat'.

references to Stowe. He learnt to fly, went shooting, and studied medieval bestiaries as a prelude to taking up falconry. One of the Governors remembered sitting down upon a chair in his room when 'a snake emerged from the cushions and slithered across my knees'. After he left, he asked Roxburgh in 1941 for a reference for the R.A.F. Roxburgh replied jokingly that he would testify to White's 'moral spotlessness' as 'a necessary act of perjury'. White thanked Roxburgh for the good moral character he provided, adding, 'At least I succeeded in leaving Stowe without actually being chucked out, which I shall ever esteem as my highest claim to the above.'

Not all masters made the same impact though one near-contemporary, Mr Dungey, used to smoke a pipe up to the last moment before lessons began, then hastily stuff it away with the result that on occasion smoke was seen to issue from his pockets. A.V. Ireland was a relative of John Ireland, the composer, and a choral scholar of King's Cambridge, but he changed his name back to that of his forbears and became the Baron Velleman von Simunich. It was not a propitious moment to adopt vestiges of German nationality. In June 1935 a lady called at the War Office in order to draw its attention to the anti-militarist propaganda at Stowe by a German master. Hinting at secret funds from the Third Reich, she deposed: 'Up to two years ago the Baron was a poor man known as A.V. Ireland. Today he is the richest master in the School owning several motor cars.' Her son at Stowe said this master spent fifteen minutes of every lesson persuading boys of Germany's guiltlessness in the Great War, her pacific intentions for the future, and the futility of military service. The boy decided along with others that he would not join the O.T.C. The son of a famous admiral had declined to join the Navy. She added darkly that von Simunich intended to open a school in Austria where boys would be allowed a degree of freedom that would undermine their moral character.

At masters' meetings Roxburgh occasionally spoke forcefully against imposing ideologies upon the young but he regarded the Baron as a sufficiently good teacher to ignore the complaints. At the Film Society, which showed masterpieces of the highest quality such as *La Kermesse Heroique* and *Carnet du Bal*, one foreign film, *Gribouille*, was introduced by the Baron with a memorable speech which makes one surmise on how it would be received in the 1990s:

Gentlemen, you are to see tonight a film which I have had some hesitation in presenting. I have heard it said in certain quarters that some of the films I show you are unsuitable for people of your years and may even have a corrupting influence on you. I feel sure that is not the case. The film tonight is a story of adultery and bloodshed, of a tragedy that overtakes those who give way to unbridled passions . . . Should it ever be the fate of any of you (and I pray it may not be) to stand on the brink of crime may you remember this film and withhold your hand.

Life with the Baroness, a local girl, was unsettled and he left in 1938 to teach in Switzerland. He returned to teach at Eton during the war where he also became something of a legend.

Very different was B.R. Miles of Hawarden School and Jesus College, Oxford. He became tutor of the Medical Side and until the Second World War was in charge of P.T. and boxing which he took over from D. Simmonds, an Oxford Blue, who was another to join the Inspectorate. Miles was a county hockey player and an immensely keen golfer who devoted great energy to the modernizing and improvement of the Stowe course. George Gilling-Lax was a brilliant Marlburian Classic who had First Class Honours in both Classics and History from King's, Cambridge.[2] He came in 1931 and eventually became housemaster of Grenville. He compiled a valuable though unpublished History of Stowe in its days of private ownership. Imbued by his researches with a great love of the mansion and the throng of characters who had passed through its spacious halls, he explained his reasons for joining the R.A.F.V.R. in the dangerous role of night fighter although as housemaster and almost over-age, he could have accepted

---

[2] The preparatory schools were adept at finding out which masters set the scholarship papers at the public schools. At Stowe, Gilling-Lax set the Latin translation and, in 1938, chose the Martial epigram, 'Non amo te, Sabidi', famously rendered by Thomas Brown (1663–1704): 'I do not love thee, Dr Fell'. P.M.Ward, a candidate, devised the paraphrase:

> I do not love thee Gilling-Lax,
> The reason why my brains I tax,
> But this I know up to the max,
> I do not love thee, Gilling-Lax.

Discretion became the better part of valour and he did not submit it, although it would certainly have pleased the examiner.

exemption from military service. 'I have been privileged to enjoy the beauty and freedom of Stowe and it is incumbent upon me to repay the debt and help to preserve these things for others.' He was killed in 1943. Roxburgh wrote to an American Old Stoic, 'I cannot help feeling that if any man gave his life for his country it was Gilling.'

George Rudé and Alasdair Macdonald also came in 1931 again enforcing the belief that Roxburgh enjoyed contrasts in his appointments. Rudé, despite a fascination for Bentley cars, was a radical who later became a distinguished historian of revolutionary thought. He took part in the anti-Fascist demonstrations of the 30s and a (quite untrue) story circulated that he had been involved in a brawl with a constable. Roxburgh murmured urbanely, 'My dear fellow, I don't like to enquire into your private life but is it true you were seen knocking a policeman off his horse?' He moved on to St Paul's where the High Master was less sympathetic. A parent saw him addressing a left-wing rally near Earl's Court and his resignation was procured immediately. Macdonald, from Fettes and St John's, Cambridge, first had his attention drawn to Stowe when he shared rooms at Yale with an Old Lancing boy who put up Roxburgh's photograph. As Stowe was seeking a master to teach Latin and French he spent a month in France. As a married man his position involved all the usual difficulties with housing. At the outset he ran Hill House in Buckingham where twelve to fifteen boys spent their first term. Roxburgh, in writing to ask him to keep the problem of accommodation to the fore, added 'I always thought that the Parable of the importunate widow, though ethically dubious was full of worldly wisdom.' When, during the Second World War, Ivor Cross decided to leave Chatham his decision vacated one of the very few desirable residences for a married man. Playford immediately made plans to win the hand of the sanatorium sister but Roxburgh declared that he would only consider the application when he saw the necessary announcement in *The Times*. The Macdonalds moved from Cobham where he was acting housemaster and remained in Chatham from 1943 to 1962. He wrote two valuable histories of the house and school and eventually became second master. His Saturday morning gramophone sessions won many converts to opera, including Julian Budden, biographer of Verdi.

1932 brought J.A. Tallent, a Cambridge and England centre

three-quarter. Roxburgh hoped that he might achieve the same success as Ian Clarke enjoyed with the forwards, but he left after four
years for the Stock Exchange and was later President of the English
Rugby Union. Rex Hamer was an Uppinghamian Classic who
joined Capel Cure on a record-breaking ascent of mountain peaks
in the British Isles within a time limit. He had a successful war, and
returned to be housemaster of Grenville, moving from there to a
headmastership in Trinidad. In addition to Tallent who, from the
Epicurean seems also to have been nimble on the dance floor, there
were two other Rugby Internationals in the Common Room.
Donald Crichton-Miller was a Wing Forward for Cambridge and
Scotland and D.I. Brown, later housemaster of Cobham, also
played for Cambridge and Scotland. J.R. Hands came in 1933, a
Modern Linguist with a good tenor voice who played Frederick in
The Pirates of Penzance. After the Second World War he served in
the Allied Control Commission in Austria. Julian Budden, attending a performance of *Der Rosenkavalier* in Graz, looked up at the
Imperial box and saw his old schoolmaster resplendent in the midst
of Habsburg ornamentation.

The Reverend T.C.P. Brook succeeded Habershon as chaplain.
He was twin brother of P.W.P. Brook, another International
Rugby player, and was himself an excellent sportsman. He ended
his time after a brief period of headmastering and teaching at
Sherborne as a parish priest, where he had the distinction of having
the ex-Archbishop of Canterbury, Lord Fisher, as his curate.

There were other notable figures. Robert Skene, Oxford Cricket
Blue, took over Grenville when Ian Clarke went into Walpole,
married the sister of a Grenvillite, John Langley, and was later the
Director of Gabbitas Thring. James Todd, mathematician, after a
headmastership at Newcastle-under-Lyme became the Oxford
Secretary of the Oxford and Cambridge Examination Board. In
early days the application form for an assistant master's post at
Stowe contained merely the words, 'Public School', as if others
did not exist. Raymond Walker attended Consett Grammar School
in County Durham, from which he leapt to King's College, Cambridge, as a scholar and Wrangler in the Mathematics Tripos.
Although clearly a very desirable catch for any school his arrival
at Stowe in 1933 was delayed for a number of reasons. Roxburgh
thought that the Depression might affect staff numbers: 'The world
is in such an unstable condition that one simply does not know

what may happen between now and next Autumn to the class of English people who pay school fees.' Roxburgh himself was unwell: 'The Headmaster, who has been in the doctor's hands for some time has been compelled to give up work completely for at least a couple of weeks', came a note in December 1932. Even when his appointment was agreed the start of the Autumn Term was delayed as the result of the granting of an extra week of holiday at the request of the Prince of Wales. Walker was assistant housemaster to Skene in Grenville and acting housemaster for a period. Roxburgh had to plunge into a very considerable correspondence to retain his services as a mathematician in wartime. He pointed out the national need for technicians in the future: 'I cannot get anyone to teach them except a highly inefficient woman'. Walker was a good amateur musician, a bassoonist and pianist who was able on one occasion to stand in as relief pianist at a school dance. In 1945 he married Biddy, daughter of the commander of the ordnance camp which occupied part of the school. This meant leaving Grenville. Stowe houses were always at the mercy of matrimonial events. 'You will understand', he wrote, 'that as a married man I become a nonentity (in one way!) here and being a Wrangler I don't view working as second string to AGA (Archer) for ever with much satisfaction.' In fact he waited until 1955 before becoming Maths Tutor though he had the distinction of becoming senior tutor after Patrick Hunter in 1962.

The position of senior tutor had been created for Hunter in 1933. It comprised responsibility for the timetable and a certain degree of overseeing the efforts of assistant masters. 'I have a strong feeling that enough is not being done to help the younger masters with their work, nor indeed to keep them up to it', wrote J.F. 'Yet I do not see how I am going to do much more myself in this way than I have done in the past. Hence the proposed devolution and departmentalism.' It was one of the few moves he was ever to make in this direction. As boys stayed for shorter periods owing to the economic climate (prep schools often wished to hang on to pupils for as long as possible for the same reason), the burden of dealing with registrations, university entrance and careers intensified. The tasks of remembering twenty-first birthdays and replying to Old Stoics multiplied as the numbers swelled. A larger staff meant more interviews. Roxburgh did however have great good fortune in being able to make appointments which established Stowe in the forefront in music and art.

In 1928 he had written rather dolefully to the Governors that Henry Marten (Vice-Provost of Eton) had recently praised Radley in *The Times* for its outstanding musical strength. 'If he had wished to mention the school in which music played the smallest part, I fear he might have chosen Stowe.' It was timely that Leslie Huggins (Rugby and Balliol) felt that he had little more to achieve at Radley and, having private means, was able to contemplate the small salary offered with equanimity. At the 1930 Speech Day Roxburgh was able to say, 'When I was trying to persuade Dr Huggins to come here eighteen months ago I found that what most attracted him to Stowe was his conviction that the Headmaster was totally unmusical, and either would make no suggestion on musical matters, or would be easily crushed, if he did.'[3] He added that 'apart from singing in Chapel, which our worst enemy could not say was lacking in vigour, the School boasted a Choral Society, a Madrigal Society, two orchestras, a band, – and a panatrope.' He might also have mentioned that Stowe produced a ballet which was not ordinary fare in H.M.C. schools at the time. The 'Polovstian Dances' from *Prince Igor* were staged as well as sung. *The Advertiser* reported 'a whimsical flying dance', 'a vivacious kick dance', 'a combined war and flying dance', then 'a final terpsichorean skirmish' performed to 'thunderous applause'. J.C. Saunders, a young master who came with Huggins in 1929, was a member of the Folk Dance Society and arranged the choreography, bravely dancing himself . This balletic work rose to the the attention of *The Times* with particular praise for the costume and scenery designs of G.J.B. Wright of Grafton, 'in the manner of Komisajevsky', though the *Times* critic thought that the Khan should have had a

---

[3] Roxburgh rather enjoyed his unmusical reputation. It was said he listened only to the 'Kreutzer Sonata'. Writing in 1945 to a mother enquiring about recorder lessons he declared: 'I don't know whether we run to recorders; we certainly have performers on the clarinet, flute and oboe (probably sackbuts and shawms too)! This is a very musical school and it enjoys that character largely because it has a totally unmusical headmaster. There is, therefore, no one to interfere with the musicians, who develop their habitual initiative in every direction, happily for the most part at a considerable distance from my rooms.' How many headmasters, one wonders, would have risen to this epistolary flight in answer to a very mundane request?

hookah rather than a pipe, even if the smoke 'rising up continuously gave ethereality to the movements of the dancers in scarlet'.

Dr Huggins was a superb Director. ('It is a blessing to find
anyone who, though being so musical is at the same time so easy
to live with and so normal', wrote Roxburgh.) He was also a full
participator in school and county life. He helped the Stoics to
found scout troops in local villages long before community service
had become part of the 'hidden curriculum' and was for a time Joint
Master of the Grafton Hunt. He personally paid for many of the
celebrated artists who came to give recitals at Stowe. In 1933
subscription concerts were launched. One hundred supporters
were needed to make the programme viable and this number was
exceeded in the first week. By the end of the year 260 serial tickets
had been issued and many more were taken for individual concerts. The programmes were far from populist and included
quartets by Ravel, Fauré and music for sophisticated tastes. He
raised funds for the organ from unknown donors. 'It is rather hard',
wrote Roxburgh, 'to thank an anonymous abstraction, but I am in
fact full of thankfulness towards the impersonal source of this
unexpected help – and also, as you know, towards you.' He edited
and contributed hymns to *Cantata Stoica* and collaborated with
Roxburgh to reduce the Psalter. 'Most of the savagery and most of
the nonsense has been cut out', said the latter with satisfaction.

In 1933 the tenth anniversary was celebrated by opening a
subscription list to renovate Queen's Temple as a Music School.
Saplings were growing through the steps and the roof leaked badly.
A Roman pavement discovered at Foxcote was inserted in the floor
and the department's new home opened in 1934 with the Bach
Concerto for three pianofortes. In 1935 there was an ambitious
production of *Boris Godunov* with the professional, Dennis Noble,
in the title role. Possibly fearing what he was to encounter he had
imbibed rather freely *en route* causing 'The Major' to enquire
whether 'Boris' was 'Good enough'! The orchestra under W.L.
Snowdon, later Director of Music at Haileybury, had to pick up
Noble's interpretation of the part with one rehearsal only, which
lasted far into the night, and was played without lights for part of
the first performance. Noel Annan, head of school, First XV,
Under Officer in the O.T.C. and prominent in several learned
societies, played the Simpleton and Huggins considered it the finest
acting in the production.

Art received a similar lift when, on the death of H.W. Neville who had founded the department, Roxburgh appointed Robin Watt to inaugurate the new building given in memory of Pilot Officer G.D. Watson O.S., killed in training. Robin Watt was born in Canada, but commissioned from Sandhurst into the Green Howards. He was four times wounded in the First World War, won the M.C. and Bar and Croix de Guerre. He had studied in Paris and Rome but his influence at Stowe, and that of his wife Dodie, went far beyond his department. The Art School became the best club-room in Stowe and a real engine of art appreciation. He served as an officer in the O.T.C. and Home Guard and many 'came to believe that there must be something in military discipline when such an artist believed in it and something in art when such a soldier practised it'. Dodie was also a considerable artist and worked tirelessly creating costumes for plays and for puppets even during the wartime clothes rationing. She had very decided views on the good and the bad in art. At a wartime 'Brains Trust' in Buckingham when the panel had to choose which member of the opposite sex they would most like to have been she unhesitatingly selected Michelangelo. (Roxburgh chose Cleopatra.)

Ewald Zettl brought to the Modern Language Department a wide knowledge of Europe and its literature. He was strongly recommended by Pickard-Cambridge from Sheffield University. At the University of Innsbruck he had been an Austrian ski champion and he joined with Bill McElwee in organizing visits to Europe and cultural excursions.

There were changes in the houses too at this time. Ivor Cross was moved from Temple to Chatham where it was deemed a rod of iron was required. He was followed in Temple by Capel Cure. Timberlake, housemaster of Grafton, was obliged to give up the house on marriage and moved on to Rugby. His place was taken by Clifford, then a bachelor. Walpole House opened at the end of 1934. J.T. Hankinson, a biologist, succeeded Acland in Cobham when the latter moved to Norwich and, with the help of D.I. Brown and his own ability to stay awake beyond 10 p.m., a new and ambitious policy was introduced.

Boris was in rehearsal for much of 1934 and, while the Tsar lamented the plots and insurrections which were destroying his empire, Warrington was enduring feelings which were similar. The impulse to found schools was still unsatiated. In response to a request from the Bishop of Mombasa he established Limoru School for the daughters of Europeans in Kenya and it was quickly filled. He was also moving into higher education. St Peter's, Oxford was founded as a memorial to Bishop Chavasse of Liverpool to provide education for those who could not afford the fees at older colleges. In 1933 he came to the aid of a Bible college and founded Clifton Theological College so that the Principal, a Dr Carter, could continue his work. He was also buying up advowsons and presentations to livings. Even after his empire was reconstructed Allied Schools still owned 181 advowsons. Like many successful financiers he had begun to attribute unlimited capacity to himself and fallen into the temptation to confuse private and company funds. He was a strange mixture of religious zeal and rough opinions. Clifford recalled that he was once dining with J.F. when Warrington called and had to be asked to join the party. As the meal progressed he launched into bawdy jokes, much to Roxburgh's embarrassment: 'I have known him baulk at Shakespeare in full sail in a play-reading circle!' The building was still costing large sums in maintenance. Roxburgh complained of the North Front in 1932,

> Large pieces have fallen from one of the cornices, one or two of them being quite big enough to have killed a man. We cannot hope that there will not be further falls especially in Autumn and Winter. I have had to forbid the boys to approach the North Wall at all on one side of the steps. As the North Front is the first part of the building which a visitor sees its dilapidated condition has naturally attracted a good deal of attention and it is certainly one of the causes of the many absurd rumours now circulating about our financial position. One Preparatory School Master wrote to me the other day, that many of his parents believed Stowe to be bankrupt because the building was falling down and 'there was no money to put it right'. I do not suggest that we need pay heed to these rumours but I am convinced that the repairs cannot be delayed much longer without the possibility of unfortunate consequences.

Interference in small matters intensified. A charge of £14 for typing of examination papers was disallowed. Roxburgh had to explain that papers set in plain English were typed by his own secretary, Lucas, working far into the night. Those requiring Greek or German letters or mathematical formulae had to be sent to Oxford. A suspicion of light entertainment pervaded enquiries into the Film Society, particularly on the installation of a 'Talkie' projector. 'I would willingly have avoided installing a "Talkie",' replied the headmaster,'but we were driven to it by the fact that silent films are now practically unobtainable.' When the normally loyal Haworth complained about masters' conditions he replied, 'I understand your feelings very well about the apparent indifference of the authorities to the personal welfare of masters. I will have one more try to get better service and more consideration for you. But my own position here is not an easy one because it involves responsibility without power. I am expected to keep my masters and bring in a good type of boy but I am not able to spend the money necessary to make these things possible.'

It was not surprising that in the chilly financial climate of the early 1930s the creditors should have had misgivings. The Legal and General, now the major lender, refused further loans unless they were given nominations to the Council in 1932. By 1933 the debts of the Martyrs' Memorial Trust schools amounted to £1 million, a huge sum for the time. All sources of credit were exhausted and creditors were pressing for payment on all sides. Roxburgh was informed that the banks were likely to refuse cheques for salary payments and provisions. The closure of Stowe and its fellow foundations seemed to be threatened. The abandonment of a dozen schools would have left the parents of 2,500 boys and girls seeking places elsewhere, and it would have clouded the reputation of the whole independent school structure. Heroically, the Legal and General agreed to prevent the disintegration of Warrington's empire provided that each school would accept a scheme of management that would override the existing articles of association and give the Society complete financial control of their affairs. The mortgages of other companies such as the Norwich were taken over and the sums which had to be found by way of interest were reduced. One or two of the less viable schools were sold. The chivalry of the Legal and General was remarkable. During the war no interest was charged at all and in the post-war years the low rates, 3 per cent or less, enabled sinking funds to be established with the result that the 1934 debts were discharged by the year 1980.

A new constitution replaced the old. A central committee sat under the chairmanship of Sir Cyril Norwood, now President of St John's College, Oxford and, after a discreet interval, Lord Gisborough was succeeded as Chairman of the Stowe Council by the experienced Pickard-Cambridge. The appointment of Governors lay with the Legal and General but the Martyrs' Memorial Trust were allotted places in the ratio of 1:6. The Allied Schools Agency Ltd. was formed to give substance to the organization. It employed central office staff, acted as trustees of reserve funds, composition fees and appeal monies. In the early days the sub-committee of the Allied Schools Council met almost weekly to scrutinize the cash flow but as the position improved, schools were given more autonomy and there was less interference in local budgets. Despite the continued stringency, financial rectitude prevailed and, in so far as the governing body set itself the more modest task of preserving Stowe rather than overthrowing the Vatican, it was more likely to achieve its aims. Had funds permitted, a second Temple of British Worthies might have been raised with assorted busts of the Legal and General Directors in the niches. It is worth noting that one of the first reforms was to improve the food. Writing to answer a parental complaint in September 1934 Roxburgh reported a new head cook, an additional second cook, hot plates, pastry rooms and a new bread contract.

Meanwhile Kenneth Adams, a young accountant with Price, Waterhouse and Co., following on the removal of Warrington from his Secretaryships, delved into the accounts and made some astonishing findings. The schools' trusts had been administered from Monkton Combe. Each school had a No.1 account from which cheques were paid, signed by Warrington and one other Governor. Adams found wads of blank cheques signed by other Governors. Auditors checked the No.1 accounts against the schools' ledgers and from time to time sent Warrington lists of payments which they could not identify by reference to local school bursars. Warrington sometimes gave short descriptions of the items and these appear to have been accepted by the auditors without further enquiry. Original evidence of much expenditure was not produced and some of the statements had been fabricated. Expenditure through the No.1 accounts had been over £2½ million, much of that on the re-financing of bills. The arachnoid techniques of Warrington defied simple analysis. While the profit-and-loss accounts might be regarded as substantially accurate in total, they were not accurate for individual schools. In many cases payments which should have been spread over several schools were paid for by one. Fittings, carpets and movables had been transferred from one school to another without inventories of adjustments. Large sums had been spent with antique and picture dealers for which neither receipts nor invoices were available. There was, said Adams, no evidence that the valuables had *not* been delivered to the schools but 'it may be that a considerable proportion of such purchases were for the Reverend Warrington (sic) himself.'

Under the headings of 'Preliminary Expenses' in connection with purchases of property, salary and expenses and personal payments a sum of almost £70,000 had been advanced to Warrington. In only two cases had authority been given by a school council for relatively small sums. Warrington, while insisting that the governing bodies had known about and approved these sums, had to admit that the majority were not recorded in the minutes. The personal payments included over £10,000 for antiques and pictures and £1400 for the gardens at Monkton Combe. Cheques cashed locally to the tune of almost £2500 were believed to have gone on domestic wages. He insisted that it had always been intended that Monkton Combe should become the headquarters of the schools organization and the proper furnishing and upkeep of properties there was a legitimate charge. As Roxburgh had once written of a boy who had pasted '– from his Grandfather' over a school library label (oddly enough in the *Koran*), 'I am afraid – still does not know the difference between meum and tuum.' Many years later, writing to Hankinson at Canford he recalled memories of Warrington's regime, 'when the School only had one painter who was always painting Warrington's own home – while no one knew what happened to our profits'. In fact Kenneth Adams seems to have shown that in comparison with other foundations Stowe had not suffered disproportionate raids on the exchequer. An important feature of his enquiry was to show that, shorn of extravagances and missionary enterprises, the Allied Schools were viable.

Warrington was allowed to depart the scene on grounds of ill health, (he had suffered from influenza two years before) and Norwood announced that the educational purposes of the schools would remain the same, being 'neither narrower nor wider than the simple aim of training boys and girls to become in their generation worthy members of Church and State'. Writing to a prep school after the revolution was over Roxburgh said 'I hope that before long – certainly in September – we shall have a new and improved Prospectus (incidentally showing a new and improved Governing Body).' Parish warfare between Monkton Combe School and the vicar for influence in his parish long continued. Sometimes he would extol the breadth and importance of his work for education. Sometimes he would confide that the Monks of Downside were plotting his death.

Warrington died in 1960. There was no representative at his funeral from any of the public schools he had founded. In 1963 an application was received from the rector of Bath Abbey, to whom a request had been made for a memorial in Monkton Combe churchyard describing Warrington as 'Founder of many schools including Stowe'. The Governors decided that it would be 'quite incorrect to describe Mr Warrington in those terms', although he 'had been associated with others in the foundation of Stowe'. One of the Stowe School carpenters long remembered having to remove Warrington's name from his Founder's Stall in Stowe Chapel.

Derek Bateman, an Old Etonian, came in 1936 to support Kenneth Adams in the administration of Allied Schools. On the whole the system worked well though the feeling persisted that Stowe was, to some extent, being drained to support its fellow foundations. In 1939 the vicar of Holy Trinity, Brompton Road, during a visit to preach at Stowe, had remarked in the presence of several boys that it was a pity that Stowe's profits should be used to support other schools. This was repeated to McElwee, who was in receipt of much schoolboy intelligence, and he conveyed the gist of the conversation to Roxburgh. It appeared that a parent, Lord Kennet, had expressed similar views to McElwee during the holidays. The matter had been highlighted by the gloomy consideration that masters' salaries might have to be cut to meet wartime conditions. Roxburgh replied,

I am quite sure that I have never categorically stated that Stowe's profits never could be used to support other schools. What I have doubtless said many times and can say again now is that, since the departure of Warrington, they never have been so used and probably never will be. Actually my remark in the Masters' Meeting was not meant to refer particularly to other schools. I was actually trying to assure people that, if the masters became poorer, nobody else would become richer and, in particular, the Insurance Company would not gain what we lost . . . The situation about other schools is, I believe, that theoretically the profits of the various schools could be pooled. But if that were done I should know immediately from the audited accounts and I can say with conviction both that it has not been done and that it is not likely to be done.

The danger that Lord Kennet has pointed out to me once or twice is concerned not with profits but with capital. Warrington arranged that the schools should guarantee each other's capital debts and the Insurance Company has hitherto been unwilling to let these guarantees be undone. At the same time, as Lord Kennet himself made clear a year ago, the danger is a purely theoretical one, as it could never pay the Company to cripple a prosperous school in order to pay some shillings in the pound on a bankrupt school, both being their property. However, the danger, even if theoretical, does exist, and to the best of my knowledge I have never denied it.

What I have denied is that the old Warringtonian system by which the profits we earned were used for any cause or school in which he was interested still persists. It does not still persist.

Certainly Roxburgh had achieved much greater freedom on the educational front and the new Governors do not seem to have been too demanding. To a parent whose son was going to be over fourteen on entry, and who was concerned about a recent Council ruling that all boys should come to Stowe under that age, he replied: 'I am not going to do any such thing. Every case is different.'

The change also put an end to the doctrinal disputes which had led to accusations of intolerance and sectarianism during the early years. In 1930 it had been rumoured that Roxburgh might shortly be moving on to Eton. He wrote to Andrew Croft:

I feel that these silly rumours have done me a good turn in that they have brought me a protest such as yours. There is only one thing more impossible than that I should be invited to Eton and that is I should accept if the invitation came! Curiously enough the only school to which I should feel any attractions would be my own school – Charterhouse. But it is not in the least likely that I shall be wanted there and it is quite certain that, if all goes normally, I shall not dream of leaving here until things are fully established and until there seems a real need for a new Head and fresh blood.

Working now under an unbigoted Council with greater expertise in its ranks he was vastly reinforced in his belief that the creation of Stowe was his own particular challenge.

The strong desire to enter external competitions which had marked Stowe from the outset was bringing some remarkable performances. In 1933 the school won all three competitions in the Public Schools Fencing Championships – Sabre, Foil and Epée – instituting a new record. P.B. Lucas, in the same year that he was playing in the school cricket team, reached the sixth round of the English Amateur Golf Championships, beaten there by the eventual winner. In 1936 J.D.A. Langley, while still a boy in Grenville, reached the final of the English Golf Championships at Deal, came fifth in the American equivalent and represented Britain in the Walker Cup. Two years earlier he had taken part in the Boys' Championship as did Reginald Maudling from Merchant Taylors', the future Chancellor of the Exchequer. Also in 1934 Langley captained the English team in the International Schools Match. According to the *Daily Telegraph* 'he gave an insight into the quality of his golf at the first hole. This measures 500 yards and though the wind was behind Langley, who is by no means a powerful youth, he was on the corner of the green with a drive and a No. 5 iron.' At a Boys' Golf International there were six Stoics in the lists. This provoked comment and onlookers were heard saying, 'Of course they have got a first-class golf course at Stowe.' 'Some of us overhearing this,' said the *Stoic*, 'wished that it were true, and vowed that one day it would be.' In April 1964, the *Stoic* cast a retrospective glance over this golden age. In 1937 the Cambridge Captain of Golf found himself on the horns of a dilemma. There were four Old Stoics in the side already and three candidates including one Old Stoic, for the remaining place:

Comparable sentiments must no doubt have passed fleetingly through the minds of Old Etonian Prime Ministers as they formed their Cabinets, but with a similar disregard for criticism the Cambridge Captain backed his judgement, gave R.O. Booth a Blue and five Old Stoics . . . contributed to Oxford's defeat that year.

All this had been originally based upon nine primitive holes which covered the ground along the South Front eastwards from the Rotunda and then crossed Armoury Field. They had little architectural merit but they were loved (as much in nostalgic retrospect as in the present) as few holes can ever have been loved before. They were largely designed in the mid-1920s by the first housemaster of Grenville, Mr I.A. Clarke and by a Stoic, himself a good golfer now resident in America, A.S. Anderson. The contribution of these two pioneers to the building of Stowe's golfing tradition was massive.

Old Stoics of the first generation were no less enterprising. Jack Dunn, the 'Nijinsky of the Ice', came third in the European Figure Skating Championships and second in the World Championships in Budapest. In the United States he partnered Sonja Henie and reached Hollywood where he was cast for a film on the life of Valentino, though tragically he succumbed to a rare illness and died at twenty-one. J.C. Monteith, shooting for the Conan Doyle Statuette at Bisley, took part in what the *Daily Telegraph* called 'one of the most marvellous rifle duels ever seen'. He and his opponent each obtained six bulls followed by an inner and then a further fifteen bulls. Monteith lost the match by one point. E.R. Avory played for the English tennis team against Ireland. P.B. Lucas was also selected for the Walker Cup Team. E.A.F. Widdrington was a member of the British shooting team which toured South Africa, Australia and New Zealand. He made the top score at Sydney beating all previous records and helping to win the Empire Trophy. On 13 February 1932 Bernard Gadney was playing scrum-half for England and the Grafton Chronicle reported that 'a large and appreciative number of convalescents listened in to the broadcast of the match and thoughts of the House were with him even during our own Match.' At the Stowe Sports Day at around the same time Roxburgh was able to say that the school had arranged for the University Boat Race and the Grand National to take place at times that did not clash, but they were still all faced with the choice of watching the sports at Stowe or Gadney at Twickenham. In 1933, Gadney was Captain of the English Rugby team which won all its international matches. At senior level H.D.H. Bartlett won the British Amateur Foil Championship. P.D. Ward, a Cambridge Running Blue, having won the 5,000 metres European Universities Championship in Budapest was a finalist in the Olympic Games in 1936, and British record holder for the Three-Mile event.

In wider spheres, Andrew Croft was a member of the British Expedition across Greenland from west to east. Lieutenant R.A. Gardiner working on the Survey of India discovered a plateau and mountain pass in the Himalayas. P.J.K. Pike passed out of Cranwell as top cadet and was awarded the King's Medal. His brother, J.M.N. Pike, followed suit and achieved both distinctions. Nor were the arts of peace neglected. The Poet Laureate in 1934 presented the Royal Medal for Poetry to Laurence Whistler. C.B. Cash won first prize in a national art competition sponsored by Winsor and Newton against thousands of competitors. In two successive years J.P. Searight and K.G. Rice won the Lilley and Skinner Photographic Trophy for Stowe. David Niven was making a name for himself in the cinema; there was great excitement in the local press when he brought Merle Oberon on a visit to Stowe in 1937.

E.A. Bonvalot wrote a Suite for Orchestra, one of the first large-scale pieces to be composed and conducted by a member of the school. Thirty Stoics attended a Toscanini concert in Oxford while others listened to the wireless relay in Dr Huggins' room. For the Stowe Show in aid of the Pineapple the Duke of York's Theatre was commandeered and well-known artists appeared including Arthur Marshall and the Western Brothers. Naunton Wayne was the compère. Sir Thomas Beecham travelled overnight from Paris and joined the London Philharmonic Orchestra with two minutes to spare for a concert at the school. Sir Henry Wood and Sir Adrian Boult followed, the former conducting the Choral Society in his arrangement of choruses from Handel Operas. Forty-two volunteers offered their services to strengthen the string sections of the orchestras and had to be taught in groups. For a brief while a mouth organ band flourished. *Boris Godunov* was followed by *Der Freischutz* in a new translation by J.C. Saunders who also played Samiel, the Demon Huntsman

The *Epicurean* provided outlets for parody and satire. During the political turmoil of 1931 there was a clever parody of Milton's *Comus* in which the Labour politician Arthur Henderson endeavoured to tempt Britannia from the protection of her conservative brothers Samuel and Simon:

Drink but one draught from this my magic cup
That is brimful of harmless T.U.C

He is thwarted by the timely appearance of the nymph, Baldwina, 'in a cloud of smoke'. 'The Delirious Drama' of 'King Cluph' (McLaughlin was known as 'Cluffy') related conflicts between a motley assortment of 'Courtiers, Vitruvians and Slaves' climaxing as in Shelley's 'Prometheus Unbound' in the arrival of Demogorgon, though he quelled the oriental tumult with the more familiar line: 'My dear fellow, we don't do that sort of thing here'. The 1934 Speech Day edition, as a result of pieces of scandal it was presumed to contain, proved to be the last for twenty-five years, indeed for the remainder of Roxburgh's time. The entire edition was confiscated; surviving copies having something of the rarity of Gutenberg Bibles.

Sometimes, however, in public-school life truth outstrips all the inventions of the satirist. In 1932 there was an outbreak of polio and the boys were sent home for a short period. When school resumed, the *News Chronicle* printed a photograph of a party of Stoics waving cheerily from a train window as they left London. A gentleman who described himself as a 'middle-aged independent bachelor' sent the photograph with one Stoic heavily ringed and the others as heavily scored out saying that the boys' cheerful countenance had so impressed him he would like to set him up financially and have him as a lifelong companion. Even Roxburgh, who had a wide experience of human nature, seems to have been nonplussed by this outlandish suggestion and wrote somewhat archly: 'I am afraid I cannot help you. All the boys here already have parents or guardians to look after them. Otherwise they would not have been sent here. I must say also that I do not feel justified in giving you the name of the boy to whom you refer.'

Life was still pleasantly informal. In October 1931 an airman who had run out of petrol made a forced landing in the Bourbon Fields. A group from Grafton fetched some from the Science laboratories and he continued on his way. Parties listened to wind-up gramophones in the Grecian Valley in summer and skated to Strauss waltzes on the lakes in winter. Nevertheless there was some social awareness also. The Reveille Club was founded in 1933 and the Toc H spirit was strong. Three members read papers on 'Duty', and there were experiments in social service which were common in schools during the 1960s and 70s but less usual in the pre-war years. Stoics founded a scout troop at Thornborough and helped to start a Boys' Club at Leckhampstead which had eighty members. Boys helped individually with old people and assisted with household tasks. A group was formed to carry out relief work on Toc H lines by renovating village halls and tackling the results of poverty. The steam coal used at Stowe was traced to a particular colliery and the district visited. By 1938 such contacts had been extended. Seven boys and two masters spent a week in a mining community near Sheffield to work on the allotments of old and disabled colliers. The following year fourteen boys carried out similar tasks in South Wales where they were shocked by the dangers of mining work, the reasons for dismissals, the small amounts of food and the homes, with their odd mixtures of lodgers and relatives.

The difficulties of recruiting Old Stoics to work at the Pineapple, however, remained a constant problem as more went off to universities where time and talents were fully stretched. The increasingly popular motor car and weekend trips into the country provided counter attractions. Gifts of clothes, sports gear and second-hand books were still sent from the school though, as one note rather sourly observed: 'It is difficult to find a use for books like Caesar's *Gallic Wars*.' Those who did work at the Pineapple did so zealously. The future Labour Peer, Stephen Taylor, reported: 'The State takes no interest whatsoever, in boys between fourteen and sixteen so that long hours and minimum wages are the rule. It is to these boys – and to those who are sacked as soon as they become sixteen – that the Club is perhaps the greatest help.' He added that it sometimes took the boys months to save the 4s/6d for the annual camp near the Cobham Monument. The Warden ran a boys' employment agency. A warrant officer from the Scots Guards took P.T. classes and there was football in Hyde Park. 'The Centre does not stop them looking for work', said a report on the 240 members 'and many are up and about at 6 a.m. doing so.'

The major sports had settled into a recognized pattern by the end of the 1930s. There was no longer the excitement of the first emergence of senior teams but, despite the difficulties of moving into the orbits already established by older schools, there were fixtures with Radley, St Edward's, Rugby, Bedford, and Oundle.

Though the inter-school fixtures increased slowly there were many gentlemanly amateur or college sides which welcomed invitations. In 1933 the collapse of the Free Foresters provided one of the most exciting close encounters of the time:

> Nothing seemed more remote at half past six than a win for the school. The Free Foresters then wanted no more than 30 runs to win with six wickets in hand and Melville . . . not out 100. The bowling was beginning to wear a distinctly tired look which, in view of the terrific assault made upon it and the memory of three dropped catches in the slips, was not to be wondered at. Suddenly Lucas galvanised the side by bowling Sherrard [a Stoic pressed into service because of a manpower shortage]. Ling in the next over bowled Melville and followed this up by getting Colonel Clarke caught on the leg-side. Twelve to make and three wickets to fall. The new ball was wisely called for and Lucas yorked Awdry who had looked as though he would finish the match off quickly. With only four runs required to the winning of the match the ninth wicket fell, Krabbe bringing off a wonderful one-handed catch in the slips off a shot which the batsman might be pardoned for thinking had decided the result. The last batsman scored two of the runs required and then Lucas produced another yorker which finished the match. As the team came off the clock struck seven.

In 1934 Stowe for the first time scored over 400 runs in an innings against Westminster; the first Oval match was played against Oundle in the same summer when both sides made large scores and the match was drawn. There was disappointment in the mid-30s that George Geary could not be lured as the professional. Finance and the lack of housing, always a problem at Stowe, caused him to refuse the invitation. In 1937, however, A.D.G. Matthews, who played in the Test Series that year, greatly strengthened the cricket coaching. On the Rugby field Oundle long remained the invincible opponent. Even in 1936, a season in which Harrow was defeated at 1st, 2nd, and 3rd team levels, Stowe lost to Oundle by only one point. In 1938, the final pre-war season, the citadel was at last stormed. Oundle had not suffered defeat from any school for three years but the wheel of fortune had brought to Stowe a generation of good athletes. During the 1938 season the XV recorded 117–17 points in school matches, 292–62 in all matches. The score of 67 against Radley, usually strong opponents, was a record. For the Oundle match, the North Front became the Plains of Troy. The score went from 3–3 to 11–11 at which point the Stowe forwards, sensing the possibility of victory, spent themselves in effort. A.V. Farnell-Watson, against the wind and from a distance of fifty yards scored from a penalty. D.A. Yellowlees scored a try and the final score was 17–11. 'It was a game which will live in the memory, one of those games which will deservedly be recalled in after years by all of us who were lucky enough to see it', declared the *Stoic*. 'We shall call to mind the graceful agility of Hastings, and the power and speed of Yellowlees, but, for one spectator at least, what will arise most vividly in his memory will be the remembrance of the tired forwards who won the game for Stowe.'

Peter Hastings also held four athletics records and captained the Stowe team, which in 1939 beat Eton and Lancing in the annual triangular match by one point, another exciting finish as he appeared in all the later events, just as the Stowe totals seemed to be trailing.[4] At the Sports Day Roxburgh announced that he had gathered together a collection of ladies who were mothers of captains of football, cricket and athletics, and the competitors who had established four new records in the Stowe Sports: Mrs Hastings would be representing them all!

The last pre-war summer also saw a memorable cricket match against Tonbridge; after twenty five breathless minutes a comfortable Tonbridge win changed into a tie. Tonbridge was reported to have such a strong batting side that their No. 11 had his pads on for two years without ever being asked to bat. On a cold drizzling day Stowe had made 183 runs and at 6.30 p.m. Tonbridge had reached 154 for the loss of only three wickets. The spectators were huddled behind windows or under rugs beside the trees. Within minutes the scene had changed and there was a vociferous crowd on the boundary. M.B. Scholfield, head of school, took three wickets in four balls to make the score 154 for 6. In the next over a single-handed catch by R.H. Marten brought the fall of another wicket with the score unchanged. Twenty minutes to play, three wickets to fall and thirty runs to make. Everything created uproar: a ball that was not

---

[4] At one such athletics match Playford noticed on the programme that every single member of the Stowe team had three initials. The Captain (it is not known which), when questioned, admitted that many were fictitious but the general effect was impressive.

scored off, a batsman sneaking a run, a fielder reducing a likely two runs to one. An eighth wicket fell: fifteen minutes to play, two wickets to fall, nineteen runs to make. An appeal for a catch was followed by the umpire raising his finger but only it seemed to scratch his face or remove a fly. The ninth wicket added eleven more runs before Scholfield bowled an unplayable ball.

Eight runs to make and ten minutes remaining. The Tonbridge No.11 did not seem daunted by his unwonted attendance. He hit the first ball for three and the next, from the other end, for four. This brought the scores level. He called his partner for a run. Martin threw in to Peter Hastings. The appeal came as a universal roar and this time the umpire's finger meant what it said.

It is out of such occasions that the great set-pieces of school life are made, but other forms of recognition came to Stowe in the period. Clifford had taken over command of the O.T.C. as Major Haworth had served the full time allowed. When Captain Liddell-Hart wrote in *The Times* that General Wavell was the country's best trainer of men Clifford tried to secure him to inspect the Corps. Wavell was then G.O.C. Southern Command. Clifford found the two necessary sponsors, one in the War Department, the other a Brigadier in the Black Watch. Unfortunately the document failed to arrive and, after waiting in vain for some time, Clifford sent a personal letter. Wavell told him to re-apply and said that he would look out for the missive. On the day appointed he flew to Bicester and was met there by J.F's car. The inspection was held on the Bourbon Fields. Roxburgh accompanied the party wearing a homburg. The recruits marched in school blazers, grey flannels and trilby hats as they had not yet passed out and earned their uniform. The machine gun section mounted on a boy scout trek cart aroused interest but at the close there was a worrying silence, worrying because Neil Blair, a military Old Stoic, had warned Clifford that if Wavell did not like a contingent he tore it apart. The ice was broken when Clifford apologized for the absence of a horse. Wavell said that he never saw his own horse as his daughter used to commandeer it and go riding herself. At lunch, when Clifford said that Wavell's *Palestine Campaign* was always given as a prize to the best Certificate Part II candidate, the General became positively communicative. His complimentary report was, however, well deserved. Four years in succession the Stowe O.T.C. won the competition for the best guard in camp, in 1935 with record marks.

The Royal Imprimatur continued to be placed upon Stowe with what seemed more than usual frequency. H.R.H the Prince of Wales attended the tenth anniversary celebrations; H.R.H. the Duke of Gloucester, the fifteenth. The Prince travelled by air to Buckingham and then drove to the North Front where it was estimated that there were 3000–4000 visitors and that 1143 cars had passed Stowewards through the town. Roxburgh had written to a parent: 'Tall hats will not be wanted, I gather. I rather wish that they were to be. But H.R.H. does not like them out of London. He will probably wear a beret himself.'[5] Old and present Stoics gave an exhibition of fencing and tennis. The Prince planted a copper beech, which had been raised from seed sown in 1923, and said in his speech: 'You have already sent men to all the leading professions and if, as Lord Beaconsfield declared once, the air of Buckinghamshire is favourable to political knowledge and vigour, who knows that there is not being brought up here a future occupant of No.10 Downing Street.' At a tea with the prefects he confided that his concerns were more immediate: his Mother had told him forcibly to ask for a week's holiday lest he should be thrown in the lakes, the reference being to a boy who had burnt the Union Jack and been treated to an immersion, reported in the press some days before. Roxburgh was presented with a silver bowl to mark the tenth anniversary by the original ninety-nine entrants.

H.R.H the Duke of Gloucester visited the school in 1938. He had been in Major Haworth's company at Sandhurst, though the guard of honour on this occasion was commanded by the art master, Robin Watt. The most impressive event of the day was an equestrian display, which included a musical ride and jumping in pairs, fours and eights. E. Reynard demonstrated Stowe's constant ability to surprise by giving a display of acrobatics on a small grey pony. Roxburgh reported that a development plan had been drawn up and admitting that there had been some errors in the siting of

---

[5] In fact H.R.H arrived in a straw boater with a pipe between his teeth. Purcell's *Dido and Aeneas* was performed by a group of musicians from Oxford in the setting provided by the Temple of Ancient Virtue. The Prince left early from this struggle of Love and Duty, and many of the guests missed his departure. In fairness one should add that he gave his full and friendly attention to a party of ex-servicemen waiting in the Grand Avenue.

buildings, concluded, 'our successors will have no excuse for making any at all.'[6]

Between the royal visits came the Speech Days. In 1931 the guest of honour was the Lord Mayor of London, Sir Phené Neal. Roxburgh based his speech upon a refutation of a recent pronouncement that it was the duty of schools to produce efficient salesmen. 'I should like to think that whoever goes out from here was efficient in whatever line of life he chose; but the idea that efficient salesmanship is the highest possible activity of the human spirit is to me intolerable.' The Lord Mayor turned this rather nicely by saying that Roxburgh was the best salesman he ever knew – 'He is almost irresistible'.

Speech Day in 1934 was addressed by Viscount Hailsham, who had been Member of Parliament for Marylebone when the Pineapple opened; in 1936 by the Marquis of Willingdon, former Viceroy of India; in 1937 by Sir Thomas Inskip, Minister for Co-ordination of Defence. In the summer of 1937 Stowe opened its doors to a conference of the Northampton branch of the National Union of Teachers at which the Permanent Secretary at the Board of Education commented on the extremely cordial relations which existed between Whitehall and the N.U.T.

International tensions assisted a much greater degree of political seriousness than the comparatively static conditions of the Cold War. John Cornford, already a boy of decided views, who supported the Hunger Marchers and regretted that Parliament had not been blown up, spoke in a debate on the country where he was one day to die: 'This House regrets the departure of King Alfonso from Spain'. Ivor Cross was a prime mover in founding a branch of the League of Nations Union which had a full quota of famous speakers: Gilbert Murray, Lord Lytton and Lord Robert Cecil. Committees were formed in the Midde and Lower School to produce reports on the subjects with which the League grappled at Geneva. The first came from Mr Robinson's Middle School committee on 'Science as applied to modern warfare'. The Hon. R.D.G. Winn gave an account of aeroplane construction and explosive, incendiary and gas bombing. This was followed by a practical

[6] The only discordant note was struck by the vicar of Stowe Church, the Reverend C. Fernihough who, to pay off some ancient score, rang the church bells loudly throughout the speeches and ignored all Roxburgh's messages that the pandemonium should cease.

demonstration which aroused great excitement. A tree stump was blown up in Chatham Field; ten pounds of gelignite were used, and substantial pieces of the tree were blown one hundred feet into the air. There were 239 members of the League of Nations group, 36 matrons and staff and 203 boys. A Colonel Victor Haddick spoke on the organization of German youth and his description of the regimentation and fervour was received 'with incredulity but also a certain awed admiration'. Sir Philip Sassoon urged Stoics to apply for Cranwell. In fact there had always been an interest in flying. As early as 1927 the R.A.F. had given a display over the grounds. Fighter planes dropped smoke bombs over a target and ammunition by parachute. A night bomber flew past but could not land as there was insufficient space to take off again. Casualties too came early. A.M. Cowell, one of the ninety-nine, was killed testing a 'Flying Flea' for the British Empire Air League. George Moorby, a founder member of Chatham, was one of the first Stoics to be commissioned in the R.A.F. He was a daring pilot and was killed in civil flying in 1935. In the same year Pilot Officer T.B. Hunter of Grafton was killed in action in Palestine. The plane controls were shot away by Arab gunfire while he was low flying in support of ground forces.

The generally right-wing opinion that prevailed in public schools in the post-war years was not present. Passionate opinions were expressed on both sides. H.S.L. Dundas at the League of Nations Union defended the Republican government of Spain. By his act of rebellion Franco made reform impossible. Captain Victor Cazalet spoke to the Union on behalf of Franco, depicting anarchy in the 'Red' territories. Rather more presciently Dr E.P. Gooch pointed to the North-South/East-West axis in European affairs and prophesied that Prague was the danger spot. The turmoil of Europe came close when it was learnt that John Cornford been killed in the Spanish Civil War, fighting on the Republican side. A great-grandson of Charles Darwin, he had come to Stowe with an entrance scholarship and before his seventeenth birthday had been awarded a major scholarship at Trinity College, Cambridge. Writing to Jim Butler, the Trinity Tutor, Roxburgh declared, 'I cannot keep pace with him at all in his views on politics, economics or literature. But he is very charitable in his attitude to elderly schoolmasters and, though he disapproves entirely of the public school system, he takes no active steps to interfere with its workings at Stowe. In personal appearance he is very striking as he wears his dark curly hair startlingly long and has a contempt for people who bother at all about their clothes.' At Cambridge he lived openly with a mistress. Clifford recalled, 'Cornford merely twinkled nicely at me when I gave him my stock talk on Sex, etc.' He gained Firsts in both parts of the Historical Tripos but, in the summer of 1936, became convinced that duty called him to Spain. He joined the International Brigade and was soon in action on the Cordova Front. After one day in hospital – he refused to stay longer despite having been wounded in the head – he went out in advance of his men to reconnoitre an attack and was killed. It was the day before his twenty-first birthday.

About the time of Munich the *Stoic* strangely reported that a Hitler Youth cricket team had visited Stowe. No one can recall such a visit and this may have been a hoax entry although it was not a publication given to jesting.[7] Writing to an American Old Stoic Roxburgh made a strong defence of Munich: 'If Chamberlain had acted as his critics would have wished, London and Paris would now be in ruins and there would have been precious little civilisation left in Europe. I hope the time will come when we are strong enough to stand up to Hitler but we definitely are not at present and unless something can be done to strengthen France (which looks doubtful at the moment) we never shall be.' Earlier in the decade war had still seemed something in history. 'If war ennobles a few individuals it degrades whole nations', Roxburgh said in a Remembrance Day sermon. 'It cannot begin without hatred and it cannot continue without lies. To look at the old newspapers of England and Germany in the war years is to gain a new conception of the blindness and folly of the human race. To read the sermons and prayers of the clergy in both countries is to gain a new conception of the weakness and venality of our religion.'

---

[7] This unlikely tale had odd reverberations. Another story relates that during the Second World War a German aeroplane came out of the clouds and flew low over the playing fields. The boys threw themselves on the ground expecting to be machine-gunned. The plane, however, gave a friendly roll of its wings and flew off. It was surmised that the pilot must have been a Hitler Youth visitor in 1938, who recognized the house. After the war when Roxburgh was attempting to move on the master, P.F. Wiener, the latter claimed that his unfair treatment stemmed from the Fascist nature of Stowe as evidenced by this German party. Among the witnesses at Stowe at the time, Patrick Hunter recalls a German youth team arriving. But it would be odd to be playing cricket in the early autumn.

His sermon preached a few weeks after Munich was more sombre and contained presages of the approaching conflict.

The demands upon us will be such as can only be met by men who have within them (in the words of tonight's Lesson) 'the holy spirit of discipline', men who keep themselves always ready for high endeavour or steady endurance. The man whose body is out of training cannot stand a physical strain; the man whose character is soft cannot stand a moral one. It is therefore our duty owed by each one of us to England and to the world to make 'the holy spirit of discipline' reign in his heart, to keep his will-power unweakened by indulgence and his ideals undimmed by selfishness. Our statesmen may speak for righteousness in the world but they will speak in vain if they have behind them forty millions of weak and superficial people, who cannot feel deeply or act strongly and who care nothing for the great issues of life. Every indolent avoidance of effort, every frivolous refusal to think, every deflection from honourable dealing in any one of us weakens the power of England to save the world. You, personally, cannot give the nation another aeroplane or another ship, but you can give it another citizen able to think seriously, resolve highly and perform steadfastly.

In the face of such eloquence it is perhaps surprising that Roxburgh was often under attack from Ivor Cross for failing to make sufficiently strong moral judgments. He had sometimes been forced to guide Ivor Cross through rather intemperate quarrels with parents. In 1930 he wrote an admonitory letter, which is a model of its kind, about a family closely identified with the school.

Here is a copy of what I have written to Colonel —. I mean all I say in it but I am extremely sorry all the same that you have not 'managed' the — s better, unreasonable as they are. A situation like this is the culmination of a long history of mutual irritation and should therefore never have been allowed to arise. It seems to me your first business is to put it right. There is not the least need for you to climb down in order to do so but, of course, the attitude that peace is only to be obtained at the price of the other fellow's submission is a hopeless one and rather ridiculous too. I do not want to think that in future any Temple parents who are inclined to be difficult or unreasonable (as a certain percentage always are) will only be able to keep up friendly relations with their boy's housemaster, if they learn never to give any trouble and always to toe the line. If they could do that they would not be unreasonable.

Cross, in turn, reproached Roxburgh with the inevitable effects of a tolerant regime: 'Once at a housemasters' meeting', he wrote, 'you broached the subject of post-Stowe failures – at Oxford and Cambridge chiefly. Do you think that the staff as a whole and housemasters in particular are giving enough attention to the essential part of their profession? I myself feel that, judged by its application to conduct and the prevailing standard of morality (general sense) in the School, religion in so far as it is taught is not getting across.'

As Roxburgh ran Stowe on an intense and personal level disharmonies could be amplified; there were several masters who felt that their rapport with him had a special quality. As Cross wrote, 'I want to make this claim, if you will allow me, that I am nearer to you than anyone else here and have greater personal understanding. Hence "paradoxically" the "differences" between us. They are nervous and unreal – as I believe you are aware.' He hoped that more housemasters would preach in Chapel on general themes arising out of school circumstances. 'I am concerned about the spirit of Stowe. It started so bravely. We must stick to principle. We must feel that we have something to achieve beyond the release of personality. Now is the time, having established Liberty, to make of it a holy and acceptable thing.'

The correspondence with existing staff, however, was as nothing compared with that to and from those who had moved on. The story of McLaughlin reads as if Dostoevsky had wandered into the pages of public-school fiction. Needless to say work in the Inspectorate proved unsatisfying and he was soon hankering to return. The results of Roxburgh's hints that this might be possible show the suffering which infinite tact can cause. He could not persuade the more staid members of the Common Room to contemplate McLaughlin's return:

> The resulting reaction in a certain quarter stimulated my desire to get you back at all costs. It had no other effect as you may suppose . . . Reactions elsewhere revealed nothing so unpleasant though I cannot help feeling that it might have been a little hard on some people to be thrust again into the background

from which they have been recently emerging. But all this is neither here nor there. There is no money and (except for the little slum Vancouver) no home either. And there we are. I cannot send you the invitation which you know I personally am longing to send just as I cannot send one to the Archangel Gabriel. (He is probably quite as expensive.) [He praised the continued progress of McLaughlin's pupils at university.] The debt on account of scholarships can be reckoned in figures because it amounts to twice as much as all the other Sides have contributed and to a considerable fraction more. But the debt on account of the boys themselves can be represented only by a curious sign habitual to Mathematicians but known neither to me nor my typewriter which signifies infinity.

McLaughlin wrote a wild letter in March 1934 referring to 'jealous little people. I believe that you think they had nothing to do with my departure, plenty of other people think that they had . . . And after all you had no need to tell them that any return was imminent: that was surely asking for trouble.'

Much of Roxburgh's time must have been spent in writing testimonials but McLaughlin's boasts that he would raise intellectual standards in any school that would appoint him and qualify for a housemastership within a year did not please prospective headmasters. To an official at the Board of Education, Roxburgh confided, 'The wretched man . . . spoils every chance he is offered by his preposterous affectations. The pity of it is that he drops these when he gets to work . . . I wish to goodness you people on the Board would do something for him and get him off my chest. At present I get a letter from him daily and a visit once a week.' After a short spell at Bryanston, which he left hurriedly, McLaughlin invested in a small school of his own in Perthshire. He sent constant letters asking for rejected pupils which Roxburgh did not have, for introductions to the Duke of Montrose and other dignitaries, for Roxburgh's help as a Governor and for news of Stowe and his ex-pupils. Eventually his school was commandeered by the Forces and for reasons of health he had to move south. Life became a series of disasters. Wolfenden at Uppingham took him for one term and dismissed him after twenty-two hours. He had been presented with a desk by the boys at Stowe when he left and this he wished the school to have. His solicitors were obliged to write and state that he was of unsound mind and ask if Stowe would keep the desk in safe custody until it reverted legally on his death. With the twist of bitter comedy that intrudes into such narratives the desk went to a mystified headmaster in Stow-on-the-Wold and it was some time before it found its rightful home. In 1964 his hospital in Oxford was telephoned to say that he had been found lost and derelict in the lanes of Shropshire at night and taken into Shrewsbury General Hospital, where he died.

The story of J.T. Hankinson, housemaster of Cobham, has a happier ending though he also caused Roxburgh much anxiety. In 1936 he was beguiled into the business world, but things went seriously wrong and it is likely that a good deal of family capital was lost. He too was desperate to return and rehearsed all the crises and achievements which had beset him in Cobham. Stowe parents were also the recipients of anguished letters. Fortunately he secured a post at Canford, wrote a series of books on games skills and became in time something of an elder statesman in the school.

In addition to the labours of dealing with masters who moved on and then wished to return there were problems with others who did not move at all. There were a number of very able masters who deserved promotion and Roxburgh always wrote very warmly in support of applications, but headmasterships were rare. Possibly the fact that Roxburgh distanced himself from the Headmasters' Conference, or that Stowe was regarded as more experimental than in fact it was, were determining factors. Certainly disappointments, as they accumulated over the years, must have added to an autumnal feeling in the Common Room.

One of the features of the Summer Term was the annual outdoor Shakespeare production by the Historians under the direction of Bill McElwee before the Queen's Temple. His wife, Patience, displayed enterprise in collecting the costumes. Those for Julius Caesar came from a projected film of *I Claudius*, those for Macbeth from a film called *The Ghost Goes West*. On the last Speech Day before the outbreak of war Pickard-Cambridge was in the Chair. Vice-Chancellor of Sheffield University, he was an experienced guide and friend. He was able to announce that the first Old-Stoic Governor, John Boyd-Carpenter, had been appointed so that the average age of the governing body (Pickard-Cambridge had himself heard Gladstone speak) would be suitably lowered. The guest of honour was the Canadian High Commissioner, the Hon.

Vincent Massey. He opened his address by saying that they were in the open season for Speech Days. Boys must feel like grouse on the twelfth. But game could sometimes be missed; the targets of the merciless Speech Day platforms could not. He made a comparison between Stowe and his own dominion, both young in years and spirit but with roots deep in the past. He called for a closer and more thoughtful study of the Empire. 'Critics of the public schools might be usefully reminded that the dictators would never tolerate them. They are the very symbol of the freedom which the dictators destroyed. We reject regimentation; we rejoice in differences. The totalitarian loves the goose-step conception of life which has no place in the British Empire.'

The evening was more sombre. The Historians had chosen *King Lear*. As night closed in, the avenues loomed up like the nave and transepts of a dark cathedral and the final lines of the play had a prophetic ring:

> The weight of this sad time we must obey,
> Speak what we feel, not what we ought to say,
> The oldest hath borne most: we that are young
> Shall never see so much, nor live so long.

5

Stowe in Wartime

In the first weeks of September 1939, there was a feverish blacking-out of over a thousand windows. Neighbouring Farmer Davies was a Special Constable who watched for infringements of the blackout regulations with especial zeal. Hay stacks were set up on the South Front to make the landing of enemy aircraft difficult. As Chapel could not be used after dark, Evensong became voluntary and the Aurelian Room, redecorated, reverted to its original role. The sheer scale of Stowe precluded the removal of all blackout screens by day and hence many waking hours were spent in 'perpetual penumbra'. Cellars and changing rooms were reinforced and part of the ground floor of Cobham sandbagged, all of which added to the depressing effect. Petrol rationing affected school teams. The cross-country race against Charterhouse was cancelled and another arranged with Rugby, closer to hand. The Corps summer camp had already been a casualty of the commandeering of tentage by the military but the Air Section were able to visit Norton Priory, where Duff Cooper made a patriotic speech so stirring that he was shoulder-lifted around the aerodrome by wildly cheering cadets.

Such scenes would not have appealed to Roxburgh and he viewed the future with pessimism. Introducing the fiftieth term of Stowe he wrote: 'Darkness has come down upon the road before us – the road which was once illuminated with so clear and cheerful a light. We planned a future that was to be full of new achievement and was already full of hope. We dreamed of the service that we could render to an England steadily advancing towards justice and happiness.' By October, 1939, he was worried about boys listening to the nine o'clock news, not for the sake of censorship but because of distortion. McElwee too, discouraged boys: 'They waste not only the time they spend listening but much more time afterwards in futile speculation. I should have thought we were doing something educationally harmful.' As the war progressed Roxburgh became even more critical on this issue and in September 1941 in a letter to Habershon confessed: 'One of the facts that depresses me most is the futile and childish tone of announcements by the BBC. The German utterances, if not more truthful, are at any rate more dignified and so are the Russian. I feel that, if the BBC news bulletins are to be taken as the voice of the government, we have a government which does not deserve to win the war. They certainly cannot be taken as the voice of England.'

The unexpected death of Ian Clarke just as war began left a serious gap in the Common Room. The loss of a lieutenant whose loyalty was not interwoven with emotional dependence deprived Roxburgh, in particular, of a stalwart 'counsellor in adversity' and 'companion in prosperity'. The staff had expanded with the school and there were more frequent changes to which a further impulse was given by the housing shortage. The situation is well illustrated by the story of Edward Dewing, head of Science during the years of growth who, after four years of dealing with landlords, threats of accommodation being put on to the market over his head and other insecurities, had a serious breakdown. Roxburgh had wished to appoint R.G. Gilbert, a scholar of Tonbridge with a First in Classics from Pembroke, Cambridge in 1932. But, as Gilbert announced his intention of marrying, his arrival was delayed until 1938. He was English tutor from 1945-60, after war service in the R.A.F., and housemaster of Temple from 1961, where, as a traditionalist who believed in discipline of mind and body, he had to contend with all the difficulties experienced by those called in to quell disorder. His meticulous garden reflected a lifetime of devotion to Virgil's *Georgics* and in his last years at Stowe he was a strong opponent of the policy of exchanging woodland for buildings.

Bruce Barr, who came in 1937, was also an expert on the forestry and wildlife of the park. Originally a natural scientist, also of Pembroke, Cambridge, he studied for a second degree in Ireland in order to teach Biology. He published monographs on the birds and trees of Stowe and helped to establish a Young Farmers' Club. At

Cambridge he narrowly missed a Rugby Blue and remained one of the very few masters to have dropped a goal against a school XV.

A.B.E. Gibson was a rugged and formidable figure, who as head of Lower School, was as severe upon untidy appearance as upon lightweight intellectual effort. The *Stoic* referred to 'the sudden terrible quietness of voice which warned that an almighty storm was about to break'. As master in charge of the school shop he was able to hand over thousands of pounds to the Roxburgh Hall for stage equipment and to the games and athletics sections but, having had problems with disposing of unwanted stock when dress regulations changed, he followed the discussions at masters' meetings, lengthy as they were, like a Hound of the Baskervilles. He was a keen cricketer who once took nine wickets in a masters' match against the First XI. Grenville House under his rule was reckoned to be good at all corporate efforts such as the P.T. competition and the Coldstream (O.T.C.)Cup. Large-scale house plays such as *Treasure Island* included almost every boy in the cast.

While the Western Front remained inactive, life, in many respects, continued as normal. Stowe won its first match at First XV level against Rugby in the autumn of 1939 and turned a fresh page of history by defeating Oundle on their home ground. In the wartime Varsity Match that year there were three Old Stoics: J.E.C. Nicholl and J.P. Stephens for Cambridge, P.R.H. Hastings for Oxford. The first winter of the war was uncommonly severe. There was skating for the first time for several years and Temple won the Ice Hockey Cup from Grenville which the latter had held since 1933. Pipes burst, flooding areas of the school and making them uninhabitable. The cold and the absence of both light and petrol brought about, as elsewhere, a revival of homemade entertainment. At the end of Saturday mornings there was 'school singing in the gymnasium' and in May 1940 a mixed group of masters and boys with the assistance of two lady vocalists from Buckingham produced *The Pirates of Penzance*. In the same month a popular revue, *Swinging the Gate*, was running in London, described by the *Evening Standard* as a 'Stowe Old Boys Reunion'. Geoffrey Wright, who had designed the costumes for *Prince Igor*, wrote the music, Gerard Bryant the lyrics and Robert Macdermott, later a well-known BBC quiz-master, the book. But the Summer Term had not advanced far when Hitler unleashed his forces on the Low Countries. The mood remained remarkably calm: there were no television cameras roaming the land to stir up feelings of apprehension and woe. Stoics organized a fête on an impressive scale in aid of the Buckingham Hospital. Playford and Bruce House, the Watts and the Art School played a large part. School artists had already developed skills in painting and decorating the blackout screens. Watercolours and oils by the boys were sold, as were caricatures by Colin Welch, future political correspondent and editor. Shilling teas were served by the matrons while boys did the washing up. Melodramas, impersonations and sketches were performed in the Aurelian Room and Library. Walpole provided musical entertainment which ranged from the Walpole 'Rhythm Boys' to Chopin piano pieces.

Continental musicians with exotic names came to Stowe to perform. Prince George Chouchavadze gave a recital for the Red Cross. Miss Jelly D'Aranyi, great-niece of Joachim, played gypsy music on the violin to great acclaim. During the collapse of France and the evacuation from Dunkirk the Choral Society was rehearsing Vaughan Williams' Five Tudor Portraits and a choral version of Weber's Invitation to the Waltz. With floodlighting banned, the Historians moved from Queen's Temple for an indoor production of *Twelfth Night*. W. Hilton Young, later Lord Kennet, played Feste and composed his own setting of 'Come Away Death'. Various string quartets met regularly to practise. Cricket matches tended to be played against more local teams from Brackley and Buckingham, but A.V. Farnell-Watson scored 421 runs in the season and E.P. Hickling 411 (averages 82.4 and 82.2). 'It must be a long time since any School could boast an average such as these two', declared the *Stoic*. As Hitler consolidated his grasp on the European coast there was even a match at Lord's. Clifton had cancelled and instead Stowe met Tonbridge who had had victory snatched from them the previous year.[1] Humphrey Playford left for France to assist with ambulance work. Roxburgh wrote to the Chairman: 'Playford (Parson, Housemaster, Aged 44, Teacher of Bottom Form) has been invited to take charge of a number of ambulances which are being sent out by the Anglo-French Ambulance Corps to deal with the French wounded . . . He has

---

[1] During these momentous days the scribes of Grafton continued to relate every house cricket match over by over in the heavy bound volumes which detailed all house activities.

many times motored the whole length of France under conditions of every sort. He knows more about motor cars and keeping them on the road than any ordinary mechanic . . . I don't feel I have any right to dissuade him from taking on this emergency job.'

By 26 June the Debating Society was considering the motion: 'In the Opinion of this House Anglo-French Union is the only hope for Western Christendom', but events quickly consigned Churchill's proposals on that score to the flames.[2] Facing the threat of invasion and fought over in the skies, Britain was mobilized for total war. Most Stoics over seventeen joined the Local Defence Volunteers, went out on dawn and dusk patrols to search the grottoes and temples for parachutists and spent fortnights in the holidays back at the school working intensively at Home Guard duties. Major Haworth took command of the North Bucks force. Clifford later recalled the night exercises when tea had to be brewed without a light at midnight during forced marches across country and when 'a comradeship in arms was forged between educated boys of 17–17½ and much older farm-hands, hedgers and ditchers, roadmen, ground staff and poachers.' Voluntary services were held in Stowe church for the holiday residents and were well-attended. Collections were given each week to the BBC's 'Good Cause'. Night exercises often came to centre upon the capture of the White Hart Hotel in Buckingham where rival platoons that had crawled and clambered around in the vicinity would be given cups of cocoa.

The windows were checked for fissures of light, by boys after dark and masters in the late evening. Carpenters and painters had little time for any other work and the condition of the interior suffered as a result. Under Hart Dyke sixteen first line and sixteen reserve fire squads were trained to deal with incendiary bombs and find their way over the hazardous rooftops. The Matrons' Mess – 'that distressing room' as Roxburgh described it – became the heart of Civil Defence activities. The telephone was manned permanently, by two boys from different houses in daylight and masters

---

[2] A local vicar blamed the barbarity of the Germans on their nation having been outside the Roman Empire so that 'they had not enjoyed four hundred years of Latin'!

(correcting exercises) overnight.[3] A large area of the Bourbon Fields was ploughed up to be sown with oats and potatoes. In various gardens the boys planted large quantities of onions and other vegetables. Humphrey Playford kept the estate work going. Notices began to appear: 'There will be voluntary digging for the following . . .' A forestry camp took place in Westmorland where conditions were far from luxurious. The sun disappeared behind the hills at 5 p.m. when invariably a bitter wind began to blow. The merest trickle of a stream was the only supply of water for washing and, when the school party dug a 'Lido' and diverted water into it, cattle and ducks staked an indisputable claim. There were no drying facilities and when the lakeland rain fell the reappearance of the sun had to be awaited for clothes to dry. Because of the blackout no camp fires could be lit and everyone tumbled in to bed as soon as the nine o'clock news was over. Work lasted seven or eight hours a day. One hundred and eighty acres were felled representing 50,000 lineal feet of wood. For one day before Scottish professionals got to work Stowe held the record for the largest tree felled (a Scots pine of twenty-eight feet in circumference). On farming parties at Westbury, Mixbury and elsewhere boys stacked flax, helped with threshing and cleared out sheds.

It was generally considered that wartime food was not too bad. Dried egg was popular and scrambled for tea. The bursar took pleasure in sending back ration books with notices such as 'You will observe that a full five weeks' rations are enclosed as against a holiday of only 33 days.' For the Home Guard squads, however, things were less easy as the school furnaces and electric plant were closed down in summer. Cooking had to be done on an outdoor range on the West Lawn. One of the first efforts of peace was to cover this unsightly spot with dahlias and other blooms. The outside shelters were rarely used although as German bombers droned overhead to Coventry and the windows of the school

---

[3] J.F. himself once undertook the overnight manning of the A.R.P. post. As there was only a camp-bed on which to snatch some sleep the masters were sure that at least once they would find him crumpled and dishevelled in appearance. To make doubly sure of such a coup the relieving watch turned up half an hour early to find Roxburgh with perfectly creased trousers and groomed to the usual standard.

shook as a result of the bombardment of the city it was deemed prudent to bring everyone down from the dormitories to the basements.

Staff had to be recruited to replace those leaving for the services. Some of the appointments were colourful but surprisingly successful. G. Wilson Knight, Professor of English at Toronto University and an eminent exponent of mysterious themes in Shakespeare plays, wished to return to Britain in 1940 as he regarded it as a sacred place guarded by supernatural forces. He applied to Stowe and, to illustrate his interest in play production included a photograph of himself in the role of Timon of Athens. Most headmasters receiving an image of this wild-eyed and hairy apparition would have placed the application in the out-tray with a pair of tongs, but Roxburgh's gamble was well rewarded. He was worried that the standard of English might be below the great man's level ('There is a saying about a steam hammer and a nut'), but Wilson Knight was happy to be given lowly work wherever he could be helpful. 'I have been teaching Geography of late', confided Roxburgh, 'and with Hitler's help have progressed very well in it during the last year or so.' He derived benefit from the exchange of views and reviews with this scholarly figure of whom Anthony Quinton wrote, 'To be taught by him was to attend a master-class by Macready. He was a splendid and kindly man but too remote in his empyrean of romantic speculation for us to enter into much closer relations with him than we might have had with the Aurora Borealis or some other glorious natural phenomenon.' When Roxburgh heard that Knight had been reading *The Poetic Procession*, a work written when Roxburgh was at Lancing and dedicated to Capel Cure, his head of house, he observed ruefully: 'I cannot help feeling rather sorry that my youthful indiscretion . . . has come under your scholarly eye.' While at Stowe Knight produced *Chariot of Wrath*, 'a study of Milton and National Greatness'. A copy was sent to Princess Elizabeth and it was reported that H.M. the Queen had read it before handing it on. Roxburgh was less happy at the prospect of a book on Stowe and its place in the missionary role of Britain. He was particularly worried that H.M.C. colleagues might consider it 'advertising'. This was an abnormally sensitive subject in wartime as numbers shrank and a pupil shortage prevailed. Spencer Leeson, headmaster of Winchester and Chairman of H.M.C., was reassuring, suggested a preface in which Knight made clear he was writing as a free agent, and exhorted Roxburgh to go through it and 'remove anything that would upset our brethren'. Roxburgh did in fact make some suggestions, pointing out that the Temple of Bacchus had been small, ruined and never beautiful, that the Temple of Concord had been collapsing and the substitution of brick wall for pillars had saved its life and that most of the wood in the Chapel Chancel was new, the original having been found to be partly veneer on deal. He finished with the endearing remark: 'The following small points have been brought to my notice by the sub-editor which lurks in my sub-conscious'!

He was somewhat sardonic on being the dedicatee of a book which dwelt upon the transcendental radiations which Stowe gave forth:

My only claim to such an honour could be that I have fought to preserve the freedom and kindliness which have struck you in this place against the encroachments with which masters brought up in another tradition and the herd instincts of the boys themselves have from time to time threatened them. I realise after reading your book that even this, which I have always believed to be my sole merit, is really owed to the Spirit of Stowe itself, which only an unimaginative die-hard would have attempted to combat. So the 'sole merit' has gone! but I have seen it go without regret.

John Davenport arrived in 1941 aged 35. He talked with authority on modern literature, European thought, films and music. He was short and round but muscular and energetic, having boxed for Cambridge in earlier days. He enjoyed being a grown-up among adolescents, hinting at friendships and excitement in the world of left-wing intellectuals. He was a gifted mimic and taught the subtleties of style by making his pupils write parodies, the best of which he would collect and lose. He is remembered as a stimulating teacher by Anthony Quinton: 'The dissipation of his talent over absolutely everything of cultural interest in his age made him a quite ideal introducer of younger people to that rogue-gentlemanly culture of the thirties.' He must truly have been forceful to make such an impression as he left after only two terms. He took over the Library and was reputed to have spent liberally upon unconventional purchases. A gift was made to the school in memory of Hugh

Barbour, the first non-scientist to win a Science Prize. Roxburgh suggested that sets of Jane Austen or Trollope would be suitable, but Davenport found unwarranted gaps among the Restoration dramatists! When Playford made a complaint about holiday duties such as fire-watching, Roxburgh reminded him that only Davenport had so far refused and his resignation had been requested.

Other temporary appointments who brought in a knowledge of wider spheres included Martin Cooper, Music Correspondent of the *Daily Telegraph*, and Roy Meldrum who combined coaching the Cambridge VIII with erudite work at the University Press. In rain, snow and nights as black as pitch he cycled the route from Chackmore via the Corinthian Arch to lessons and tutorials. When leaving he expressed the hope that Roxburgh in retirement would write his autobiography – 'a Chartreuse in words'.

Every school, of course, had its disasters among wartime masters. Writing to Bill McElwee, who was doing army training in Scotland, Roxburgh confided, 'We had a poor little Austrian doing the Maths but he couldn't get on with anybody and was always having soul-storms. When he had soaked my hearth-rug with his tears for the third time I thought it better to suggest a move to a day-school!' Many stayed longer. A.A. Dams had sung in Westminster Abbey choir as a treble and revived the Walpole House Glee Club. At Trinity, Cambridge, he was a Hockey Blue and helped to establish hockey as a major sport at Stowe ('A game I have never understood' wrote Roxburgh to an American O.S. in 1945). He founded the Congreve Club and directed it in dramatic productions until 1956. His wife, Marjorie, had once understudied Edith Evans. As lay reader and churchwarden at Stowe parish church he often had to maintain parish life during periods when there was no parson. Immediately after the war he suggested a specialist department of drama. 'A School of Drama would be a delightful thing to have', replied Roxburgh in a typically ornate refusal. 'I reckon that it would cost about £50,000 and that we should get a licence for spending that money in the neighbourhood of 1990. You will see that the project is a perfectly practicable one and no doubt we shall soon carry it out.'

E.H. 'Digger' Boyd from Tasmania stayed until 1947 teaching Science. He was small and assertive with a thick Australian accent. He and secretary Lucas made a strong tennis pair. The 1944 school team was only once beaten – by the masters. The Reverend

Windsor-Richards came in 1944 and stayed to be housemaster of Temple. The Warden of Glenalmond had given him a good reference as a lively chaplain, but mentioned that his rumbustious manner sometimes led to brushes with other members of staff. 'Our staff here is no more angelic – a bit less I sometimes suspect than anyone else's', said Roxburgh, though he made the appointment. Windsor-Richards had been an engineer for several years before entering the Church and his experience was to prove valuable in clearing and restoring the lakes after the war. Brian Stephan, who also came in 1944 to take the brightest of the younger forms, became housemaster, tutor in Classics and English, senior tutor, second master and for a term acting headmaster. A.J. Chapman remained as Economics tutor until 1966, as did H. Rutherford, tutor in French who came in 1945. Rutherford had the distinction of having replaced Evelyn Waugh as a master in the prep school which served as the model for Llanabba Castle in *Decline and Fall*. He is best described in Crichton-Miller's reference written in 1961:

> Dr Rutherford accepted the challenge of getting the lowest Certificate Forms through their Latin examinations by a combination of persuasion, bullying and a mysterious third ingredient known only to himself. Later, as Head of French at Stowe, he gave his time unsparingly and made a surprising number of surprised Stoics find they had passed where failure seemed inevitable. His European tours with Stoics in the summer holidays have extended from Turkey to Morocco and produced a crop of stories which would seem incredible to anyone who did not know Dr Rutherford.

B.E.N. Fawcett, who had been appointed in 1937, acted as History tutor during McElwee's absence in the Army. The wartime years were quite good for open awards. In the season 1941/2 there were eight scholarships and two exhibitions and the historians maintained their share of the total. Fawcett wrote modestly to Roxburgh on his departure for a headmastership at Rishworth in 1946: 'When you asked me to be History tutor I was terrified – but habit and a measure of success caused me to imagine that I might perhaps be numbered among the intellectuals, a misapprehension I soon realised when Bill McElwee came back.'

The Summer Report in 1941 from the headmaster to the governing body contained a new sub-section:

'Enemy Action'. At 2.30 a.m. on Friday May 9th a 'stick' of light bombs fell in the grounds, the nearest crater is 180 yards from the South Front. A very large number of windows were broken and some window frames were also damaged. There was a small fall of plaster from the ceiling of the South Front Portico and the master on watch was hit on the head. His 'Tin Hat', however, saved him from injury. One small piece of bomb case went through an open window in Chatham and struck the wall above a boy's head. There was a full moon which lit up the buildings brilliantly. The craters formed a curved line and it was generally agreed the German plane had not been aiming for the School.

In fact one piece of shrapnel went as far as 'George' and boys clambered around in the muddy crater collecting others. Farmer Davies was convinced that Hitler was after his new elevator. For a brief while the idea of camouflaging Stowe was discussed and the R.A.F's Director of Camouflage was consulted. Both he and the Ministry of Home Security decided that the concealment of the mansion was beyond human ingenuity. Only one other 'Enemy Action' report appeared, in 1942. It was noted that on 7 July at 6.25 a.m. four small bombs were dropped 600 yards from the school. There was heavy rain and low cloud at the time and only a few panes of glass were broken.

Roxburgh was for a long period pessimistic about the outcome of the war. John Boyd-Carpenter was staying with him on the memorable night when news came of the German invasion of Russia and felt able to reassure him, but in the first years he believed certainly that the Nazis would take over the school he had created. Numbers gave cause for concern. In September 1941, Roxburgh wrote to Habershon: 'We are considerably down in numbers, being now about 460 instead of 520 and I suppose that the drop will continue. No less that thirty of my small boys were evacuated last Summer and parents who have to pay half their incomes to the Government cannot afford Stowe fees.' Boys were leaving earlier, either to join the Forces or to squeeze in a year at university before they did so. (The correspondence with college tutors sorting out this last point was vast.) Of seventy leavers in the summer of 1941, thirty-one were under 18, two under $17\frac{1}{2}$. The early leaving meant that a higher replacement rate was required. By the summer of 1942 the average age of leavers was 17 years 7 months. In deference to increasing youth the junior cross-country course was shortened to a bare two miles. Although there were still around 450 pupils, entries were at less than half of the pre-war average. Roxburgh ascribed the drop to the belief that Stowe was an expensive school and to the shortage of petrol, as well as the high rate of income tax. In H.M.C. circles there was even some discussion that Stowe might possibly have to amalgamate with another school, but by 1943 things had begun to improve. The petrol shortage affected not only entries but staff relations as many had to travel to school (A.A. Dams from Lillingstone Dayrell, seven miles away, for example), and wives were frequently in competition for petrol to shop in Buckingham. They believed that Roxburgh's eloquence would move the heart of the Divisional Petroleum Officer.

The isolation of Stowe made it the bemused recipient of a number of surgical specimens rescued from the bombed premises of the Royal College of Surgeons. Equally unexpected was a huge collection of stuffed birds, formed originally by Edward Hart of Christchurch, Hampshire and continued by a Stowe parent, John Hall. By July 1942, only one third of the birds had arrived but they already occupied a room forty feet by twenty. An ornithologist, N. Aldrich-Blake, was appointed to look after them, but wartime conditions made display difficult and they remained in their boxes.[4]

What had been re-named as the Junior Training Corps was over three hundred strong and the reorganized Air Training Section contained over seventy cadets. In 1942 it took over a second afternoon each week. Colonel Worsley, the Inspecting Officer in 1942, praised the Corps highly: 'This is a very good contingent, well commanded and officered and with cadets of excellent quality. Smartness and good turn-out are admirably combined with sound field-work. The School may be assured that the J.T.C. is fulfilling its function with energy and success.' The field-work included night endurance exercises during which the Stoics frequently disturbed sleeping cows and horses. Training was not restricted to termtime. Fifty N.C.O.s helped units to train in their home localities during

[4] The birds had mostly been shot by Mr Hart as they returned over his Hampshire property after migration. The collection included relics of extinct birds, an egg of Aepyornis-Maximus, largest known bird, the egg being over 34 inches in circumference, and a reconstruction of the Dodo (Didus Ineptus) last heard of in Mauritius in 1681.

the holidays and at the school. Officers and cadets ran six-day courses at Stowe to enable Cadet Force officers from other areas to take the War Certificate 'A' examinations. As the Scouts were in abeyance Archer organized a six months' 'Field Intelligence' scheme, developing self-reliance and powers of observation for young recruits. These were the famous 'Freddie Boys'. The syllabus included darning socks and wood-fire cooking. Robin Watt commanded the Senior Platoon doing the Certificate B. Syllabus, and Bruce Barr directed the two platoons of trained cadets. Over 100 cadets joined the parade which opened the Buckingham War-Weapons Week, marching in formation both to and from the town as well as in the march past. On their way down the Grand Avenue they also practised anti-aircraft dispersal and re-formation. 'Wings for Victory' and other patriotic events followed a similar pattern. Life was certainly not relaxed. The compulsory P.T. had been cancelled in the Spring Term 1942 because of the weather and was therefore introduced more intensively than ever in the summer. The Air Section had exercises such as a contest between 'Bombers' and 'Fighters', based upon plane recognition. Points were scored for the correct recognition of the types of aircraft printed on a card and held by the contestants. 'Fighters' were allowed to run, 'Bombers' had to walk, though even so the latter won by 150 points to 70. As well as commanding two Home Guard Sections, Clifford ran the J.T.C. throughout the war. His vigorous militarism sometimes brought him into conflict with members of Grafton House (who thought the regime too Prussian) and with the less enthusiastic cadets. But Clifford was proud of the number of times that the Stowe contingent was called upon to instruct the officers of other groups. 'Come and be my guest in your own School', he wrote to Roxburgh during one of the holiday courses. 'Have a bit of fun and hobnob with these splendid men.'

Cricketing hours had to be shortened as no motoring could be undertaken in hours of darkness. Against Bradfield stumps had to be drawn at 4.30 p.m. to enable them to return home. Bedford had to leave at 6.00 a.m. to make the train connections for Stowe. In the summer of 1941 the Lord's defeat by Tonbridge was avenged. Stowe declared at 269 for 8. Tonbridge were all out for 41. W.R. Mallory enjoyed a hat-trick, took six wickets in all and had the impressive analysis 10.2.8.6. There was a similar success in the summer of 1942 by W.M. Savery against Radley. Stowe, having started before daybreak, were put in to bat by Radley who thought they might be tired. In the Radley innings, however, Savery took a wicket with the third ball, two more in his second over, two more in the third and one in his fifth. The analysis at this moment read 5.2.6.5.

Youthfulness made it harder to turn out heavy and experienced Rugby teams. Contrary to the impression he sometimes gave Roxburgh felt the games results keenly. In the arid reports he submitted to the Governors the only sparks of life are to be found in the games sections. In December 1941, he reported that the XV had been young and inexperienced. 'We played against Uppingham without our full-back, our hooker or our fastest three-quarter', he reported, showing a more than academic interest. In the spring, having blamed illness and injury, he concluded, 'But the results are none-the-less regrettable.' By 1943 he was uncharacteristically critical: 'The Fifteen was again young but it is undeniable that it was also incompetent . . . My own impression in watching matches against such schools as Oundle has been that *our* boys play as amateurs against professionals.' Of a boy who had just been given his First XI Colours in 1943 he said: 'He has just got his cricket colours – although I admit that the team of which he is a member is the worst we have ever had.' He thought there were too few cricketers willing to take advice or to practise hard. Fawcett, who looked after First XI cricket during the war, was more kindly: 'This was a good wartime side. The fact that most of the important school matches were lost . . . militates against this opinion. But wherever the side played it invariably gave intense pleasure to the spectators by its fielding and, in match after match it received well deserved praise in this department.' To which Roxburgh appended the comment, 'It is evident, however, that in other departments it was weak.' Bruce Barr, who coached the Rugby, was at times quite vitriolic in his comments on the Stowe XVs.

As the war moved into a more global phase and there were heavy losses both in the Mediterranean and the Far East, each event in the school calendar revived memories and added to the burden of sombre news that came of losses among Old Stoics. In retrospect it seemed that in sport these men, as boys, had sustained a constant flow of success. Up to Easter 1941 there had been only 30 fatalities in almost two years of fighting. In the Remembrance Day Service of that year there were still only 47 deaths recorded, along with the names of three missing for over six months. Even by July 1942, there were only 79 fatal casualties. Then the Desert and Italian fronts and fighting in the Far East led to a huge increase. By November 1944, 201 fatalities had been recorded. Other schools had figures of equal or greater magnitude but they did not represent so large a percentage of the Old Boys in action. The Old Stoic Society was more than decimated. For Roxburgh – who had endeavoured to establish a personal and sympathetic link with each individual named, who had corresponded with colleges and tutors, crammers and all manner of institutions on their behalf, and who now had to comfort the bereaved families with whom he had enjoyed friendships which transcended a merely professional association – the losses built up a huge load of inner grief. He felt, too, the years growing upon him. When he heard that Acland, first housemaster of Cobham, had retired from Norwich School, thinking that he 'ought to give way to a younger man', he found it 'disquieting that Acland thought himself too old at 52 years after 12 years service (I am 54 and Stowe is almost twenty years old).' He found it even odder that Acland about this time announced his intention of marrying. 'Hart Dyke and I', wrote Roxburgh, 'feel that you have given new hope to bachelors and although I am your senior by a great many years I feel that even in my case a faint glow of hope is now to be seen on the horizon.' His letters occasionally contained wistful references to matrimony. One interesting aside came in a letter to Bill, now Major, McElwee in Scotland: 'Years ago I used to play golf at Dornoch and very nearly became engaged to be married there. The lady is now the wife of a Major-General and I think he has done better for her than I should have. But the Dornoch Golf Course still has a kind of golden glow over it in my memory.' To an old friend, Sam Pike, headmaster of Cothill House prep school, he wrote in sympathy after a child's illness: 'When one brings a family into the world one gives hostages to fortune. But how much more happiness one has than ever comes the way of a bachelor. At least so things have always looked to me.'

Despite the two minor incidents of German bombing, greater disruption came to the school from friend rather than foe. There had been some worries that the building might be taken over by the Admiralty, either as a headquarters or as a training camp for the W.R.N.S. Clifford remembered seeing the Gothic Library stiff with Admirals on one occasion and, indeed, pushed the J.T.C. camps to counter such a move. In September 1942, 500 troops, part R.A.O.C. and part Pioneer Corps, arrived and the authorities requisitioned eleven classrooms, the masters' hostel, the cricket pavilion and scout hut, as well as setting up tented camps along the Grand Avenue and various verges. As winter approached the majority of the soldiers moved to billets but a N.A.A.F.I. was set up in two central classrooms where the constant radio competed for attention with nearby instruction. Fortunately the commander was a keen Rugby player so the occupation of the pavilion did not greatly interfere with the First XV fixtures. There were E.N.S.A. entertainments and dances. Raymond Walker married Biddy, the commander's daughter. Many years later Mrs Warden, a retainer in the school since 1923, interviewed by *Middle Voice*, one of the informal school magazines, remembered Benny Goodman playing to billeted troops in the Old Gym. In practical ways the school gained as the Pioneers laid the pipes connecting Stowe with the North Bucks water supply at government expense.

The presence of the R.A.O.C. betokened supplies of ammunition and equipment. Nissen huts were placed in dale and grove. The Grand Avenue was ideal for providing cover and here there were about 100 huts, not particularly well secured, some with only sacking at the entrances. The hunt for souvenirs was inevitable. Andrew Vinen, later a master, recalls Roxburgh addressing Assembly: 'Will the gentleman who removed a box of hand grenades from Hut No. 33 kindly hand them in to me. It seems that the Army wants them back.' There were no serious accidents as a result of these raids save to fish, on occasion blown out of the lakes by unsubtle methods. But it is doubtful whether the headmaster's genteel approach was adequate. Eric Reynolds recalled collecting two truck-loads of ammunition during his early days at Stowe. In December 1944, the Army decided to prosecute and there were appearances at the Juvenile Court. 'I think the Magistrates will refer the boys to me,' Roxburgh informed the parents of one offender, 'in which case — will have nothing to fear. At the best, however, it will be an unpleasant experience for the boy and I would gladly have kept him out of it.'

A repeat of the Stowe Fête was held in 1942 in aid of the Red Cross. Members of Bruce fashioned a bandstand out of scaffolding. The raffle prizes included a portrait to be painted by Robin Watt. Buckingham shops contributed custard powder and boot-polish but, by 1942, there were not many luxury products on display. 'The White Elephant Stall did good business', said the *Stoic*, now issued in very slim volumes, 'considering the patent inutility of its wares.' The long period of total war was having its effect. David Wynne, the sculptor, also interviewed by *Middle Voice* recalled 'the grey dead feeling of wartime [which] slowly rose like a tide during my time at Stowe – rations, cheap clothes, horrid hairy paper for books . . .'

No doubt all these things contributed to the frustrations of the Common Room. In pre-war days the staff lived at close quarters but there were holidays and travels abroad to ease tension, even on the meagre salary scales of the times. Now holidays were occupied with farming camps and A.R.P.duties. As so often, relief of tension came in the form of letters to the headmaster. Ivor Cross in particular hankered after the lost innocence of the 1920s. While Nazi High Command was laying its invasion plans he pressed Roxburgh on greater support for the chaplain and better attendances by masters at the early services. He wished also for a 'campaign of infinite duration against petty dishonesty by enforcing *sanctions* to show we mean business . . . Nothing else will work and both the times and the spiritual condition of the School will call for deliberate effort'. By 1942 the mood was reproachful: 'I am oppressed by the "negative spirit" – the soullessness that seems to be developing here . . . How many Masters back the Voluntary Service on Mondays? We have had two (Masters') Meetings so far this term and this is the beginning of the new school year as well as Confirmation Term. But you have not talked about religion or (I believe) about Confirmation except to give us the date.' Roxburgh had ignored the point he (Cross) had made in a recent sermon that the war was a spiritual conflict. 'Whether you agreed or not personally is not the main point . . . Why should I be made to feel that I don't exactly win your favour?' At the same time he urged Roxburgh on into a decidedly unspiritual conflict with the Petroleum Officer who was not won over, first suggesting that the Crosses might share with the Cliffords and Kinvigs in their journeys and finally replying tersely that 'the number of coupons released for domestic use to Stowe School is considered more than sufficient'.

All this did not prevent Roxburgh from paying an eloquent tribute to Cross, whom he had known since the age of twelve and who was, apart from 'Moss' at the school shop, the sole survivor of May 1923. Cross left Chatham at Easter 1943, to found a small preparatory school, Lapsley Grange in Cardiganshire, which prospered under his care: 'He has provided an element of strength, of high purpose, of idealism both civic and Christian, and a devotion to duty which demanded the most from himself and the best from us all.'

Playford continued to wage a private war against the bursar, Major Russell, long after the latter had left in 1940. Playford wrote in 1942 of 'the treatment meted out in 1939 when for three weeks a small group of people worked strenuously to make it possible for the School to open . . . Stowe School appeared almost to resent their presence and made no effort to house and feed them adequately'. After an onslaught on the food and service, he refused to do holiday fire-watching: 'If the truth be told blatantly but not boastfully, one has endured the conditions for the sake of the boys and because Stowe seemed worthwhile. But endure them beyond the limits of a term I cannot.'

Roxburgh replied reasonably,

I cannot seriously believe that the deficiencies and absurdities of Russell, as exhibited in 1939 are regarded by you as sufficient reason for not helping us two and a half years later . . . I think that you should remember when you hit back at 'Stowe School' for the defects of its treatment of masters you do not hurt 'Stowe School'. What you hurt is the other masters! The fewer men who do holiday work the worse it is for those who do it. And surely the discomforts of the holidays affect others just as much as they affect you. Is it reasonable you should be the only person to avoid them?

In reply to Roxburgh's assertion that the school and the boys afforded 'an entirely delightful job', Playford replied, 'The job involves an isolation from the world which is far from delightful and which is not shared by many schools', and concluded, 'I am not willing to prolong the discomforts of the term into the holidays.' In November of the same year he raised the issue of the respective roles of headmaster and housemaster over a number of incidents which the frustrations of the time no doubt heightened. Roxburgh defended a beating which he had inflicted on a boy who had shouted bad language from the scorebox. 'A public offence had been committed with which the School reverberated and it was most necessary that punishment should be inflicted at Headquarters and as a School affair.' Playford claimed that a housemaster knew a boy's record more closely especially in matters such as smoking and drinking and it mattered 'how recently he had spoken to individuals or to the House as a whole . . . these points will have a bearing on the offence.' Roxburgh replied (with regard to smoking):

> The offence is just a breach of rules and whatever the boy's history may have been he must learn that, if you touch an electric wire you will get a shock and that, if you are late, you will miss your train irrespective of any moral question . . . What is more, it is most necessary that the boys should believe that rule-breaking of that kind is treated exactly the same in whatever House it occurs. The last thing that they should be allowed to feel is that people who smoke in House X are beaten but people who are in House Y merely reprimanded.

Roxburgh disliked beating only a little less than Playford but probably he suspected that Playford defended members of his house too readily. Playford was thanked for 'the amicable tone in which you put your points' (not it may be said a feature that everyone would notice) but he had the last word: 'There is only one thing I would say, if I may be so bold. You might more often say to a master or prefect "Take this to the Housemaster to be dealt with" instead of feeling that you yourself must deal with every case that is reported to you, and even let it be known that it should be the exception to go to you.'

Despite his unrelenting industry Roxburgh's diffused dealings with every boy did sometimes blur the issues and the chain of command. His preference for addressing the school privately left some of his colleagues uncertain about disciplinary priorities. Even Clifford, to whom loyalty was the cardinal virtue, complained in 1942, 'In not knowing what disciplinary points you were making to the School on two occasions this term I have honestly felt at a loss in helping to carry out your wishes. It doesn't matter *how* we know so long as we do know from you. I have refrained from pestering you and from cross-questioning boys but I should like to bring to your notice how invidious the position may be.' Following a statement at a masters' meeting in February 1942 on working with determination to bring Certificate failures up to the mark Clifford expressed the feeling of many veterans. 'I hope you will drive us hard and be neither considerate nor generous, but exacting. It may seem odd to you perhaps, but we shall welcome it in these days and respond, or I'm very much mistaken.'

War conditions revealed other stresses within the system. It was no longer possible for Roxburgh's own fastidious standards of behaviour and taste to percolate down and influence the majority. Human stupidity and cussedness provided blockages which gentle urbanity could not breach. Peregrine Worsthorne more than once has denounced the bullying during morning breaks and at other times when masters were absent. The same things happened in other schools but other headmasters did not speak so devoutly of the blessings of freedom. Throughout the war there was a prodigiously long correspondence between Roxburgh and Patrick Hunter, senior tutor, on the dangers of identifying the school too closely with one individual. 'I still feel that the School is too centred upon you', wrote Hunter in May 1940, 'and I fear for the successful transition when it comes to a successor.' Clothed in gossamer webs of compliment as all Roxburgh's correspondence to and fro inevitably was, there were real and important points at issue. Of the masters Hunter added,

> They are loyal to you because you can carry them where you will in two minutes by an infallible touch. But the moments are in some cases rare and so they do not understand Stowe . . . I know of a number of cases where you could have turned conscientious work into devoted service. Some would have kept up their quality better, others would never have left and many, when they talked abroad, would not talk so freely of the shortcomings of Stowe School Limited but would think first of the pride they feel in your Stowe . . . Ultimately surely a school must depend upon its staff. That's why I so want you to have time for what you now have little time for, and what you can do so superbly well.

It would appear that Roxburgh had criticized some masters for being too ready to punish. In November 1940, Hunter wrote that many moral principles could be inculcated by classwork. 'I think there are many men who work really hard to cure certain shortcomings in the boys which sometimes justify stern measures. Very often they have acted . . . as they have because they have been prepared to take more and not less trouble.' Roxburgh had been in the habit of handing out high grades to those he taught which nullified the more stringent comments and marks awarded by others. 'Conscientious masters have felt this an indirect snub for them and have had much heart taken from them on that account . . . We are not weaned from the time when you, almost of necessity with a young staff, were the complete centre of things . . . Give us a goal and the routes to it can be many and various, but they will have direction.'

It was the age-old argument between pattern and impulse, classical and romantic. 'We have too often considered a boy's feelings before his good', wrote Hunter in 1941. 'We have given boy nature too often credit for possessing qualities of judgement and control and perception beyond what he can usually have developed at his age.' In particular Hunter wished Roxburgh to curtail his lower school teaching, which would have struck at the principle that he taught every form and every boy, but was a great demand on his time and energy. 'In my opinion,' he wrote 'the only possible way to influence boys fully is through the staff. That is why I think that you spend too much time with the boys as a whole to the considerable detriment of the staff, instead of with the staff and senior boys.'

Roxburgh refused to curtail his Lower School teaching: 'When the War is over, or perhaps sooner, you will doubtless have a new Headmaster. His methods will perhaps be more in accordance with your ideas and I am sure they will be better methods. But I cannot change my methods now and I hope that you will not again ask me to do so.' He believed in allowing masters to teach according to their own natures and idiosyncrasies. Hunter responded, 'Men who have not the welfare of the place at heart are allowed to get away with what they please. Unless one pulls oneself up and remembers that you are generous to a fault (and therefore the cause is one that may be admired) one is in danger of wondering what does matter and what does not.' Despite the compliments the temperature of the correspondence was high. One can appreciate Hunter's wish that Roxburgh should give up his crippling teaching load and ensure that he handed on a well-organized and unified Common Room at the end of his time. 'If direct contact with all boys is the central pillar of the Headmaster's policy, it cannot help implying an imperfect trust in his colleagues.' There was also a strong case for releasing Roxburgh from the prison of his own methods. He was constantly penning letters of congratulation on engagements, marriages and births, for example, which the Old Boys of other schools might have expected from housemasters but not from the headmaster personally. (Rosemary Hill recalled finding him at his desk one Christmas morning and his being surprised at her seasonal greeting, having forgotten the date.) Yet not only could he not change but, against the background of war and the grief over casualties, he became distressed at the exchanges. 'I have read what you say with profound disappointment and with a kind of hopelessness . . . The whole thing is disheartening and seems to involve such a waste of emotional energy that I cannot bring myself to discuss it with you for a moment' (5.12.41.). Nor can genius be easily tamed.

Because of the fears of diminishing numbers the standards of entry often had to be lowered and a number of pupils, whose capacities and motivation were doubtful, were quite enthusiastically admitted.[5] One result was a division between the intellectual élite and the remainder. Letters to the *Stoic* began to contain criticism of hallowed institutions like compulsory Chapel and the prefectorial system. References to the fear of revolutionary ideas and 'bolshevism' indicate a certain amount of friction. Open Awards were comparatively numerous. The results of the average performers fell slightly. In 1941 Stowe enjoyed an 81.94 per cent success rate at Higher Certificate compared with a national average of 62.77. A year later the national average had risen to 66.36 and Stowe had fallen below this figure. Visitors to Societies were less frequent although Eileen Joyce and members of the London Philharmonic came to give a concert in 1941 as did Leon Goossens in 1942. Dr Zettl made valiant efforts to find foreign films for the Film Society but for obvious reasons they were rare and expensive. Home-made entertainments prevailed. The subjects of debates were mostly escapist. Peregrine Worsthorne deplored the detective story; Anthony Quinton supported *Old Moore's Almanack* against *The Times*. George Melly seconded the motion: this house views

[5] 'It would be an abuse of language to say he had passed', wrote Roxburgh to the prep school of one young man, whose mother had been a friend of Lord Gisborough. He scored 11 per cent at his first attempt, was given a second shot and, having raised the total to 17 per cent, was accepted.

with disfavour the present popularity of classical music. In his autobiography *Owning Up* he refers to the small cells of jazz enthusiasts which flourished. He gave a paper to one of the learned societies on 'Surrealism' and played Lady Macbeth in a production by Wilson Knight which only the most strenuous efforts by the stage manager prevented from achieving a surrealism of its own. J.E. Richardson won the British Boys' Chess Championship in 1940. Dodie Watts organized a Puppet Club which performed *Alice Through the Looking Glass* with the marionettes based on the original Tenniel illustrations. Iona Radice who helped in the Library and elsewhere organized the Sunday Concerts. A performance of the Brahms-Haydn Variations by two of the music staff was so popular that a second performance had to be arranged. Wilson Knight helped to found The Symposium, a club for aspirants to the essay society known as the XII.

To the XII itself J.E.M. Irvine read a paper on 'The Novels of Disraeli' and it is sad to reflect that no sixth former today, battling with three or four 'A' Levels, could possibly make such an original excursion. Stowe Film Productions for a time produced monthly news reviews after the manner of Pathé and Movietone, recording Bruce house corporately felling a tree, the floods in Buckingham and the substitution of pony traps for the motor car. Like many other boys in schools across the land Stoics found themselves knitting helmets and scarves for the Armed Forces. It was said that conversation revolved not around the use of a mashie or a number four but whether it was preferable to slip or knit the first stitch. Miss Richardson, one of the lady teachers, founded a Junior Science Society. Biological gardens were in operation in addition to the farming camps. Rabbits were reared for dissecting work and microplots cultivated to report on the culture of potatoes and turnips to Rothamsted Laboratories. In the summer of 1942, when the fortunes of war were at their bleakest, the School Concert featured the Single, Double and Treble Concertos of Bach.

In 1943 the horizon began to brighten. Eighty-seven new boys came in September, a figure only once before equalled in the previous nineteen years. Nine boys returned from Canada and the U.S.A. Future registrations were improving. By September 1944 numbers had risen to 509, fifty-two more than in the previous year. At the end of 1943 the military occupation of the classrooms ended and the stuffed birds were assigned to the

Temple of Concord to make way for fee-paying residents in the dormitories.

1944 brought the 21st birthday of the school and telegrams flooded in from battlefields all over the world. McElwee, waiting for D-Day along with an Old Stoic, Ian Munro, wrote:

> At present trying to get a telegram off to you from both of us, not I fear the correctly witty scrap of Latin for neither of us was properly educated but full of goodwill . . . The War will have deprived you of the comfort and serenity which ought to have been your personal share. There is neither the time nor the mood for satisfaction . . . but as some compensation I think the War has given you even more to be proud of. Your personal achievement is not to be assessed in words at all. But I would like to record my own gratitude for having been allowed a hand in the job even for a few of those twenty-one years.

The Pineapple Club was a casualty of the London Blitz and was forced to move to the premises of another club in Maida Vale. 'The heavy hearts shown at leaving the Old Pineapple have revealed the deep appreciation which exists among the lads for what Stowe does', reported the Warden. 'Never was it clearer than when they first rallied to clear up the mess of broken glass and debris.' On Empire Day 1941 incendiary bombs set ablaze even the ruins that were left. Many of the London Committee of Old Stoics were called up and it could no longer meet. John Lilley O.S. who had worked tirelessly for the club and wrote the *Pineapple Newsletter* was one of the first to leave for France. As the newly appointed Warden anticipated his entry into the R.A.F. his place was taken by Mr A.E. Crewdson who among fresh features introduced a boot-repairing class, rehearsals for a revue and a discussion group for the Pineapple Old Boys. The club provided a temporary shelter for those who were bombed out of their homes and soon it, too, had its casualties to report both from abroad and in the London streets and cellars.

As almost all Old Stoics were serving in the Forces there were fewer distinctions to report, and most were in sport. E.P. Hickling, three years in the First XI, played for the Southern Public Schools. P.C. Holden won the Three Mile Race at the Cambridge Freshmen's Sports and, in 1942 and '43, the same event at the Inter-University Sports. P.R.H. Hastings represented England against

Wales in Rugby football in 1942 and against Scotland the following year. A.D. Thomson and J.E. Murray both played Rugby for Cambridge in 1942 and R.D. Lightfoot was Cambridge Secretary of Athletics. Hastings also won the Quarter Mile for Oxford in the first wartime University Sports when J.M. Thomson won the 100 Yards for Cambridge. In 1944 J.S.B. Butler was President of the Union at Cambridge. Noel Annan was elected as Fellow of King's, Cambridge.

The summer of 1945 brought the seventeen terms of war to a conclusion. More than a quarter of the school's history had been passed under blackout conditions. The spectacle of the South Front with light pouring from the windows was a strange one and took more than two months to achieve, the blackout proving, in Roxburgh's words, 'much more difficult to get off than it was to put on'. The bursar's heart fell when the massive task of redecoration was revealed.

The school had been due to reassemble on 8 May but it was left to parents to decide whether boys should travel on that day or not. On VE Day plus 1 a celebratory bonfire was lit on the site of the bomb crater of 1941. The school in September numbered 519 and would have been larger but for the delay in moving the stuffed birds. Registrations in the first half of 1945 were among the highest recorded.

As if to toast a return to pre-war ebullience the Summer Term brought a most successful cricket season. All four school matches were won. On a dark and drizzling day, Bedford was beaten by 97 runs, their first school defeat for two years and the first Stowe victory over Bedford since 1940. J.F. Chance, who was described by Roxburgh in a letter to an Old Boy as 'the discovery of the Season', enjoyed a hat trick. But even this was eclipsed by the match against St Edwards which gave Mr Fawcett an opportunity to indulge his reporter's talents.

Stowe had scored 207. St Edward's were 99 for 7. Then the St Edward's Captain was out. 99 for 8. It now looked as if Stowe would win with a little time to spare but Graham and Rutherford had other ideas and batted most courageously. 25 runs were added and – sad to relate – catches were dropped. Once again a draw seemed certain.

Then the miracle happened. There were seven minutes left to

play and Young went on to bowl. For the third time this season he was to prove that he could bowl straight to the tail-end batsmen when he had to. With his second ball he had Rutherford lbw; off the next Herson who, to Stowe supporters had seemed an unconscionable time coming in to bat, made a single; off the fourth Graham made 2. Then came the fatal fifth ball; Graham played it hard to second slip where stood the faithful Illingworth who held another catch in his right hand. Lattey came to the wicket with such deliberation (not to mention a little practice he had in the course of his stately progress) that it would obviously be impossible to start another over. There was thus one ball to go. Could Young bowl a straight one? He could and Lattey for all his practice found it too much for him.

6

Persto et Praesto

The courage of Leonard Chesire V.C., D.S.O. and Order of Merit, and the confidence he inspired in his bomber crews have passed into the nation's history along with the deeds of Drake and Nelson. It is the simple purpose of this chapter to show that these qualities, which have been fully described by others, were not uncommon among the Stoics of his generation. It is in no sense a complete history of Stoics in battle in the Second World War. The total number recorded as having served was just under two thousand: 270, a proportion of one in seven, lost their lives. There were 242 decorations, a proportion of just over one in eight. The list included 2 V.C.s, 28 D.S.O.s, 21 D.S.C.s, 111 M.C.s, 46 D.F.C.s and 34 other awards. Stoics were too young to take higher command in war but they were represented in every major and most dangerous engagement. The following pages do no more than recount extracts, impressions and selections of feats that were by no means unique. All schools received news of brave deeds and tragic losses. At Stowe the significance was heightened as Old Stoics were still few in number and the generations were better known to one another by reason of the founding of the houses one by one. So this is less a chronicle than a tribute, to those who are not mentioned directly as much as to those who are.

The first casualty was John Busk, ironically a keen lifesaver at Stowe, killed in the bombing of Scapa Flow. For McLaughlin as late as May 1940, Roxburgh had news of only two other casualties, in air accidents. When the German offensive through the Low Countries began there came the first decoration: to

E.R. Farnell-Watson, whose brother, head of school, was given the task of taking the news from class to class. Farnell-Watson was with the Royal Tank Regiment and, with all but two carriers out of action, succeeded in bringing back crews and weapons to safety. Tufton Beamish won an M.C. at Steenbecque. While driving a truck he ran into five enemy tanks and two motor cyclists. He managed to escape and defend the position, continually moving among the men and 'setting a fine example to other companies in the battalion'. A.C. Geddes returned under heavy shell fire to help his battery commander evacuate a forward troop. The commander was killed beside him but, although wounded himself, he rescued two guns and, from a motor cycle, organized and ensured the rescue of the wounded.

On the same day as Farnell-Watson's decoration Joe Kayll was awarded the D.S.O. and D.F.C., both within twenty-four hours. He was Officer Commanding 615 Squadron, the last still equipped with Gladiator biplanes. As the Germans advanced it was ordered to Le Touquet and re-equipped with Hurricanes. With unfamiliar planes and with the hazards of operating from continental stations the squadron succeeded in destroying thirty-two German planes while the battle for Northern France was in progress. Kayll himself, as Roxburgh informed the Council, accounted for nine. 'Under his inspiring leadership and training this officer's squadron has responded to every call made. The Squadron Leader combined flying leadership and administration in an exemplary manner throughout', said the citation. Kayll had come to Stowe as his father had been a comrade of Ian Clarke in the First World War. T.S. Lucas M.C. formed part of the garrison defending Calais where he was wounded. There were many Stoics in the Rifle Brigade and reviewing the Regimental History by Lieutenant-Colonel R.W.S. Hastings O.S., J.C. Saunders described the defence of Calais as 'glorious as Thermopylae'. Lucas was taken prisoner but escaped from his German escort and despite his wounds walked twenty miles to a remote part of the French coast. He rowed himself across the Channel in a dinghy and after twelve hours was picked up only half a mile from the English coast. P. Gammidge was lost at sea during the evacuation from Dunkirk on board H.M.S. *Keith*.

In the Battle of Britain Stoics shared fully in the heroic exploits. John Dundas had proceeded from Stowe to Christ Church where he gained First Class Honours in History and a Half Blue for Squash. He also earned an award which enabled him to study at the Sorbonne and Heidelberg. He was one of the most promising journalists of his generation and was sent on a number of European assignments by the *Yorkshire Post*. He was in Prague at the time of the German entry and on his return joined 609 Squadron convinced that the Munich Settlement was dissolving.

At the start of the war he had only sixty hours flying time before being sent up solo in a Spitfire. His first flight with the squadron was not auspicious as he had engine failure on take-off and ended up in someone's back garden. At Christmas 1939, he was by coincidence stationed at Kinloss in Scotland and helping to guard the Home Fleet. In May 1940 he moved to Northolt and one of his first tasks was to patrol the skies above Dunkirk. The Yellow Section which he commanded ran short of fuel on a return journey and lost its way in fog. Planes were lost but he made a successful forced landing at Frinton-on-Sea. Twice he escorted Churchill across the Channel on missions to seek out the French Premier, Paul Reynaud. As an ex-journalist he edited the 609 Squadron Journal and set such a compelling standard of reporting that it was said to have been read with great interest by King George VI.

On 11 August 1940 a huge formation of enemy planes was circling above the Portland-Weymouth area. John Dundas was able to penetrate the enemy formation and attack from within. On 7 October he was sent to intercept German planes attacking the Westland Helicopter Plant at Yeovil. He destroyed one 110 but was hit from behind by a cannon shell and landed with several pieces of shrapnel in his leg. On the following day he was flying with his leg in bandages. Late in November he hosted a party of officers and cadets from Cranwell but there were two scrambles which interrupted proceedings. The second was called as a sweep of some fifty 109s was bearing down over the Isle of Wight. Their purpose was unclear as they did not have any bombers with them, but it was a crack force which included Major Helmut Wieck, one of the German air aces. They came down out of the sun. In the mêlée which ensued John was heard to shout 'Whoopee, I've got a 109', and this was the last message received. It is said that the Luftwaffe came up on the international distress wave length to ask the Air Ministry if they had any news of Wieck. It was clear he had been John's victim but Wieck always flew with a protecting plane covering him. The body of John Dundas's No.2 was washed up on the French shore but no trace was found of Dundas or Wieck. A Bar was added to his D.F.C. posthumously.

In a series of engagements fought from Biggin Hill with No.92 Squadron Tony Bartley, of Grafton, brought down eight enemy planes and was awarded the D.F.C. He came down to Stowe where he had been a member of the Rugby XV and was given lunch in the Common Room. David Brown spotted him and said that, as he had just lost a left-wing three quarter through injury, Bartley must play that afternoon against Middlesex Hospital. An hour or so later he found himself running out on to the pitch wearing the familiar colours. As he described it: 'Rumour quickly spread among the spectators that the rather breathless substitute . . . was an Old Stoic veteran of the Battle of Britain and everything I did from then on whether good, bad or indifferent was greeted with cheers.' He came to Stowe, which was close to his home, on another occasion with his top button undone in the approved fighter pilot fashion. His housemaster, Clifford, did it up for him saying in Roxburgh accents, 'My dear fellow you must not let the boys see you looking slovenly'. Clifford told the story against himself: 'Boys like their old housemasters to be silly. They feel sophisticated men of the world.' He spoke of many visits from pilots: 'They used to come down to Stowe on leave and walk to and fro with me on the South Front saying what heaven it was out of the Battle of Britain, or throwing their bomber about to escape the cone of searchlights' glare over German territory. I could only listen while they commanded words and made me feel very humble.' Bartley later flew in almost every theatre of war and was awarded a Bar to his D.F.C. After VE Day David Niven helped him to word his telegram of proposal to Deborah Kerr, the actress. He brought Deborah down to see Clifford who was greatly impressed, not least because she spontaneously drew out a cheque for the Pineapple. When Bartley and Deborah Kerr were married the car was discovered to have a flat battery and they were pushed from the doors of Claridges by a bunch of cheering fighter pilots 'whose combined air victories exceeded one hundred'.

While still a boy at Stowe Fred Gardiner was taking flying lessons in Northern Ireland and was surreptitiously allowed solo flights, although under age. On one of these he had his first experience of a forced landing. At normal height his engine continued at full take-off power. He eventually switched off the ignition and succeeded in descending to the air-field safely. The throttle lever had become disconnected from the carburettor. It was the first of several such adventures. Joining the University Air Squadron at Cambridge he was sent to summer camp, again in Northern Ireland. Returning in formation he noticed the oil pressure was low and discovered his feet were covered in it, so again he force-landed on Irish turf. On the outbreak of war his engineering degree qualified him as an engineering officer but this was not the employment he wished to have and after Dunkirk he was allowed to transfer to Hurricanes and was posted to 610 Squadron. On the 25 August 1940 he was shot down having destroyed an enemy plane, and landed by parachute near Dover. He was moved to Coastal Command as a Squadron Leader and led torpedo dropping raids against German convoys in passage from Kiel to Rotterdam. For this he received the D.F.C., 'mainly for surviving I often think'. Assignments in Egypt and the command of an anti-submarine squadron followed and his varied R.A.F. career closed with the monitoring of vessels bringing illegal immigrants to Israel.

D.A. Pemberton, who came to Grafton in 1926, spent six terms in the Fourths and three in Removes. If his academic progress was barely perceptible his house reports descended with noticeable speed from the initial 'cheery and irresponsible'. Squadron-Leader Pemberton was one of the most gallant pilots in the Battle of Britain, killed late in 1940 while flying in bad weather conditions. His citation spoke of his outstanding leadership after the return of his squadron from France. Led by him on almost every operation, it destroyed or damaged fifty-one enemy aircraft. It is salutary to reflect that this total, significant in the history of the war, was achieved by someone whose school reports had lamented a 'failure to gain respect'.

Hugh Dundas, brother of John, also fought in the skies during 1940, covering the evacuation from Dunkirk and intercepting bombers making for the East Coast. In August he had the narrowest of escapes from death when shot down by an M109. He struggled with the hood of his cockpit which was jammed and refused to open. Escaping with seconds to spare, he saw his Spitfire explode in an adjacent field. He survived to fly in formation with the great Douglas Bader, experimenting with manoeuvres which would protect the rear of the squadron in the daily dogfights over the Channel. He was selected for the hazardous task of proving the worth of the new Typhoon planes in combat, and fought in Tunisia from airstrips bulldozed from the mud and covered with a species of netting. He commanded a wing based in Malta which covered the invasion of Sicily and at twenty-three was in command of five squadrons of fighters guarding Montgomery's assault across the Straits of Messina. He flew above the Allied Armies as they advanced up Italy, carrying out low-level attacks on enemy positions behind the front. At one moment, while the ground battle hung in the balance, he and his men had to carry out these missions with bombs from a suspect cargo that had unsafe detonators and might blow up the plane in flight rather than the enemy.

One of the strangest stories of the war, though of a different kind, concerns P.F. Baker. He had been head of school, gained a First at Trinity and returned to Stowe for a brief period of teaching in 1939. In February 1940, he left Brighton by car to rejoin his unit in Gravesend, driving part of the way along the coast. Neither he nor the car was ever seen again, although in wartime there was a much closer watch for missing persons. The mystery remains unsolved.

Squadron-Leader R.G.A. Barclay D.F.C. fought in the two decisive Battles of Britain and Egypt and was killed at El Alamein in the summer of 1942. His record in the O.S. Register is necessarily brief but his life was remarkable. He had been intended for Chandos but chose Bruce, along with other friends from prep school. He came from a serious clerical family and took a place in Remove on the good results of his Common Entrance. In his second year he had a severe illness and spent several months away from Stowe. 'We must be thankful enough that we have George's life given back to us and that he has recovered so wonderfully', wrote the father. He too did some peacetime flying at Cambridge and wrote to Roxburgh from Cranwell in March 1940, 'I have always wanted a flying career from the time I was in the Stowe Aero Club . . . The War has saved me temporarily from the office stool as I went down from Cambridge last June to start a job in Barclays Bank.' In reply to Roxburgh's congratulations on his D.F.C. in December 1940 he wrote, 'At the end of November I stupidly let a hun fighter get the better of me and made a graceful descent on the end of a parachute near this hospital! My wounds which were never bad are getting on well.' His mother told Roxburgh, 'He had a thrilling three months defending London with his Squadron 249 which did very well . . . He had the nose of a cannon shell and shrapnel extracted from the elbow.' 249 Squadron could claim one of the highest totals of German planes destroyed during the Battle of Britain. Barclay was twice offered safer postings but wished to return to action. In September 1941 he was reported missing over France but in November there came a telegram: JUST RECEIVED WIRE GEORGE SAFE. REJOICING. BARCLAY. Roxburgh replied THANK YOU FOR GRAND NEWS. GOD BE PRAISED. Behind this exchange was quite a remarkable story. He had been too low to bale out when his plane was hit. He managed to land in a ploughed field but had hardly got into the undergrowth when he heard motorcycles making for the spot. He turned his tunic inside out, ruffled his hair and pulled his trouser legs down over his boots. He then rolled in the mud and leaves. It was not a very convincing disguise but, together with a bundle of sticks on a bent back, it deceived a lorry load of Germans who went by on the road. A few minutes later he found a warm welcome in a peasant's house.

One day a small girl arrived with a civilian suit and instructions that he should catch a certain train for Paris. He spoke French well but there was a danger in his appearance as he was a handsome young man and noticeable in any crowd. As he stood on the platform a German officer with his batman came and stood a few yards away. Barclay noticed that he was being eyed suspiciously. The officer whispered a word of command and indicated to him. At the same moment a group of old women with baskets clattered on to the platform. Without hesitation Barclay gave a cry of joy and rushed towards them, throwing his arms around the first and whispering as he kissed her, 'Aidez-moi, je suis aviateur Anglais'. In a flash she grasped the situation, accepted all the risks and gave a performance worthy of the Comédie Française. She went into torrents of French, everyone kissed him and welcomed him home. The German mounted into his reserved compartment and Barclay climbed in with his band of rescuers.

On his safe return from Spain he was not given long to rest but transferred to command a squadron with work of special difficulty in the Middle East. He was assigned to No. 238 Squadron which particularly needed to have its morale reinforced. Before he left he visited his parents. His father was in the middle of taking a communion service when he arrived at the church. He had just reached the Prayer of Consecration when George entered and knelt at the altar rail with the family. He fought with his squadron throughout the desert retreat and was last seen engaging impossible odds in an antique Hurricane. His body was found by a party of South Africans. Another Old Stoic, W.B. Hay, wrote to Playford,

> Not long ago we were given a new C.O. Imagine my pleasure and surprise at finding it was none other than George Barclay. He was only with us two weeks before he was missing in action. Recently word has come through that his grave has been found. During two weeks he was with us his leadership was of the highest quality both on the ground and in the air. He shot down two enemy aircraft in that short time. One of my friends said that although he didn't believe in hero worship he would follow him anywhere because he was giving everything he'd got. Nearly everyone in the ground crews I have talked to mentioned his name at one time or another with real devotion . . . It was a real honour to have been in the same squadron and I was particularly proud in view of the fact that he was not only an Old Stoic but also a member of Bruce. No word of praise could be too high and I wanted you to know how we felt.

Both at school and university George had been a member of the Christian Union. His grandfather, C.T. Studd, had been a noted cricketer and evangelical. Found in his pocket was a small tract on 'Loyalty'. Writing in reply to Roxburgh's letter of sympathy, Mrs Barclay said: 'I feel sorry for you as your family is so vast'. She was to lose another son in the defence of India at Kohima but she and her husband carried out an imaginative plan of holding a party for the French men and women who had shielded George during his four months in France. At the memorial service, his favourite hymn, 'Be still my soul, the Lord is on thy side', was sung to the special tune used in Stowe services.

Not all bravery brought decorations. Cyril Berger was a member of Grafton from 1936 to 1938. The relationship had not started auspiciously as his mother, a widow, had written asking for a Lancing prospectus. Roxburgh, warm-hearted and sympathetic to every kind of victim, had a curious blind-spot regarding Jews. A name like Rosenberg might be followed by an exclamation mark, and writing to Berger's prep school the correspondence contained phrases like, 'Well grown, pleasant and looks like an Anglo-Saxon'. Yet his relations with Cyril were cordial and he sent the boy a handsome wallet when he succeeded in passing his School Certificate in hospital. He was put to endless trouble when Mrs Berger suddenly opted for an education at the Sorbonne without having made any arrangements. Roxburgh was obliged to do the work of finding families that took in boarders and arrange tutoring through his old Sorbonne acquaintances. One, Professor Marouzeau, sent the splendid letter: '*Votre lettre me rejoint à Vichy où ma femme soigne sa bile éprouvée par les évènements* [of Munich].' It was Cyril's Jewishness which made him fanatically determined to fight Hitler when war broke out. At first graded C for fitness, he was so persistent in his efforts that he was accepted for R.A.F. training and was one of the first to be sent to America for this purpose. This involved an exciting Atlantic crossing during which his ship was pursued by the *Bismarck*.

Although he suffered severe discomfort after flying and was told he would be invalided out, he refused to accept the decision and put such pressure on the authorities that he returned to Britain in 1942 as a qualified wireless operator/air gunner. He could have obtained the post of Instructor which he would not take and, after a spell in hospital with severe phlebitis, extracted a letter from R.A.F. Medical H.Q. which stated that he could be retained as aircrew although he was not to be posted to any station that involved long walks. On 27 September 1943 an air-crew from Caithness 612 Squadron were carrying out an anti-U Boat patrol in the North Atlantic and were due to make a landfall in the Shetlands at 3.45 p.m. At 3.30 a faint S.O.S. was picked up but nothing further was heard or seen. A heavy sea was running and it was thought unlikely that the men could have launched a dinghy successfully. Earlier in the year he had spoken with a friend of his revulsion at the Nazi atrocities. As the friend related the conversation to Roxburgh: 'He seemed to see it all so vividly and he felt the need for action. Indeed he must have died in the consummation of his heart's desire to do something about it.'

James Pike had won the Sword of Honour at Cranwell. He was awarded the D.F.C. for his low-flying machine gun attacks against enemy aerodromes in the Middle East and he was responsible for the confirmed destruction of eight aircraft. On one occasion he arrived over an aerodrome as three fighters were taking off and they intercepted him. He immediately dived on the leading plane and put it out of action. Before either of the other aircraft could engage him, he attacked four grounded planes, one of which caught fire. By skilfully manoeuvring he then enabled his air gunner to disable one of the fighters and did not leave the target until he had set fire to four enemy planes in all and damaged three others. On another raid he succeeded in setting fire to four bombers, photographed the result and returned to his base by night.

During the ceaseless bombing of Germany and Europe there were many courageous exploits to recount in addition to the heroic missions of Leonard Cheshire. Flying Officer G.F.B. Newport Tinley of Cobham was captaining a plane flying at 1400 feet over the North French coast when it passed over heavy anti-aircraft fire. He completed his mission but on the return journey the engine caught fire. The fire was extinguished but the engine failed and the plane lost height. When it reached the English coast it was at sixty feet, in bad visibility. By what was described as 'superlative airmanship' he brought the plane down on the sea and saved the lives of the crew. A similar exploit was recorded of Flying Officer R.A.P. Allsebrook, returning from a mission over Mannheim. The port engine seized and, jettisoning all possible material, Allsebrook flew on one engine for four hours. After bringing the plane down on water he and his crew were rescued from their dinghy fourteen hours later. The Sub-Lieutenant of the naval unit that picked him up wrote to Allsebrook's father:

> I would not have written this letter only I thought you would like to know of the magnificent spirit and courage shown by your son in greatest adversity. He refused to board our craft until all his air-crew had been safely embarked and did much to cheer up his subordinates until they had fully recovered. It really was the greatest pleasure to meet someone so unassuming and enthusiastic and we in the Navy cannot express our admiration sufficiently for him.

Ralf Allsebrook and his brother Geoffrey were greatly esteemed by Roxburgh. When the parents asked if they could take the boys home after a concert he replied that he could not release Geoffrey, the elder, who was a Prefect. 'By all means take Ralf home with you . . . Geoffrey being a pillar of the state cannot be withdrawn without producing a collapse of the fabric. I prophesy that Ralf will not be less "columnar" when his time comes.' In 1943 Ralf had been taking his squadron to one of the aerodromes near to Stowe. 'I flew around the place for a while and probably moved you to a frenzy . . . for which I am very sorry, but I could not resist when I found the O.T.C. marching up Armoury Hill, and my crew were so intrigued by the whole place.' The reply came: 'It was nice to hear from you. Never bother to apologise for taking off our chimney tops. We are quite accustomed to it now. As long as it is by an Old Stoic (though of course one cannot be sure) we shall not object to being beaten up. When I suspect that you are the guilty party then I positively like it.'

In July 1943 Allsebrook added the D.S.O. to his D.F.C. 'It means quite a lot when it is given to a Flight Lieutenant aged 23', wrote Roxburgh. On the night of 15 September, Ralf and his crew disappeared following a raid on Hamburg. 'I wonder how many people there are who, like Chris Barlow, will say when they get the news, "this is the bitterest blow so far" ', wrote Roxburgh to the family.

War with Japan and the fall of Singapore brought only bad news. Simon Acland had been admitted into Grenville with some reluctance because of low Common Entrance marks but the boy came from the same prep school as P.B. Lucas and Roxburgh had made a commitment to take him. His career oscillated between bouts of dutiful toil and disheartening lapses during which Roxburgh had to supply frequent doses of encouragement and hold discussions with the parents. He had always wished to join the R.A.F. but having finally scraped some academic qualifications he was rejected on health grounds. He subsequently entered the aircraft industry, hoping to make a career on the commercial side. War altered the situation and in 1940 he was made a Pilot Officer as an engineer and sent to Headquarters at Singapore. When the Japanese invaded some managed to escape. One Stoic wrote 'We were ordered to rendezvous in the docks early in the morning . . . I got away in a rowing boat with another officer in my regiment and six men. Helped by a home-made sail we made Sumatra in eight days.' Acland was listed missing. 'There are so many officers of whom nothing whatever has been heard . . . that one simply must assume that the Japs aren't telling us whom they have got', wrote Roxburgh. 'It means an anxious time for many mothers and friends but I firmly believe that in most cases the anxiety will be relieved in the end . . . May it be so in Simon's case.' There were reports that he had been seen on an island and then had vanished. When the Friends of Stowe organization was revived on the school's twenty-first birthday in 1944, the parents wished his name to be included even though there had been no news for two years. There were only rumours that he had been seen in Java, then in Sumatra the day after an attack by Japanese paratroops. Finally news came that he had died of pneumonia in No. 3 Camp, Tokyo, in December 1942. Somehow a fountain pen, a present from his sister, and a Dunhill pipe given by workers in his Bristol factory as a leaving present were brought home by a P.O.W. friend along with some notes he had left. 'I have the little possessions, and the notes containing material in his own handwriting helps', his father told Roxburgh. 'Actually we feel almost as if the Almighty had allowed us a direct message from him.'

Reggie Allen had also been a lucky admission though for different reasons, for with the delays in building work in 1926 Roxburgh had found himself with 125 boys 'promised – or nearly promised – and 21 places'. Allen was in the Rugby XV for three years and Captain in 1931. He worked in Thailand before the war, was taken prisoner and died working on the railway at Sankrai.

John Burns, also of Grenville, had been bursting to enter the Services. 'It is quite impossible for us to make sure that an active and enterprising boy of seventeen and three-quarters cannot bicycle to a Recruiting Office if he wants to', Roxburgh informed the parents. Having joined the R.N.V.R. and been consoled by Roxburgh for a second failure to obtain a School Certificate ('Cheer up my dear Johnnie and don't distress yourself too much about this disappointment. After all it is not as bad as Hitler and you will have forgotten all about it by the Autumn.'), he was shot down over the Malacca Straits. He resumed flying and in August 1945, in the last days of the war, was forced to make a sea landing by fire from a Japanese convoy off Sumatra. He and the crew drifted 250 miles in a dinghy and were washed up on an uninhabited island without food and, more seriously, without water. Four days later some Japanese fishermen came and took them off to the mainland where he was imprisoned in Bangkok until rescued by the Allies.

Alister Campbell was a contemporary of the two V.C.s, Jock Anderson and Leonard Cheshire, in Chatham. He seemed destined for the highest positions in the Army. The Colonel of Probyn's Horse had considerably annoyed the Governor of the Punjab by placing Alister in order of preference above the Governor's well-qualified son. General Sir Alan Hartley declared that in forty-five years service he had never met a more promising young officer. In the Burma Campaign he won the M.C. and Bar and the D.S.O. His training and enthusiasm at the Tank School in India contributed to the success of the 7th Light Cavalry Regiment in action. All the Indian cadets wanted to go into 'Campbell Sahib's Regiment'. His squadron's tanks were the first into Mandalay. Although wounded, having been shot through the right arm, he carried on with it in a sling and would not leave the squadron. At Allamaya his tank was blown up and turned over backwards on to him. His General personally ordered his return to England by stages, in a plane with a doctor and nurse in attendance, but he had to put down in Calcutta and died during a blood transfusion.

One of the most striking features of the Second World War was the courage of parents. In earlier days Campbell's mother and Roxburgh had been sparring partners on many subjects such as cold Sunday lunches and the nutritional value of Stowe cabbage. 'I always enjoy corresponding with you. Your frankness does me good and cheers me up at the same time', said the Headmaster gallantly in 1934.' There is no doubt about the iron fist but the velvet glove prevents it from hurting too much. . . Personally I always eat the cabbage provided by the Chef because I think it is excellent.' After Alister's death she was sustained by Roxburgh's sympathy. 'You wrote me the most beautiful and helpful letter I've ever been fortunate enough to receive and your real understanding and true sympathy have touched me deeply.' She forwarded a letter from the Colonel: 'I have heard Senior Generals down to newly joined soldiers speak of his [Alister's] magnificent qualities of courage and leadership. Later one heard similar accounts of the magnificent fight he was putting up in Hospital . . . One after another the men have come up to me to express their sorrow and I can truthfully tell you that all ranks feel his loss as a personal one.'

Lieutenant-Colonel Dudley Baker of the R.A.M.C., who was later Chairman of a major post-war appeal, was also in the attack on Mandalay and Mentioned in Despatches. There were echoes of the Grafton Hunt in the tactics of Lieutenant P.F. Greenwell of the Durham Light Infantry in the jungle fighting. He told his men to wait for a special signal blown on his hunting-horn. As he raised it to his lips it was shot from his hand, but undeterred he summoned the platoon by more orthodox means and reached a Japanese post under heavy fire and despite multiple injuries.

There were many exploits recorded in the Desert and North African Campaigns. Raymond Alderson of Chandos, who had also given Roxburgh pastoral concern from time to time, left to study German in Bonn whence came complaints of flirtations from his German host. 'I did not think he was the sort of fellow who would fall in love with a tobacconist's daughter', replied the headmaster rather ruefully. He had pacifist views but joined the Friends' Ambulance Unit and did such brave work in the Blitz that he was given a commission to command a transport section allotted to the Free French Forces. In Syria he set up clinics which became a consuming interest but had to leave the work when he was moved to Libya and a forward position near Tobruk. He was killed by a direct hit on the slit trench where he was taking cover. Lady Mary Spears who was with the unit wrote of his dedication: 'Two nights before he died he gave two pints of blood in an unsuccessful attempt to save the life of a British Officer.' The Red Cross, which the Germans generally respected, had been clearly marked and it was thought that the bombing had been carried out in error. A lighter moment was recalled by an Old Stoic under wartime anonymity in the *Stoic* for 1942:

All of a sudden I took a prisoner. I was never so startled in my life as when a little man in German uniform popped out from behind a bush and put his hands up. I had to pull the car up quickly and felt more annoyed than hostile. However, seeing that he insisted on surrendering I became suitably ferocious and drew a gun on him – a process somewhat hampered by my gun being in a suitcase at the back of the car. However, in a matter of five minutes or so, during which my obliging prisoner waited patiently, I had discovered my gun – it was in my pyjama pocket – and found some ammunition, loaded the gun, cocked it and then put him in my car. He was a very nice fellow from Bavaria. We agreed that we disliked Africa, in saying which he had probably more justification than I had.

Another unusual encounter with the enemy was recorded from the desert:

After lunch and an air-raid we drove on westwards to deliver some messages to a Divisional H.Q. Alas! It proved to be an enemy H.Q. I turned the car round (the engine stalling three times on the way) and then drove away on the narrow road which was dead straight for a mile and so full of holes that speeds would normally be low. It is probably an exaggeration to say that I went faster than the rifle bullets which followed me down the road – but believe me it was not for want of trying. And so back to Tobruk and from there to Cairo by air.

1943 brought the first Victoria Cross. 'Jock' Anderson came to Stowe in 1931. Tragedy had stalked the family's first association with the school for his elder brother, Robin, was a sleepwalker who had been killed one night falling from a high window on the North Front. 'Jock' was one of the Stoics who fell victim to the streptococcal germ and there were signs of heart trouble, as a result of which he spent some time away from the school, though it did not prevent him becoming President of the Boat Club at Trinity College, Cambridge. At the beginning of the war he was sent to France with the Argyll and Sutherland Highlanders but was part of a force surrounded near St Valéry with little or no ammunition. Nearly 200 escaped from the German encirclement, Anderson among them. Hiding by day and marching by night they eventually reached a small port near Cherbourg and found a boat by which they reached England.

It was on St George's Day, 1943 that he played an epic part in the battle of Longstop Hill, west of Tunis and about six miles from Medjez al Bab. It was a position which the enemy defended fiercely. Anderson was the only surviving company commander but rallied the men, personally led assaults on three machine gun positions and one mortar unit and finally captured the hill with four officers and forty men, taking around 200 prisoners. Strangely enough the incident bore a resemblance to one of the more famous of Lord Cobham's acts of daring at Venlo. News of the award came to Stowe on 30 June. Moss rushed from the shop to the headmaster's study when it was announced on the nine o'clock news. In reply to a telegram, Anderson wrote: 'I never exceeded my plain duty in winning it but that doesn't seem to have deterred the publicity men at home. All the same I shall always be proud of having been the first Stoic V.C. and I look forward to the day when my name will be at the head of a very long list.' He mentioned another Stoic, A.F.R. Porcher, in his battalion who had just been wounded. 'I remember him well as a Prefect and find it rather embarrassing to have him as a subaltern.' In August Roxburgh wrote, 'I wonder whether anyone has told you that the School had a whole holiday when the news of what you call "your recent medal" came through? We were all agreed that nothing less than a whole holiday would do and the speech in which I announced your honour and the holiday was the most popular I have ever made in Assembly.' Sadly the hero's welcome never took place. John Anderson was killed in October of the same year.

A.R.P. Ellis, who had been the Public School Javelin Champion in 1932, was a Captain in the R.A.M.C. During the battle to take the Mareth Line he attended to the wounded under a heavy machine gun and shell bombardment, evacuating them on the twin stretchers of his scout car. During a tank battle he went forward and rescued men who had been wounded in their tanks and were still under fire. His car was hit by shellfire and he was himself wounded in the leg. He rapidly changed cars and carried on dealing with the casualties until ordered back by his commanding officer. Arthur Buchanan, one of three sons of a Stowe Governor and benefactor, died in the same battle with the Grenadier Guards, crossing a dangerous minefield which surrounded pockets of German defenders.

One of the ways in which a certain Stoic individualism was evident was the strong participation in some of the clandestine and secret operations carried out by small, highly trained groups. Andrew Croft served with the Independent Companies in Norway, landed subversive parties on the Italian coast from Corsica and finally joined the Maquis in France. Brooks Richards in the naval section of Special Operations transported agents between Cornwall and Brittany in refugee fishing boats and in 1942 had the task of landing seven tons of weapons to be ready for the allied landing in Algiers, an operation soon followed by rescuing French Gaullists from the Vichy forces. For seven weeks he held a strategically placed lighthouse near Bizerta from which the German air-bridge from North Africa to Sicily could be monitored. Two Stoics took part in the first parachute raid upon enemy territory, which was directed against an aqueduct in the ankle of Italy. The raiders were commanded by Major T.A.G. Pritchard, Royal

Welsh Fusiliers, and the demolition party by Captain G.F.K. Daly, Royal Engineers. Pritchard, who had been in one of the first senior Rugby XVs had also been an Army heavyweight boxing champion. Gerald Daly, one of two Grafton twins, had an engineering degree from Cambridge. His brother gained the M.C. with the R.A.M.C. Airborne Division. This first precursor of the S.A.S.-type operation took place in 1941 and was carefully rehearsed in England. Photographs had shown that there were two aqueducts about 200 yards apart and it was decided to destroy the Eastern one. With mission accomplished the parachutists were to make their way to a point on the West Coast of Italy where they would be picked up by a submarine.

Eight Whitleys left Malta in evening light, six with the party and two with bombs to create a diversion. Unfortunately one was late in starting owing to a mechanical defect and did not reach the dropping area until one hour and a quarter after the appointed time. This plane carried Captain Daly. The parachutists made their descent in good formation. There was snow on the hills and bright moonlight. When Daly arrived he found that three of the piers inspected were not of masonry but of reinforced concrete, much harder to destroy. It was decided to concentrate on one pier, the most westerly. Some containers of explosives had not left the aircraft but there had been a large margin in calculating the amount. By 12.15 all the explosives were laid. A small bridge nearby was also mined to hinder repair work. The main charge went off at 12.30; the bridge blew up 30 minutes later. Major Pritchard divided his small force into three groups. He and his party set off westwards and when dawn broke they hid in a wood. At dusk on the second night they moved again, skirting the villages. When they struck south-west expecting to find more woodland they reached a terrain of rock and snow on which their tracks were visible. The search was on and a farmer who found their path gave the alarm. Dogs were brought, village children followed the dogs, mothers rushed to protect the children, and menfolk to protect the women. Gradually, organized parties trapped the paratroopers in a cave. They could have shot their way out but it would have involved a massacre of the women and children clustered excitedly around their hiding place and Major Pritchard had no choice but to surrender.

The Duke of Wellington was a member of No. 2 Commando Unit, along with J.E.C. Nicholl, later housemaster of Cobham, and ten other Stoic officers. Among other hazardous assignments they were landed behind the German lines while the Allies fought to break out of the Salerno beachhead in the Italian Campaign. Because of a signals error he led a charge upon what turned out to be a strongly held position on a hillside and was killed in the assault. 'He always struck me as being a remarkably different person from his illustrious ancestor', wrote one of his comrades. 'It was not until we were in the thick of it that he really showed himself. Then, indeed, a fire burned in his kind friendly soul which I for one had never seen before. The orders he gave for the final assault with the bayonet on a terrifically strong German position were the coolest and calmest possible but he led the charge like one inspired.' His troop had been wont to put over their hut door the innocent tribute 'The Dook's Boys'.

The Italian Campaign was long and costly. The M.C. was awarded to Lieutenant J.S. Wingate of the Queen's Bays because of his actions which ensured that the San Salvo Ridge remained in Allied hands. His tank was hit and he therefore carried out his reconnaissance on foot. Having located a German Mark IV Special Tank he brought up his own, engaged at 300 yards and destroyed it. He made several such reconnaissance during the day and at one moment forced twelve enemy tanks to suspend a counter-attack. When his own tank was completely destroyed he took over another and, under heavy machine-gun fire, towed his own back, unshackling it from the tow-rope only when it was totally ablaze. At this time Americans and British were fighting together. R.K.V. Andrews was a young Stoic who went to America in 1939. He became a Private in the U.S. Mountain Infantry and was awarded the U.S.A. Bronze Star. Near Abetaia a forward observation post was in need of vital equipment for communication. Andrews made his way over treacherous and rugged terrain to bring them supplies which assisted the following attack. *The Times* in 1989 noted in his obituary that he was a 'distinguished Philhellene scholar'.

When the Armistice was signed with Italy Frank Benitz, another contemporary of Cheshire's in Chatham, was in a P.O.W. camp and with the help of some Italians he escaped through the back of the camp while the Germans were marching in through the front. He was chased through the woods and some of his companions were recaptured, but he lived disguised as a dirty old shepherd for five weeks and eventually found his way to British lines. Unlike

Cheshire he had lasted only two years of the Stowe academic course but nevertheless received Roxburgh's air-graph in 1942, in hospital in Alexandria, after winning the D.F.C. and being wounded. By 1944 he had rejoined his squadron, which was now in Malta, but in November was reported missing. When his plane was shot down into the Mediterranean it sank after thirty seconds taking all the emergency supplies with it. The crew had no food or water for ten days though mercifully it rained on the fifth and they survived. They were picked up by an enemy hospital ship (the Germans were to use photographs of the rescue for propaganda purposes). 'Laddie' Lucas also took part in the Battle of Malta in 1942 and commanded No. 249 Spitfire Squadron, described as the top-scoring unit in the British and Commonwealth Air Forces in the Second World War. It was the first of three operational tours with Fighter Command of which the last was with the Second Tactical Air Force in support of the Allied invasion of France and North-West Europe. News of D-Day came to Stowe during a Corps exercise so was quickly relayed by the signallers to almost all the pupils. One Old Stoic wrote in the school magazine,

> It was curiously inspiring to see that vast concourse of shipping searing its way across the Channel . . . I don't think I have ever loved England so much as I did at the moment when I had to sail away and leave it. The Germans – foolish fellows – seemed to resent our presence and made determined efforts to prevent us landing. But I'm glad to say they had no success, though it was a good many weeks before we eventually persuaded them that perhaps after all Germany was where they belonged . . . We were eighty-three days in battle without a proper rest and when we eventually reached the Seine we had had about enough, especially as we had to walk most of the way.

David Barrow of Chandos was one of the first to land on D-Day. His battalion of the Queen's Royal Regiment suffered heavy casualties but he himself survived the initial assaults. When nominating him for the Army Roxburgh had declared: 'I know well enough that David will make a success of his career as a soldier and that people who meet him in later life and learn that he comes from Stowe will have a higher opinion of the school than they had before they met him.' He behaved with conspicuous gallantry during the landings and took an enemy position which was surrounded by wire obstacles. Because many fellow officers had fallen he had to carry out the same process under heavy mortar fire, again in the forefront of the fighting. A few days later he was wounded and died. In more peaceful times he might have gained prominence as a writer or artist. *The Times* expressed the hope that some of his poems might be collected or his paintings exhibited. Peter Bosanquet was in the same regiment and had pressed to be released from a safe staff appointment to be with his men at the front. He too was killed in the Battle of Normandy. The details of Bill McElwee's M.C. were reported in the *Buckingham Advertiser*. He was in command of a company near Caen when the Germans attacked with tanks and infantry. He was with a forward platoon but by good siting of machine guns and anti-tank weapons he drove back the initial German thrust. He moved back to company headquarters and thwarted an attack on the right, knocking out one tank himself. In the difficult, thickly wooded terrain, and when communications with battalion H.Q. had broken down, he moved his small forces with skill as sole commander on the spot and held his section of what was known as the 'Scottish Corridor'. On the news of his award Roxburgh wrote: 'My thoughts go back to the conversations we had before you decided to join the Army. In those days we both thought you would be a schoolmaster soldiering. But I think that it has now been proved that you are in reality a soldier who did a bit of schoolmastering before he joined. Anyway it is a fine thing to stand so very high in two professions.' In 1949, when Bill produced a regimental history of the Argyll and Sutherland Highlanders, Roxburgh praised it:

> The fighting was, of course, very different from anything I met in World War I but some of the incidents and some of your phrases recall those days quite vividly. I suspect there is a family likeness between all infantry battles. Doubtless in the Peninsular War (and I dare say in the Trojan War too) infantry officers felt that 'baffled lost feeling' or had 'no certainty down to the last minute regarding the exact area to be taken over' or were 'just starting breakfast when called for' or that 'at least six plans had been issued to the battalion' or were sickened by the smell of decaying transport animals.

Derek Davies of Temple spent his twenty-first birthday guarding the Nijmegen Bridge. He replied to Roxburgh's greetings and told him how Rollo Spencer, head of school, and like McElwee in the Argyll and Sutherlands, had come to the aid of his company under bombardment in Normandy while setting up defences: 'He was careless about himself and is really a great loss to the world.' Shortly before Rollo Spencer's death they had spent the night in the trenches talking of Stowe. McElwee also recalled a moment with Rollo and with the wounded Peter Hastings in the later stages of the war.

I had three good Stoic moments during my short battle. The first was in a wood right out in the air where I was hanging on with the remnants of three companies, out of all touch and with no flanks at all. In the evening I got a quite wild message which only told me that the tanks in the rear believed that they had come up to cover the withdrawal of a battalion, but I could get no definite orders and refused to move without any. And when the definite orders came in a spectacular dash by an armoured car it was a very cheerful Charles Alexander who stepped out and said, I suppose with characteristically 'historian' lack of respect: 'Now Bill, no pompousness. You're to come back at once.' And the next morning, after a vile night of disengagement and with-drawal finished off with a few hours sleep in a ditch, I was wandering around, dirty, hungry, unshaven for three days, wrapped in a blanket against the cold, my morale at its lowest ebb, when I was hailed by poor Rollo Spencer out of a neigh-bouring ditch: 'I say Bill, do you think Noel Annan really planned this very well?' He had some tea boiling and a flask and was very kind and completely restored me. The last was on a hospital train on the way back when I found myself in the same compartment as Peter Hastings, very cheerful and quite unchanged in spite of a legful of mortar splinters.

I saw quite a lot of Rollo before he was killed and got to like him very much. Both of us had got more tolerant, I think, though we never actually quarrelled even in the old days.

The end of 1944 did not bring about the collapse of the German forces hoped for, and there were accounts of street fighting in Belgian and German cities and of the winter cold in the Ardennes. In February 1945, Major A.C.C. Brodie of Bruce, an officer in the Black Watch, seized a house and strongly held trenches. At 200 yards, having been subjected to withering fire, he rushed forward with a few men, shot dead with his revolver two enemy machine gunners and forced his way into the building with revolver and grenades. He was twice wounded in the legs but paid no heed. The company was so inspired they followed him and took the house with thirty-seven prisoners. He pursued the fleeing Germans into the orchards nearby and, though wounded twice more and weak from loss of blood, would not allow himself to retire for treatment until he had fortified the position against counter-attack.

Another example of close conflict was recounted by an O.S. writing from a French orchard where he was still under fire. 'You'd laugh if you saw us all diving into slits and under our vehicles when the old whistle starts. One moment lots of men standing or sitting about and the next not a soul. After one rather big and close bang yesterday I yelled to my Sergeant Driver to see if he was still O.K. and his voice answered from underneath me! I had no idea that anyone could have moved quicker than I did.'

One of the narrowest escapes of the Arnhem battle was recorded by John le Bouvier who had been scheduled to take a reporter on a bombing raid. They had only one parachute between them and, when the plane was hit, le Bouvier gallantly gave this to the reporter who jumped safely. Naturally the news of this self-sacrifice was announced so the sorrowing family and later Dr and Mrs Zettl, who knew him well, were surprised when he walked in through the door. The rest of the crew having made its escape he had hurled himself from the plane seconds before it crashed, had been found by members of the Dutch Resistance and given passage back to England. Eric Brown, who had been in the First XV and XI, fought for six days with the First Airborne Division to keep the corridor with the 'Bridge too Far' open before being killed. He had also turned down a staff job as being too detached from the struggle. His mother was another whom the war brought closer to Stowe. In more peaceful days she had waged a campaign to have brown bread provided with meals. Roxburgh replied that the boys did not like it but, 'I will see whether I can induce the School to change its taste in this matter'. In October 1944 she replied to Roxburgh's letter of condolence: 'One of the first letters I write must be to you for the glorious tribute you have paid to Eric.'

Andrew Croft was parachuted into Southern France to work with the Maquis in ambushing and destroying the German columns winding their way north. Following the liberation of Montpellier

Roxburgh wrote; 'I should like to call this award D²S.O. for it commemorates a job that was more than just distinguished.' When the Third Reich finally crumbled there was an Old Stoic present at the surrender of the 25th German Army, which took place

> in a huge concrete block at least 100 yards long with walls of concrete and a ceiling some twenty feet thick . . . At about five minutes to three we asked for a wireless in order to hear Churchill's VE Day speech. There we stood with four or five German senior staff officers beside us listening to the P.M. announcing and explaining the utter defeat of Germany. When the speech came to an end the B.B.C. began to play 'God Save The King'. Immediately the German officers snapped to attention and stood rigid.

There were some light moments recalled during the war itself. Ian Craig, commissioned in the 10th Hussars, met D.I. Brown, the huge and formidable Rugby master, a Corporal in the same unit. We have all been delighted, wrote Roxburgh, to think of you being saluted by Mr Brown and respectfully addressed as "Sir". I am sure he enjoyed the experience as much as you did.' Early in the North African war a Stoic reported that he was riding a grey Arab stallion which had been specially chosen for Mussolini to ride when entering Alexandria in triumph. Another interviewed a fanatical S.S. officer in liberated Brussels. 'He demanded transport to German-occupied England. Vive le Docteur Goebbels!' One O.S. spotted another who had been given the posting of Flag Lieutenant to the Commander-in-Chief Malta. 'Poor —. When I last saw him, he was sitting in the back of the Admiral's Barge holding the Admiral's dachsund.'

There were many references to Stowe in letters and reminiscences. On D-Day, Tony Bartley, attached to an American brigade, carried an Old Stoic tie in his pocket to put it on the moment the French shore was reached. 'The other day I did a deal with an Arab', wrote Peter Bates, 'and bartered a battered old cricket shirt which I had had at Stowe for three dozen eggs and limitless goodwill.' Waiting for a second burst of fire from the *Scharnhorst* in the Arctic waters on H.M.S. *Norfolk*, Gordon Forsyth asked his friends what went through their minds. All replied, first home and then school. 'I kept thinking about Stowe, particularly periods of waiting there – waiting before matches, waiting to be sent for by the authorities when something had gone wrong. It all seemed very near; and then a four-inch shell exploded ten yards away.' Somewhere in the Mediterranean a ship's company were holding a service: 'In five minutes time we shall be having Prayers. I have supplied the Captain with the Stowe Assembly Prayer No. 2 ("Stretch forth, O Lord"). I expect it has been stretched round the world anyway by now. It is funny the way one keeps such things in one's mind for years.'

What is noticeable in these accounts is an absence of jingoism. There was admiration for the deeds and grief for the loss of friends and a strong yet innocent belief in the time-honoured qualities of an England that was under mortal threat. Edward Harding, a glider pilot at the time of the Rhine Crossings and a trainee transport pilot killed in 1946 on a night exercise, was a boy of fifteen in the sanatorium at the time of Dunkirk and opened the first of many poems with the lines:

> Our praise for them shall never cease
> Who gave their lives for England –
> And for peace.

John Benson, killed in experimental flying, had sent a poem to his mother, 'The Dawn':

> Tomorrow shall be ours, and we shall
> Cast a girdle round the world
> Of mutual amity and lay upon
> Earth's sweating brow the garland of Eternal Peace.

As Roxburgh wrote upon receiving it: 'The more I think of John's life and death the more bitter I feel about those foul men who brought all this upon the world.'

7

Roxburgh's Final Years

In the 1945 General Election four Old Stoics were elected to Parliament: Major J.A. Boyd-Carpenter and Major T.V.H. Beamish M.C. for the Conservatives and Captain S.T. Swingler and Dr S.J.L. Taylor for Labour. 'When I first came to Stowe in 1925,' recalled Patrick Hunter, 'I lived above the newly built Chatham House. Within the House itself John Boyd-Carpenter and Stephen Taylor shared a study rich in political argument. It is amusing to think that in due course both became Life Peers, on opposite sides of course.' The results of the mock election at the school were not so evenly balanced. Peace had released high spirits: the Liberals with a little quiet practice disconnected the carillon on the North Front clock and played 'Rule Britannia' to herald their meetings, on one occasion competing for attention with the Labour candidate, who shared George I's pedestal, and the Conservative high on the balustrades. A smoke bomb was detonated during a Labour Party rally in Assembly while Conservatives held the doors closed and left-wing supporters emerged choking on to the South Front. The Conservative candidate, J.V. Bartlett, won by the sort of majority which Roxburgh would have liked to have seen on a national scale. He wrote to a mother that the election news 'does not suggest that the country is very good at showing gratitude to those who have saved it.' The remaining years of his headmastership were to be spent in the radically changed conditions of post-war socialism.

Public schools in general were pushed further towards the periphery of national education as the Butler Act began to take effect, but immediate concerns lay with the novelties of peacetime living. The car once again became a status symbol. 'No longer the tired pair of taxis,' wrote the editor of the *Stoic* in the spring of 1946, 'but a host of cars, bright and with a few exceptions burnished, now sweep round the curve of the colonnades in that exciting quarter of an hour before lunch on Saturdays . . .' The names that once crowded under the Blue Book heading "Absent on Active Service" have migrated to other pages and now represent real and known people . . . And then, of course we have had bananas – the first fruits of Peace.'

Bananas notwithstanding, strict rationing continued and austerity intensified rather than relaxed. Arranging to meet Acland at the Athenaeum Club in 1946 Roxburgh added, 'I expect we had better make the hour one o'clock or even 12.45 – otherwise the bishops will have eaten all the beef.' Masters of the week were urged to show the greatest vigilance in preventing the waste of bread at meals and married masters were excluded from school meals unless they were taking games or had other duties. In May 1947, Dr Bostock reported that the food situation had deteriorated markedly since the previous year. A boy needed 3,000 calories daily but rationed and 'points' goods supplied only 1,400. The remaining 1,600 had to be supplied from non-rationed goods, root vegetables, salads and fruit. But at Stowe storage space was limited and, since tradesmen were still rationed, stores had to be ordered well in advance. This prevented lightning raids on the shops when produce appeared at bewildering times and places. Replying to a master's request for extra petrol coupons Roxburgh declared: 'I think you are a bit of an optimist in asking for enough petrol to do some shopping trips. I am only allowed to send Mrs Tompkins down once a week.' Vegetables and salads were not popular in that they were often badly prepared by non-specialist staff and Dr Bostock pressed for an increase in the storage space.[1]

If there was plain living there was also high thinking, especially on the music front. Dr Huggins was one of the first to return, as he had been one of the first to leave, and took over from

---

[1] The quince tree in the Masters' Garden rose to the situation. Already a friend to many in days of shortage, in 1947 it produced 242 pounds of fruit. In 1948 the J. Arthur Rank Organization came to make part of the film *Trottie True* in the grounds. A sumptuous Edwardian picnic, with game pie and champagne was laid out near the Palladian bridge. To the dismay of Stoics who pounced on the remains the champagne turned out to be water and the game pies bounced.

W.L. Snowdon who moved to Haileybury. He had kept the department alive during the war despite a depleted staff and many J.T.C. encroachments upon practice time. The musical fare on offer at Stowe in this period resembled rather the programme of an international festival, albeit the concerts were spread over a number of terms. Denis Matthews, Cyril Smith, Solomon, Moiseiwitsch, Eileen Joyce and Louis Kentner were just some of those who gave piano recitals. The war had encouraged musical appreciation. Kathleen Long's recital included Chopin's B Minor Sonata and the report ran: 'She had to play three encores before the school would allow her to leave'. A song recital was given by Heddle Nash and a guitar recital by Segovia. In 1948 some 60 per cent of Stoics belonged to the Music Society, all three concerts were full to overflowing and almost every item in the concert version of *Merrie England* was encored. And which C.C.F. today would seek to entertain rival schools with piano pieces by Grieg and a rendering of 'The Yeomen of England' at summer camp, as the Stoics did in 1949? M.E. Harding played the César Franck 'Symphonic Variations' with the City of Birmingham Orchestra under George London, with only the briefest of rehearsals. A performance of the Rachmaninov Second Concerto was broadcast in America. The house competitions in music, 'always notable for their Procrustean treatment of every conceivable type of work', were boldly submitted to the notoriously caustic tongue of Professor Jack Westrup of Oxford.

The winter of 1947 was memorably harsh and February 1948 the coldest since 1841. The school was isolated. On 5 March the bread supplies from Brackley could not get through and on the following day coal and other supplies from Buckingham failed. The bread was finally brought in by use of a special lorry loaned by the Agricultural War Committee and manned by German prisoners of war. For almost a week all masters living at a distance had to come and go on foot so the timetable had to be altered. Milk lorries were sealed off by snow in Banbury and Farmer Davies supplied milk in churns manhandled up the hills by pantry staff. For a while there was skating and Walpole's victory in the ice-hockey cup was attributed to 'a good team and a proper ice-hockey stick'. The Natural History Society noted that cold and food shortage were bringing certain local species close to extinction: barn owls were cut off from mice and voles by the blanket of snow and a kittiwake blown off course by the gales was found dead in the grounds. There had been twenty-eight degrees of frost at one point in February. The cross-country race against Uppingham, run in a blizzard the previous year, was now run on thick ice and the report ran: 'the relief at seeing the runners return at all was only increased by the knowledge that Stowe had won'.[2]

Roxburgh welcomed back D.I. Brown, 'undamaged except by matrimony'. His re-appearance was welcomed by the Rugby fraternity, but the problem of housing was further increased. The bachelor schoolmaster had been a typical figure earlier in the century. As late as 1936 the Inspectors had commented on the paucity of female influences at Stowe. After the war the bachelor was in a minority. At the same time housing and building were limited not only by the perennial lack of funds but by government regulations. Roxburgh drew up a memorandum on the subject:

> The School has always been short of accommodation for masters. In the early years we had to house five masters in a large house in Buckingham, transporting morning and evening by car, and for fully twelve years only one of the housemasters could be married. Since the present Governors took over much has been done to relieve the situation but great difficulties have been caused by the shortage of houses to let in the neighbourhood and by the increase in the proportion of married men on the staff. Ten years ago 14 were married and 29 were bachelors. Now 27 are married and 17 are bachelors (one being engaged). Even so we are short of Masters' rooms at the School (and even married men must have studies there). Two of the three (Field) Houses intended for married men have been used for bachelors ever since they were built. One of these two must be given to Mr Brown, who has returned to Cobham House as a married man with three children. We can only secure it by providing married quarters for the four married men who are at present living as bachelors.

What the paucity of rooms and the incessant draught-board moves must have meant in terms of human irritation we can only surmise. Roxburgh's concluding comments show that he was originally contemplating retirement in 1948:

[2] It was in the 1946 race against Uppingham when visibility was down to thirty yards that I.B. Calkin lost a shoe almost at the start and ran barefoot in the snow for five miles.

Next year a grave difficulty will arise for the remaining Field House will have to be cleared . . . and offered to the new Headmaster unless the Governors are to limit applications to unmarried men. We therefore need eight houses for married men – four immediately and four by September 1948. Towards these eight we have secured one – a cottage in Dadford which has not yet been provided with water, light or sanitation. The Governors will not therefore be surprised that when a small house in Buckingham was offered to us – and I was informed it could not be purchased – I felt and expressed grievous disappointment.

The Governors, he concluded, must either face the need to buy properties in affluent Buckinghamshire or build some relatively humble dwellings (£1,200 houses) in the grounds. 'The gravity of the present situation can hardly be exaggerated and drastic steps must now be taken to meet it.' There were no drastic steps taken and the shortage was eventually solved in piecemeal fashion, but it was unfortunate that it prevented the headmaster from making appointments from the large pool of returning ex-servicemen, often very well qualified. There was another problem. The rapid increase in staff between the years 1923 and 1930, as the number of boys grew, had produced an uneven age spread in the Common Room. Apart from Major Haworth there was not a single master approaching retirement, which meant glacial progress in staff mobility and advancement. In 1946, B.E.N. Fawcett left to be headmaster of Rishworth, J.M. Selby went as a lecturer to Sandhurst and R.M. Hamer, just appointed to be housemaster of Grenville, to a headmastership in Trinidad. He was succeeded by Brian Gibson, the sixth change of housemaster in twenty-four years. E. Cawston left to take over Orwell Park preparatory school partly because of the housing difficulties. Some of Roxburgh's successors were to be critical of his failure to appoint a strong post-war team but it is clear that he had little room for manoeuvre. He did secure W.H. Bradshaw, a Blue in cricket and association football. It is said that at his interview a mouse ran across the headmaster's study and Bradshaw stamped upon it with such athletic speed he was appointed on the spot. Chris Deacon, another well-qualified games player, came in 1947 and John Uttley at the start of the same year. All three became housemasters. Martin Burke who joined the music department had been a medallist at the Royal Academy. There was also an inspiring appointment made as bandmaster when E.J. Webb succeeded Mr Geoghagan. Webb was a medallist of the Royal Military School of Music. Within months he had trebled the number of brass players at Stowe and in sixteen years he raised the level of the military band to one of the highest in the public school world. It not only played for ceremonial parades but gave concerts which were among the most popular events in the calendar. In the unlikely role of David to King George V's Saul he had played the harp to his monarch during the latter's convalescence in 1928.

The Common Room was not only static and growing more elderly and set in its ways. Many of the concerns which Patrick Hunter had expressed were at least in part realized. Roxburgh's comments at masters' meetings are revealing. In January 1946 he addressed them, including a number who had returned from war service. They would want to know how the school had fared in their absence. In some respects the most serious threats had not materialized but the school had received a 'crushing set-back in the shrinkage of numbers which had caused acceptance of many pupils below standard.' Such pupils and their heirs and successors had to be subjected to remorseless improvement. Too often in Stowe's temperate way bad work had been greeted with 'regretful smiles on the one side and amiable grumbles on the other'. An irate father claimed that his son, who had passed in French quite comfortably at Common Entrance, now thought the feminine of 'Monsieur' was 'Masieur'. An Old Stoic had written recently to say he was 'geting a comission'. On the prevalent misuse of the double consonant he declared that, 'A new Stowe language appears to be growing up in which people are said to be "sliping" or "droping" but oddly enough to be also "dinning" and "comming".'

He contrasted the success which the Army P.T. instructors had had in improving those who were physically puny and thought the same methods could be employed with those who were mentally supine. In commenting upon masters' reports he had his own brand of gentle irony. He thought, for example that the phrase 'he is not quite disinterested' might be read as making an 'imputation on the boy's motives'. A master who says in a final term report something quite incompatible with what he stated at half-term, 'somewhat undermines the confidence of parents in his judgement'. Sometimes he could be quite censorious. 'If after eight terms we are not doing 100 per cent better at work and games than we are doing now,' he said in 1946, 'it will be time for us to shut up shop.' In 1947 he reminded tutors and housemasters that admissions to university were likely to become more difficult. Even when the flood of ex-servicemen had subsided there would be great numbers of clever boys from state-aided grammar schools whose expenses would be paid by the state. A year later he passed on the news that Trinity, Cambridge, a major destination of Stoics, had announced that henceforth it would not accept anyone without a good School or Higher Certificate.

That extremely good work was done in certain departments cannot be doubted. There had been rejoicing in 1945 when a record number of pupils, 97 out of 101, gained School Certificates. For two years the tide ebbed but in July 1948 came the best results ever: 98 Certificates out of 100 candidates. The problem of entrance and university scholarships was harder to resolve. Too few bright boys were put forward for the entrance scholarships. The competition, he declared in 1947, had been fading and had almost vanished altogether. He requested masters who had friends in the preparatory-school world to make the value of the Stowe awards better known. In 1948 he was able to announce that some interesting and promising candidates had come forward, but 1949 brought a degree of disillusion.

University open awards remained elusive. In 1948 there had been only three, all in History. It brought further appraisal of the benign and charitable attitude to life. He had often been struck, he told the masters, with the light-hearted way in which boys referred to scholarship examinations. They did not seem to realize that to gain a scholarship was an exceptional achievement requiring more than average ability and much more than average hard work. Were Stowe masters too ready to praise an essay, a paper, a speech, a dramatic performance, when the effort had in fact been undistinguished? Benevolence, though a social merit, was 'dangerous when applied in the critical field'. With depressing frequency he urged masters to avoid missing lessons without notice, to set and correct work meticulously and to concentrate upon the standard of English. He confessed that too often he had to suffer from inadequate setting of prep. He could not go round Cobham Court every evening banging on every door whence noise was proceeding or tracing 'the muted tones of a radio at low volume'. His reminder that dogs should not be taken into lessons or Chapel does not suggest that professional standards were impeccable.

His final masters' meetings displayed his endeavour to hand on an efficient school even though much of what he said contradicted his own practice in pre-war years. More than once he made reference to the fact that Stowe was still inferior in its buildings and equipment to many great schools (in 1946 he told the masters that the gym had recently been repainted and 'now looked almost like a solid structure') and must therefore rely on the dedication of masters as its *point d'appui*. It was necessary to offer boys something of a 'spiritual and personal' nature which could not be found elsewhere. In January 1949, he expressed the opinion that petrol rationing and the inroads of domestic chores had led to a shirking of obligations. When this raised a measure of protest he retracted and expressed 'his wondering gratitude' at all the voluntary work done uncomplainingly. Subsequently he stated that in the public-school world a master had 'to sell his soul' in termtime as the price of three months' holiday. Masters could not expect to have weekends in addition to long vacations. Chapel attendance by masters was a hardy perennial. 'Was it really impossible that except when something amusing was afoot the School must do without the presence of married masters throughout the whole of every Sunday?' He wished to see a sharper competitive edge in both work and games. There appeared to be some danger that the tradition of relaxed informality was undermining this. 'There is a lack of temper in our metal which does not show until the last moment but shows fatally then.' Showing clearly that he was becoming aware of the gap between his post-Victorian world and the ethos of modern Britain he affirmed that 'the true schoolmaster' could never be just a friend: 'He could never be rid of the responsibility as older man and as a man trusted by the School and the parent to take charge of boys'. He deplored the use of Christian names for masters, the keeping of late hours and displays of cynicism before pupils.

The absence of a strong field of entrance scholars may partly be attributed to Roxburgh's own generosity in accepting borderline candidates from prep schools over the years. The comparative rarity of open awards is more mystifying as the intellectual life of Stowe in these years was almost unparalleled. Distinguished lecturers came in great numbers: A.J.P. Taylor on 'Eastern and Central Europe', Lord Brabazon on 'Aviation', Sir William Holford on the 'Replanning of the City of London', Sir James Grigg on 'The War Office', Réné Massigli, French Ambassador, on 'Problems of the Fourth Republic', Richard Crossman on 'Politics'. There was even a visit from a Miss Margaret Roberts, future Lady Thatcher, President of the Oxford University Conservative Association, for a debate with her Labour counterpart. John Betjeman spoke to the Vitruvians on Victorian architecture and conducted a party of Stoics around Blenheim Palace. The Earl of Halifax spoke on 'Anglo-American Relations'.

There were moreover, in this final pre-television era, many lively initiatives within the school itself. Alasdair Macdonald founded the 'Ephemerals' to bridge the gap between the XII Club and the Symposium, so the air reverberated with learned papers. The Toxophilites (a pun on its President's name) catered for those outside the more literary groups and heard essays on Radar, Jet Engines, 'Exploring in Newfoundland', and 'Labour in the Middle Ages'. A '46 Society was addressed on the new science of chemo-therapy. Masters too played their part. R.E.J. Davis, President of the XII, gave what was described as 'a mordant dissection' of the 'Influence of Dr Arnold', and we have an interesting glimpse of Raymond Walker instructing the Toxophilites on 'Tops' in 1948. 'From behind a maze of machines large and small Mr Walker revised a large amount of the Higher Certificate Mechanics syllabus. We heard why tops spin, why cats always land on their feet when dropped upside down, how a torpedo gyroscope works, why the Secretary always falls into the ditch when cornering on a motor cycle and why the President [Mr Archer] loses so many golf balls due to slicing.' The Natural History Society began work on the first of its post-war publications and reported that the Black Redstart had been spotted several times in the grounds – a bird which had 'invaded these islands through the bombed sites of London and should find the temples and mouldering ha-has of Stowe to its liking'. David Shepherd O.S. spoke to the geographers on the 'Wild Life of East Africa' and R.J. Roberts and D.L.E. Evan-Hughes illustrated ancient and modern methods of discus throwing and wrestling to the classicists. The Modern Language Society read Marcel Pagnol and foreign films began to return: a

French film on eighteenth-century Russia, *La Tarakanova*, and the Swiss film *Marie Louise*. In the ordinary Film Society reports there were touches of sophistication worthy of C.A. Lejeune, the famous *Observer* critic of the day: 'Dark Waters revealed Merle Oberon in some sort of peril in the Louisiana swamps but it was a little too dark to discern exactly what'. Illuminated windows no longer being a cause of prosecutions and fines there were longer and better play rehearsals. A.A. Dams produced *St Joan* in 1946. Toby Robertson as Archbishop of Rheims, 'spoke his brilliant lines with icy splendour demanded by the part and his commanding presence dominated the stage whenever he began to speak'. To present *The Importance of Being Earnest* in Buckingham Town Hall, Lord Neil Primrose (later a noted stage lighting designer) and others had to construct a stage and proscenium arch and install a cable to amplify the electric current. The Historians were able to resume outdoor performances and gave *Richard II* after which Beverly Baxter, critic for the *Evening Standard* and a parent, wrote of the 'authority, pathos and dignity' of Toby Robertson as the King. Roxburgh urged the masters to ensure that the immense efforts put into house plays should result in memories stored with great literature. It was a waste of effort and time for boys to 'learn low American', and 'it cannot be right that they should "study human nature only at its lowest levels".'[3]

One of the new boys in September 1945 was Simon Coke, the first son of an Old Stoic to enter the School. He beat William Eddy by a term as the latter came from Argentina and spent a term acclimatizing to the English system with Ivor Cross in Wales. It was estimated that 175 Old Stoics had 214 sons registered for the school. For six years boys had passed straight from school into the forces and this, combined with the high casualty rates, broke to some extent the continuity on which registration lists depend. In November 1947, Roxburgh informed the Governors that registrations had passed their peak. In the world in general changes were coming in the relations between schools and families. Debates on the 'Future of the Public Schools' had previously been principally

---

[3] There was further sage advice in a *Stoic* review of Crichton-Miller's time: 'It would appear a fruitless task to perform a thriller at a school, since it is hard to imagine anybody being frightened by his intimate friends, even if they are on the other side of the orchestra pit.'

jeux d'esprit. Under the Labour Government and with the implementation of the Butler Education Act, university entrance began to widen and the belief in a hierarchical society began to crumble. There had always been multiple registrations at several schools. The entry forms of the 1930s show that clearly enough. But now there was more caution and an evaluation of traditional routes. The break-up of wartime marriages meant that plans were changed, and the enterprise of Old Stoics often took them off to distant parts of the world where English-style education was available. In February 1948, Roxburgh told the Governors that of 200 registrations only a proportion had come forward to take Common Entrance. There had been 57 candidates, 28 postponements and 25 failures to answer enquiries. He attributed the losses to fears over rising fees and the continued petrol restrictions. He still dealt in detail with all entries and, like many colleagues, built up lists in the present as an insurance against dearth in the future. In autumn 1947, the Medical Officer pointed out that there were twelve too many boys in the dormitories and numbers should be at 525. Yet by the following year they had risen to over 550. The result was not only overcrowding in dormitories but in studies too. The congestion militated against the proper cleaning of the premises and adequate storage of food and property, and also against the best possible conditions for work, especially as the majority of housemasters were non-resident. As no headmaster wished to display diminishing numbers it was many years before these problems were solved.

The retirement of 'The Major' in 1947 snapped a link with the pioneering days. In his first terms he had had to expend much midnight oil to keep abreast of the syllabus in the lower school and in the 1930s some of the more precocious members of the school had been subversive about his appointment, but his integrity and the ability to inculcate gentlemanly behaviour by a regime devoid of tyranny had made him an influential figure. As soon as he saw Eleven Acre Lake on his first visit he pictured it flecked with sails and he not only founded the Sailing Club, which defeated Oxford University in its first match, but he maintained it financially for many years. Despite his war injuries he was a man of great vigour. He worked with Ian Clarke's foresters and helped to level the Bourbon Fields with pick and shovel. For many seasons he led his form XI out on to the cricket field and no day was rounded off until he had taken a long walk over open country. Even in retirement, when the winds were favourable, he would sail down to the prep school at which he taught on Lake Windermere. In September Roxburgh wrote: 'It seems strange to be starting the new term without you. The only familiar element is the arrival of a gift from you to the Benevolent Fund which quite reminds me of old times.' When Roxburgh himself retired Haworth told him: 'I remember you once said, when for some reason I was a trifle fractious, that you and I had never had a row. It was the happy understanding which I like to think existed between us that was one of the chief factors in creating the spirit of contentment that filled my life at Stowe.'

His departure emphasised the need for an established second master who could relieve Roxburgh of some of his burdens. In early days Earle and Cross, with whom, according to Clifford, Roxburgh could sometimes be 'astonishingly brusque', had automatically deputized. During the war and after, Haworth had been much the most senior figure. The choice was now between Playford, Capel Cure and Clifford himself. Capel Cure, consulted, gave the modest opinion that his views corresponded so closely to the headmaster's that the school would not benefit from diversity of experience. 'In practically every important matter I have the identical opinion as you do, to most sudden happenings my reactions are the same as yours, I think the same things important and the same things unimportant: A.B.C. (Clifford) I put first for exactly the same reasons the other way round.' He finished the letter, 'Luckily the time that I am due to go into school has come before I get moved to urge my personal claims . . . and that *would* become intolerable.'

Roxburgh wrote to Pickard-Cambridge:

Owing to Haworth's seniority and personal prestige there was never any doubt that when I was ill or absent he was in charge of the School. I never described him officially as Second Master but everyone knew that he was in fact Second in Command. When he has gone, however, there will be no-one who so imposes himself (in the French sense) and a firm appointment will be necessary . . . Clifford commands so much respect here and has such strength of character that it would not matter if Playford did resent his appointment . . . which the rest of the staff would accept as right and proper. In earlier years it did not matter much who took over in my absence because I was absent so rarely. But I have now been ill four times in the last two terms and was off work in the Spring of 1946. Bostock is doing what he can for me and sending me to see various experts in London, but I cannot count on not being ill again.

To Playford Roxburgh was even more pessimistic about his health: 'Bostock does not hold out much hope of better things in the future.'

'Now what I want to see you about, my dear man, is something quite different and far more important. [Clifford was often wont to recall the interview, word by word.] Fritz, you know that nowadays I am often ill in bed. I should like to feel that someone is running the place as I should like it to be run – and my Governors are behind me in saying this to you.' To Capel and Playford he wrote: 'I hope most sincerely that in so deciding I shall not have made either of you think that I am ungrateful for what you are and what you do and what you mean to Stowe. Surely you know that is not so . . . In any case I am certain that your regard for Clifford will be in no way lessened and that whenever he needs it he will have your backing and your loyalty.' Playford in reply stressed that he harboured no personal grudge but feared that the appointment might herald a less liberal regime:

Clifford stands for the stern disciplinarian and the traditional school system. Stowe, one had hoped, was aiming at something more free, more friendly, more enlightened . . . With the probability, as you seem to expect, (and I hope that it isn't so) of your being absent and with the inevitability of a new Headmaster one day with a possible interregnum the bias is bound to be towards a rigid and stereotyped educational system. I cannot do other than deplore that.

Roxburgh endeavoured to mollify:

I am sure that though he [Clifford] is more of a disciplinarian than many of us, he values the Stowe spirit as much as we do. What he can contribute and what is so badly wanted is a tightening up of the purely organizational side of my job. I want him to make up for some of my deficiencies on the practical side as well as relieving me of some of the work not connected with the boys. I have no intention of allowing the appointment to have any effect upon my policy and, if my successor is not capable of having a policy of his own, he will not be fit for the job.

Playford was in any case hardly the man to impose strict attendance and punctuality upon his colleagues. Patrick Hunter had tried to see masters who were lacking in these matters: 'Three accepted criticism, a fourth countered with self-laudations but squirmed. But with Playford – *he* had the victory.' He said he never asked permission to be away, 'adding with unconscious humour that life would be altogether too busy if he did'.

The athlete, dancer or musician who has trained for life will be carried on by technique after talent has begun to wane. To some extent this was true of Roxburgh though on occasion the technique faltered. The problem of the succession loomed as large at Stowe as ever it did in the last days of Queen Elizabeth I. Patrick Hunter continued to plead for 'direction': 'To recognize that you have not quite the prodigious energy that you had ten years ago is only a compliment to the fullness of a life devoted to Stowe.' There was some alarm for the imminent future, scarcely veiled by the cirumlocution. 'Where you do intervene in the administration of the School the intervention is apt on occasion to seem – I mean "on occasion" for of course it is not always; and I mean "seem" for I know it is not the intention – the intervention is apt to seem rather capricious.'

It was a tragedy that Clifford, who during the war had been housemaster, head of Modern Languages, commander of the J.T.C. and an officer in the Home Guard, and whose family had been in America necessitating a midnight correspondence (a habit he was incapable of relinquishing), had overstretched his energies. His tendency towards unfocused activity was a sure sign of overwork. Finding Roxburgh's independent methods frustrating he was, within a year of his appointment writing: 'By last holidays I felt desperate and I sat down and drafted a well-considered letter in which I offered you my resignation as Second Master. I had worry without responsibility and, in the circumstances I just couldn't see daylight through the problem.' He disapproved of Capel Cure. Playford too still rumbled ominously. Chapel, as so often, offered a rich minefield for controversy. Microphones had been installed without consultation. 'I have taken trouble to be audible at the back of Chapel. Yet you announced publicly in a masters' meeting last term that no one at the back ever heard anything. I fear you have started a snowball. When added to my other grievances I find no appreciation of my effort.'[4]

Roxburgh, however, could still handle the old guard. Yet even he was baffled by the megalomaniac behaviour of a more recent arrival: P.F. Wiener.

It would require a companion volume to relate all the tribulations which he brought upon the hapless Roxburgh. He arrived with a laudatory reference from Hugh Lyon, headmaster of Rugby, and all manner of credentials including a doctorate from the Sorbonne which he should have had but did not, as the Gestapo had pointedly extracted and destroyed his qualifications after the fall of Paris. His correspondence bristled with phrases such as 'I shall not bore you with the many people who have asked me so far to give you their regards, apart from Harold Nicolson . . .', 'I am seeing quite a bit of S.M.R. The Prince de Bourbon who is a contemporary and a great friend (also a relation) of Elizabeth and Philip – I would either suggest he comes down to Stowe for a weekend or that he finds out what the form is for a royal visit', 'I had a quiet tea yesterday with Irene Ravensdale when in stormed three Old Stoics'. He was engaged to teach the less able linguists but Side 8A soon became Side 9 with Wiener wielding full tutorial powers. He did in fact change the lives of these pupils who had no great examination goals and arranged trips to places of interest such as Scotland Yard and the *Daily Express* and *Evening News* offices, 'which Lord Rothermere has kindly arranged for me'. His fifteen Stoics were entertained to tea at the Foreign Office by Hector McNeil, Minister of State and, lest the day should have been deemed wasted, they proceeded to the House of Lords for a lecture and discussion with Lord Jowett. Wiener took a very successful party on a trip to America which included a visit to the Roosevelt home.

A comet's tail of essential 'Thank you' letters accompanied his progress and Roxburgh was obliged to write to all sorts and

[4] The sound system in Chapel was never totally tamed. In Bob Drayson's time the Headmaster of Eton was invited to preach. He arrived late, the microphones broke down and Clifford claimed that he heard nothing but the opening text: 'Whom say ye that I am?'

conditions of men, from ambassadors and cabinet ministers downwards. Dignitaries were wished upon him to entertain. Referring to an arrangement to receive Kingsley Martin at the same time as he was expecting the Bishops of Oxford and Maidstone he wrote: 'For Heaven's sake don't unload Joad on us at the same time. Such a weight of intellect would sink me – and in any case there are no beds.' A book by Wiener entitled *Martin Luther – Hitler's Spiritual Ancestor*, the Preface of which was addressed 'Stowe School', brought down on Roxburgh and Pickard-Cambridge the wrath of the World Evangelical Alliance; libel actions brought by or against Protestant reviewers waxed and waned.

It was in March 1948, that *The Times*, in a correspondence dealing with criticisms of the quality of entrants for the Civil Service, printed next to its leading article a letter from Wiener, addressed from Stowe, which lamented the poor standard of many teachers and the 'starvation wages' paid to the profession. Pickard-Cambridge demanded his removal and recent arrivals in the Common Room were outraged. Wiener launched into the proposed legal battles with zeal. E.G. Wykes, the solicitor to Allied Schools, received a thirty-five-page letter which Wiener intended to publish along with the replies of Roxburgh. Wiener did not lack literary power – for example his thrust at the Chairman: 'I did feel sorry for the aged scholar whose main contribution to world affairs during the last decade has been a work on *The Theatre of Dionysius at Athens*' – and the prospect was alarming. Wiener intended an 'Areopagitica' and accused Roxburgh of sacrificing 'the rule of law, the dignity of man, the sanctity of the individual and all human rights' to a utilitarian concern for the reputation of Stowe. It was here that he asserted that Roxburgh had concealed the pre-war visit of a Hitler Youth Party lest he, Wiener, should then have withheld his services from the school.

Eventually the controversy petered out, leaving many untidy ends, not least demands from Paris hotels where Wiener had reserved rooms that had not been occupied or paid for and from Harrods' Library requiring the return of volumes that appeared to have been sold along with the borrower's own. From the U.S.A. Wiener wrote to express sorrow that Roxburgh would not be joining him there in retirement! J.N. Buchanan, a Governor who had a special interest in American links, wrote in 1952 to say that a man who purported once to have taught at Stowe was making scurrilous attacks on American schools in the *Manchester Guardian* and endangering Anglo-American relations. By then Eric Reynolds, who knew Wiener from Rugby days, was headmaster: 'I regard him as one of the most dangerous influences that I have ever met in the confines of a Public School. He is utterly unscrupulous and disloyal and I frankly think there will be trouble wherever he goes.' Wherever he went is not clear, but he was last heard of being pursued by the 'Church of Our Lady of the Prairies' of Dakota who were 'interested in his views on Luther'.

Departures in 1948 much more sincerely regretted were those of Robin and Dodie Watt who decided to return to Canada. They had, as partners, run a most notable Art department at a time when the subject was regarded as secondary in many public schools. The Art School had been something of a gathering place for Stoics of all ages and temperaments. As Roxburgh observed, they 'had inspired so many artistic boys to make the most of their talents, given to so many philistines a first understanding of beauty, made the difference between happiness and unhappiness for so many boys at different moments in their lives and given so much personal delight to us all that it was difficult to see how we should ever get on without them.' Dodie Watt had dressed many Congreve productions with what seemed miraculous skill in the age of clothing coupons and shortages.

A retrospective exhibition was arranged and eighty Old Stoics whose work had shown promise were circularized. Twenty-five responded with 200 works, including some painted in prisoner-of-war camps. J.C. Saunders, matching the colourful display in prose, pondered the question whether there was a 'Stowe School'. He concluded that the trees, arches and skies of Stowe had provided sufficient material to train powers of quiet observation. 'If they had learnt to paint beneath a pall of soot and among the walls of clammy yellow brick they might have dug into their subconscious in search of the marsh gas of originality or, from very desperation at the dreariness of their surroundings, have turned to the grotesque or to the strident to relieve their feelings – they might have preached, they might have shouted. Instead they have learned that what is worth saying will be audible however quietly

it is spoken.'[5] Robin Watt was not to realize his wish to paint
Roxburgh's portrait. The commission was given to James Gunn, a
leading portraitist of the time, who produced what Roxburgh was
wont to call 'that libellous square yard'. Viscount Buckmaster
presented it on behalf of the Friends of Stowe on the occasion of
the school's silver jubilee.

The jubilee did not bring a Royal Visit. Roxburgh told Haworth
that they had tried but failed: 'We did not do anything to celebrate
the birthday but a kind parent provided vast quantities of iced cake
for the school and some champagne for the Masters.' In 1946,
however, there had been an acclamation only marginally less than
royal for Field Marshal Viscount Montgomery, who presented the
Library with the accounts of his campaigns and told the young
Stoics that he had come across many Old Stoics in the war and had
always been highly impressed by their attitude and achievements.
He took tea in the headmaster's rooms and then returned to meet
the school in Assembly where, to renewed cheering, he asked for
a day's holiday.

Roxburgh's Jubilee message in the *Stoic* was not triumphalist:
'Our standards of achievement in work and games fell during the
war and, though they are rising again, they are not rising fast
enough: there is not the old tingle in the air, the old tingle of effort
and achievement. When are we going to get back such University
Scholarship Lists as those of 1938 and 1939? When are we going to
repeat some of our great Rugger and Cricket Seasons of the past?'
Certainly the report on the Rugby season of 1945, by Bruce Barr,
had been a diatribe, including a cutting comment on a heavy defeat
by Oundle: 'A description of the Match would necessarily be to us
a rather dull chronicle of many tries and can be found by those
interested in the Oundle School Magazine'. The 1946 season,
though it began with a disaster against Bedford, turned out to be
quite successful and brought to the fore R.M. Bartlett, a future
Cambridge Blue and International, who set an example of 'hard
tackling, good kicking, courageous falling, and the will to win for

[5] Among the artists who could not be represented was Kay Irgens, a Norwegian
who came to Stowe in 1938. His large-scale Rubenesque drawings of horses and
men in combat were outstanding and his promise is still remembered by contemporaries. He was killed serving with the Coldstream Guards in France.

the sake of the team and the School'. By the end of the season there had been victories over a number of old foes such as Radley, Harrow and St Edward's. The return of David Brown to coaching boosted morale. Eventually he had coached Rugby for so long at Stowe that he was able to shout, 'Boy, you're as lazy as your father', across the touch line. In 1947, when things were going well, a 6–6 draw with Oundle was considered a disappointment. 'Even the thoughtful granting of a half-holiday could not prevail against cuts in the basic petrol ration and only a few cars accomplished the fifty-mile journey.' Results in 1948 were evenly balanced but the appraisals of Stoic effort were warmer: 'I have not had a more pleasant and willing lot to coach', wrote Brown. 'They have not needed American coach methods to stir them to action. They have given themselves unstintedly to the game and Stowe.' As petrol restrictions eased Cheltenham came into the fixture list. R.G. Macmillan played for the Scottish schoolboys after passing first in the Sandhurst written exams.

With improved coaching and the return of Austin Matthews as professional, cricket had a good 1948 season with some moments of high excitement. Against St Edward's W.R.G. Short took wickets with his 2nd, 3rd, 9th and 14th deliveries, plus two more: 6 wickets for 12 runs. The last St Edward's wicket fell to a catch by J.F. Conington who misjudged the flight of the ball, struck it high up behind his head, snatched it a second time, lost it and caught it finally just above the ground. Bedford, which had not lost a school match, were defeated despite the distractions of cheers from the crowd (during a Conington brothers' partnership) at news from Henley, where the Bedford crew were winning the Princess Elizabeth Cup for the third time. There was a famous and much-photographed score board at the Bruce v. Temple house match in July 1948 which read D.E. Conington 140, J.F. Conington 131, during the Bruce innings.

A word should be said of the swimmers for, with all the impediments of training in the lake often in low temperatures, they beat, in the 1947 season, Rugby, Bloxham, St Edward's and Oundle. In 1948 they won all matches and the water-polo team visited the Channel Isles winning five out of eight matches. Misled by the notepaper the team was hailed by the Guernsey Press as coming from 'that very famous Buckingham College, Chatham House, near Stowe.' In the same year the tennis team won the Glanvill

1. John Fergusson Roxburgh (1920s)

2.. Roxburgh greets the first arrivals, 11 may 1923

3. The first arrivals on the North Front, 1923

4. The Prince of Wales with the headmaster and Governors, 1933.
Lord Gisborough leads on the Prince's left; Roxburgh and Warrington follow to the left

5. A 1st XV rugger match against Oundle on the North Front in 1938

6. A well-drilled approach to sport; tennis coaching with R.E. Lucas in the 1920s *(above)*, and P.T. on the South Front in the 1950s

7. The O.T.C. being inspected by the Duke of Gloucester for the fifteenth anniversary, 1938

8. The C.C.F. in the Grecian Valley, 1990

9. Skating on the Octagon Lake with the South Front behind, 1933

10. Boys at the feet of George I watching the Stowe v. Oundle rugger match, 1938

11. The two Stoic recipients of the Victoria Cross: Group Captain Sir Leonard Cheshire V.C. O.M. D.S.O. D.F.C; and 'Jock' Anderson V.C. D.S.O. *(below)*

12. Queen Mary lays the foundation stone of the Chapel in 1927

13. The Queen Mother with Donald Crichton-Miller and head boy, I.A.H. Sitwell, leaving Chapel on the occassion of the school's 40th anniversary in 1963

14. Eric Reynolds by A.E. Cooper (1958)

15. Donlad Crichton-Miller by David Shepherd O.S. (1963)

16. Temple house room, 1956

17. Boys' and girls' studies today

18. Robert Drayson
by David Shepherd O.S. (1979)

19. Christopher Turner
by David Shepherd O.S. (1989)

20. Community service in the 1970s: teaching at a local primary school and serving at an OAP's Christmas party

21. The 'new' swimming pool (late 1970s)

22. Approaching Kang Nar Gorge on the 1987 Stowe Himalayas Expedition

23. A Duke of Edinburgh Award party on Bleaklow near Glossop, 1970

24. The Beatles give a concert in the
Roxburgh Hall, 4 April 1963

25. The Jubilee Concert in the Chapel, 1973

26. A Trio in the restored Music Room

27. A performance of *Twelfth Night*, the Senior Congreve play, 1977.
The set was designed by William Dady, Director of Art

28. Time-keepers at the finishing line, Sports Day 1985. From left to right: J.B. Dobsinson,
C.P. Macdonald, J.M. Temple, R.M. Potter, M. Waldman, F.A. Hudson,
and Mrs Pat Iles, matron of Cobham

29. The Computer Centre, 1987

30. Sixth form Geology group tutorial with Michael Waldman in Bruce House

(Doubles) Cup for the second year and reached the Final of the
Youll Cup, being beaten by Eton. N.R. Cunningham Reid and
G.W. Scott in 1947 represented the public schools. John Downing
was in the Tennis VI for four years and was picked out for his play
by the correspondent of the *Star*. In 1948, the squash team also
won all their matches. When boxing was reintroduced there were
over seventy entries for the championships. Riding, which somehow had continued during the war, was celebrated with a
gymkhana in which each house had to produce a team of four to
compete for the Haig Cup. Bruce won the event overall, but
Grafton was superior in the jumping.

With the return of peace Old Stoics were able to participate in
many and wider fields. Geoffrey de Havilland, a founder member
of both Cobham and Chatham, had joined the family company in
1928 and ten years later became its chief test pilot. During the war
he tested many high-performance military planes – Mosquitoes,
Vampires and Hornets – and was regarded as the finest demonstration pilot in Europe. A successful athlete in the first Sports
Days, he won the de Havilland employees' mile race three years
in succession without any apparent training. Tragically, he was
killed flying the D.H. 108 experimental jet a week before an
attempt on the world speed record. He was awarded the Segrave
Trophy posthumously for the 'courage, initiative and skill by
which he worthily upheld British prestige before the world'.
Squadron Leader H.S.L. Dundas won the International Air Race,
flying a Spitfire at 294 miles per hour. P.B. Lucas was Captain of
the Walker Cup Team and won the President's Putter at Rye.
G.C.W. Joynson represented Great Britain in the Winter Olympics
of 1948 in the bobsleigh team. At Cambridge, M.B. Scholfield was
Captain of Golf and G.P. Lloyd a Quarter Miler. The school had
its first Wrangler in Mathematics in O.G. Taylor; J. Stoye became
a Student (Fellow) of Christ Church Oxford; and Noel Annan won
the Le Bas Prize for Literature. A.R. Barrowclough won the Eldon
Scholarship for Law; J.L. Nicholson, the London University Prize
for Economics and the Frances Wood Prize of the Royal Statistical
Society.

Laurence Whistler published a biography of his brother, Rex,
recalling how much inspiration his brother had derived from visits
to Stowe. Speaking to the Vitruvians he reminded them that
Rex's murals in the tea room at the Tate contained a number of

decorative themes based upon the landscape architecture around them. There was an award of the B.E.M. made to A.P. Dewing whose coolness and initiative had enabled wounded Italians to be evacuated from what was then known as Mogadiscio, who, said the citation, 'if he had made a mistake, would have undoubtedly been murdered by Somalis'.[6]

During the war Roxburgh had made attempts to buy from Farmer Davies the avenue east of the Boycott Pavilions and the principal approach to the school. Makeshift fences and wandering cattle robbed the drive of dignity and trees which were old and failing had been compulsorily felled.

It was presented as a gift by J.N. Buchanan D.S.O., M.C., a long-serving Governor, associated with the names of his three sons. They were all officers in the Grenadier Guards, Arthur Buchanan having been killed in Libya in 1943. There began to be a revival in interest in the grounds and Christopher Hussey published a series of articles in *Country Life* drawing attention to the work of Kent, Bridgeman and Thomas Pitt, describing the plans as 'a vast poem in the medium of visual instead of verbal images designed to elevate the mind and implant virtuous ideals'.

That they were not universally successful was illustrated by the Silverstone incidents in the summer of 1948. The Humber Car Company had stored a large number of vehicles in the hangars at Silverstone, awaiting export. Their existence was discovered by free-ranging cyclists and two parties of boys broke into the hangars and drove round at speed on the premises. Damage was done to the engines and to the lights and, as the thrills of the chase grew, dried-up cars were abandoned and others taken out. Sir William Rootes of Humber generously agreed not to prosecute if compensation was paid but, as Roxburgh informed a parent, 'the matter does not end there'. Three boys late for the roll-call or 'Stance' drove back to Stowe, returning the stolen car late at night, thereby committing all manner of traffic offences. Roxburgh had to accompany them to Towcester Juvenile Court, which was not too severe, although the press reported the incidents. The episode was an

---

[6] When Anthony Davenport O.S. became engaged to a dashingly dressed Wimbledon tennis player who featured prominently in the press Roxburgh was perplexed over the sending of his customary congratulations: 'He has become engaged to someone called "Gorgeous Gussie". If she has other names I have not heard them.'

illustration of Roxburgh's failing touch which had given rise to the worries evinced by Hunter and Clifford and the concern over capriciousness. Writing after the court appearance he was almost jocular in his report to the parents: 'X and I are feeling happier than we were a few hours ago'. At the end of term he reassured the worried family that X was 'nice and sound' and 'will become much more steady at 18'. Yet this escapade could have resulted in deaths or serious injuries. A few months before, a boy who had played for the school in XIs and XVs and had an excellent record, left for some unspecified lapse in responsibility. Despite the most touching letters of contrition and apology he was banned for two years even from representative cricket teams which had no connection with Stowe and his appeals were coldly received.

All cares, however, were subsumed in the farewells of the summer of 1949. A few weeks before Roxburgh's retirement the War Memorial was dedicated by the Archbishop of Canterbury. The Edinburgh firm which had made the stalls for Sir Robert Lorimer in 1929 still had some of the original oak available. In material and style, and in the craftsmanship of the Scottish carvers, it harmonized with the interior. The names of 270 Old Stoics were recorded in gold leaf. The Book of Remembrance placed under a canopy contained 270 pages, illuminated in black, gold and red. Because of the large concourse 350 members of the school were seated outside and heard the service relayed. Roxburgh's formal eloquence remained undimmed:

> Heroic souls do not think of themselves as heroes, they act no part before their fellows, they make no appeal to posterity. If questioned, they say they act as they do because they must. It is what the occasion required of them and how could they be unfaithful to it? To default at such a time is to forfeit one's manhood. To be equal to the demand is to rise to a new level in selfhood. In the hour when a man gathers his whole self to the deed to which no conditions are attached he asks for no reward and looks for no applause. Perhaps he has his uncertainty and his reluctance still, but something great has come upon him and he obeys.

As the term moved towards its last days the mood swung between gaiety and nostalgia. With amazing temerity the musicians mounted a performance of *The Marriage of Figaro*. As Alasdair

Macdonald observed: 'If the actor forgets his part the prompter can quickly and quietly hand him back the thread of his discourse but, should the singer forget his words or miss his entry the conductor has a very large number of mystified mortals on his hands.' J.C. Saunders produced and, mindful of the inanities of operatic translations, made his own. Michael Mounsey, successor of Robin Watt, had no mean challenge in designing the sets and creating the illusion of space on the tiny gymnasium stage. The boudoir of the Countess was decorated with a magnificent Gobelin tapestry in which the South Front made an appearance. Few boys had ever seen an opera. K.A. Henderson (Susanna) associated the name Figaro solely with the Rossini aria from *The Barber of Seville* and the cat in *Pinocchio*. All but one of the trebles, coached by Martin Burke, were in their first or second terms. The script had been typed somewhere in the school offices and those with smaller parts had to share the third or fourth carbon copies. There was only a single copy of the vocal score, in which Saunders had transcribed his version and this had to be passed from hand to hand while each player learnt his lines. The voice of the Countess began to break two weeks before the performances and a future director of the America International Bank took over at the age of thirteen and with as many days in hand.

Leslie Huggins took the cast to dine at Simpsons and see the opera at Covent Garden from the stalls. He and Saunders gave no indication that the venture might not work and, representing the essence of adventurous education, it succeeded. Recalling that Mozart had composed the work in a month Macdonald opined that he would have been the first to applaud the spirit which prepared and performed it in two.

The Historians gave *Richard III* reviewed by Peregrine Worsthorne O.S. who, while suggesting that the Plantagenets might be re-titled 'This Unhappy Breed', praised the brilliant exploitation of the setting. 'To sit in the elegant grounds . . . on a fine summer's evening is to taste life at a ducal level. The play is essentially not the thing. Stowe is the thing and in such a triumphantly artificial setting any performance, unless it is of Olympian splendour, becomes a play within a play.'

More than a thousand Old Stoics came to the headmaster's farewell party. The prefects presented Roxburgh with a Crown Derby Service, a tribute to many years of courtly entertaining. The

Old Stoics gave him a Sunbeam Talbot Ninety, a clock which reproduced the Stowe chimes and a cheque for £5000 for him to do with as he wished. This last he gave back to the school as a spur to the building of wood and metal workshops. There was, he said 'a touch, a suggestion about these presents which might have struck them; a clock to tell him that his time was up, then a motor car to drive away in and finally journey money enough to take him to the Antipodes.' With a backward glance at the motor races he had had with Leslie Huggins and Dr Bostock returning from Buckingham he commented on his new automobile: 'It is called a Ninety because it reaches 90 miles per hour in the distance from the sanatorium to the Boycott Pavilions. To a poor old gentleman who has never driven over 30 miles per hour in his life that does seem an overwhelming present.' (Clifford was one day having his hair cut at a London barber's and doubtless talking volubly about Stowe when a silver haired gentleman approached and said in hushed tones: 'May I say, Sir, that I once had the honour of having my car run into by Mr Roxburgh's'. He retreated and the silence was only broken by the snipping of scissors.)

On 17 August Roxburgh wrote to Andrew Croft: 'Tomorrow I am being sold up – all my possessions except the few that will fit into my cottage are being auctioned. The effect is strange; all the accumulations of years are being brought to light; intimate things are being made public; everything is being numbered and catalogued. Already a big marquee is being erected in Cobham Court and men with green baize aprons are carrying furniture out of every door.' Those who had been young under his care felt that their own youth had gone with his retirement. Letters poured in from generations of Stoics and from parents. One small boy in the school concluded his farewells very sweetly: 'My sincere wish is for your everlasting happiness'.

After visits to Paris and Ireland he set out on a cruise to South Africa where a band of Old Stoics gathered to meet him from the boat at Durban at 4.30 a.m. Post-war restrictions prevented him from building at Great Brickhill the gracious retirement home he had planned but he had a cottage on the property, cultivated prize-winning vegetables and blooms and indulged his hobby of photography. For a time he taught at the Old Ride, a local preparatory school, whose headmaster bravely accepted this Gulliver into his

Lilliputian world. He enjoyed the work and his more pronounced mannerisms found an appreciative audience.

His self-imposed isolation in retirement made Great Brickhill a kind of Avalon where the past lay veiled from the present. Despite efforts by the Stowe Templars and others to entice him to visit the school he came only once, to the funeral of Leslie Huggins in 1952. In 1954 he travelled to Ambleside to the funeral of 'The Major' and with a great effort of will read the lesson. On the return journey he could not bear the noise of the engine and sat in a compartment with Clifford who talked to him of the time they dined with Admiral Lord Keyes of Zeebrugge, 'like dining with Nelson'. Later Roxburgh wrote of 'our wonderful talk in the train'. Clifford's last glimpse of him was as he disappeared into the crowd on the London platform, walking slowly and purposefully and not looking back. He died in May 1954 in his cottage and his funeral fell on the anniversary of the school's foundation. The seven pall bearers were those who had given the longest service to Stowe and were led by Edward Hart Dyke.

Roxburgh was a phenomenon whose career is hard to summarize. There were some glaring faults in his institutional legacy, such as the non-residence of housemasters and the uncertain roles of his chief lieutenants. Yet to have tried to persuade him to mould Stowe in a fashion different from his own, as others sometimes did, was like attempting to instruct Wagner in the writing of music drama by correspondence course. Two addresses given early in his career illustrate vividly his approach to his role. Giving the prizes at Wycombe Abbey in 1928, he spoke on literature and declared, 'Truth is said to be stranger than fiction but Mr Lytton Strachey's History is more entertaining than both. If you want to know about Queen Victoria or Queen Elizabeth I do not know what books you should read, but if you want to see the English language superbly used and to enjoy the art of writing as practised by a perfect craftsman I recommend you to read everything that Mr Strachey writes.' Style, in short, could sometimes marvellously blur reality. He himself could turn the most prosaic issues into occasions for unique and touching comments. A boy in Cobham had a severe kidney illness and the father was worried about paying the fees while he might have to spend many months at home. Roxburgh replied, 'So far as Stowe is concerned the fee question can easily be dealt with. I will put the boy down as definitely leaving at

Christmas which means the School will have no claim on you after that. When the time comes for X to return we will make a place for him by some means. To the Auditors he will be a new boy but to us he will be an old friend.' Sometimes style had to cover the slow growth of the school's essential foundations. Sometimes it seemed to exploit the receptivity of those dependent upon him.

The second address was given to the pupils of the Royal Latin School in 1933, a sermon on the text, 'They brought forth the sick into the streets that at least the shadow of Peter passing by might overshadow some of them', Acts 5.15. He pointed out that each of us, wherever we are and among whomsoever we move, casts a shadow. He had a deep appreciation of the interaction of human beings, and the English public school afforded a unique theatre in which to act and observe. At times the shadows he himself cast were sharp and unmistakable. 'Laddie' Lucas remembered once suggesting that it would be better for a particularly habitual offender not to return the following term and seeing Roxburgh move to the French windows so as to set his words to maximum effect: 'Has it ever occurred to you that X can probably do something rather better, is capable of performing some service rather better, than anyone else in this school, you included?' And, when the rather ineffectual negative came, 'Then I must tell you that as the head of X's house and head of school, it is your job to find it out.'

At times his shadow was quite invisible but nonetheless effective. A final story will illustrate. He had taken into the school a boy of very moderate abilities, a relative of a distinguished Old Stoic for whom he had high regard. Because there were financial hesitations Roxburgh placed a sum in a bank account on which the family could draw should some crisis with the fees ever arise. Concerned with the boy's slow development he found the name of the best endocrinologist in London (he was very skilled in the knowledge of specialists) from his doctor brother and a consultation was arranged. Nothing untoward was diagnosed, but a few months later, when a younger brother seemed to be overtaking the boy in school, a further opinion was sought from a second expert. When the boy left with a rather uncertain future and the parents reported that the sum in the bank was still untouched, Roxburgh gave back to the Benevolent Fund the half which had come from it, but asked that the remainder, which was his private contribution, should remain where it was until it would 'make a difference to the achievement of some ambition.' He had already paid for the second and more valuable consultation.

As Barbara Cross, widow of Ivor, wrote after his death: 'Behind the persona there was a great, good and spiritually minded man. Speaking to Ivor once of his responsibilities and feelings towards the pupils, he had used the striking phrase: "Pro eis me sacrifico".'

8

Eric Reynolds

The task of the sub-committee of the Council which met under the Chairmanship of Pickard-Cambridge to select a successor was not an enviable one. Certainly the Governors did not swallow the cynical advice of a well-known Cambridge pundit on public-school politics who advised that they should appoint a hopeless dud and dismiss him after three years when he had drawn all the expendable fire. There had been some hopes that William Darling, headmaster of Geelong, might step into the stupendous gap, but he was not persuaded. A popular Winchester housemaster withdrew. It was rumoured that Stowe's financial future was far from assured and accommodation in one of the Field houses, no grander than the others, was not enticing for married men. Roxburgh himself was favourable towards the candidature of Eric Reynolds, a bachelor Rugby housemaster, and gave him some assistance over the likely topics to arise in interview. In the 1920s Rugby, under Dr Vaughan, had been in the ascendant and masters openly spoke in the Common Room of the headmasterships that would be distributed among their number. The tradition was still powerful enough for Wiener to boast that he had prophesied the appointment of Reynolds to Stowe. In March 1949, Roxburgh wrote to Andrew Croft: 'Reynolds, the new man, is good. Everyone thinks very highly of him and I like him personally very much.' To Habershon he said more openly: 'We have secured an extremely good man who is I think a good deal more than the conventional Rugby housemaster, though I trust he has all the virtues of that uninteresting but effective type.'

Reynolds was a Scholar of Haileybury and had read for the Modern Language Tripos at St John's College, Cambridge, though his final examinations there had been interrupted by the General Strike when for ten days he drove a London bus. His cultural enthusiasms were genuine. At Haileybury he shared a study with Robert Speight, the actor, and at Cambridge was Secretary of the prestigious Marlowe Society. He worked for a time as Lecturer at the University of Leipzig, which was then the musical capital of Germany, and there he gorged on the musical fare on offer. He gave up the opportunity for a career in the Foreign Office in favour of teaching and taught not only at Rugby but, on exchange, at Upper Canada College in Toronto from which he toured the United States. American History was a subject he taught with great success at Stowe. At Rugby he had commanded the J.T.C. and restarted Stanley House after its wartime closure. To do this he had been allowed to select fifteen boys from other houses and thus his experience had been similar to that of several of Stowe's housemasters.

He was familiar in the Rugby staff plays as the dashing 'man about town' in Ben Travers farces, and played Darcy in *Pride and Prejudice*. If a headmaster has to be to some extent an actor the Rugby *Meteor* did not question his skills: 'Mr Reynolds in white flannels, Mr R. in evening dress, Mr R. in natty gent's suiting, and above all Mr R. in riding-kit. Yes, well inside the part of the society cracksman, Mr Reynolds always knows exactly where to stand, where to look and how to move, so that it is as much a pleasure to watch his stage craft as to hear his carefully modulated voice bringing out the best of every remark.' His talents for make-up were so marked that he was sometimes suspected of taking part in Stowe plays anonymously!

He was accomplished and witty. When, in 1951, Capel Cure expressed a wish to give up Temple, he did so in a poem of several stanzas entitled 'A Ballad of Approaching Senescence' which concluded:

> This matter then I beg you expedite,
> For to my heart it is so very near,
> It's good for Stowe, no need to be polite,
> And good for Temple, both things I hold dear.
> The Governors won't surely shed a tear,

When they are told of this my great desire,
They must admit my keenness now is sear,
Next term from Temple, please may I retire?

Reynolds straightway replied in kind:

Ballad to hand. Its matter conned and vetted;
Its themes of resignation, lack of zest regretted.
Your Muse's flight made sour news taste much sweeter,
Reply herewith – forgive my halting metre.
Your wish is granted I add in all humility,
Before senescence changes to senility,
Succession apostolic, cardinal or papal,
Provides no answer for the cure of Capel,
With time a Deacon may become a Rector,
So for the present 'Templa quam Dilecta'

When his sleek and stately cocker spaniel swallowed a watch which McElwee had just dropped he remarked with surprise: 'The value of that dog has just gone up considerably'. In one of his interviews with prospective parents he noted: 'Father was at Harrow; thinks all Old Harrovians are either Churchills or wasters (doesn't say to which he belongs).' When Capel Cure used the word 'compensation' in connection with his retirement from Temple Reynolds told him to eschew the word utterly: 'If it is ever used in the hearing of a Commissioner of Inland Revenue we shall all be sunk as irredeemably as the Oxford Boat'. Like Roxburgh he too had lost surrogate offspring in war. A favourite godson, who had been also his first head of house and a noted athlete, had been killed serving with the R.A.M.C. in Cyprus.

Yet although Reynolds had much in common with Roxburgh, and the Governors had done their work well, Rugby was an organization very different from Stowe. At the former the headmaster in his castellated domain supervised his own School house and left the internal affairs of other houses to the housemasters. There was no general desire for direction or motivation from above and many boys met the headmaster on rare occasions only. Discipline was maintained by dividing and ruling, the academic tradition had long ago acquired its own momentum and did not need constant promptings. Staff discontent there must have been, but it was fragmented by the scattered geography of the place. When Clifford expressed worries that the masters at Stowe, many of whom felt that they had been first in Roxburgh's estimation, were campaigning to (putting it at its kindest) bring back the 'good old days', Reynolds was not unduly concerned and said that he too had been a rebel as an assistant master.

He suffered from a staffing position static almost to the point of ossification. George Clarke, one of his first appointments, remembered occupying the same stall in Chapel term after term. Housemasterships were similarly motionless. If nothing were done there would only be one vacancy after five years and another after ten. He introduced a plan whereby tenure would be limited and those with unlimited franchises would be placed on a sliding time-scale. Age and weariness also brought inevitable illness and there were several absences by senior men for whom substitutes had to be found.

His objects were practical enough. With memories of the ponderous Memorial Hall at Rugby he wished Stowe to have a dignified and spacious home for public occasions. He expected the Headmaster's house he had been promised, not least because his cook was periodically cycled into in Plug Street while conveying his meals from kitchen to table. He wanted to improve the salary scales which had not been amended for twenty years. He was more interested than Roxburgh in matters of accountancy and tax. He tried, as Clifford remembered, to give masters their major increases in mid-career when family expenses were highest. Such measures won appreciation. When Capel Cure discovered that he could claim back certain overpayments he wrote: 'As the original conception of expense allowances came from you it is only fair that the announcement that it is turning out better than expected should come from you too.' Of the 1951 increase Clifford voiced the general feeling about 'the vital part you personally have played in bringing about such improvements'. In 1953 a fresh scale of expenses was agreed with the Inspectors and in 1956, after further gestures, Patrick Hunter wrote, 'In case the pleasant task has not been undertaken by someone more suitably placed than myself, I write to thank you for your efforts once again on behalf of the staff'. For the first time the public schools were in competition with the state system as the Burnham Awards not only gave overall increases on the basic scales but gave graduate teachers with good degrees more favourable remuneration. The figures involved seem ludicrously small today. The entire cost of the salary improvements of 1951 was £2200. But an effort was made to bring housemasters' emoluments closer to those prevailing elsewhere and to prevent masters with the best academic qualifications from moving into maintained schools by giving more weight to the tutorial allowances. Inflation had not yet begun to establish the tradition of annual or even termly salary increases and such things still had the charm of novelty.

The construction of a headmaster's house would do something to relieve the chronic shortage of masters' accommodation. One of the Field houses intended for married staff was still occupied by bachelors and the hostel west of Chapel had, in 1950, been taken over by the bursar for offices and rooms for secretaries who had to work through the holidays. Kinvig, housemaster of Walpole, strangely did not use his private side which housed six masters, but they might at any time be dispossessed. In the main building masters lived in a diverse assortment of studies and bedrooms with far-flung bathrooms shared between them. But this was still a time of building licences and strict control of building materials by men with titles such as the Regional Priority Officer, and the Ministry of Education had bureaucratic powers even in the independent sector. The Governors thought it would be easier to obtain permission to convert rather than build and, for a time, there was an extraordinary plan put forward to eject the stuffed birds from the Temple of Concord and consign the headmaster to its cold embrace. Fortunately, the central committee of Allied Schools favoured a new house, perhaps because, when Reynolds remained at Stowe in the holidays, heating and services had to be continued. They persisted with the Ministry, but it was not until 1955 that Reynolds was able to write: 'I consider we can now say that the headmaster's house has begun; workmen are scrambling about the ground but, what is more important, they have built themselves a little hut in which they can make tea.' He had himself selected a site to the south-east of Chatham, but there were many hurdles to be overcome before Kinloss was completed.

There was, however, at the start of the 1950s, a general feeling in the country at large that at last austerity was lessening while, at the same time, the social problems of modern Britain had not yet appeared. Life membership of the newly founded Stowe Templars

Cricket Club could be purchased for one guinea. Even the Pine-apple Ball at the Grosvenor House Hotel in Park Lane cost only two guineas per head. The official school handbook brought to the attention of those interested that the 6.22 from Marylebone could be halted at Finmere by a request to the guard (except on Satur-days). In celebration of the Festival of Britain in 1951 four Old Stoics in New Zealand subscribed to the unusual gift of 150 lbs of bacon for Stowe. The *Epicurean*, banned for twenty years, reap-peared and there was a revival of the school dance for which Reynolds had to arrange partners *en masse* from Bicester. When the names of the Council were for the first time printed in the Blue Book, the reference in the *Stoic* to 'our tyrannical governors' was pure banter and the first Speech Day and Old Stoic Day combined reappeared in the calendar after an interval of twelve years. The military band brought its ceremonial uniforms out of store from the armoury and appeared thirty-strong at the Annual Inspection. As part of the Festival, *Merrie England* was revived. There were no empty seats and, said the *Stoic*, 'Never before has there been such a demand from the audience for encores'. The old gymnasium was packed to capacity while the audience encored the Earl of Essex confidently extolling The Yeomen, 'free as the winds that span, The broad breast of England'. The Corps, now called the C.C.F., under Major McElwee had a record 398 cadets. It was the largest con-tingent at the 1950 Warminster camp and won the competitions for the best laid-out lines and guard mounting. The Stowe Air Section at Hullavington achieved such success in the proficiency exams that a special letter of congratulation came from the Air Marshal in charge. In the summer of 1950 there was a production of *Carmen*, Leslie Huggins had been injured in a hunting accident and the task of training the chorus and orchestra fell to A.A. Negus. J.C. Saunders had again composed a new translation substituting in the famous 'Habanera' the more poetic image:

> Love's a bird you cannot tame him.
> You cannot chain him to your wrist

for the ancient:

> Love will like a wild birdling fly
> Careering whither he may choose

which, as Alasdair Macdonald remarked, reminded him of a toy aeroplane. The Carmen of K.A. Henderson was received with ovations and was dramatically powerful; Escamillo was sung by Colin Graham, later the international opera producer; and Don José by Nicholas Hordern, a stalwart of the Cricket XI, who had to rush from the perils of the crease to those of the Flower Song. Michael Mounsey was again an ingenious designer and the sets included an adroit perspective giving spectators a glimpse of the bull ring through a grille. The Historians followed with *Julius Caesar* in which the Queen's Temple was besieged by the mob brandishing flaming torches. The Rhythm Ramblers, a jazz group in which Charles Macdonald, future second master, played the trombone caused a dispute between Reynolds and Capel Cure who threatened to incite Temple to unruly behaviour if the Ramblers gave a concert in Assembly, adjacent to his house room. 'If Temple were to upset a concert or do anything to create a bad impression I should not hesitate to move the House-Room elsewhere', said Reynolds. 'I have already told you of my attitude to the Rhythm Ramblers and so I consider your last remark as mere melodrama.' It was eventually voted by the masters at a meeting in 1952 that 'the Headmaster would practise euthanasia on the Ramblers at the end of term', but they reappeared from time to time. A second school dance was less tentative than the first. Three hundred balloons were released from the Assembly ceiling and the 'lucky number' ticket was won by the headmaster. There were further celebrity concerts, Frederick Thurston on the clarinet, Gareth Morris on the flute and the Dennis Brain Ensemble. Constant Lambert's 'Rio Grande', Roxburgh's least favourite work, was revived and it was said with awe that J.C. Saunders had mastered sixteen different percussion instruments for his part in it. The whole school learnt five choruses from the *Messiah* and a large group of aspiring string players, so numerous they had to be taught in groups, performed 'Three Blind Mice' to tumultuous applause. There were visits to concerts in London and Oxford including one long remembered when, as Dame Myra Hess was *en route* through a Chopin Sonata, a large lady fainted during the Marche Funèbre and had to be borne from the Sheldonian to its doleful strains.

Nostalgia deceives: the period was in fact not free from anxiety. The war in Korea brought news of casualties, the Cold War was global, and the nuclear threat pervaded the atmosphere of debates

and political lectures. Yet there was still insulation from all the
world's troubles carried daily and nightly in the media and the old
social structures were beginning to reassert themselves as socialist
rule came to an end. A lively picture of Stowe at this time was given
by an English Speaking Union Scholar, Brainerd Stranahan from
Massachusetts, who spent a year in Grafton. He noted the difference in the approach to games. The American played to win; the
boy who showed ability received thorough training and did little
else athletically but his main sport. At Stowe, almost everyone
played and tried their hand at a variety of sports. 'Rugger is played
not so much for victory as for the game itself. As long as a match
is enjoyable no one seems to mind which side had the larger
score – a real contrast to the dolorous grief which enshrouds an
American school when the team loses.' Boy power was still a reality
in houses and he had to discover all the nuances of prefectorial rule;
'Studying the Grafton punishment book like a Bible and inter-
rogating house authorities until they turned a deaf ear away I eked
out my scanty knowledge with ferocious scowls at my small
charges, who, in the first week or two of my reign could have
revolted with complete impunity . . .

'The Winter Term had its Rugger matches in the bitter cold (all
American winter exercise is indoors) with the winds whipping the
rain across the fields in sheets like a deck scene from "Ten Years
before the Mast".' There were house plays, 'to punctuate the dark
skies of the Easter Term; more recently immaculate figures in white
flannels contrasting vividly in the summer sunshine with their
green background; and always such nostalgic memories as P.T.
(an entirely English institution), House Prayers, hymns in Stowe
Chapel and innumerable debates and discussions on various
aspects of Anglo-American affairs . . . Having visited a fair
number of English schools I have become a fanatically loyal Stoic,
and remain convinced that it has been my good fortune to attend
the friendliest and most attractive Public School in England.'

The country was still subject to the notorious 'Smogs' and one
Rugby match, in 1949, against King's School Canterbury, was
played by 'spectres with a phantom ball, watched by invisible but
vociferous spectators'. George I came to the rescue and by revealing himself occasionally through the murk gave the home team
time to re-orientate themselves. For a brief experimental period
Sports Day, often defeated by the spring weather, was moved to

the summer and plans were made to curtail the time spent on house cricket matches and give more attention to the coaching and selection of school sides. Other sports slowly extended their activities. A Stowe sailing team entered the public school races on the Clyde in 1950 and came fourth out of twenty-seven schools, the first three teams having been entered by Scottish schools and hence knowing the waters more intimately. The squash team in 1950 won all matches including those against Eton and Harrow and the tennis team was praised in the *Telegraph* (which like *The Times* devoted many columns to public-school sport) for victory in the Glanvill Cup. Stowe had to win 3–0 because of the complicated arithmetic. R. Lush and J.R.J. Burnham defeated Manchester Grammar School in the last three deciding matches and won the cup for the third time.

Different forms of exercise were taken in the maintenance of the gardens and grounds. With Home Guard and farming duties there had been little time during the war to do estate work but the 1950s saw the beginnings of real concern to study and preserve the Stowe inheritance. Reynolds had first heard of George Clarke through a lunch with a fellow headmaster in Edinburgh. After his visit for interview, George wrote: 'I can't believe that anyone who has wandered round the Park would not want to live there' and he was to devote many years to the study and restoration of the eighteenth-century splendours that seized his imagination at first sight. He was later to give lectures to learned institutions on the subject, but these were based upon practical labour as well as anti-quarian research. Volunteers opted for the work during certain games and Corps periods. Vistas were cleared in the Grecian Valley to and from the Temple of Ancient Virtue and there was clearing carried out in the marshy reaches of the Alder River. 'We reasoned', said George Clarke, who had a great ally in Michael Mounsey, 'that if prehistoric man could build Stonehenge without fork lifts or tractors there was little that twenty intelligent boys with levers and ingenuity could not achieve in Stowe's woods'. Eleven thousand crocus bulbs were planted behind the cricket pavilion in 1951 and Capel Cure began the formation of a water garden. Investigations were made into some of the features that had disappeared, such as the Chinese House raised on poles on an island near the Grotto, the Heliconian Spring near the Doric Arch and the Temple of Contemplation, whose absence as a possible place of detention must sometimes have been regretted. Admiration has to be expressed for the labours of a noble army of martyrs who worked in all weathers in thickets, briars and reed beds for paradise regained. Accumulated silt in the lake by the British Worthies had to be washed away by the school fire engine and the *Stoic* described the scene: dozens of Stoics 'covered in slime and up to their necks in ooze' clearing the swamps. Yet, as one remarked of the house matches that were missed: 'The whistle goes and there's an end of it. But I can come back here all my life and see how this avenue is growing.'

The first years of the new regime also saw broadening Old Stoics' success. In the 1950 General Election, Boyd Carpenter, who had tried in vain to win a public honour for Roxburgh from the Labour Minister of Education, and Tufton Beamish were joined on the Conservative benches by P.B. Lucas. The Labour MPs were defeated though Stephen Taylor who had been a keen biologist ever since his studies with Hankinson, produced a prophetic book, *Shadows in the Sun*, on the conquest of malaria in which he stated that the overcoming of disease would lead to threats of starvation in the Third World. In Australia, P. Howson was elected a member of the House of Representatives. Anthony Quinton became Stowe's first Fellow of All Souls' and J.J. Hartland Swann, a Fellow of the Royal Society of Literature. A.R. Barrowclough came first out of 349 candidates in the Inns of Court Examinations. Lieutenant-Colonel D.B. Drysdale of the Royal Marines led commando troops in the Korean War and was awarded both the D.S.O. and the American Silver Star for gallantry in action. G.B. Michler, an American in Walpole House, was awarded the U.S. Air Medal with four clusters. John Langley became English Amateur Golf Champion fourteen years after his first appearance in the tournament. G.P. Lloyd won the Cambridge pentathlon and quarter mile and J.V.H. Hippisley who had been Captain of Stowe Swimming gained a Cambridge Blue, as did P.C. Murphy. On the Cambridge stage Julian More wrote numerous lyrics and sketches for the Footlights Revue, 'A Flash in the Cam'. Andrew Croft spoke to the Geographical Society at Stowe on his expedition across the wilds of Canada and Kinvig found it hard to bring the meeting to a close. The *Stoic* decided that, for all its brilliant coverage, television could not provide the electricity of the 'personal sharing of time and space with the lecturer who is master of his subject'. It was a

comparatively eventful time for Kinvig for under his auspices the
Geographical Society visited a company at Denham which had
recently developed the ejector seat for jet planes. Several members
of the Society, the President included, were strapped to the pilot's
seat and ejected fifty feet upwards on a vertical runway.

During the summer vacation in 1951 Eric Reynolds travelled to
Skye for a climbing holiday with Simon France, an ex-member of
his house at Rugby. They motored up and stayed at the foot of
the Cuillins. On 2 September, although the weather was a little
uninviting, they decided to climb but, after an hour or two, sensing
worsening conditions, they abandoned the ascent. They were coming down by the eastern gully that splits the 1000 ft rock precipice
of Sron na Ciche when a cartilage gave way in Reynolds' knee and
he began to tumble down the hillside, which was excessively
rough. The cornea of his eye was scratched and his skull cracked.
After a long fall he landed almost at the feet of a party of climbers
who, fortunately, were led by an experienced mountaineer, Edward
Judge. 'For one agonising moment', said Judge, 'no one moved.
Then we dashed to his aid and found that he had suffered such a
severe battering about the head that it seemed doubtful if he could
survive.' France was guided off the crag and he and a novice in the
party despatched to find help. They had to descend several steep
scree slopes and cross a stony hollow at Coire Lagan before
reaching the lower reaches, a journey of about an hour. The team
had just reached a corner on a shelf and this made an easy passage
for a stretcher impossible. Judge and a friend descended the
gully to a point just above a sheer drop and regained the shelf,
fixed ropes along the route and waited for help. 'The gully was an
awesome place at any time,' he recalled, 'but was the more so now.
In the rapidly ebbing daylight thin wisps of mist clung to the
buttresses as if looking on the morbid scene for a while before
drifting away to join the all-enfolding clouds. Our concern was lest
the stretcher would not come in time for us to move the man before
we were enveloped in the approaching darkness.' He had to go
down to encounter the stretcher party and repeat the exhausting
climb again. Reynolds was strapped to the stretcher and brought
down a route that was perilous enough in daylight. 'I remember',
said Judge, 'being amazed at the skill of some of the climbers; with
ankles flexed they seemed to have no difficulty in clinging to the

slabs that but a short while back we had felt it necessary to treat with great respect.' In getting the stretcher off the shelf it was for a time suspended in mid-air on ropes, but eventually it was lowered on to willing shoulders. A steady jog-trot was maintained to Glen Brittle where an ambulance was waiting to take Reynolds to hospital.

The proximity of a potential rescue team had been fortunate. The following night was stormy. A lone climber fell 150 feet and died of injuries before he was discovered. The bad visibility and raging winds forced the climbers who had discovered him to spend the night squeezed into clefts in the rock.

Eric Reynolds, described in one press report as 'a Cambridge schoolmaster', was moved to hospital near Glasgow. When he had recovered sufficiently he was brought back to his home in St Albans. Kenneth Adams, Secretary of Allied Schools, and the Governors arranged for the attention both of a distinguished eye specialist and the president of the Royal College of Physicians. Considering the gravity of the accident, Reynolds made an excellent recovery. He returned to deal with the Certificate Results at Christmas 1951 and resumed his duties in the Spring Term. In March 1952 writing to the Master of Clare College to apologize for a Stoic who had left the Entrance Examination abruptly, feeling he had done badly in the first papers, he added, 'I am now completely restored to health and have thoroughly enjoyed being back this term'. The accident in itself did not shake the fortunes of Stowe but unfortunately it was the first in a series of changes and calamities that were to follow in succession. For the first part of the Autumn Term Clifford acted as head. Ever the disciplinarian, he caned a senior boy for shooting at a matron's cat, but managed to save Rutherford from the consequences of a more than usually disastrous car journey with Stoics abroad. He submitted an interesting report to the Governors. Roxburgh's had always been surprisingly terse and Reynolds followed the same format. Clifford included some information to show that Stowe, contrary to popular belief, was not a school for plutocratic families. The average weekly pocket money was $1/10\frac{1}{2}$ d, the average sum banked with housemasters £2, the average bill for extras £14.10. Although the charge for riding lessons was 7/6d per hour only twelve boys availed themselves of the opportunity. The headmaster of Bedford was a passionate supporter of his Rugby team which he followed to other schools, making forays up and down the touchline and lunging with his umbrella almost into the scrums to indicate which direction the ball should take. 'I am the well-known Headmaster of Bedford', he said to Clifford on arrival. 'And I am the bogus Headmaster of Stowe', came the reply. But Clifford did not survive in office long and went into hospital for a duodenal operation. Capel Cure, himself far from well, saw the school through the remaining weeks. In addition to the administrative upheavals a series of bereavements struck the community: George Clarke's first experience as editor of the *Stoic* was to compile a list of obituaries. A monitor in Walpole died suddenly and inexplicably in the night. Leslie Huggins who had not fully recovered from a riding accident died on Easter Sunday leaving £5000 towards the costs of a new Music School. Harry Webb, Roxburgh's chauffeur for many years and a familiar Stowe figure, died. So too did Pickard-Cambridge who had only recently retired as Chairman of the Council. To secure his services and expertise on their governing bodies the public schools had hunted him in packs, but he retained a particular affection for Stowe which he had first inspected in 1925. He was succeeded as Chairman by Lord Wimborne who had been a Governor of Stowe for little more than a year though his family had a long connection with the Church of England Trust. Clifford was summoned to dinner and recollected the footmen in white gloves who attended upon the meal. There were changes at Allied Schools also where Kenneth Adams, who had long kept watch on the finances of many schools in all their complexity, was replaced by Derek Bateman.

At the October meeting of the Council in 1954 Lord Wimborne paid tribute to all that Reynolds had achieved since 1949. The scholarship entry in 1953 had been higher than for some years and eight were awarded, three to the sons of Old Stoics. In 1954 all ten were awarded for the first time in five years. In March 1955 numbers in the school were the highest ever at 570 and future registrations appeared strong. In 1953 although the year began slowly there were 329 names entered, the highest total since 1947. Nor did supply seem likely to diminish. On 2 September 1952 five 'Old Stoic' births were announced in *The Times* on the same day. Noel Annan, staying overnight in Grafton and noting the familiar names on the lists remarked upon how 'philoprogenitive' his contemporaries were.

Reynolds had also been effective in bringing to the school some outside funds to assist in capital projects. Michael Colston, a boy returning from Canada at the end of the war, had been accepted by Roxburgh on condition that he lost 'that appalling colonial twang' and subsequently his father endowed the Colston Trust to assist with engineering workshops. Sir Aynsley Bridgland provided an endowment fund for buildings and Sir Leslie Plummer another for equipment. In 1951 the possibility of co-operation with the Ministry of Works to begin restoration of the temples was explored and the long process was begun which culminated eventually in the participation of the National Trust. A Ministry grant was made on condition that the school supplemented it. The Temples of Venus and Concord were examined along with the Boycott Pavilions where renovation would help with housing. In 1957, one of the hind legs of 'George's' horse collapsed and the statue was taken to London to await events. The school was in the throes of an economy drive and the Governors did not feel justified in committing funds to repairs. It was hoped that the Ministry might oblige but no rapid decisions were forthcoming.

The Industrial Fund was swifter in action. This Fund had been established by industrialists to remedy what was seen as a national deficiency in scientific and technical education and to make grants to public schools who promised to donate also from their own resources. A team of assessors came to Stowe where a need to strengthen the Science Department had been recognized in the Inspectors' Report of 1955 and in a letter to the Vice-Chairman, Noel Annan. The headmaster was anxious for his part that all boys should have an opportunity of studying Science to 'O' Level. The first proposal was to move the maintenance workshops from Stonemasons' Yard at the back of the school and replace them with laboratories. The cost would be £20,000 partly covered by a grant of up to two thirds but still requiring £7000 to achieve. Eventually the Industrial Fund offered less and the school had to find more but Legal and General thought the opportunity should not be lost and offered to advance 75 per cent of the school share with an additional mortgage. In the final scheme the Gibbs and Adams classroom blocks were adapted, as a migration of all the school's resident work force would have been expensive and disruptive.

Inflation was beginning to make its impact and everywhere capital projects, of the kind so necessary at Stowe, were outrunning the estimates. Plans for a School Hall had to be revised, but it was one of Reynolds' chief projects and he was anxious that it should not be abandoned. He reflected that the legacy of Dr Huggins for the building of a Music School might be used if that were to form part of a new Hall. Since it had ceased to be considered as a potential headmaster's house, Concord had been earmarked for Music. Aylesbury museum had expressed an interest in the bird collection as well as a collection of stuffed animals, a later benefaction, which remained at rest in a London storehouse. G. Forsyth Lawson, an architect from Banbury, was instructed to draw up a double design for Hall and Music School at an estimated cost of £16,000 as against the original figure of £12,000. (At one moment there was even a suggestion that masters' studies and bedrooms might be included in this potentially least peaceful corner of the school.) The level was to be raised by 7 feet to give more spacious dimensions to the aircraft hangars which formed the basis of the construction. In 1954 Reynolds could report that the Friends of Stowe had offered just over £8000 and this, combined with the Huggins request and £3500 from the Plummer fund, would produce about £17,000. The death of Roxburgh in 1954 had brought a further £2500 to the Friends, and £1500 had been subscribed as a memorial to him. In 1955 Reynolds was writing to say that the architect had done a superb job and that 'there is nothing to suggest that the building will look like a hangar in search of an aeroplane'. But the costs had soon risen to £27,000 and, as the school was fully stretched by the headmaster's house, the delivery of bricks for the Hall was for a time suspended. Eventually the Friends guaranteed up to £23,000, the costs having mounted to £33,000 during construction. At Reynolds' last Speech Day in 1958, Peter Sherwood, on behalf of the Friends of Stowe, handed over the keys of the almost completed building to Lord Wimborne. It was an amenity without which the school would have been greatly embarrassed in the years following and it owed its inception to the persistence of the headmaster at a time when rising costs were a new and alarming phenomenon.

The story of the headmaster's house, his other chief concern, followed much the same pattern. When a licence was finally granted the Governors stipulated that it should not cost above £10,000 but the surpluses of 1952/3 quickly changed to deficits as the salary scales and costs of living rose. The Legal and General offered a special loan though Mr Lawson's plan was discarded in favour of one by the company's own architects. This plan, too, turned out to be well in excess of £12,000 and the scale had to be modified, an attic floor being added to compensate for the reduction of the ground floor area. The final account came to almost £15,000 but, as Reynolds pointed out, it gave the Governors much more scope in their choice of successors to himself.

The 1955 Inspectors' Report had commented on the absence of younger masters with high academic qualifications. It is generally agreed that when the rare opportunities for appointments arose the headmaster made good use of them. George Clarke has already been mentioned, Colin James, who came as chaplain, went on eventually to be Bishop of Winchester. Angus Watson, who joined the Music Department, was later, at Winchester College, one of the foremost Directors of Music in the country. Joe Bain, from St John's College, Cambridge, did for Stowe drama what Huggins had done for music and produced a series of plays which would have been deemed impossible in many schools at the time. David Donaldson, an Athletics Blue, went on to be headmaster of Kimbolton. R.J. Morris was a Cambridge Cricket Blue. R.C. Pinchbeck who came from Durham University to help with Rugby and swimming and take charge of Physical Training, later commanded the C.C.F.

Colin James had been working as a curate in Stepney, (the East End press referred to him jovially as 'the ginger-haired jester of St Dunstan's') and had to await the return of his superiors from a conference in the U.S.A. before he could accept the post. 'The Bishops of London and Stepney have now returned in their Stetsons and Ten-Gallon hats', he wrote, 'and both have given their approval to my leaving this parish.' Windsor-Richards had misgivings that he might move too far from the Low Church position of the school. In Stepney he was 'Father James' and the Confirmation Service was announced as the 'sacrament' of Confirmation. Both Reynolds and Windsor-Richards lamented the absence of Pickard-Cambridge who had taken an interest in doctrinal questions but both felt that in the growing secular mood of the time a slightly more 'Catholic' approach was probably a more successful one with the public schoolboy. The question of Confession was more dangerous and James set out a long memorandum on the subject preliminary to discussions with housemasters. Kenneth Adams of Allied Schools was horrified when he learnt that the idea had even been mooted.

James enjoyed working with Reynolds whose commitment to the school and friendliness as host he respected. Reynolds he felt was free from any deviousness, a quality which Clifford also singled out in his recollections. 'Like Reynolds you were speaking your real thoughts', he once wrote to Christopher Turner.

Brian Stephan had followed Major Haworth in Chandos and Windsor-Richards succeeded Capel Cure in Temple. In 1955 Bruce Barr took over Grafton from Clifford and two years later John Uttley followed Kinvig in Walpole. Kinvig had been a sick man in his final terms with two major operations and a long absence, but it was recalled that he and Archer in the Heroic Age had once saved the day for the masters' XI by scoring a century in partnership with the last wicket.

Clifford also, though only 54, had aged considerably, worried unduly about the growth of faction within the Common Room, even cutting himself off from the Old Graftonian Dinners, and trying the patience of the governing body. He made the delays in building the headmaster's house the subject of a crusade and came into collision with the Council over extensions to the Grafton private side added by an architect of his own choosing. E.G. Wykes of Legal and General who had a grandson at Stowe did not like being called 'Grandpa' at governing body meetings, which was trivial enough but part of the concern at Clifford's spontaneous combustion. On his Brackley property he launched a market garden. 'The poultry and flower business is using up a great deal of his energy', wrote Reynolds to Annan who was by now the most influential member of the governing body, 'and when he is not actually giving each "petit poussin" the sort of House magisterial treatment that he used to give to Grafton he is writing effusive advertisements for pedigree daffodils and narcissi.' Annan suggested quiet disengagement and in a letter, the draft of which was covered with erasures and rewritings, Reynolds accepted Clifford's resignation with full acknowledgement of the loyal service that had been rendered. In retirement, Clifford made long sea voyages, one to visit his son in New Zealand, on which he must have taken his typewriter as reams on school and family history arrived in the post. A great deal of panache survived. On crossing the international dateline he dated his letter, 'Tomorrow and tomorrow and tomorrow'. He continued to attend the Pineapple Ball and sometimes visited the prefects' mess and recounted tales of the 'quaint masters who taught long ago and could drive J.F. to distraction'. He viewed the rise of the Drayson Sports Hall with suspicion as a luxury which ran counter to the old spirit, which dug the tennis courts and levelled the playing fields with voluntary labour; he became a devoted, if exhausting, admirer of Christopher and Lucia Turner, 'Oxbridge United'. The innocent purchaser of the house of Peter Agnew, a later Chairman of the Governors, wrote to complain that he was receiving telephone calls at all hours of the night from 'a gentleman called Fritz' who demanded stern and immediate action on Stowe.

The declining powers and departure of Clifford left an unhappy situation. Capel Cure had died of cancer in 1953. Had he been in good health and cooperative he could, in the fashion of the eighteenth-century politics which Stowe had witnessed so often, have brought a considerable 'political interest' over to Reynolds' support. He was regarded as 'the unrivalled interpreter of J.F.'s constructive liberalism'. Playford was close to retirement and even that was giving problems. Although nominally one of the chaplains he had played no part in services for many years. Patrick Hunter, on a visit to Eton, had discovered that Eton masters were not given leave freely for Henley Week and expressed forcible views on the nurture of this legend at Stowe in the interests of Playford. In 1953 he had reluctantly to give up Bruce but, in order to qualify for a full pension, would have to stay until the age of sixty-two. This had been agreed in 1948 and, as Reynolds pointed out, was an exceptional concession. Even so there was some friction over the precise term of his departure and the repercussions on pension, and he would have liked to stay on longer. Reynolds, who was good with figures, indicated that the effect upon pension was £210 per annum and 13/4d decrease in the lump sum: 'In the next school year considerable readjustments will be made in the time tables and it will be necessary to replace you by a man who is possibly a scientist. I am being continually urged to cut down on staff and, although this is clearly impossible, there would certainly be no question of extra manpower which your retention would mean.'

Like many bachelors young and old who left Stowe Playford rapidly became a happily married man. Returning to Stowe with his wife and a young relative, he drove straight past a notice saying 'No cars beyond this point' and drew up beside a huge pile of logs. Deprived of the lusty axemanship he had enjoyed at Stowe he advanced rubbing his hands and exclaiming: 'Ah! these are just what I need' to be told by a boy that they were on the contrary 'reserved for the poor of Buckingham'. He was a gentle giant who was said to have only once used his cane, when a boy's wrongdoing caused a soldier to lose his rank, but a sturdy defender of the members of Bruce. Experts in the lapidary style adopted by school magazines will discern what lay behind the sentence in the *Stoic* valediction: 'He could be over-sensitive in their defence, which led him sometimes to under-rate the good faith of his colleagues'.

Patrick Hunter succeeded Clifford as second master. No one knew Stowe better and his credentials in administration and tutorial work were impeccable, but he had not been a housemaster and it was in the area of morale and discipline in houses that weaknesses in the organization began to appear. With the majority of housemasters non-resident the control of events often rested with the matrons who, though they might be ladies of stature, were unlikely to be equal to every occasion. They were assisted sometimes by junior house tutors but, while a housemaster can go anywhere in his house without supposedly snooping, a junior master cannot. The tasks were not easy. The houses had grown by occupying rooms and dormitories as the need arose and as workmen finished the conversions. House distribution within the main building resembled an ethnic map of the Balkans and the inflated numbers and over-crowding did not help. When Reynolds himself was secluded in Kinloss the ultimate deterrent of the headmaster's close proximity was abandoned and advantage could be taken.

Externally there was ample evidence of continued excellence. In July 1957, Earl Mountbatten made the inspection of the C.C.F. which was over 400 strong. In 1953, for example, out of 57 boys eligible to join as recruits, 56 had done so. Mountbatten's visit was regarded with some apprehension. Rumours flew that he had given one other famous school an extra parade, the Survey Section was given a full term's notice to polish up their brasses, the portico of the South Front was renovated. All went well and Mountbatten, who was attended by Lieutenant-Commander J.E.C. Kennon, a future Chairman of Governors, duly signed the Distinguished Visitors' Book in the traditional green of the First Sea Lord, expressed his pleasure and had particular praise for the band: 'Many cadet forces hire or borrow bands for the occasion; others I have heard one wishes they did! But here, I must say the band is second to none.'

The aunt of a boy in Temple, herself an experienced teacher, wrote after attending a Chapel service to Capel Cure in 1953: 'The quiet reverent conduct of the boys, the dignity and beauty of the surroundings, the appreciative singing, and memorable reading of the lessons by a senior scholar have imprinted themselves in my mind for all time.' Capel Cure who had played a part in the compilation of *Cantata Stoica* replied of the hymns: 'Even we who hear them very often never stop loving them'. Five years later a correspondence arose in the *Telegraph* about the selection of a public school and a Stowe mother wrote of her impressions: 'When I sit in Chapel and watch the quiet and orderly manner in which nearly 600 boys take their seats and listen to the well rehearsed singing and fine accompaniments and prefects reading the Lessons, I realize this is the heart of the matter.'

Old Stoics, however, scattered and mobile during the war were now able to meet in frequent session and make comparisons with the past. All schools have good and bad seasons in sport and fixture lists would be illogical if the results over the years did not have a reasonable balance between victories and defeats. In the early 1950s Stowe had to face Ted Dexter of Radley who was held in awe as much on the Rugby pitch as the cricket field. In 1952 he scored 20 of Radley's 27 points but even so Stowe was the first school side that had not been beaten by more than 30. The XV finished that season by defeating St Edward's and (against predictions) Harrow. D.I. Brown described the 1955 season, when preliminary coaching was given by R.M. Bartlett O.S. of Cambridge and England, as 'The best possible answer to the slings and arrows from outraged Old Stoics including "my special critics from East Anglia".' Bedford, St Edward's, Radley and Harrow were all beaten without any of those teams crossing the Stowe line. Satisfaction was compounded by the fact that the Second XV of that year won all but one of its matches. Success continued into 1956 and the season was compared with that of 1946/7 when Bartlett himself had played. One try by A.J. Arnold 'will live in the memory of spectators for years', said the *Stoic*, whose prose in the sports section did not scorn hyperbole. The new pitch at Oundle was 'at the top of a mountain underneath a leaden sky', the Stowe defence on one occasion 'continued to die obstinately in the last ditch', and P.L. Morris felled the Oundle full back 'with a peculiarly murderous tackle'. The mud at Harrow made it 'impossible to distinguish individual forwards, except perhaps McConnell by his feline pounces'.

The 1953 cricket season seemed to revive memories of pre-war contests. There was a young and harmonious side and J.C. Witham scored Stowe's first post-war century. When the Radley team came to Stowe and the 'almost legendary Dexter' was stumped by Dew, the Stowe Captain, the appeal rocked George in his saddle. It was an exciting match with the Radley XI which had not lost, so it was said, for six years, 100 runs behind and fighting desperately for a draw. The fielding was alert and there was an excellent catch by the Warden of Radley beyond the boundary – in defence of local VIPs and parents. The last Radley pair did not even run lest they were run out and for the final ball the entire Stowe team was within a yard or two of the bat. The Radley player missed and a draw resulted.

There were triumphs in other sports also. In 1952 there was a premature heat wave. The swimmers cleared the reeds from the lake and pursued a course of intensive training under Mr Pinchbeck. Most of the matches were won and for the first time, Wellingborough, which possessed an indoor pool, was defeated, Stowe taking first and second places in every event. Late in 1952 Henry Cotton came to give a golf demonstration and soon afterwards the British Golf Foundation began to give help with coaching. The Stowe golfers were invited to join a select competition between Eton, Harrow, Winchester, Rugby, Charterhouse and Marlborough instigated by Gerald Micklem. Under the captaincy of L.G.B. Williamson Stowe won the Micklem Trophy for the first time in 1952 beating Harrow by 4 matches to 1. Work was begun on the reconstruction of the golf course. In 1954, the tennis team, including a second generation of Avorys, won all thirteen matches though the prestigious Youll Cup still remained elusive. R.E. Lucas, the school secretary, whose time at Stowe went back to 1923 and who had been principal tennis coach, died in 1955, unhappily just before the period when victory in the Youll Cup became almost automatic. In 1955 the tennis team defeated Repton, a school with a strong tennis tradition, in another uniformly successful season. The Sailing Club continued the tradition of self-help by felling trees on the Boat-House Island and clearing the lakeside to build a jetty and make a dinghy pool. A grant was made for two Cadet sailing boats.

There were still many, however, who thought that sporting conquests should build up in an arithmetical progression. Others, with more reason, wished to see the number of open awards increase for these were always good indicators of a school's academic status and at Stowe the totals in the 1950s rarely rose above an annual four or five. The strong links between the school and Oxford and Cambridge had rested on the pre-war ease of entry and Roxburgh's persuasive and often apologetic letters of application. Times were changing. State scholarships and supplementary awards were enabling many more grammar-school entrants to compete with a single-mindedness that the distractions of Stowe did not allow. Reynolds thought the autonomy of the Sides in different subjects led to rivalry rather than the creation of an academic *corps d'élite*, but the system was too deeply entrenched to alter. There was ample intellectual activity: the XII Club heard papers on subjects such as 'Platonic Idealism in Shelley' and 'Gerard Manley Hopkins'. The 100th Meeting was attended by Gavin Maxwell and Noel Annan and discussed 'Chinese Communism'. The Symposium heard Nicholas Lyell on 'Atomic Energy in War and Peace' and S.J.F. Ramsay was allowed to bring the snakes essential to his address into a meeting. There were papers on 'Thomas Creevey' and a gastronomical comparison between England and France. The Classical Society studied the maps of Eratosthenes and Ptolemaeus, heard C.A. Rodewald, Clifford's brother-in-law, on 'Xenophanes, first of the Sophists', and Charles Macdonald on 'Greek Astronomy from 585 BC. A new society for scientists, 'The Nucleus', was established to investigate some of the higher problems of modern science; the Vitruvians met Sir Stanley Spencer; and A.E. Hopwood of Grenville spoke to the Natural History Society on the 'Wallabies of Staffordshire', one of the few wild herds in Britain. The Young Farmers were instructed on 'Heredity in Cattle' and the Music Club on 'John Dowland'. The Young Farmers also demonstrated the technical wonders of the new Land Rover, which could battle up slopes and cross the roughest terrain. Unfortunately it sank in the marshes with the Chatham matron on board and had to be rescued with capstan and winch.

Year by year the Historians contended with nocturnal chills or buzzing insects to present Shakespeare before the Queen's Temple. *Othello* in 1951 evoked the definitive observation on the play from a mother: 'I'm just terrified of losing my handkerchief ever again';

Hamlet followed, with the Temple setting accentuating the Court elements. In the *A Midsummer Night's Dream* Freddie Archer's C.C.F. recruits swung in the lighted trees to enhance the magical atmosphere. In *Coriolanus* Oliver Plowright plunged in a spectacular fall down the Temple steps. Modern schoolboys sharing the accents of disc jockeys and television presenters would be surprised at the upper-class tones which still prevailed at this time. J.C. Saunders, reviewing Mounsey's production of *Richard of Bordeaux* by the Congreve noted that 'for the first time in our recollection "power" was not "pah" though occasionally a "Juke" took his place among the aristocracy.' During a performance of Galsworthy's *Escape*, life imitated art. There was a genuine breakout from Dartmoor and two convicts were still at large when the curtains parted. During a roadside scene involving a stolen car, the machine started suddenly of its own volition and cleared the stage more speedily than intended. When the Historians' *Julius Caesar* was beset with drenching rain the togas had to be dried for the next evening and the McElwees' garden was said to resemble a sail-maker's yard. As the new Roxburgh Hall rose the last productions were given in the old gymnasium, more forlorn than ever after a tree had fallen across the roof. Andrew Rudolf, future head of History, appeared in *The Merchant of Venice* and was described as bringing 'a touch of Danny Kaye to the part of Launcelot Gobbo'. Brian Stephan wrote: 'Perhaps the sentimental here and there, past and present, may spare the passing tribute of a sigh for the ram-shackle building which, with its whimsical shortcomings, has for so long tried tempers and challenged resourcefulness and has seen the first tentative efforts of not a few now established on the professional stage.'

There were house plays. Temple mounted *Trial by Jury* and *H.M.S. Pinafore* with orchestra and a staff play, *Hay Fever*, was the first since 1940. George Clarke, 'looking no older than the Sixth Form', said the *Stoic*, played the juvenile lead; Marjorie Dams the actress-mother and Clifton Kelynack, the new Music Director, the shy young diplomat. The Cine Section, as well as making newsreels of school events, began a feature film based on Orwell's *Animal Farm* in which the boys ejected the masters only to be subjected to the tyranny of the First XV. There is no record of who played the part of Boxer, though perhaps the bursar saw himself in the role. Combined with a host of other commitments, the relentless programme of drama, valuable as it was, must have militated against the long evenings of study which boys from the grammar schools or the great day public schools could pursue unhindered. Rising standards demanded longer rehearsals and the March 1953 editorial of the *Stoic* commented on the tiredness which prevailed: 'shortly before the performances it scarcely seems worth while going to bed at all'.

The range of musical concerts was no less wide. There were recitals by Kendall Taylor on piano, and Alan Loveday on violin, Archie Camden on bassoon, and Joan and Valerie Trimble on two pianos. Colin Davis, then unknown as a conductor, played the clarinet in the Mozart Quintet in A Major. The Harvard Glee Club included Stowe in a very restricted tour. J. Carter Brown who had been an American Scholar at Stowe was the Narrator in Stravinsky's *Oedipus Rex* and was later to hold the prestigious position of Director of the National Gallery of Art in Washington. *The Beggar's Opera* was put on in 1955, younger string players were able to participate in the *A Midsummer Night's Dream* Overture with specially edited parts, and the whole school had a unison role in *Behold All Flesh is as the Grass* in the Brahms Requiem. Energies were also absorbed by the house art competitions which Michael Mounsey had established. By 1954 all houses participated and in the Speech Day exhibition of 1955 there were 150 Stoics with work represented.

Following success in clearing the Alder river, which had been neglected for twenty years, the Landscape Force turned its attention to the Oxford Water. Windsor-Richards had been an engineer before he entered the Church and took charge. In 1938 a breach had been made in the retaining bank through which the contents of the lake escaped. This had now to be filled, and a concrete dam constructed with a sluice at the base. The biggest task was the removal of thousands of tons of sludge into which the trunks of trees and other large objects had sunk. Fortunately the school had strong links with the McAlpine family and machinery was generously supplied to complete the operation. After seven months of labour the sluice was closed at 4 p.m. on 11 November 1955 and within twelve days the Oxford Water had returned to its old level. The picturesque Oxford Bridge was restored and the entry to the Park and the first glimpse of Stowe which visitors received was by these efforts greatly enhanced.

By 1957 it could be said that a new Stowe was being revealed – forgotten vistas and long-obscured groves. Houses were allotted different areas to manage. With block and tackle trees were hauled from the Oxford Water, the Grecian Valley and the environs of Concord were cleared of brambles and saplings, views across the lake were opened up as the islands were pruned of vegetation. On 9 May 1957, two Stoics were out running near the Cobham Monument in a thunderstorm when there was a dazzling flash and a titanic burst of thunder. They raised their eyes to heaven and Lord Cobham had disappeared. The lightning conductor had been severed and the statue dashed to the ground. The head had been parted from the body but, as Reynolds sadly reported to the Finance Committee, the crock of gold, which it was said to contain, proved to be a myth.[1]

Old Stoic distinctions were now coming so thick and fast that they must be briefly summarized. One of the most notable intellectual achievements of the time was the publication in 1953 of the researches of Michael Ventris on Linear B in the *Journal of Hellenistic Studies*. In 1936 there had been an exhibition of Cretan finds in Burlington House and Sir Arthur Evans, conducting a party from the school, told the Stoics that certain inscribed tablets defied interpretation. Ventris, aged 14, ventured a question and conceived a strong wish to take up the challenge. He was to be an architect by profession but philological puzzles always fascinated him. Working on the assumption that the Minoan signs were syllables and a form of Greek, he had his theories given credibility when American archaeologists discovered more tablets accompanied with drawings in Pylos and Mycenae. The unravelling of the mysteries of Linear B also pushed Greek civilization back into a remoter past and proved for the Greek language a continuous history of thirty-three centuries, rivalled only by the Chinese.

In 1954 S.A.M. Adshead won the Gladstone Memorial Exhibition at Oxford and S.E. Digby the Derby Studentship at Cambridge, a remarkable double. M.A.R. Freeman of Corpus, Cambridge was awarded a Special Prize for the best Science degree

---

[1] One sign of the growing interest in Stowe was the arrival of Sacheverell Sitwell and entourage unannounced who came across Eric Reynolds and demanded a tour of the Gothic Temple. They were quite unaware of his identity and at the close of the visit Sacheverell paused meditating a tip – then decided against it.

of the year. Noel Annan was awarded the James Tait Black Prize for his biography of Leslie Stephen and three years later was elected Provost of King's College. R.A.L. Black became Professor of Mining Engineering at the University of Witwatersrand. In 1953 J.W.R. Kempe, later headmaster of Gordonstoun, achieved the first North Face ascent of Kabru, a Himalayan peak of 24,000 feet, reaching the summit on the same day as the conquest of Everest. P.J. Ellam, with one companion, crossed the Atlantic in a $19\frac{1}{2}$ ft half-ton yacht, part of a longer sixteen-month voyage. P.S. Ashton joined a Cambridge expedition up the Amazon and gave a vivid account of dangerous encounters including the sight of an Anaconda snake swallowing whole a fully grown sow. Sir Harold Robinson, one of the first prefects in 1923, became Stowe's first Knight. John Boyd-Carpenter became Minister of Transport and Aviation. An exhibition of the published writings of Old Stoics ranged from Michael Ventris to the Highway Code for which the Minister had responsibility. A.A.D. Montague Browne was Private Secretary to Sir Winston Churchill.

In sport, R.M. Bartlett was capped for England, R.B. Skepper was British Junior Ski Champion in 1956 and V.V. Pope Army Bobsleigh Champion in 1957. D.P. Wells was the first Stoic Rowing Blue, a member of the Oxford crew. R. Lush was Captain of Squash, also at Oxford, and P.G. Harris, Captain at Cambridge. W.P. Cooper was Captain of Cambridge Golf. W.M. Patterson in 1956 was a further Rugby Blue for Cambridge. R.S.L. Pearman played golf for Oxford and won the University Skiing Championships.

H.J. Bonning won the Queen's Sword on passing out of H.M.S. *Devonshire*; it was the first time that the sword was won by a member of the Technical Arms. In the same year, 1952, H.I. Meynell was runner-up for the Sword of Honour at Sandhurst. In Korea, Major C.H. Mitchell won the D.S.O. for gallantry, Commander Cradock-Hartopp the D.S.C. and Major C.E. Taylor the M.C. Second Lieutenant R.J. Ruhemann, a scholar of Stowe who had been an outstanding head of school, was killed in the Korean War after having engaged the enemy in hand-to-hand fighting with four comrades, enabling the remainder of his patrol to withdraw to safety. He was Mentioned Posthumously in Despatches. Major J.A. Lloyd-Williams won the M.C. for gallantry in Malaya. Old Stoics were prominent in motor racing.

P.N. Whitehead won the Grand Prix d'Endurance at Le Mans in a Jaguar XK 120 in 1951, the first time that the event had been won by a British driver for sixteen years. In 1954 he won the Twelve-Hour Sports Car Race at Rheims as co-driver at an average speed of 104 miles per hour. N.R. Cunningham Reid won the 1000 Kilometre Race at Nurburgring in 1957 as co-driver of an Aston Martin.

Another Old Stoic venture was the founding of Aiglon College in Switzerland by J.C. Corlette who had left Stowe at sixteen and been sent to the Alps for health reasons. After the war, without buildings or assured supply of pupils, he founded a multilingual school with aspirations towards international understanding. The college grew rapidly in the 1950s and 'J.C.' became as familiar a centrepiece as 'J.F.' at Stowe.

The decision of Eric Reynolds and the governing body to come to a parting of the ways in 1958 has very little explanation in print or in writing. There were still some who unrealistically wished for the pre-war meteoric rise of Stowe to continue. There were rumours of indiscipline and unrecorded Common Room arguments and comparisons with the days of Roxburgh. The governing body itself had little cohesion. There were the appointees of the Legal and General, the 'insurance magnates' as Clifford called them, who guarded the finances; the elderly or retired clergymen nominated by the Church of England Trust, regularly replaced as they fell ill and resigned; some in public life such as Boyd-Carpenter and W.S. Morrison, Speaker of the House, whose public duties made attendance difficult; and a group of Old Stoics, Noel Annan, Peter Agnew and Peter Sherwood, who were not altogether happy about the ties with Allied Schools and wished to see a more independent and dynamic Stowe. They were subjected to frequent, sometimes acrimonious, criticism by Old Stoics who considered, to quote one apropos the Cricket XI: 'The School does not count as it should and did'. Reynolds' capacities had not been diminished by the mountaineering accident but his facial injuries had been severe and slow to heal and were a set-back to one who had played debonair roles on the stage and had an authoritative presence in public. Masters who came for interview found themselves on occasion talking with a profile or silhouette. The new establishment at Kinloss was remote from the main trade routes of school business. In addition many of the older masters were now reaching the end of their time and it was thought that a new generation would benefit from strong direction and a sweeping away of the last vestiges of the older liberal style. Hart Dyke, Archer and Kinvig retired in 1957 and E.S. Dewing a year later. Modest to the last Hart Dyke had offered to leave at any time when a suitable replacement could be found. On the eve of his retirement came the familiar letter: 'Dear Reynolds, I am going to give you the shock of your life. I am now engaged to be married and hoping naturally to be married as soon as possible . . .'

Tales of lack of discipline were the harder to counter as the very isolation of Stowe and its removal from public gaze made it a subject of conjecture. Nevertheless, it seems that all was not well. In Roxburgh's last years Dewing had complained about aimless groups of boys in Buckingham. In 1954 there was a small shoplifting incident which reached the Sunday press and grew as sides were taken over the merits of private flogging or public prosecution for rich or poor. One of the items taken had been a bean slicer valued at 2/6d. One reader who had been wanting to find this rare unobtainable implement delightedly wrote to the shop and sent a postal order. The governing body thought the headmaster had dealt properly with the offence but asked for fuller information in such matters. Greater affluence began to disrupt the careful supervision of adolescents. Pre-war Stowe had been part of a class system but parents controlled the purse strings tightly and the young were not over-indulged. Now there were new problems. Eric Reynolds received an enquiry from the publishers of marriage guidance literature about the despatch of a tome called *Planned Families and Sexology* ordered through the *News of the World*. 'It was far-seeing of you to make an enquiry', he replied, 'and I very much appreciate the trouble you have taken. Your correspondent is only a comparatively small boy and I cannot see any reason for bothering to send him the literature which he has asked for.' Alasdair Macdonald in masters' meetings had already raised the question of new types of magazines now obtainable unknown to previous generations. There were a few isolated incidents which seemed to show that the housemastering left something to be desired. When George I was lifted from his horse and sent for repairs the animal was left on its plinth. A group of boys filled the frame with buckets of water by night and the result was a performance more usually associated with the Brewer's Dray, which lasted interminably and became a subject of unedifying interest.

House dances became noisier and more energetic affairs and there were the first signs of the growing reluctance of seniors to wield authority.

A few years earlier a Stoic had written of the significance of the cedar tree where on warm summer evenings 'when there is no Prep' boys could clamber and recline, chatting idly and gazing out supposedly over five counties'. Opportunities for such moments of calm and pleasant idleness were departing. The building programme had now been achieved and the staff salary scales were beginning to match those elsewhere. The tumult of the 60s had not yet fallen on schools but, since the months of Suez, there had been a widespread feeling in many places that the old order was crumbling and needed some stern reinforcement. Early in 1958 Eric Reynolds announced his retirement for the summer and his battle for recovery of health gave ample grounds for the decision. He could never have been able to establish the close links that had bound Old Stoics to the school under Roxburgh, who had followed their lives from childhood, but one parent expressed the regrets of many at his departure: 'It may please you to know that you hold an exceptionally warm place in the hearts of my son and other Stoics whom I have met in the last four years which may be some recompense for the trials and tribulations they undoubtedly cause you.'

9

Donald Crichton-Miller I

Donald Crichton-Miller first came as assistant master to Stowe in 1934. To attract him from Bryanston he had been offered the post of head of the lower school. He was ambitious and in little over a year Roxburgh found himself writing in support of applications for more responsible posts. Although he remarked, 'Personally, I had hoped that Mr Crichton-Miller would stay a little longer before he moved on', his comments were wholly complimentary. Crichton-Miller, Cambridge Blue and Scottish International, was famed as a dauntless Rugby player: 'The boys regard him as an unequalled coach of Rugger forwards. He is genuinely interested in Education. His honour is undoubted and I have never found him lacking in tact.' At 29 he was headmaster of Taunton School and probably the youngest member of the Headmasters' Conference. The war provided a test of his administrative skills at first. Eltham College and later, after Dunkirk, King's School, Rochester, were evacuated to Taunton and had to be housed and educated in all manner of makeshift premises. The war had also brought a personal loss. His younger brother, a Balliol Scholar and a brilliant physicist ('very bright and much more like the old man than I am') was lost while parachuting at night to carry out tests on airborne troop equipment.

In 1945 he went back to Fettes College, Edinburgh, where, as a boy, Selwyn Lloyd had been his head of house and he had risen to be head of school. There was a great deal of modernizing to be done at Fettes in 1945 and so he was well accustomed to battles over building regulations and maintenance. He epitomized the

forceful Scottish dominie and was well thought of by Brendan
Bracken, the politician and great friend of Loretto, for his work in
Edinburgh. Bracken suggested his name to the Stowe Governors
through Buchanan, who knew that Stowe was seeking someone
who would impose a bracing regime on a supposedly indolent community. Whatever the school, choice of one of its former masters
for headmaster is never without risk. Stowe had more than its
share of men who had sought promotion unavailingly. In Crichton-
Miller's case the situation was aggravated by the fact that he had
been master of the lower school with certain public privileges, such
as addressing Assembly, which had not been shared with contemporaries. The Governors also considered Oliver Van Oss, Eton
housemaster, who was later headmaster of Charterhouse. He was
an expansive and warm-hearted man who swept all before him, but
Old Etonians on the Council were divided and Crichton-Miller's
record appeared to be proven.

He was in no doubt that he had been charged with the task
of enforcing a more rigorous regime. Lord Wimborne, who had
had his share of admonition and advice from Old Stoics, assured
him that changes of staff would have his full support. Heavy satire
in the *Epicurean*, 'The New Sheriff comes to Town', had a ring of
truth: 'All right, you guys! The game's up. I've come from the
North Country where men are real men, where the coffee's so
strong you can float a horse-shoe on it, where men speak with their
fists and never read books.' His opening address to the Common
Room was later a bone of contention. His homily on efficiency, to
which the audience was already well accustomed, was accompanied by the veiled threat that some of the listeners might not
be in their posts a year hence. Crichton-Miller, suggesting fuller
reports than those given by his predecessors, (welcomed by the
Governors) submitted one that teemed with unpalatable facts. The
summer's 'O' Levels, he declared, 'had been almost the worst' in
the school's history, 'through misguided policy rather than bad
teaching'. Progress on repairs had been slow: 'We have been at
work for nearly two years on the Temple of Venus, not a large
building, and it looks as though two years will be needed to effect
repairs on the statue of George I, about which many questions have
been asked.' (George I was found languishing in an East End
warehouse as Allied Schools had been unwilling to pay for restoration.) A planning committee was needed: 'It is difficult to see how

some new buildings have been sited where they are.' He found seventeen 'temporary' huts around the grounds, some disused, some unjustified. One had been appropriated as a garage by a master who lived out but liked his car to be under cover by day. The unsafe Leoni Arch had from early days been supported on brick and concrete fillings, 'a prominent reproach' which had greeted generations of parents on arrival. Stowe Church bore the scars of disrepair worsened while 'a feud between High and Low Churchmen' on the staff delayed action. He particularly blamed Allied Schools for allowing fabric and gardens, which should have been unique assets, to become symbols of poor stewardship, though it might have been wiser to recognize what Clarke, Mounsey and the boy workers had achieved by their own recent efforts. The bursar and his men had in 1957 stemmed the worst breaches in the roof of Stowe Church, always a financial burden to the governors, and redecorated part of the interior as a memorial to Marjorie Dams, to designs by Michael Mounsey.

Crichton-Miller was particularly scathing on the distribution of salaries. Although increases had been given the scales were complicated: 'Our present system is neither simple enough to be understood and therefore attractive to young masters, nor sufficiently equitable to the more senior.' A patchwork of small allowances covered the duties of assistant housemasters, those in charge of minor sports and responsibilities such as the cinema: 'Even the number of them seems to be in doubt, as I recently discovered that some houses had two official assistants while in another case I found that the housemaster did not know which of his assistants was being paid, if either. The fact is that an enterprising young man can collect three or four of these small payments while other people are undertaking equally important work without payment at all.' Benefits in kind ('Ever since the War Independent Schools have sought methods of remunerating their staff which will defeat the Inland Revenue') could soon be taken for granted. 'A limit of usefulness can be reached in attempting to give Masters unseen and therefore untaxed remuneration. Eventually it becomes invisible not only to the men themselves but, even more important, to people who are considering employment at the School.' Nor was there aught for the Governors' comfort in his survey of the fire precautions: 'There is very little knowledge of the alarm system and when the Captain of the Fire Team (Clerk of Works) showed me where the main switch was he received an electric shock as it is not properly insulated. When I asked a Housemaster what he would do to fight a fire at night I was told, "we must not have a fire at night after the men's canteen closes".' He thought that fire drills were well carried out but was doubtful about the chances of the bursar and his men drawing water from the lakes in less than half an hour.

One of the first changes to be made was the addition of an extra half-holiday each week, the better to accommodate games fixtures without mass absences from lessons. As teaching hours could not be reduced, changes in the timetable had to be made. There were promises of reform in the arrangements for promotion in the middle and lower school and examination of the old system of Sides which was unequal to the business of providing pupils with Higher Certificate or 'A' Level results in three subjects. Down in the lower school large numbers of boys laboured on a full range of subjects, were promoted or delayed on aggregate marks, 'took up to seven 'O' levels simultaneously and failed the lot'. If this process occupied four years they were left with only one year in which to specialize, which was quite insufficient for 'A' levels. Noel Annan lent his support to improvements in this system. He wished to see the average boy take three years for 'O' levels, sitting them in stages: 'As George Hirst said (or we are now told he didn't say) to Wilfred Rhodes, "We'll get 'em in singles".' Reinforced by the fact that the school gained only two exhibitions in the winter of 1958/9 Annan suggested that the cleverest scholars should have the Oxbridge scholarships as their goal and push 'O' levels out of the way as soon as possible, otherwise boredom would set in as they repeated the syllabus they had covered at prep school. Even 'A' levels could be taken early to leave time for the very different type of study demanded by scholarships. 'The real point', he concluded, 'is that Stowe education has always lacked drive. Boys aren't pushed hard enough and it is this which, in part, has led to the "country house" atmosphere. It is essential that a boy is pushed – otherwise larger classes, greater freedom, a multitude of outside interests militate against the nose to the grindstone.' He appreciated that parents were not sufficiently aware of the mounting barriers to Oxbridge entry. He suggested a Letter from himself, Anthony Quinton and Crichton-Miller to the parents of 16 year olds, giving a realistic picture of the multiplied competition. 'Not only are parents ignorant of the present situation but hope often springs eternal that by some miracle the headmaster or housemaster will wangle a place at a college.' The point about the boredom of the bright scholar new boy was apposite and had wider implications. In Roxburgh's day, as many autobiographies testify, preparatory schools were often small and spartan tyrannies and arrival in the liberal atmosphere of Stowe was occasion for delight and stimulus. But the post-war preparatory schools had reformed and the change to a public school did not now bring the same experience of release. So too was the point concerning the failure of parents to comprehend that the public schools possessed no magic key to Oxbridge. One father in Eric Reynolds' time had made a complete hash of his elder boy's chances by dithering between colleges, though in the end, with a passionate appeal, Reynolds had obtained a place at his own old college. It did not prevent the father from pressing for early action over a younger brother, bearing in mind the school's 'ineptitude over the older boy'.

Changes in lower school organization were hampered by the opposition of Brian Gibson who controlled these matters with defensive and conservative vigour. Moves to tighten discipline could not be made without wounding feelings in a more personal fashion. Windsor-Richards was counselled to beat a dignified withdrawal from the housemastership of Temple. Though he was a lively preacher and a dedicated contributor in activities such as swimming, life-saving and the work parties in the grounds, a cherubic attitude to misbehaviour and penitence had undermined control. Appointed as a bachelor, he had married the matron and was an additional non-resident housemaster. He had great influence with the headmistress of a famous girls' school who despatched bus-loads of girls to the Temple house dances where the colonnade at the hour of their arrival, since the Classics were not dead, was known as the 'Mercatorium'. There had not been any warning of his removal and there was talk of litigation though Crichton-Miller endeavoured to dissuade the Governors from considering compensation. Bearing in mind that there were other masters who could be moving on, he wrote with what must have appeared sweeping intentions: 'It seems to me that the Governors face a situation in which they will be paying for one staff to work at Stowe and another on the retired list.' He said that, if the matter did come to the courts, he would give evidence 'to the effect that a headmaster who invites parents to send boys to a housemaster whom he believes to be below standard is defrauding them. I made it clear in my original letter that failure of this sort does not mean failure with all boys; but it means failure with or harm to a greater number than a reasonable headmaster can contemplate.' He gave a chilling forecast of what a cross-examination in court might elicit and concluded: 'When I saw the Masters on arrival at Stowe I warned them that recovery would be a painful business. I don't think they believed me then but they would probably agree now.' They may have agreed when Kelynack, Director of Music, was removed. There was no lack of musical activity but music was not the force in the land that it had been in Huggins' day and in Angus Watson there was a brilliant deputy who had the gift of gathering talented performers about him. Nevertheless the manner of Kelynack's going was abrupt and nervousness grew. In 1960, J.C.T. Uttley, housemaster of Walpole, took sabbatical leave and tendered his resignation. He had served in Sicily and Italy as a battery captain and been wounded by a mortar at Salerno. He spent two years as a Japanese prisoner and the effects of this were understandable nervous exhaustion and a diffidence about his abilities which at times became almost self-destructive. He had been presented with the challenges of Walpole after the collapse of Kinvig and had to endure de-monitorings and complaints. But he had helped with First XV coaching, brought some good Worcestershire cricket players to matches at Stowe and had stepped in at the last moment to command the C.C.F. for the Mountbatten inspection. Tragically he committed suicide by driving his car over a cliff in Guernsey. One must agree that a question mark could have hung over his suitability as a housemaster, but his departure cast a further shadow. Reynolds thought that he had been harshly treated and Uttley complained to D.J. Robarts (successor to Lord Wimborne as Chairman). One of the school secretaries with a taste for melodrama spoke of 'a smell of fear'.

Yet there was also support. The father of a boy who had come in 1958 wrote, 'I can only say how thankful I am that you are now Headmaster of Stowe, as at one time, prior to my son going there I had, frankly, misgivings.' Noel Annan, in the summer of 1960, met a group of younger masters at Vancouver Lodge, home of the McElwees, which was generally considered a haunt of mild sedition, and found a lot of goodwill. Pinchbeck had exclaimed: 'Stowe was a modern school in 1923 and it has just woken up to the fact that it is modern no longer.'

It was probably impolitic to raise the issue of relations with Allied Schools at the same moment as other changes, but finance remained a besetting hindrance to the solution of practical problems at Stowe. Old Stoics frequently raised the matter also. To one who had left Temple in 1947, the headmaster explained the matter in some detail. The Schools owed Legal and General about half a million pounds with rates of interest around 3 per cent. When the debt was paid off it was possible that the Alliance might be dissolved. Annoyance arose because some schools had paid off more and faster then others and felt they should be able to draw on the hypothetical surpluses for capital projects. But because of the differences between schools these assets were frozen. The matter was complicated by the fact that Lord Wimborne was Chairman of Allied Schools as well as Chairman of Stowe and by the fact that Crichton-Miller regarded Kenneth Adams, the chief officer of Allied Schools, with his London premises and staff, much as a Eurosceptic might regard Monsieur Delors in Brussels. Adams had in fact given a lifetime of patient attention to disentangling the finances of the various schools and a certain amount of personal feeling entered into relations. B.R. Miles had died suddenly in class at the very start of Crichton-Miller's time. There had inevitably been inquests and post-mortems and arrangements for the funeral had not been easy. Adams was hurt that he had not been informed of the date and intimated that Miles had had an excessive workload during the laboratory extensions, which had not always been appreciated. Old Stoics were now rising to positions of eminence and thought they should have a larger share in the direction of the school, as happened elsewhere, but power was still monopolized by the Legal and General and the Church of England Trust. To give a further discomforting twist to the whole business, E.G. Wykes and other Legal and General representatives were liable to come under fire from their own shareholders as nursing public schools was not the most profitable of investments.

Derek Bateman, an Old Etonian who succeeded Adams, argued that, although Stowe had contributed more than other schools up to the time of the Warrington crash, since 1933 the balance had been even. The argument in favour of the existence of Allied

Schools was that the small surpluses of each school formed in total a substantial fund which enabled big projects to be undertaken at any one in rotation. Wimborne suggested that this was a good moment for Stowe to put in a bid for a big new building, but the fact that he informed the central committee that Stowe was restless offended Crichton-Miller, and Crichton-Miller certainly offended Wimborne. The headmaster confided to a Governor, 'the most offensive series of disjointed accusations I have ever heard . . . It was quite astonishing and I can see that if he ever did anything of this sort with Reynolds it might well have proved fatal.' Old Stoics, especially those who subscribed through the 'Friends of Stowe', would like to have seen one of their number as Chairman, but Noel Annan was Provost of King's with its boundless commitments and, him apart, the succession was not clear. 'I still think we might make a go of it with Wimborne,' wrote Crichton-Miller, 'but he must be made to understand that Stowe is the dog and not the tail.'

He asked for the position to be investigated, outlining the duties of the Stowe bursary office which included entering 20,000 items on school bills each term, and unearthed details of the amounts paid by some wholly independent schools for legal and investment advice. D.J. Robarts, a near neighbour, whose family had long given Stoics the freedom of their property, succeeded Lord Wimborne as Chairman of the Stowe Governors. Wimborne held on to the title just long enough to brandish it at the gate-keeper when removing his son before the permitted hour on Speech Day, 1960. Crichton-Miller, who had certainly not made allies of the Allied Schools nominees, had hoped that an Old Stoic might be Chairman, but an executive committee with four Old Stoics in a majority was formed and Allied Schools were prevailed upon to allow more capital projects to be financed from Stowe's own resources. Sir William Holford was asked to prepare a plan for a teaching block in the Old Stone Yard.

There were other innovations. From 1959 onwards a Guest Night, subsequently the 'Commemoration Dinner', was held to bring college tutors, prep-school headmasters and prominent well-wishers together. An estates bursar was appointed and a development plan drawn up to remove huts and builders' yards and to prevent what Christopher Hussey had termed 'empirical ribbon development'. A waiting house, Nugent, was formed out of the masters' common room, some music rooms and the old

Biology preparation area. It not only gave the opportunity to increase numbers but also flexibility in dates of entry. Martin Burke of the music staff was the first housemaster and alternative space for the masters' common room was made in the headmaster's old apartments east of the Gothic Library. By June 1960 there were thirty-three more pupils, bringing in additional revenue of £14,000 and some talk of a new house. The Bridgland Trust gave generous grants towards the refurbishing of the Chapel and Stowe Church organs. To less popular acclaim the headmaster announced his discovery that Stowe had been functioning at less than thirty-six weeks per year and six days of teaching would now be added. Only pupils who were post 'A' level were permitted to work in studies. A new 'Tutorial Centre' was created for others and some were required to work under supervision in the Library. Four stages to 'O' levels were reduced to three and it was envisaged that all boys would begin working towards G.C.E. and the Science course in their first summer. In the lowest forms symbols recording progress were substituted for the marks system which Gibson stoutly defended. In a rather feline way the *Stoic* printed the proposed changes and juxtaposed quotations from Roxburgh on the limits of compulsion.

The masters who came to Stowe at the same time as Crichton-Miller included John Hunt, geographer, who subsequently made history as the first headmaster of a major girls' school, Roedean; Andrew Vinen O.S., a Cambridge Wrangler, later tutor in Mathematics and housemaster of Temple; and Muir Temple, housemaster of Grafton and second master. In the following year the Reverend J.E.C. Nicholl, first Old Stoic to preach in Chapel, arrived and was soon afterwards appointed as housemaster of Cobham, replacing D.I. Brown. Dr Bostock had served as the school doctor for ninety-nine terms and his numerous appearances in the *Epicurean* bear witness to the affection with which he was regarded. (When Russia first opened its gates to tourism a poem began: If you drive through Vladivostock/With the speed of Dr Bostock). He retired in 1962 and his deputy, Dr Clive Priday, succeeded. The penicillin treatment pioneered by Sir Alexander Fleming, a Stowe parent, had done much to eliminate the epidemics which, in the days of Roxburgh and even Reynolds, had sometimes caused two or three hundred boys to be out of action at a given moment. A.B.E. Gibson also left in 1962 along with

M.M. Maynard, Patrick Hunter and Bill McElwee. Patrick Hunter had served at Stowe for thirty-seven years, the longest tenure of all. He was held in awe for his knowledge of the school and its workings. On his departure he was presented by the Old Stoics with a goblet on which Laurence Whistler had engraved appropriately the vista of the Temple of Ancient Virtue. Bill McElwee, who had published several books on Stuart and Modern British History, went as Director of Modern Studies to Sandhurst. M.M. Maynard had founded the Air Section of the O.T.C. before the Second World War and served in the R.A.F. Seasonally each year the wall of his room in Plug Street had to be breached in order that his oversized boat could be extracted for use. He was an unconventional artist and claimed to have an unfinished symphony awaiting completion. The Hon. Simon Stuart, who came in March 1959 but left for Haberdashers' School two years later, was a lively teacher of English and well connected. On one occasion he asked if he might attend a memorial meeting for his grandfather. Crichton-Miller looked suitably mournful and granted permission. Stuart then flew off for the opening of the Guggenheim Museum in New York.

Under the scheme devised by Eric Reynolds housemasterships were no longer held in perpetuity. In addition to the more sudden changes imposed upon Temple and Walpole, where R.G. Gilbert and R.V.P. Adams (first Old Stoic housemaster) succeeded Windsor-Richards and Uttley, three veterans – Alasdair Macdonald, David Brown and Brian Gibson – handed on Chatham, Cobham and Grenville respectively, to W.H. Bradshaw, the Reverend J.E.C. Nicholl and G.B. Clarke. The new regimes appeared to give scope for the implementation of further change of policy, had energies not been diverted into the conflict described in the following chapter. But there were other initiatives of the Crichton-Miller period which should be mentioned as they coloured the future of Stowe considerably.

When R.C. Pinchbeck took over the C.C.F. from Uttley moves were made towards combining travel and adventure into training in the approved modern fashion. From 1959 to 1963 camps were held with the French Chasseurs Alpins and the Bataillon d'Infanterie Alpine. The Stowe contingent, 'évidemment l'élite de la nation Britannique' as the French commander later wrote to Drayson, performed manoeuvres on skis after minimal instruction, climbed through soft snow to the Lac de la Partie at over 8000 feet and built igloos large enough for four under the direction of a French colonel. There were diversions such as a gastronomic French picnic by Lake Annecy and basketball matches against the Chasseurs who were regional champions. At home there were arduous training exercises of a testing kind. At Easter 1959, the cadets were dropped in pairs at York and given a map reference fifty miles distant to be reached on foot with heavy packloads. At Dusseldorf, Stoics were drilled by a Guards regimental sergeant major and entrusted with hand grenades in platoon attacks. The naval cadets, sailing from Dartmouth in the HMS *Sheraton* encountered a force-9 gale and were reported as having shown 'true seamanlike qualities'.

The founding of a beagle pack was a project very close to Crichton-Miller's heart. The intention was to develop links and raise Stowe's standing with the sporting fraternity, of which there was a strong one in Buckinghamshire and neighbouring counties. Since the death of Leslie Huggins the hunting connection had diminished but it so happened that the headmaster's secretary, Rosemary Hill, was an enthusiast and knew many Old Stoics in the hunting field. A friend of the headmaster, Philip Burrows, presented the school with a brace and a half of hounds, and hunts all over the country gave assistance. In 1962 the pack was created at no overall financial cost to the school. John Atkinson, from the North of England, recruited by Rosemary Hill, was a champion breeder and for many years Stowe carried off the trophies at county shows and major competitions. A supporters club formed from the squirearchy and local farmers helped to link the school with the local community and the holiday travels of the beagles spread the fame of Stowe from Northumberland to the West Country. In term time the care of the pack provided a small but enthusiastic minority with an alternative to team games, but more importantly it played a part in bringing entries from the shires. Stowe did not, like so many, become a 'regional school'.

Rosemary Hill was also a tennis enthusiast and drove to the Public Schools Championships at Wimbledon each day from her office. The first victory in the Youll Cup came in 1959 after four unsuccessful appearances in the final since 1947. To the disapproval of the *Daily Telegraph* the team had been strengthened by the cricketers but it was pointed out that they had kept up tennis coaching through the season. The Cup was won again in 1960, indeed Stowe was to break Eton's record of three consecutive wins with four. In the final against St Paul's, B.K. Huffman, an American E.S.U. scholar, defeated a Surrey Junior and at the crucial set point, 'rather than have it on his conscience for the rest of his life', as he put it, said that his stroke was out and asked for the point to be replayed, which he then won. D.R. Sabberton and R.B.B. Avory played First Pair for the Public Schools against an All-England Team and did not concede a set. Sabberton, who by 1962 was head of school, played in all four of the victorious Youll Cup sides.

The cricket captaincy of Chris Atkinson in 1959 brought confidence. Oundle came as ever with a high reputation and three batsmen who had built up averages of over 50. At Stowe, Oundle made 100 runs exactly and 78 of Stowe's 103 were contributed by David Costain who was described as one of the best batsmen since the war. In the shadow of such successes house matches witnessed stronger competition and, according to the *Stoic*: 'The weaker teams, instead of wearing their weakness as a badge of intellectual superiority, have endeavoured to conceal their incompetent members or drill them into some co-ordination of hand and eye.' The 1962 season was another that seemed to brighten the horizon. The number of good cricketers was small but there were few injuries and hence greater continuity and team spirit, combined with the quickest fielding for some years. The Oundle Match was won with eight minutes to spare, J.W.O. Allerton scoring fifteen in the last over, bringing his total to 117 not out. The closing moments of the Bedford match were even more tense with 'masters in charge restlessly on the prowl'. Bedford's ninth wicket fell with the scores even. The Bedford last man was in the side only because the Captain had gone to a wedding and came in to face M.W.G. Fisher who had already taken six wickets. He managed to scramble a run and a victory. In the summer of 1963, though, the results generally disappointed expectations. R.N. Goodchild scored 166 against the Dragonflies, the second highest total ever, Howland Jackson's 204 remaining impregnable. The success of athletics underlined the need for a proper track and a site was found by the old orchard which would not destroy the landscape. Michael Mounsey and David Donaldson led the parties which cleared the ground and a parent lent heavy machinery. With the cinder track in use athletics became a full summer sport. Stoics were well represented in the county youth competitions and teams. Four Stoics competed for Buckinghamshire in the Inter-County Sports in 1962. M.J. Summerlin broke the javelin record at Radley with a throw of 196 feet 4 inches and, at the national competitions at Hull, went on to throw 202 feet. D.H. Temple won the County Junior discus event and D.E.B. Walker the 120 yards hurdles. The greater contacts with local schools also pointed the way to other future enterprises.

Archery made its first appearance and a Judo Club was founded in 1962. Under the influence of two American students, T.A. Galyean and B.K. Huffman, basketball figured as a sport. K.I. Meldrum who joined the Common Room in 1960 and later became the principal of an outward bound training school founded a Mountaineering Club and led winter expeditions to the Lake District. M.C. Penney, an Athletics and Fives Blue, took over fives and a junior fives league was introduced. Nine Stoics represented the county in the National Swimming Championships and the swimming team continued to defeat virtually all the schools that did not have an indoor pool. Sculling attracted over eighty active rowers and W.G. Fletcher at Peterborough was one of the first Stoics to reach the final in a regatta.

In Crichton-Miller's first Autumn Term an O.S. Rugger Day was held when matches were arranged for anyone willing to turn up and play. There were three XVs: the Worthies, the Vitruvians and the Palladians. On the academic front it was the Classical Society which continued to offer the most uncompromising fare. In 1959 Nicholas Sturch O.S. returned to recreate the wars between Chalcis and Eretria for the Lelantine Plain. The Debating Society become a little more serious and in 1960 there was a debate in which Sir Isaiah Berlin and Anthony Quinton spoke on the motion: 'In the opinion of this House the best brains in the modern world should be found in the Board Room and not in the Common Room'. Despite the efforts of the two visitors the house, mindful of self-interest, voted to reserve the best brains for the Common Room. An International Society was founded to promote awareness of foreign affairs. There were lectures on Israel and the Middle East and Stephen Whitwell O.S., who had served in New Delhi in the diplomatic service, spoke on India and Pakistan. Leavers were given a series of addresses on public speaking, civic service and finance. With a grant from the Royal Society a dedicated band built what was believed to be the first amateur radio telescope ever constructed. Its components included two commercial TV aerials and a wartime receiver, but various emissions from the galaxies were studied. Under Dr David, a Science tutor appointed in 1956, an Archaeological Society worked on sections of the old Roman Road. *An Account of the Birds of Stowe* was published by the Natural History Society, which described not only the regular visits by the Great Crested Grebes, whose unpunctuality caused alarm, but the rare appearance of the Whooper Swans last seen in 1956, a waxwing first seen by J.C. Saunders in his garden and the male bearded tit spotted in 1959 which, it was thought, must have followed the course of the Ouse in search of a mate as there had been no strong winds to blow it from East Anglia. A study was made of badgers at Stowe and a Mercury Vapour Moth Trap caught eighty different species. *A Winter's Tale*, *Richard II* and *Macbeth* were produced by the Historians, but Joe Bain provided some ambitious stage ventures including plays by Ionesco and Anouilh, and even *Hedda Gabler*. The Reverend P.T. Hancock came as chaplain in 1962. A John Bunyan Society was instituted to discuss contemporary religious issues such as the New English Bible and the Bishop of Woolwich's *Honest to God*. It had a junior section, the Augustinians, open to first-year Stoics.

The Roxburgh Hall, with acoustics much finer than any Stowe had experienced in the past, opened with the Overture to *Russlan and Ludmilla*, the Brandenburg Concerto No. 3 and movements from the 'New World' Symphony. Recitals were given by Paul Tortelier, who gave a memorable performance although suffering from a temperature of 103, by Julian Bream and Fou T'song. Sir Adrian Boult returned with the City of Birmingham Orchestra. At a second school concert T.W.J. Waine played the Grieg Concerto. One concerto player in a generation would have pleased most schools; at Stowe they came forward year by year. Angus Watson arranged chamber concerts in the Library and the musicians had a dual concert exchange with Radley. Simon Stuart reviewing this musical equivalent of the Oundle Match declared: 'I will not be accused of chauvinism when I say that Stowe would emerge creditably from the comparisons I do not intend to make.' Peace had her victories no less renowned than war and Stowe and Oundle combined in a programme which included the Handel Sonata for two celli, played by the respective teachers. The military band was tackling works by Gordon Jacobs and Vaughan Williams and in

1959 Boosey and Hawkes, in honour of forty years of patronage by Mr Webb, gave the cup for a Wind Instrument Competition. To celebrate the birth of Prince Andrew the band played a fanfare and the headmaster spoke in Buckingham marketplace. The Town Fathers asked Crichton-Miller particularly not to be late 'as Mr Webb was a very busy man'.

Old Stoics were by now rising to high places in many walks of life. Stephen Taylor who had sat on the Labour Benches became a Life Peer. There were three Old Stoic Heads of Diplomatic Missions abroad; J.P.E. Henniker-Major, Ambassador first to Jordan and later to Denmark; Colin Crowe, Ambassador to Saudi Arabia; J.D. Murray, Minister and later Ambassador in Belgrade. John Boyd-Carpenter was Chief Secretary to the Treasury; Lord St Oswald, Parliamentary Secretary at the Ministry of Agriculture; and R.J. Maxwell-Hyslop MP for Tiverton. A.E. des C. Chamier headed the list of entrants for the senior branch of the diplomatic service. J.F. Nye was Professor of Radiology at Johns Hopkins University, Baltimore; J.F. Tuohy, Professor of English Literature at Cracow; J.C. Simopoulos, a Fellow of St Catherine's College, Oxford; O.A.W. Dilke, Professor of Classics at Rhodes University, Grahamstown; J.J. Hartland-Swann, Professor of Philosophy at the University of Malaya. D.P. Choyce was Hunterian Professor at the Royal College of Surgeons and noted for his original contributions to eye surgery; Dr P. Sainsbury was Director of the Medical Research Council's Psychiatry Unit and Dr A.K. Thould a leading authority on congenital deafness. J.D. Dwight became a Fellow of Magdalene College, Cambridge. P.G.H. Gell was Professor of Immunological Pathology at the University of Birmingham. At Oakham John Buchanan was transforming a small country school into a large and progressive public school, pioneering co-education and instituting on ambitious building programme.

In 1962 the Old Stoics reached the final of the Halford Hewitt Golf Tournament and were beaten on the last green by Oundle.[1] P.R. Hastings-Bass was training the Queen's horses. C.R. Selby was awarded the Silver Cane as the best cadet at Mons. It was noted that at least nine regiments were commanded by Old Stoics. C.J.G. Shillington ran for Ireland in the Empire Games, broke the

---

[1] They were, however, victorious in this tournament in 1979 and 1988.

Northern Ireland record for the Half Mile and won the Mile for Ireland in an International Match in Wales. A. Cameron was a member of the Irish Olympic Equestrian Team and in 1962 came in fourth at 100–1 in the Grand National, at one moment leading the field. W.G. Fiske and R.K. Middlemas were in the Queen's Hundred at Bisley. W.P. Cooper, J.M.E. Anderson, and L.G.B. Williamson all played golf for Cambridge and C.M. Hill won a Blue for boxing, C. Atkinson (Hockey) and C. Wates (Rugby) were Oxford Blues, R.B. Skipper represented Great Britain in the Winter Olympics in 1960 and R.J.W Utley driving a Lotus won the Whitsun Handicap at Goodwood.

T.E.B. Sopwith in 1961 won the Offshore Power Boats Race in 'Thunderbolt'. David Niven was awarded an Oscar for his role in the film *Separate Tables*; J.M. Diack won the Premier Prize at the Grenoble Conservatoire; Colin Graham produced the 'Hoffnung Interplanetary Festival' and David Wynne received some major sculpting commissions including the head and hands of Sir Thomas Beecham. C.G.L. Shankland was architect in charge of the planning of the Liverpool Centre, one of the first to experiment with glass-covered malls and open-air cafés, etc. D.H. Villiers, at one time the youngest squadron leader in Bomber Command, had shown a great talent for making documentary films and won a First Prize at the Venice Film Festival.

It was still unusual for school leavers to set off on global travel but M.C. Houghton, hitch-hiking and on bicycle, toured Rhodesia. He was reported to have swum a swollen river carrying his bike and been attacked by baboons. M.L.A. Andrews and A.B. Howarth, members of the Cambridge Explorers Club, travelled with a party in two Land Rovers the 25,000 miles from Cape Horn to Alaska studying animal husbandry *en route*.

As the older generation in the Common Room were reaching retirement so too gaps appeared in the ranks elsewhere. Miss Butler, one of the original matrons, retired and Miss Whittington, first matron of Temple, died. A.E. Warden who had worked from 1923 and had risen to be head houseman, storing trunks, moving furniture and, in early days manning Messrs. Merryweather's fire engine, died in 1961. Harry Hutchings, another survivor from the first days, who nightly cleaned hundreds of pairs of Stowe shoes on his revolving brush, retired as did Ted Park, Physics laboratory technician, who had also been cinema operator, a cook in the old Home Guard, and a stalwart help to harassed masters mounting science equipment. H.A. Garrett who had worked in the bursar's office with seven bursars since December 1928 also retired. He was an expert bowls player and the Old Stoics presented him with a set of woods. Ted Gillett in 1962 completed his one-hundredth term as chief laboratory assistant. Sergeant-Major Reynolds had been with the Cadet Force since 1943 and helped to train over 2000 cadets under five commanding officers. As well as a fine shot who had been a small-arms instructor in India, he was a keen angler and a great source of information on fish in the lakes.

As Pinchbeck had remarked, the school had been young in 1923 but was young no longer. When the 1960s were reached, not only was the first generation of those who had established Stowe coming to an end, but there were massive social changes afoot. University competition was not the only result of the Education Act of 1944. For the first time school fees became a matter of deliberate choice for those who wished to pay. Before the war parents had frequently complained of the cost of education but the fact was that for any boy of relatively low ability there was no provision for education beyond a low leaving age and certainly no sixth-form education provided by the state. Even the old grammar schools made a charge for the majority of pupils. The new generation of parents was aware that, if one could swallow its imperfections and the absence of all the merits of the public schools, there nevertheless was an alternative system which cost nothing and could lead to higher education. They may not have wished to use it or have had any intention of using it, but its existence led to a certain feeling of martyrdom as each termly cheque was signed and was noted to be larger than the last. The slower pupil was no longer on the only road open to him and it was a toll road rather than a freeway. This in turn placed heavier responsibilities on the schools to justify their claims of excellence and their policies. Failure could no longer be shrugged off and of this headmasters and Governors were aware. It was against such a background that a crisis arose.

10

Donald Crichton-Miller II

Crichton-Miller's reports to the Governors were intended to be informative as well as critical. Noel Annan had congratulated him on the first:'It combines frankness with a complete absence of rancour. The old form of the Headmaster's Report must be completely abolished.' Crichton-Miller in reply made reference to the heavy commitments of some of the Governors: 'It is difficult to hit off a reasonable balance between the sort of account which will give you enough detail and the sort which will be sufficiently short for Sir Miles Thomas to read'! In 1960 he warned of unease in the Common Room:

> Some Governors are, I think, concerned about discontent among senior men – the top twenty say – but I hardly think this is a surprising development. These are masters who remained at the School during a period of steady decline. Most of them developed a certain tolerance for moderate standards and a few learnt to cultivate the easy life. (It is true that all, or nearly all, genuinely looked forward to reform. But in the nature of things their proposals were at variance with each other and in several cases their hopes were shattered.) I warned them at the very first meeting that the road to recovery would be unpleasant, but naturally enough each man interpreted this as meaning that his neighbour was at last to be found out!

It is difficult at this distance of time to recapture the chemistry which affects relationships in a community such as a Common Room. The masters were certainly taken aback by the vehemence of the criticisms of the status quo and the picture that had been given to the headmaster before his arrival. The school had never been noted for its rule by edict. Even at the time of Reynolds' appointment David Brown in the masters' meeting had drawn attention to the richness of the notice boards in out-dated and superfluous documents. The notices of Crichton-Miller required extra space and extra boards. Rebukes to the school *en masse* by Roxburgh had been remembered for their deft understatement and it had not been Reynolds' manner to denounce misbehaviour in stentorian tones.

At the beginning of the Spring Term 1961 Crichton-Miller told the Governors that he had decided after the changes in Walpole, 'to tear the biggest strip off the School that I have done so far. Indeed I prepared the ground by removing the smaller boys . . .' This suggests that other but not necessarily negligible strips had been torn before. On paper he was very convincing and amusing withal, but there was nervousness among the masters, which inhibited the healthy venting of feelings. Irritation was caused by some matters in which the headmaster's experience of other places left him in no doubt about the justice of his case, and rightly so. 'You may not know', he wrote to Annan in February 1960, 'that for some years before I came here the Masters had refused to accept any reliable system of signing in and out for meals. It was the duty of the catering staff to prepare dinner for the maximum every night and if the minimum arrived no complaints were made. Thus I sat down on several occasions last year with three other masters when dinner had been prepared for twenty-five!'

Sometimes he was justified in feeling irritation too. Reynolds had been criticized for choosing his dinner guests according to their sociability and conversational skills. When the Crichton-Millers entertained on a strict rotation basis the cry went up that the invitations had no thought or merit behind them. At Vancouver Lodge, home of the McElwees, independence of opinion on policies and personalities flourished. Even David Brown had protested when members of the First XV were kept up late on the nights before important matches in convivial company. It must have been difficult for Bill McElwee, an historian and teacher of great distinction, to serve under a headmaster who had been a young master at the same time as himself and who did not share the sixth-form teaching, on which so much academic inspiration in a school rests.

The tally of university awards was not rising and disciplinary problems, such as they were, showed little sign of diminishing. Apropos of a group of historians who appeared to be heading for disaster, Crichton-Miller wrote to McElwee in 1960:

> As I understand it, J.F. did intend tutors to take a large share in character training as well as mind training. I suppose we would say that this intention is now in danger of being forgotten and that, in any case, it was never entirely fulfilled. Whether the number of Tutors who pay little attention to this side of their work is greater or lower today I know not. But certainly their interest varies – to put it mildly – and the system is to some extent on trial these days.
>
> Now it happens you represent, *par excellence*, the type of Tutor who is not content only to teach boys; you want to influence them. And you have always succeeded in doing so. Many owe you a great deal and this is well known. If at this moment you suffer four casualties it will be a serious matter for this kind of tutoring . . . You seem oblivious of the risk . . . unless I got you wrong the other night.

When McElwee took exception to certain phrases which he underlined, the headmaster replied: 'As I have repeatedly said I am very unsuccessful in making myself clear nowadays – but I also find a certain amount of deliberate misunderstanding here at Stowe.' Sarcasm gleamed through the response: 'I had begun to flatter myself that I had become particularly adept at discovering the basic intention underlying your allocutions and memoranda. Please forgive me.' This landscape was different from the granite rocks on which a headmaster's authority rested in Scotland. The fact that Crichton-Miller offered to McElwee the senior tutorship contradicts the latter's suspicion 'that you believed there was some contagion spreading from me or the History Side or Vancouver Lodge which was making boys unsusceptible to ordinary discipline', but the offer was declined.[1] 'Though I fully understand and in many ways wholeheartedly appreciate the objects which you have in view and have no doubt that I could manage the job to your satisfaction it is clear that the sort of supervision you require will involve a great deal of administrative work of the kind which I

---

[1] On the death of Patience McElwee, Bill said that Crichton-Miller's letter was above all others the one she would have chosen as her obituary.

most dislike and would cut me off altogether from the sort of teaching which I enjoy and do best.' It was a great misfortune that McElwee did not accept this offer for, apart from the loss of his abilities in a key post, it set the headmaster's mind thinking on the possibilities of appointing from outside. Patrick Hunter had been both senior tutor and second master and it seemed now as if the positions might have to be divided.

Eric Reynolds had never set Roxburgh on too dizzy a pinnacle. It had been one of the sources of Common Room disaffection that at times he had displayed slight amusement at tales of J.F.'s more extravagant mannerisms. By contrast Crichton-Miller, who had known Roxburgh in his prime, had a great admiration for him and could see that the 'Roxburgh Tradition' was acquiring some of the characteristics of legend. He could, after all, recall J.F. telling his masters that he might have to seek out a Common Room that had 'rather less talent but rather more loyalty'. Differing interpretations of the past affected the copious correspondence which accompanied the efforts of head and Patrick Hunter to improve general efficiency. At the outset Crichton-Miller wrote generously: 'It happens that you are very strong in the department in which I am weakest. I abhor paperwork and in consequence of my resistance to it I do it very badly . . . It may encourage you to know that I simply can't exist without a strong partner on the paper side and I doubt whether I could get a better man than yourself to fill the vacancy.'

At the beginning of the first term Patrick Hunter, anxious to find some common ground, wrote to Annan to say that he felt the picture of Stowe painted to the incoming headmaster had been too bleak. 'It is clear to me that he has been given a very lurid picture of Stowe and that it weighs heavily upon his sense of responsibility. Now to my mind this picture is out of all proportion and potentially distorting to the future. I do not think that the disease is deep: I have a strong belief in the goodwill of my colleagues and in the quality of, say, eighty or ninety per cent of our material.' He believed that some Governors ('I do not know who nor do I wish to know') had swallowed too completely the complaints of ex-masters and a group of Old Stoics. With agreement matters could be put right and any image of the school that was untoward could be rectified. 'I wholly accept', he declared, 'that I had not given enough weight to the importance of our public reputation and the need to get that altered as soon as possible.'

While the arrangements for the more rapid promotions of and earlier taking of 'O' levels by the brighter pupils were gradually put into operation, with much cavilling over the size of forms and sets, the feeling arose that the headmaster was less interested in the potential scholar than the average boy. Crichton-Miller trusted that scholarship would grow out of a generally efficient standard of teaching, Patrick Hunter that it would be diffused by careful nurture of the best.

> Both by implication and also by direct word and action you have given a strong impression (to put it at the least) that you discount scholarship and even exalt mediocrity. . . Your general experience I know well is far greater than mine and your wisdom deeper; but I speak here in a field where I know what I am saying. I've taught Upper School boys for more than thirty years and you, I dare say, have taught them very little. And I know that, as Saunders puts it, 'scholarship is infectious'.

Crichton-Miller, after pointing to poor 'O' level results in 1958 and 1959 and saying that no satisfactory diagnosis of the causes had been made, repeated that he would like to have more scholars from whom award winners might be fashioned but, having got the boys they had, they must ensure that a Common Entrant who passed in with an average mark of 60 per cent received as good a deal at Stowe as anywhere else.

> I know (this policy) will never be popular with the Sixth-Form type of master. At the back of my mind I have the feeling that some of you chaps think it is my fault that we are getting boys of this calibre to the exclusion of the much brighter type that we had fifteen years ago. Of course this reaction is hardly rational, but I still have the feeling that when both parties are disappointed (as we both must be) there is a tendency to work off our irritation on each other.

While the entry lists were numerically strong and a number of Old Stoics were rallying, the absence of a wider range of higher abilities was not something easily solved. It may have been that Crichton-Miller's aims were not always crystal clear. 'You have a disconcerting tendency to go off either in digression or in actual person!' wrote Hunter, adding on another occasion, 'I sometimes wonder whether you are unintentionally elliptical, as I often find myself to be in matters on which I have long pondered.' What is hard to understand is the frequent stress on the need for a 'common purpose' or some unifying philosophy. The obvious common purpose should not have needed to be stated which was that, both in work and other activities, the standards should be as high as possible. That there was a need for humble competence as much as vision is illustrated by one of Hunter's own letters to Crichton–Miller. 'A second-termer at the bottom of Form A on the day before his exam asked if he might be excused to help with the Historians' scenery. Some boys arrived at a Maths exam 18 minutes late because of a minor sporting event held in the Break. The Tutor of Side 7 has missed occasions totalling $4\frac{1}{2}$ days between July 12th and 22nd, no doubt on school business, but away and not always with adequate provision for his work.' He believed that the headmaster was making progress but at the same time was suspicious of 'efficiency that was uncritical, uninformed, based on obedience to command which in the wrong setting can be unintelligent, deadening and even dangerous . . . and you, yourself, who boast yourself a 'Roxburgh' man cannot be after anything so negative.' The final compliment was rather back-handed: 'Your own day-to-day administration falls superbly short of efficiency of that kind. I take it as a good omen.'

Crichton-Miller sent Hunter notes on what he called his 'Punctuality Prowls'. He admitted that patrolling was not the headmaster's duty, but thought it effective.

Friday 17 Feb. [1961] Between Sanatorium and Fives Courts. Six people late; four of them ran when they saw me. Three boys then turned up running(just!) the other way. Evidently 'brought the wrong books' but I was unable to investigate as I would have liked . . . Monday 6 March. I was in Chapel Court at 11.45 a.m. Several boys began running from the South Front Corner when the bells started and were late. Three boys arrived later – all with the same excuse that they had been running in the last mile heat. This was interesting as subsequent events showed they were in ample time . . . Monday 13 March. I was on the North Front at 4.30. Actually I descended from the West Colonnade steps at $4.26\frac{1}{2}$ whereupon everyone began running.

This was all done with some amusement. It does not bear out the contention that he was too interested in economies and estate matters to be involved in the school.

Roger Rawcliffe, later housemaster of Chatham, said many years after this time of trouble:

> He was very aware of the performance of the staff, often to be found in the teaching area during classes and prepared to give encouragement or advice. I have not found this awareness of the quality of staff in other headmasters I have dealt with. He also was often looking at the maintenance of the school; for this he was criticized – I can only say that I found him supportive, approachable and kind and that most of those whom he appointed would probably agree.

On the other hand those whom he had not appointed and who felt that prescriptive rights were slipping away became very passionate: 'Why is it that masters visiting other schools are still greeted with sarcastic surprise that they are still at Stowe? Why in short are we mistrusted and blamed at every turn, while practically nothing is praised? Are we not human beings?' wrote one. Not surprisingly some of the discontent percolated downwards. The increased number of notice boards may not have been tactful or sightly but their presence hardly justified the charges that one of Britain's great architectural heritages was being vandalized. Two boys, tribunes of the people, had a bet of £5, quite a large sum at the time, on who could remove the most square inches of the headmaster's notices without arrest. One, falling behind in the contest, removed the results of the General Paper which contained the whole school list. The incident was slyly woven into a parody of the General Paper which was published in the *Epicurean*, a publication that had some Senior Common Room affiliations. The situation was becoming uncomfortably akin to the old pre-war stories of Red Circle School in the *Hotspur*, in which staff and boys co-operated in merry japes while a humourless deputy stood in for the saintly Dr Jerome.

Ten years before, the storm might have been weathered but the restless mood of the 1960s was mounting. Parents who had remarried after divorce, homes in which *au pair* girls had replaced the nannies and broad-shouldered domestics of earlier days, teenage affluence, the coffee-bar culture and a host of other factors blunted the weapons which schools had employed in the past. De-monitoring, which in Roxburgh's time had been a shameful blow, mattered less when student opinion resented and sometimes abdicated from the privileges of office in the first place. The warning letters to parents might produce the desired effect, but might be diluted, if there were fears of teenage rebellion. Even the sternest housemasters, in schools where the houses were fortresses, lost sleep at this time. Housemasters at Stowe, down in the field houses, were not well placed to exercise pastoral duties in buildings that remained overcrowded and unsegregated. The weapon of expulsion was still potent but on this important matter there was strong disagreement. In Crichton-Miller's view expulsion was a last resort and experience had taught him that most parents regarded it as implying failure on the school's part. He claimed that in five years he was asked to expel thirty boys, which rightly he considered too high a number: 'We gave too many boys too much rope; and when they were on the point of hanging themselves I was called in to complete the operation'.

Confidence was not restored in any quarter by the Vandervell Mystery. In February 1962, the national press was excited by the story of the kidnapping of a seventeen-year-old Stoic, Colin Vandervell, from Stowe on a Sunday evening. According to his own statement he had left the dining room after supper and was walking up some steps when two big men grabbed him and bundled him into a car which a third man drove off. He was told: 'This is a taste of what you get in future'. He awoke at 11.30 p.m. lying in a field near Aylesbury with his hands tied. Eventually he found a householder who cut him free, ungagged him and called the police. Interest in the story was heightened by the fact that Colin's father was a millionaire racing-car builder who had abducted the boy aged nine from his mother, and by the discovery in his desk of a letter in a code devised at preparatory school, which ran, 'Dear Colin, Now is the time for me to get you. I want £100 by February 5th. If not . . .' The letter mentioned that three other Stoics would die if the money was not placed outside the Oxford Lodge. Vandervell Senior had reported losses of cars from his estate. He believed that his son had been injected with a hypodermic syringe before being abducted. There were stories of kidnapping plots overheard in West End coffee bars. 'THE STOWE MYSTERY. What do the Old Boys know?' boomed the *Evening Standard*.

In the absence of credible factual information the school was reluctant to re-admit Vandervell. Father understood this to mean that his son was accused of lying and he brought a High Court action to seek an interim injunction preventing Colin's exclusion from Stowe. Crichton-Miller, probably in the light of the threats to other pupils, maintained that he could not re-admit the boy without stronger evidence or psychiatric reports. Father eventually dropped the action and it was agreed that no specific charges of lying had been made by the school, but the press wrung the last drops of drama from the case ('What school will have me now?', 'Career wrecked because I told the truth', 'Several of Britain's top schools have refused to accept the son of millionaire Tony Vandervell', etc.). A place was found at Millfield and the hostage went on to be a successful racing-driver. Crichton-Miller's opinion was that the Chairman should have got all parties together before the High Court action was brought, and his attitude was certainly more circumspect than that of a fellow headmaster: '. . . I imagine you were still tracking down your millionaire kidnappers! I hope you flogged the boy within an inch of his life; it struck me as a most ridiculous story.'

There was nothing explicitly unfavourable to Stowe in the reports but they made the Governors uncomfortably aware of the potential damage which could be inflicted in an uncontrolled situation. Their patience was beginning to wear thin as there was no indication that the disciplinary situation was improving. Not all the omens were discouraging. Larger numbers of Old Stoics were entering their sons. The dramatic improvement in games results which came at the start of Bob Drayson's time were the achievement, as he himself acknowledged, of the Crichton-Miller entrants. The lists of failures at Common Entrance were longer and the school was enjoying greater choice of entrants. Yet three years had elapsed and there were still examples of misbehaviour that came to the Governors' ears, as well as a feeling that the headmaster was equivocal over expulsion. As in the political system, mishaps could not be blamed upon previous governments indefinitely. Some felt that after initial purges in the Common Room mutual confidence should have been restored. Old Stoic Governors did not wish to have a repetition of the Old Stoic complaints about discipline as in former years. 'You were appointed to Stowe to change this reputation,' wrote the Vice-Chairman, 'and it must be changed.'

Whatever their personal feelings they were beginning to wonder whether harmonious relations could ever be achieved at the school.

That there had been clumsinesses on occasion is certain. After a Congreve play, the producer, expecting congratulations, was told to do something about the car-parking arrangements. David Brown, as chairman of the games committee, was not told of changes in the coaching of the First XV. In a smooth-running school such things would not matter unduly but they were quotable when tempers were high. The swift departure of Colin James to religious broadcasting following Crichton-Miller's appointment was made much of by critics but the headmaster's farewell was generous enough: 'You will go from strength to strength and I shall be pleased to supply references from time to time but I guess you will rapidly reach heights in which my small assistance will be superfluous.' To the father of a boy who had received some questionable correspondence from a recent leaver he wrote with tact and consideration of 'trouble generally called "immoral behaviour" though I am doubtful whether this is a suitable phrase. I hope you will not cross-examine him on this matter. [He] is on the fringe of a rather bad gang which I have been breaking up gradually.' The mother of a boy who had severe medical problems and many troublesome absences wrote to Crichton-Miller when her son left: 'You arrived at Stowe with a somewhat formidable reputation and a number of people told me you would have no time for −. I shall take great pleasure in telling them they were quite wrong.'

Raymond Walker succeeded Patrick Hunter as senior tutor but the place of second master had to be filled and Crichton-Miller, mistakenly as he later admitted, conceived the idea that the new second master should be responsible for discipline. 'Punctuality Prowls' could not continue for ever and the notice boards were not capable of infinite extension. The idea was doubtful as in the 1960s only the headmaster could really accept the relentless odium that came from contests over dress, apppearance and what our forbears knew as 'swaggering'. Hugh Carey, who was recommended for the post, was a graduate of King's College, Cambridge and an assistant master at Harrow. 'Jimmie' James, headmaster of Harrow, gave a cautious but not an informative reference. It was intended that he should arrive at Stowe some months before Patrick Hunter's departure so that an induction period could be accorded, but this led to an overlapping of duties and confusion. It transpired that Carey did not have the patience to absorb slowly all the nuances of life in the Common Room, which is the indispensable asset required of a second master. Although his experience was limited to Michaelhouse in South Africa and Harrow, admittedly very well controlled by James, he was highly critical of Stowe as he found it and soon in active opposition to the headmaster.

In making the announcement of Carey's appointment at the end of the Summer Term 1962 Crichton-Miller said to the school that he had 'failed' in matters of discipline and was handing over responsibilities to the second master. The remark may have been a piece of dry humour.[2] It may have been part of an explanation that more important issues were neglected because time was being spent upon disciplinary trivia. Somehow it was construed as an 'abdication' speech and the impression arose that, having failed to cure the present ills, the headmaster was handing over to a deputy. By the time the story reached other schools it sounded as though he had taken up sackcloth and ashes and was shouldering responsibility for all the misbehaviour of the past. The fact that, in order to buttress Carey's position, it had already been arranged that he would have certain privileges, such as a conspicuous seat in Chapel and presidency over some of the prefects' meetings, gave credence to the 'abdication' theory.

Carey soon found that he was saddled with the opprobrium which is the daily lot of headmasters. He reported that Crichton-Miller would not interfere even if he saw the most blatant disregard of rules before his eyes, which is hard to believe. The question of policy over expulsions also rumbled on and the Governors were not happy about 'grey areas' that had arisen when boys had hung under a shadowy form of suspension. They were at heart in agreement with the housemasters and there was reference made to 'rotten apples in the barrel'. The governing body had reiterated its ruling that 'other than in exceptional cases any boy found guilty of sexual misconduct or of drinking or outrageous hooliganism should be expelled forthwith'. Crichton-Miller felt that expulsion

[2] When Brian Young, headmaster of Charterhouse, decided to give up trying to run a house as well as the school he made a similar remark with wholly humorous intent. 'There is one housemaster who has been falling down very badly on his duties recently,' he began. Unfortunately all his colleagues swung round in their seats and looked at someone else.

had come to be regarded as an easy solution and that the house-masters were often at fault. In a memorandum to housemasters he repeated:

> The number of sacking cases which I have dealt with during the last four years exceed the number that were brought to my attention for consideration throughout my previous twenty years as Headmaster. The reason is mainly to be found in the conditions obtaining at Stowe during the last ten years: but a subsidiary factor is the character of the School. In my view we are likely to have more difficult cases here, even when the discipline is good, than at smaller institutions where effort is greater and home background more reliable . . . No parent can regard compulsory termination of his son's career as anything other than a major disaster. Father is likely to be unreasonable and mother may be impossible. Between them they may struggle so violently that there is an upset with the Governors, the press and so on. We may be able to look at the matter more objectively but we cannot disregard the fact that the boy has failed – and failed while under our care. Indeed there are few cases in which it can be said that the School has not contributed to the disaster.

One might add that there were few cases which did not turn out to be a great deal more complicated than they seemed at the start. Gilbert had been nearly broken by Temple, where he had been appointed to enforce discipline and, though things improved, the regime was tense and brittle. The most controversial case of all shows how hard it was to reach decisions that were clear and indisputable. Abbreviating the tale considerably one may say that X joined Stowe at fourteen having failed Common Entrance twice. In the summer of 1962 the housemaster wrote to the father complaining of indolence at work and games, giving a catalogue of offences, and requesting that X should leave at Christmas. Crichton-Miller approved. Father gave reluctant agreement but included a suggestion that the situation might be reviewed if there were an improvement. When the housemaster was shown the reply he was angry and despatched a letter which the father described as 'offensive'. Relations between parents and housemaster dropped to zero, there was no improvement in the boy's behaviour and after a few weeks of the Autumn Term the housemaster requested that

X should be sent away forthwith. Crichton-Miller pointed out that no fresh crimes had appeared on the list; the old offences had been repeated for which a promise of withdrawal had already been extracted. However he agreed to write to the father asking him to remove his son, but leaving a line of retreat which would allow the boy to take 'O' levels if there were violent objections. The boy said that his parents were in Paris and if he were expelled he would go straight to 'friends'. As he could not be permitted to drift off into unknown company he was allowed to stay until his parents were traced. They were eventually summoned over the loudspeaker system of their Paris hotel which led to X's mother ('not a well adjusted woman' said Crichton-Miller) believing the boy was dead. They returned to find he had absconded from the school though he returned after a twenty-four hour disappearance.

The headmaster did not think that the school's position was strong. If the parents sued for recovery of fees they had a chance of success and there would be publicity. They had already been to the police about the alleged existence of a local girlfriend and considered the accusations false. The housemaster refused to have the boy back and Crichton-Miller pointed out to the parents that forcible restoration would only invoke disaster. The parents agreed but asked for some accommodation somewhere at least until the examination which, disingenuously perhaps, they regarded as of *vital* importance, had been taken. Crichton-Miller offered a bed in the sanatorium and attendance at classes until the exams were over, with himself taking responsibility. It was not an ideal solution but the parents jumped at the suggestion and litigation came off the agenda. They accepted the fact that any further notable breach of discipline would mean the end and in fact when the boy broke into the sanatorium store-cupboard after three weeks of good behaviour, the parents took him away without demur.

One third of the candidates were now failing Common Entrance at the first attempt, which gave some indication that standards were rising and that the preparatory schools no longer regarded Stowe as a kind recipient of doubtful entrants. The 'O' level results had improved and more boys had qualified for the sixth-form courses: in 1962 there were 247 students taking 'A' level subjects as against 184 in 1958. Despite rising fees and the wish of Oxbridge candidates to leave at Christmas to enjoy a break before university the numbers remained strong. Among junior masters there was a very definite loyalty to Crichton-Miller, as events were to prove. However, everyone who was a housemaster at the time, or took their part, seems to be agreed that they were unhappy about presumed inconsistency and a lack of rapport. The General Purposes Committee had advised the headmaster to get on better terms with senior masters but this was not easily done. Breaches of the rules seemed to proliferate and both the housemasters who felt monitors had been too severely punished and those who thought miscreants had been too lightly treated accumulated grievances, to which Carey appears to have lent an ear.

After one committee meeting at Stowe a fateful fog descended and some of the Governors were obliged to spend the night at the school. It was inevitable that they should stay with senior rather than junior masters and a great many complaints were collected especially from the senior housemaster, Bruce Barr of Grafton. Carey thought that the headmaster should retire before the appointed date in 1966. Some members of the governing body considered, rather curiously, that any frank discussion of complaints would bring retribution on the informers. The Chairman, David Robarts, was a banker and country gentleman, and well beyond his depth in Common Room politics. He was prevailed upon to send a letter to Crichton-Miller, received on 18 January 1963, the day before the Spring Term began, saying that he must hand over the school to Carey and take extended sick-leave while three Old Stoic Governors – Noel Annan, Peter Sherwood and Peter Agnew – investigated what were called 'serious allegations'. It was true that Crichton-Miller had had a small operation before Christmas but he was fully recovered, and it has to be said that Carey had no experience of running schools.

The Chairman told Carey to explain the situation to senior masters and ask all who wished to speak to the Triumvirate to do so. One can well imagine that some would only be too happy to oblige while others with a distaste for politics would abstain. Bruce Barr, who had been quite prominent in making criticisms of the Reynolds regime, drew up a long memorandum listing complaints, which, together with the headmaster's replies, gives as full a picture of the life of a public schoolmaster and his concerns as one is likely to find.

The charges were an odd mixture of the grave and the trivial.

Much was made of the 'abdication' speech. The headmaster pointed out that for almost four years he had checked punctuality, hair cuts and general negligence. ('Previously the boys were not asked to pick up litter; a man was paid overtime to do this for them.') He had visited the cinema and dealt with bad manners on the playing field. He regretted that these duties limited his contacts with boys to a series of minor admonitions. He wished to delegate such tasks but had not handed over ultimate authority.

Barr complained that the headmaster did not wish to attend housemasters' meetings, and that he had to preside himself. Crichton-Miller replied that he had asked the senior housemaster to preside in order to give some status to what was otherwise a purely nominal title. He assumed that housemasters would like to have some private meetings – as happened elsewhere – to work out presentation of a case. He would be quite willing to reverse all this, attend all meetings and take the chair if it were considered important.

More seriously the housemasters stated that his staff appointments had been haphazard and undistinguished. For his part Crichton-Miller analysed the twenty-two most recent appointments, showing he had met the requirements for cricket (county player), hockey (Oxford Blue), tennis (Cambridge Blue), Rugby (two near-Blues), a housemaster, chaplain and a man to start senior scouting as well as five officers for the C.C F. Roger Rawcliffe, an assistant master then, was very explicit that this charge was unfounded. The appointments included D.B. McMurray, future headmaster of Oundle; John Hunt, future headmaster of Roedean; future housemasters of Temple, Chatham and Cobham; two Directors of Music at other schools; Anthony Pedder, later senior tutor; K. Meldrum, a pioneer in outward bound training; and several other well–qualified men. He reckoned the failure rate to be three or four out of the twenty-two – relatively low. The list refuted Carey's statement that no one of housemaster calibre had been brought to Stowe.

Barr referred to disaffection over a special payment to a new master which went counter to the policy of eliminating special allowances. This, said Crichton-Miller, was an odd charge as Barr had been particularly anxious to have an assistant in the Biology Department with special interest in Natural History. The master had been promised that he would not lose money by coming to

Stowe but it was found that, although the Stowe scale was higher than that of his previous school, he had been allowed more for board residence and it was felt morally right to make an adjustment. The young man had offered to forgo his allowance if it led to friction.

Arrangements for Speech Day and the economy drives came under fire. So too did the 'Study Periods' introduced to deal in part with the long periods of unemployment between lunch and supper on three days a week:

> I announced the plan in December 1962 [said Crichton-Miller] and asked for comments. I had four letters, two in favour and two against. Three weeks later I sent full details to all masters – and before term started I raised the matter again for full discussion. The scheme itself is complicated – but Form Masters are keen. Housemasters spoke so strongly against it that I have been forced to postpone its introduction. I guess their real complaint is that I should have consulted them before other masters. However this is not a House matter and I am not prepared to regard them as a Cabinet for all school business.

One of the complaints was that a wall had been put up in the ante-room of the masters' coffee room, 'On the instructions of the Headmaster without reference to any senior master'. It transpired that younger masters, especially those living at a distance, had to change into games clothes in public and a small screen wall had been put up at the request of a master half-way up the seniority table. There were objections to invigilating G.C.E. exams. 'About forty masters have to learn this routine,' ran the accusation, 'thus increasing the possibility of a serious mistake.' They wished to retain paid invigilators, but enquiries at the Headmasters' Conference revealed that all schools expected that masters would invigilate. It was true that numbers of candidates and complexities were increasing. 'I said we must adapt ourselves to these new demands as others do', commented the headmaster. 'The senior masters will not accept this and harp on the subject term after term.'

The Barr Memorandum, under the heading of 'Unnecessary Expenditure', criticized the appointment of an estates bursar, Lieutenant-Colonel E.G.W.T. Walsh O.S. and the inauguration of the beagle pack, 'in spite of rumours and hints of the critical financial position of the School'. 'I deny that I have ever said that the financial position of the School is critical,' said Crichton-Miller, 'but I have frequently said that, unless we keep expenses down, fees must go up. And high fees are against the interests of the School.' The extra bursarial appointment, he said, had been a Governors' decision, though one he favoured, and was not relevant to the headmaster's efficiency. The beagles he naturally defended with some warmth:

> From the Consolidated Extras Charge some £10,000 p.a. is available for Games and Extras Societies. I have appointed a Committee which allocates this sum – the Bursar, President of Games and the Second Master are principal members. They allocated £50, a sum smaller than they gave to Archery. Because I knew they might be prejudiced I advised the Secretary not to appeal. Instead we set about raising money privately and we have obtained at least £150 through subscriptions. Quite a number of boys are employed looking after the hounds and *their* Games Subscriptions should be available to a larger extent – but I took this line to meet criticism. (The reaction is not encouraging.)

The problem of the Blue Book (school list and calendar) raised an interesting point. Masters claimed that they had asked for the traditional list of addresses to be retained but found it had been published separately. With some sensitivity, the lack of which was the principal burthen of complaint, the headmaster replied: 'I do not think it suitable that boys should see every term the names of guardians, step-parents etc . . . It is unfair on those who have separated or divorced parents.'

Some housemasters objected to the allocation of boys to houses by the headmaster's secretary and complained of Miss Hill's 'peremptory manner'. As the headmaster decribed the situation, housemasters had full control over their lists until confirmed places were taken up two years ahead and they were permitted to have 'reserves'. After then the applicants that did not have houses and the failures in Common Entrance had to be matched. 'Vacancies in Houses must be at our disposal. Miss Hill (who rarely fails to satisfy parents) has attempted to meet Housemasters' wishes. The Housemasters now think that they are entitled to pick and choose up to the last minute. On the particular occasion quoted I had to remind a man that his wishes could only be met by courtesy of

Miss Hill whose task is not enviable. Without co-operation it becomes impossible.'

The memorandum contained a long section on discipline, and the miserable tale of X in the sanatorium was repeated. Housemasters felt that the sanction of expulsion had been softened and that boys who had lost rank and privilege had had them too hastily restored. Crichton-Miller reiterated his aversion to expulsion. 'More cases come up for expulsion or removal, than at any school I know of. There is the unusual characteristic that Housemasters are constantly pressing for this ultimate sanction whereas at most schools Housemasters are defending their boys and begging for sympathetic treatment. (This, however does not apply to all and particularly the three new men who have submitted no cases yet.)' He admitted that some boys given second chances abused them but, in favour of a less dismissive policy, he cited one case where a pupil had been rusticated and, on return, taken out of his house, lodged with a master and supervised by Crichton-Miller himself. 'He remained for two terms during which I had only one complaint – that he had been late for shooting practice. Meanwhile he took a Scholarship examination for Cambridge and is there now. He was not an incorrigible type.' The defensive statements are convincing though the Governors may have considered that the tone did not suggest that compromise was likely or that troubles would subside.

The idea of 'Form Periods' (5–6 on Tuesdays and Thursdays), a further endeavour to break the long afternoons whence disciplinary problems emanated, disturbed Raymond Walker, now senior tutor. 'You seem to have a horror of boys doing nothing', he wrote. 'Stowe is a beautiful place and I am glad to see boys sitting on the South Front occasionally, merely admiring Capability Brown's work. This is something we offer which other schools do not. I hope you will change your mind about imposing these periods upon us. If you do not, I should be grateful if Masters and boys could be informed that this is your idea not mine.' He too had been pressed by colleagues to represent his views to the Governors, though many technical matters concerning promotions and the 'setting' of particular subjects were sorted out in discussion with Crichton-Miller while these other events unfolded.

It was Clifford's feeling that the Common Room, believing it had played a part in the moves to change a headmaster once, was seeking another trial of strength. Many of the charges referred to above were capable of resolution if the goodwill had been there but behind the specific problems was a conflict between two concepts of Stowe's future: a Garden of Eden tempered, like the original, by expulsion; or a place of constant and oftimes ungrateful tillage. Crichton-Miller remarked that no one had criticized his policies when asked to take on a housemastership nor had Bruce Barr when invited to be senior housemaster. 'It would be easy for me to reply with equally general claims that I have had inadequate support from senior masters; that I receive complaints from parents about them; and that they have actively interfered with loyalty of younger masters whom I have recently appointed . . . No useful purpose would be served by a slanging match of this sort.' He added a suggestion that there should be an independent enquiry by Her Majesty's Inspectors to study academic results and appraise the masters. 'In similar circumstances in the Services eight or ten men would have been transferred and in Industry a similar number would have been paid off. In a boarding school such measures are highly undesirable for obvious reasons. As it was, we stumbled along. Considerable improvements were effected; complaints from parents dwindled rapidly. Last Summer four senior masters retired in the normal way with honour undimmed.'

At the end of his answers to the Barr Memorandum Crichton-Miller deplored his own decision in appointing Carey on the basis of one reference from Harrow. Dr James of Harrow was held in high regard in the profession. But Crichton-Miller had since been in touch with the headmaster of Michaelhouse who had replied in such strong terms that the letter was suitable for the Chairman's eyes only! He regretted the approaches to Governors: 'The situation which had arisen led to the schoolmaster's dream. Every senior master had an opportunity of saying that the School could be better run; and he could do this without risk to himself; indeed he could do it in the happy belief that he was serving the School and his colleagues.'

The first meeting of the Triumvirate was at Stowe on 26 January with Derek Bateman acting as secretary. Many younger masters were under the impression that it was a general inquiry dealing with economies and arrangements of a kind not too unfamiliar. As only masters who chose to attend gave evidence it was inevitably critical of the headmaster. Carey was the first to be interviewed.

He stated that he thought the standard of discipline lower than that at Harrow or Michaelhouse, though at both schools there were houses where behaviour was worse than the Stowe average. The headmaster was too liberal over expulsions and felt that Stowe admitted failure in employing this weapon. He took the headmaster's 'abdication' speech – 'I am handing over to Mr Carey who will be found more ruthless and quicker over the ground than I am' – somewhat naïvely to imply that Crichton-Miller felt his mental and physical powers were failing.

He was followed by Patrick Hunter, brought back from retirement, and he in turn was followed by Bruce Barr. His comments were more conciliatory than his memo. He had been at Pembroke, Cambridge with Crichton-Miller and thus had a long acquaintanceship. He did not think that the new housemasterships had caused any jealousy, nor that the headmaster bowed to parental pressure. Over a recent betting case he had been quite undeterred by threats of court action, but the case of X had caused widespread resentment.

Raymond Walker was more severe. It was true that, apart from Andrew Vinen, recent appointments had been weak in Maths, where tutorial skills for the most gifted are necessary. Walker thought there was too little searching out for brilliant specialist teachers. He disapproved of pushing forward too hastily to 'O' levels. Many boys came to Stowe because of ingrained strengths in Latin teaching at the prep schools and mathematical ignorance came to light only later. His evidence was relatively harsh. He did not like the idea of 'study' periods and considered that evasion would constitute a major headache for housemasters and tutors.

Alasdair Macdonald, housemaster of Chatham, was, as one would expect, more of a peacemaker in his observations of both parties. He thought that the 'abdication' speech had been jocularly intended, had no complaints about the way in which the headmaster had dealt with boys in his house and said that Crichton-Miller had in no way canvassed for support. Asked if the same were true of his opponents Macdonald replied that some masters had stronger personalities than others and he believed that anger still remained over the damning remarks made by the headmaster at this first meeting. 'J.F.' had been killed by routine administration and it was right that there should be delegation. He thought that some comments had been misconstrued. A statement that 'rugger is played with great spirit but very little skill' had been taken as a reflection upon the coaching whereas it was no more than a reference to innate talents.

Saunders, Brown, the bursar (K.C. Box), Gilbert and Adams were all seen in turn. Brown believed that the headmaster had been badly briefed before he came and that the persistent stress upon 'discipline' was erecting barriers within the community which were contrary to the aims of the foundation, as interpreted by Roxburgh. The bursar felt that he had had to bear too much odium for recent economy cuts, that the headmaster should have seen domestic staff to discuss redundancies and that he had extended too abrasive a supervision into the bursar's department. The Director of Music was away but he sent a letter which, in essence, thanked Crichton-Miller for the introduction of music scholars and the increase in music staff. Gilbert, who had survived a baptism of fire in Temple, dwelt upon the doubts which surrounded the finality of expulsion. 'Y' was the son of a distinguished Old Boy and an example of the malign fate which decrees that sons of the most enthusiastic Old Boys will often be the least amenable to the charms of tradition. Gilbert had wanted him out but the headmaster had transferred him to another House. 'Z' had been involved in a serious breach of the rules but had been asked to lunch with the Bishop of Oxford, which could not be right. He proffered his resignation if the headmaster stayed. Adams was secretary of the Old Stoics as well as housemaster of Walpole. He thought that edicts and proclamations were not followed up effectively with action. The conversation ranged over trouser turn-ups, blocked footpaths where notices had been put up and ignored and other matters, in which it seemed the headmaster could wield some mysterious influence divorced from the supervisory actions of others. He thought a number of Old Stoics had taken the 'abdication' speech to mean that Crichton-Miller would shortly be retiring. His own interpretation, sensibly, was that the headmaster wished to have more time to visit prep schools and attend meetings concerned with the appeal that was pending on the fortieth anniversary.

After Adams and David Donaldson, whom the headmaster had employed as a junior 'adjutant' had been seen, Mrs Crichton-Miller asked if she could put some views before the Triumvirate. She spoke fully on the social void especially for wives and married masters. As only three houses could lodge married men, some masters had been passed over and this had left resentments. Not all the wives could drive and this meant long periods of the day and in the evenings when there was little to do but dwell upon rumours and speculations. She had been surprised to find how few of the staff families knew each other.

At a second meeting on 30 January the headmaster was questioned on his replies to the Barr Memorandum. He restated his opinion that under Eric Reynolds senior masters had been independent and did not like being given instructions. He thought that the earlier interviews had been self-selected and that there had been some lobbying. One senior figure had said recently that there was little relevance in discussing the timetable for 1964 because the headmaster might not be here. He did not believe that the Headmasters' Conference would stand idly by and fail to take action on behalf of a member.

A special Governors' meeting was called for 7 February. At this meeting the Chairman announced that they were going to invite a Q.C. and two recently retired Inspectors of Schools to form a Tribunal, which would meet shortly at the school, to take the matter further. The Chairman would have done better to have quashed the whole process at this point but he was inexperienced in school politics and both parties were keen for different reasons to widen the investigation. Crichton-Miller, believing he had a good case, wished everything to be sifted 'to the bitter end'. The senior masters had put themselves in a position where future co-operation would be almost impossible. The headmaster asked if he would be expected to marshal a parade of witnesses for this new Tribunal as he was not prepared to do so. The Chairman replied that *all* junior masters would be seen, adding, 'You may have friends among them'. Crichton-Miller answered that he had never set out to be popular and had no reason to expect friends anywhere, but he wanted a thorough investigation.

The Tribunal arrived on St Valentine's Day. One of the retired Inspectors was F.T. Arnold, a master at Stowe in the very early days. C.W. Baty Q.C. and J.T. Moloney were his colleagues. They straightaway announced that they would not have time to see all masters. They would see those already interviewed and circulate a general notice to anyone interested. By this time the remainder of the staff had realized that the investigations were not related to general economies and about twenty-five junior masters signed a demand that they should be heard. The Tribunal was unwilling to see so many and eventually the twenty-five were seen either in groups or by one member of the Tribunal only.

As we have already seen the Governors who represented Allied Schools were suspicious of the headmaster's policies and would not rush to his defence. Others were not fully acquainted with recent history at the school. Nevertheless a number of masters decided that they must canvass Governors individually on the headmaster's behalf, though he himself said they should not do so unless a particular Governor was a personal friend or acquaintance. It was estimated that about fifteen to twenty masters contacted Governors but naturally junior masters did not know many personally. The action put housemasters into a difficult position nonetheless, since it was likely that junior masters' comments would contain some criticism of themselves. Dr Farmer, a relatively new master, had already submitted a long and unsolicited statement to Derek Bateman which analysed weaknesses in the system and referred to the readiness of senior men to criticize the headmaster and his policies to boys and Old Boys. Seven out of nine housemasters then burned their boats by saying that they would resign if the headmaster stayed. Sixteen other masters said they would submit their resignation if he left. At this point Roger Rawcliffe and other mediators persuaded both parties to withdraw their ultimatums and allow feelings to simmer down. The Governors were in an unenviable plight though it is hard to believe that all housemasters would have carried out their threat. They were in comfortable circumstances with commitments to families and were less likely to obtain comparable posts elsewhere than younger masters, especially as the rapid growth of the new universities led to difficulties in recruiting in schools.

The Tribunal sat for three days from 14 to 16 February. It drew up a report based upon oral evidence from the headmaster, bursar, estates bursar, Rosemary Hill and Patrick Hunter. They sifted through the qualifications of younger masters, G.C.E. results, entry figures and the files of some eighteen miscreant youths. They read Dr Farmer's memorandum which was highly critical of the school as he found it in 1961. The report covered a great deal of the ground already described and made a stout effort to see both sides of the issue. Of Crichton-Miller's first masters' meeting and the castigation of the staff, the report said that 'no feelings were spared' and the speech had been based upon 'general report rather than observation'. They had not found a coherent plan of reform, though it must have been clear that no plan was really needed except efficiency in applying the rules and in teaching. They made reference to the headmaster's 'rough-shod' approach: 'It has never been a practice with him to make his way by gentle methods of prior persuasion or to follow up his decisions with a reasonable exposition and explanation.' The liaison route through the second master had failed and certain senior masters might have acted more positively to relieve a harmful situation. Matters were not improved by the headmaster's supposition that members of the Common Room were going behind his back to the Governors.

The Tribunal commented that discipline depended upon every-one, though that was hardly newly received wisdom. On the vexed question of expulsions they decided that 'capricious and inconsis-tent' courses had provoked dissension. 'It was rightly considered that too much weight was attached to the effect of expulsion on the individual boy and too little to the effect of leniency on the position of the housemaster and on the morale of the School.'

More cogently perhaps, they examined the 'lack of academic stimulus'. 'The qualities which secured his appointment were thought to lie in other directions.' It is true that more might have been achieved if the headmaster had taught 'A' level groups or scholarship classes and led from the front in dealing with the cleverest brains. Yet the Stowe tradition had always been that the headmaster taught as many boys as possible in the Lower School in order to get to know them in the junior forms. Crichton-Miller's remark that Stowe 'was a school for the average boy' they thought had been misunderstood, but it had gained wider currency through repetition and lent some colour to the opinion that he was less interested in the intellectual minority. He had had success, though they thought it a modest one, in improving standards in the Lower and Middle School but he had not considered carefully the beneficial results of scholarship filtering down from on high.

They concurred with the view that times were not easy for recruiting academic staff as the new universities lured away the best-qualified graduates to research and lecturing, but they com-mented favourably on the personal qualities of the junior men. 'It

may well be true that not all the academic needs of the School have
been met but it has not been established that these needs have been
ignored in favour of the claims of games and other non-academic
activities or that any fail to pull their weight in one field or
another.'

The report was not decisively in favour of either camp and concluded: 'We trust that what we have recorded above will provide
the factual conclusions required as a foundation for the appro-
priate measure.' They did however go outside their terms of reference and added a supplementary memorandum on the role of the
second master: 'It is surprising that one so new should form opinions so soon and move so drastically. We suspect his motives. We
share the mistrust of him widely felt on the staff.' They considered
that his leadership of a revolt had drawn many younger masters to
the headmaster's side. They thought that Dr Farmer's memorandum should be circulated to all Governors, as an unbiased description of a situation needing reform.

Thus far, the housemasters may appear to be cantankerous and
exasperating. To give a fairer picture it must be emphasized that
the position of housemaster is one of the most exacting and stress-
ful in the profession. In addition to the demands made by classroom teaching the housemaster lives with and shares the concerns
of over sixty adolescents. He is in the front line daily for complaints
and entreaties; every waking hour of the night he has troublous
surmises lest all are not safe and sound. The task requires a flow
of encouragement and sometimes indulgence from higher authority. If they had forfeited sympathy they were suffering for it
and this was something that the Governors who were most in
touch appreciated. To add to this there was a misunderstanding
of the Roxburgh inheritance. It was seen to imply that rules were
pettifogging things and counterproductive, that a relaxed attitude
would allow natural goodness to assert itself. But Roxburgh's real
contribution had been to lift many of the troublesome burdens
from the housemasters' shoulders, invigorating the sluggish and
restraining the wayward boy, diplomatically countering parents
and accepting their concern. The range of his correspondence was
amazing and the effects of its cessation had been accumulating.
Patrick Hunter was correct when he foresaw the consequences of
Roxburgh's failure to trust and train others to act on his behalf.

The final chapter of the story was the most surprising of all. On

14 March there was a full Governors' meeting. Crichton-Miller was not present. It was by no means unanimous. The Allied Schools members had their own reasons for wanting a change, the independent members were genuinely bewildered, had been given differing accounts by older and younger staff, and did not wish to abandon the headmaster without the strongest reasons. The Chairman declared himself neutral which made everything more uncertain.

At the close the Chairman and two other Governors saw Crichton-Miller and said that it had been decided he should stay with full powers and Council support. David Robarts, the Chairman, would himself come down to Stowe on the following Monday, address the staff and appeal for unity. Carey would be asked to leave at the end of the Spring Term. There was, however, a condition: the headmaster must sign a paper saying he agreed that in future his appointment could be terminated at one term's notice. As Robarts pointed out, this did not make much legal difference but it would serve as a warning. Crichton-Miller agreed and had four communications from other Governors that the decision had gone in his favour.

On the next day he put up a notice announcing that the Chairman would address the Common Room on the following Monday. Several people were eager to know what had happened and, although it would have been politic to remain silent, it was a hard matter to dissemble. Forty minutes before the Monday meeting the Chairman and Vice-Chairman (Annan) entered the headmaster's office. The Chairman said abruptly that confidence had been breached and the Governors' decision made known. He was therefore reversing it and wanted the headmaster's resignation forthwith. The reversed decision was final: he had been in touch with what he called 'effective governors'. If there were agreement Crichton-Miller would be treated well; if not he would be given nothing.

Crichton-Miller remained insistent that he had never been warned that his victory was confidential. There was no tradition at Stowe that only the Chairman could make important announcements. Lord Gisborough had been a cipher and Pickard-Cambridge a remote administrator. When Carey had taken over at Christmas there had been no public utterance by the Chairman. He did, however, sign the ultimatum, feeling that the situation was totally bewildering and that there must be a group of Governors from whom no support could be expected. Robarts and Annan then went on to the masters. They announced the headmaster's resignation and Carey's departure, adding that if any master wished to resign he should contact 'a Governor'. Housemasters were asked to remain, were rebuked for their recent failures by Annan and told that a committee under a younger housemaster, George Clarke, would initiate a co-ordinated effort to achieve co-operation over pastoral care. When Robarts and Annan returned to the headmaster's study there was an interruption by at least half-a-dozen masters demanding to be heard. The argument was heated and outspoken.

There were many misunderstandings about the crucial Council Meeting unearthed by masters who made it their business to investigate. Peter Sherwood, one of the Old Stoic Governors who came down to discuss the press release, said that Crichton-Miller had misinterpreted the Council's decision, which was that he should go. A younger master said he had received a different account from someone else present. He was told that this Governor had left early but that statement was checked and proved false. This revelation did not quieten discontent and rumours flew that the Council minutes would be doctored.

Crichton-Miller suggested that he might stay until July 1964 when he would be a respectable age at which to retire, but this was not accepted. The Chairman held yet another meeting at the school – a curt one which began with his declaration that he had not come to listen to complaints and that masters might not approach Governors indiscriminately. One would be chosen (Anthony Quinton) to act as a channel of communication. Another Governor then read out to the masters the Tribunal's report without questions.

It is not surprising that while this turmoil prevailed morale suffered. A large number of monitors were reduced to the ranks and among candidates for expulsion were three heads of houses. Five masters approached the University Appointments Boards for new posts within a week. Nor, despite assurances, did the search for a successor seem to be an easy task. Six H.M.C. headmasters were approached, but excused themselves from applying. Two of the four who answered the press advertisements withdrew. The Headmasters' Conference made groaning noises. Four masters left but Crichton-Miller, when Robert Drayson was appointed, invited him down to Stowe to talk with twelve other disaffected masters and the dialogue secured the services of some for the future. There were eighty cancellations of future entries, twenty-seven for the following January. The affair became a matter for speculation in the preparatory schools and probably lost nothing in the telling. The Common Room had little energy left for the school routine. Ten cricket matches were lost in the summer of 1963 including one against Bradfield which began with a Bradfield score of one run for three wickets! Athletics had a poor season after four victorious years and lost all senior and junior matches. The tennis team went out in the quarter-finals of the Youll Cup. On its fortieth anniversary the school seemed to be on the edge of an abyss and facing its worst crisis since the financial problems of 1934.

Some much-needed balm was brought by an 'informal' visit of H.M. the Queen Mother for the anniversary celebrations. If she knew she was walking on a minefield she did not show it. Creative forces were mustered to present a promising image of the community at work and play. The C.C.F. provided the Guard of Honour, swimmers and scullers demonstrated both in and on the lake, the beagles paraded. When she visited the Chapel the choir were observed to be deep in rehearsal and at her own request she talked with boys at work on projects in the workshops. The prefects entertained her to tea in the Garter Room to the strains of the school orchestra. A liquidambar tree was planted near to the Temple of Venus and she left to a fanfare by the trumpeters from the school steps.

The gift of the school to the Crichton-Millers was carpeting for their new home. At a signal from the head of school a roll descended and unfolded across the Roxburgh stage, 'like a gift from Heaven' as the headmaster observed. He had the satisfaction of knowing that much of his work remained. In 1965 the existence of the Landscape Committee, springing from his concern for planned building development, was formalized and a more considered policy for new buildings followed. Although the circumstances had been unhappy Stowe had been snatched from contemplation of the past. As Granville Carr, a prominent Old Stoic, wrote at the moment of Crichton-Miller's retirement, 'I believe you have tackled a job for which future Stoics (and O.S.s) will applaud you'.

11

Bob Drayson

The task of selecting a new headmaster was not easy. Recent events did not encourage headmasters who had proved their worth to apply and it was not the time to gamble on someone inexperienced. The Council was rescued from its predicament by Derek Bateman, Secretary of Allied Schools, whose home was in the neighbourhood of Reed's School, Cobham, and who had a high regard for the headmaster, Bob Drayson. Drayson had doubled the size of Reed's and raised it from being a charitable foundation to public-school status.

He was forty-six years old and had been educated at St Lawrence, Ramsgate, and Downing College, Cambridge where he read Modern Languages and History. His university career was interrupted by the war. For four years he served in motor torpedo boats and was awarded the Distinguished Service Cross in 1943. His naval training had given him a crisp and effective manner (the Gothic Library was soon known as 'The Bridge') and he knew the importance of caring for the whole ship's company, always ready to take an approving interest in the labours of the chefs, engineers and groundsmen. He brought a breath of strong evangelical feeling to Stowe and declared on his first Speech Day that he saw Chapel as the centre of the school. He was a gifted and well-preserved hockey player who had represented Cambridge for two years, captained a Kent XI and played in an England trial. He continued to play club games well into his headmastership, though he wrote to an equally enthusiastic parent: 'I do find now that my positional play is vital!' He taught at St Lawrence and at Felsted, where he was house tutor; at both schools, as well as at Reed's, he had learned the necessity of unremitting effort to attract entries to a foundation that did not have a large natural constituency. The only critical note sounded when the appointment was announced was by Heckstall-Smith, long retired, who thought the photograph in the *Illustrated London News* looked 'too correct'.

Drayson was, of course, in a very strong position. The governing body could not possibly contemplate his resignation and another search, so he received steady support for his many building plans. Peter Agnew, who replaced Robarts as Chairman, was keen to restore confidence; their correspondence was uniformly amicable and when he gave up the Chairmanship in 1969 he described Drayson as 'an absolute joy to work with'. Alasdair Macdonald, who succeeded Carey as second master, had all the qualities and experience needed for the post. The Common Room emerged from the crisis in a state of some alarm and realized that a Temple of Concord 'not built with hands' had to be raised in its midst. The number of awards had remained relatively low for so notable a school ('I think some of the Governors . . . would trade-in 50 'A' levels for half a dozen awards at Oxbridge', Crichton-Miller had written), but academic results had shown improvement. Between 1957 and 1962 the number of 'O' levels had risen from 819 to 1079 and between 1957 and 1963 the number of 'A' level passes from 131 to 191. Because of the troubles numbers had shrunk slightly down to 560 and recruiting would have to be undertaken, but the appeal launched during the fortieth anniversary had already brought in over £80,000 towards the £200,000 target and the Bridgland Trust had granted a large capital sum, the income of which could be used to undertake restoration projects and purchases which might not be justified out of normal funds.

In education generally the most difficult years of the 1960s were still to come, but Bob Drayson enjoyed a high profile and had great self-confidence. He relished conversation and had a belief in 'communication' as a means of dissolving opposition. His notes on interviews with boys in trouble bristle with comments such as: 'I think we are getting through', 'He accepted his position', 'He appreciates the points made', etc. Speaking to the Old Stoics at a dinner in the House of Commons on 5 November 1965, he said: 'A few boys come along from time to time to tell me that the School is going to the dogs and then talk about it for an hour and by the time they go out again they have either forgotten what they came to say or they have at least realised that Authority has a reasonable point of view and things aren't going so badly after all.'

He was industrious and fielded all the questions over discipline in full and serenely amiable correspondence that swelled out the files to the size they had been in Roxburgh's day. He travelled thousand of miles to give prizes at preparatory schools and preach in their chapels. Fellow headmasters sometimes looked a little wan when he remarked that he was disappointed if a sermon did not bring in five or six enquiries for places the following week and they wondered whether the Feast of the Conversion to Stowe should be included in the Church Calendar, but they could believe the statement. Invitations to visit Stowe accompanied prep-school correspondence and links were established where they had not existed before. There were few terms when he was not committed to appeals and fund-raising and his travels on behalf of Stowe took him all over Britain and beyond its shores. Crichton-Miller's idea of the guest nights was expanded into Commemoration Dinners held in May each year (May being the month of the opening of the school and of Roxburgh's death), to which came college tutors, preparatory-school headmasters and public figures to whom Stowe owed a debt, including occasionally representatives from local education, planning and the police!

His speeches on these occasions and at the Old Stoic Dinners were indicative of a jovial approach to the rough and tumble of school life. The Common Entrance papers were sifted for quotable gems ('Wordsworth when young took full advantage of the beauties of the Lake District', etc). A parcel of overseas scripts sent to an educational assessor elicited the comment: 'I think the Stowe scripts show great originality. You should not have failed anybody who could see King Alfred saying "I came, I saw, I conquered", when greeting a defeated Rommel!' So too were the reports ('Takes time for earnest thought before deciding that a problem is insoluble'). There were anecdotes from the formrooms, as for example when a Science master found himself struggling with *The Merchant of Venice* in an English class. A pert small boy asked 'Does the word "strained" mean "pulled tight" or "passed through a sieve"?' After a long pause came the reply: 'My boy, as it says the quality of mercy is *not* strained, the question does not arise.' He liked to relate the encounter between a truculent Stoic and an Australian chef at the serving hatch: Boy: 'And don't forget I'm the person who pays your wages.' Chef: 'Good on you mate. I've been wanting to meet you. You don't pay me enough.' Then there was the episode when a young constable, on questioning a boy who had bought an unsafe motorbike, said he would take down a statement. He read it back in a dead-pan voice with no punctuation and asked if it was correct. The boy replied languidly 'Not bad. Seven out of ten!' or there was the exhortation of a young Stoic to the Stowe wives about the Fête: 'Bring anything you don't want but is too good to give away. Bring your husbands.' He enjoyed stories against himself, such as the tale of the boy to whom he said solemnly that he stood no chance of getting into Cambridge. 'Well, you did Sir.' On one of his frequent attempts to smarten appearance, he told a young man to report the following morning, 'looking like a human being', and was informed that he was addressing a member of a visiting Uppingham team who would be many miles distant. Speeches and articles in the newsletters which were circulated to the Old Boys were in the main a series of cavalry charges across the moral high ground, but he gave considerable latitude to the satirists and those who wrote for the ephemerals. The result was that his attitudes became almost indispensable to them (e.g. 'A review of the musical *Hair* by our resident critic R.Q.D.: "Too long"'). Although his campaigns of attrition on sloppiness of dress aroused opposition there was rarely profound resentment. He had no objections to being interviewed for the school magazines such as the *Voice* and gave the impression that authority was tempered with fairness.

Thus, although it would not be correct to say that all disciplinary problems were solved, they did not generate such heat or lead to Common Room tantrums. Indeed, as the prevailing view among adolescents in the 1960s was that everyone over twenty-three was out of touch and moribund the Common Room had to hang together for the sake of self-esteem. Drayson's quick reflexes and mannerisms were as essential to the schoolboy journalists as those of Harold Macmillan to the satirists of his day. At one school lecture a lady speaker was searching vainly for the name of a well-known television pundit: 'Malcolm . . . er . . . Malcolm . . .' she hesitated. 'BUGGERIDGE' boomed Drayson from the side-lines repeating the misnomer with increasing conviction as the whisperings grew. He resembled Roxburgh in seeming to put the school under omnipresent scrutiny. When he went on a world tour in 1974 the Stowe magazines were almost hurt at his absence and the cartoonists had a fine time depicting his familiar features half-hidden by the Pyramids or Ayers Rock.

He resumed control of various areas of school life such as the games committee. He knew a great deal about the practical working of departments and said once that his principal achievement had been to rescue the Physics department from an existence on five floor levels where 'oxygen cylinders and other heavy pieces of equipment had to be carried continuously from one floor to another' by the laboratory assistants. He grasped the nettle of non-resident housemasters, and during his time he brought three married housemasters into flats in the main building, making use of the new house, Lyttelton, to release more space. He was very conscious of the public image of Stowe and confident enough to let prospective parents be taken on tours by the pupils. His naval experience had taught him the importance of N.C.O.s. His reports and speeches singled out the prefects and monitors for special mention. It was hard for headmasters of the time to please everyone. When a father wrote in 1970 after his six years of checking on hair length and tidiness: 'I would like to see Stowe adopt a much firmer line on dress and general appearance', Drayson in turn wrote, 'This makes me very cross', over it. In 1968 he reported to the Governors that Speech Day had gone well and that the 'lunatic fringe of long-haired youths' (Old Stoics) became 'fortunately fewer each year'. This was a world very different from the Speech Day of 1927 when an Old Boy had returned wearing a pair of flannel trousers and Roxburgh had informed his parents : 'The indignation raised by — 's appearance was felt particularly among the boys and some very severe comments were made by the Prefects and others.'

In his opening address to boys and masters he gave a clear picture of disciplinary procedures which would follow offences: warnings, summoning of parents, expulsion. In practice it was never easy to adopt such a clear-cut pattern and discipline was never perfected, but he declared an amnesty at the outset, and even the most tortuous and complicated dealings with recidivists were conducted without rancour. In the mood of the times it was not possible to pursue a policy of total freedom and trust but by the time of his arrival many of the oldest masters had left and there were few who hankered after a return to the school as they remembered it in its earliest days. Drayson was able to assimilate the Roxburgh tradition more easily than either of his predecessors for it had become a piece of history, though he admitted privately that the anecdotes and imitations sometimes irritated him. At the end of five weeks he declared: 'We must give thanks to God for the greatness of Roxburgh but we must nevertheless realise that his work was in the past and that we must now, as a school, go forward into the future, building on the traditions with which he endowed the School.'

His arrival coincided with questions of national confidence in the public schools being addressed by the Labour Government and the Newsome and Donnison Commissions set up to examine their role in British education.[1] Stillborn as the reports eventually were, the inquiries aroused sufficient anxiety at the time. At his first Speech Day in 1964 Drayson remarked: 'We are an independent School and so, at this time, we are the butt with others of considerable criticism.' Legislative threats did not seem fanciful. The question most frequently asked at Old Boy gatherings was 'Is there any point in putting down my son for an institution that may not exist in ten years time?' Few could foresee that the push which the political parties gave to the comprehensive system and the abolition of grammar and direct-grant schools would give to the independent sector a new lease of life from 1970 onwards.

Another and quite different set of current ideas assisted the peaceful settlement of Stowe. The 1960s witnessed a new spirit of concern for the handicapped, the elderly and the disadvantaged. The community service schemes which were launched at Stowe and at other schools around this time became powerful counterweights to the C.C.F. and to its unpopularity in certain quarters. They absorbed energies and leisure time, put left-wing opinion to the test and afforded a great deal of personal fulfilment. As we have seen, there had been projects inspired by Toc H ideals at Stowe in the 1930s. Now more ambitious plans were laid and success and fame come to the Stowe community service groups as they unearthed all manner of useful and desirable activities in the Buckingham district. Nigel Eddy, who had been head boy of

[1] A female descendant of the Dukes of Buckingham was heard to remark: 'We don't live in the style that we used to, of course, but I'm happy to say I still have a manservant who can come in and switch off the television when Harold Wilson comes on.'

Grenville, noting appreciatively the closer contacts with the local community, recalled that in the 1950s he had left the grounds only three times during a whole term – on each occasion for a cross-country run. Now Stoics entered local homes to fit wiring and immersion heaters, concrete paths were laid and gardens dug. An advice bureau was formed to deal with matters such as rent rebates and housing grants. A professional decorator trained three- and four-man teams to give their services to old-age pensioners. Pledges were given to instal mains water in any house in Buckingham without it and four families availed themselves of the offer. A sponsored walk raised £1600 for materials and a mass collection of Green Shield Stamps helped to buy a van. Talent in the workshops and in the growing field of design produced solutions to the special needs of handicapped children. A greenhouse and log-store were added to the headquarters at the school. A boy treasurer kept the books and negotiated with the Inland Revenue and the Charity Commissioners. The school greenhouse aimed to produce one pot-plant per pensioner per week. Even those whose chief pleasure was to be found behind a driving wheel enjoyed the opportunities afforded by driving minibuses to supplement poor local services and by delivering over one hundred boxes of fruit and vegetables each week. Television sets were reconditioned and installed. Musicians sang and played in old people's homes.

Almost every section of the school could participate in some way and this in turn helped to put the deprivations and minor sorrows of boarding school into perspective. By the early seventies the unit possessed five vehicles and two trailers and was seeking more spacious garage accommodation. Boys went from Stowe to talk at other schools contemplating similar schemes. Community service was experiencing the huge and unexpected success which the O.T.C. had in the 1920s. There were private initiatives also. Richard Carr-Gomm O.S. preached in Chapel about the homes he was establishing for the elderly and handicapped and for those facing special problems such as re-settlement after prison. The boys of Cobham took over a house in Buckingham and adopted it as a Carr-Gomm foundation for some years.

Other increased contacts with the outside world included an expeditions day when sections of the school sallied forth to visit cathedrals, factories, stone circles and bird sanctuaries. The choir participated in a public schools' choir festival and in 1966 the bold step was taken of inviting three girls from a local secondary school to take part in *Othello*. This was one of Joe Bain's many productions which sought out unusual venues. *The Tempest*, for instance, was enacted with the Stowe cedar as a centrepiece – the masts and rigging of the ship in the storm. For *Othello* Assembly became the stage, its marble pillars providing a Venetian impression and its double doors acting as suitably grand entrances for the plenipotentiaries. A new light was shed upon the plot when Iago asked permission to take Desdemona out to supper after the performance.

Morale was further enhanced by the building programme which was almost continuous. There were very few years in the Drayson period when there was not an appeal or the opening of a building resulting from an appeal. The new house, Lyttelton, was the first fruit of the appeal of 1963/4. As it progressed accompanied by other works and clearing of the grounds, Richard Gilbert lamented that the bird life of the estate was being affected. The re-modelling of the golf course had driven partridges from their habitat by the sixth fairway and driven out the wood peckers. The clearing of the trees for Lyttelton inspired him to verse:

> I think that I shall never see
> A thing as lovely as a tree,
> In fact if many others fall,
> I'll never see a tree at all.

He wished to see the Park remain as a sanctuary for wildlife disturbed by the spread of Milton Keynes and the changes in farming methods in the surrounding countryside.

Lyttelton House was opened in 1967. The modern design by C.B. Lyster marked a new departure which was not universally popular, but boys liked the open feel of the interior and the desk and dormitory units. It had forty-seven founder members and David Donaldson was the first housemaster. Its opening enabled a 'space committee' to meet and plan a more rational use of the main building. Alasdair Macdonald was chairman and Andrew Vinen secretary and it was something of an achievement to reach a solution acceptable to five housemasters. They faced a situation where the Bruce dormitories were in the West Wing though most of the house was east of Assembly. Grenville had two dormitories known as 'the Grenville Colony' in the middle of Chandos. Chandos had a changing-room next to Power House Yard though it was situated at the far end of the building. Chandos studies were under the Cobham Matron and sick-room, etc. The solution was found in constructing study blocks in Cobham Court: one on the inner wall of Plug Street for Chandos and one over Cobham Pond. The spaces freed were allotted to suites of rooms for the housemasters of Cobham and Chandos. Eventually the Bruce housemaster was housed in the old Biology laboratories when new ones were built. The work itself was slow but, provided that the housemasters of Temple and Grenville remained bachelors, there was a totally new system in which resident housemasters shared the responsibility for the supervision of the school by day and night. More studies could be provided for the original houses, facilities which the increasing importance of examinations made ever more necessary.

Lyttelton House was followed by the Science Schools, the swimming pool, the sports hall, and an all-weather playing surface for hockey. The Science laboratories remain one of the best new additions, blending with the North Front approach with a restraint that makes no attempt to distract the visitor's eye. They are nevertheless well placed to greet the prospective parent as reminders that the syllabus has moved forward since ducal days. In his 1971 report, Drayson referred to the 'magnificent new Science building [which] provided a tremendous stimulus to both masters and boys and is the envy of other Schools'. There was a move towards Science subjects for which university places were more plentifully on offer.

Between the years 1967 and 1971 the numbers taking science subjects rose as follows:

	CHEMISTRY	PHYSICS	BIOLOGY
1967	36	71	36
1971	63	77	49

In 1972 the passes in 'A' level Sciences were 85 per cent as opposed to 75 per cent in Arts subjects. The head of Science, Charlie Macdonald, made many useful contacts with the Science departments in the newer universities.

The Science schools used up much of the money from the original appeal but efforts were renewed and, for a time, professional fund-raisers were employed. Frank Hudson, Physics master, was one of the keenest advocates of an indoor pool and on the 1972

Speech Day he organized a swimming display which added many thousands of pounds to the total. A private gift of £75,000 to help with games or athletics enabled work to go forward and building began late in 1972. Progress was hindered by the rise of Milton Keynes which frequently took away the workforce. When the diving platform arrived in a single stainless steel block it was found to be too large to go through the door, and the changing-room windows and part of a wall had to be removed. Finally, some of the sealing material used on the pool itself reduced the length by 5 mm, making it too short for national standard competitions. Minuscule shavings had to be conducted as a result. The pool was opened by Dudley Baker O.S. who had been Chairman of the Appeal Committee and the Friends of Stowe. Frank Hudson had wished to be the first to enter the water but was believed to have been beaten by a workman who fell in by mistake. The pool greatly assisted the swimming training throughout the year and in the subsequent 1973 season there was a triumphant finale in which Stowe won all eighteen events contested in the match with St Edward's.

If 'communication' and a busy building programme helped to spread a more contented and constructive atmosphere so too did the wide variety of sporting successes, for which Crichton-Miller's entrants must take a great deal of the credit. By the end of the Summer Term 1965, there had been an 'annus mirabilis' in which the Rugby XV had been undefeated, the hockey team lost only once and the Cricket XI had enjoyed its best season since 1930, winning ten and losing only one match. It was noted that in the latter part of the cricket season the opposing teams made such low scores that W.P. Durlacher, who batted No. 6 for Stowe, had only two walks to the crease. Athletics had its best season for some years and ten Stoics represented Buckingham County. J.H.G. Kinahan who trained in Northern Ireland with hurdles he had built himself achieved 14.5 seconds in the 120 yards hurdles, a time only twice bettered in English Junior Championships, and came second, in equal time with the winner, in the National School Championships. Stowe created a new record in the Achilles Club relays, 4 × 220 yards in 1 minute 32 seconds, and was runner-up in the Sandhurst Tetrathlon. On the new golf course the school was undefeated and the first hole in one was recorded at No. 5 by J.R. Green. The Micklem Trophy was won for the first time since 1957 and involved defeats for Eton, Harrow and Winchester. In the years immediately ahead Stowe was to reach the Micklem Final eight times and win the Trophy in five. In 1966 C.R. Dimpfl broke the course record of 32 held by Peter Townsend from the opening date, with 31 strokes. Other schools began to consider constructing their own golf courses. Three Stoics ran for England in the 220 yards relay team in Junior Championships and a new challenge was taken up when twenty-six boys took part in the Nijmegen March, 100 miles in four days, all completing the course.

In 1969 Drayson was able to report that the squash team directed by P.G. Longhurst, had enjoyed a run of 21 consecutive victories. By 1971 there had been 50 matches without defeat; by the date of the Old Stoic Dinner in 1972 this had risen to 65. Even when, in the following year, the unbroken run ended, the squash players won 17 out of 18 matches. I.A. Thomson, a second-generation Stoic, had the distinction of never having lost a squash match while at school and he was, in addition, Captain of Rugby, hockey and tennis, a British Junior Doubles Champion at tennis, a semi-finalist in the Junior Championships at Wimbledon and later Captain of the England Hockey team. Not all teams could produce constant success but there were some good performances. James Black, three seasons in the Cricket Xl, scored 1000 runs and took 127 wickets as well as being invited to play for the M.C.C. Schools XI at Lord's. In 1966 it was noted that he had scored 149 boundaries as against 143 singles, and had once cleared the sight-screen by twenty feet. R.G.L. Cheatle, who later played for Sussex, played for The Rest against the Southern Schools and scored more than half of his side's winning total. The archery team had two unbroken seasons of success and at the National Clout Shooting Championships S.A. Saunders won the junior under-18 class and broke the national record. M.J.H. Jackson won the 110 metres hurdles at national level and represented Great Britain in the under-20 hurdle teams. He was ranked first in the high hurdles in Great Britain under 20s.

'The facilities for Sport are quite splendid' wrote Drayson, 'with the exception of the old gymnasium which is now in a dilapidated state and could soon be dangerous. There is a vital need for a sports hall at this time.' The old gymnasium had served Stowe well as chapel and theatre, playing area and lecture hall. By the early 1970s it was as effective an advertisement for Stowe's sporting prowess as Miss Havisham would have been for bridal gowns. It was a period of strong competition between schools to add new amenities and obliterate decrepit corners and old-fashioned amenities. The appeal rolled onwards towards a modern sports and examination hall with other projects of repair and renovation added.

In 1965, with funds from the Bridgland Trust, the renovation of the Music Room, formerly the Bruce house room, began. This had originally been the setting for the talents of the Countess Temple and was designed by Valdre, an Italian who came to England soon after George Grenville, Temple's nephew and heir, had visited and admired the wall paintings of Pompeii and the Raphael loggias in the Vatican. Valdre was a romantic Italian, also responsible for the designs of the frieze in the Marble Hall. It is said that he attended Stowe Church for a wedding at which the bridegroom failed to arrive and was so distressed at the grief of the bride that he married her on the spot and lived happily ever after. For the first Marchioness he also contributed the menagerie, which is now the school shop. Restoration work on the Music Room was carried out by Michael Gibbon O.S. and it was transformed into an excellent salon for chamber concerts and intimate opera.

With the Roxburgh Hall, Queen's Temple, the Library and the Temple of Concord, music already had many places for performance. In the house music competitions of 1965 Bruce performed three sections of Orff's *Carmina Burana*, Chatham produced two composers and included 'Country Gardens' for twelve hands on three pianos in their programme. Six members of the school together with two masters were capable of playing the fourth Brandenburg Concerto and, in 1966, twelve celli were performing the necessarily limited repertoire for such an ensemble. In school concerts K.D. Frazer was soloist in the Elgar Cello Concerto and S.T.D. Ritchie soloist in Artie Shaw's Clarinet Concerto. Visiting artists were of high quality. Elizabeth Vaughan was soloist in the Brahms' Requiem and Jennifer Vyvyan and Robert Tear in the Messiah.

In 1965 Michael Mounsey retired. As well as taking charge of the Art department he taught English and had also done a great deal of investigation into the history of the house and grounds. He encouraged photography and gave much advice on the construction of stage sets and the redecoration of the Stowe interiors. His successor, W.St A.R. Dady, enlarged the department to encourage sculpture. Duncan Jones who taught Sculpture two days a week procured a bronze furnace from a London foundry and in 1969 there were four A grades at 'A' level in the subject. In 1969 an Enzo Plazzotta exhibition arranged by Dady made over £1000 for the Art School and in 1973 there was an exhibition of sculpture by David Wynne O.S.

In 1965 a Stowe Fair was organized by the Reverend 'Jos' Nicholl and opened by David Niven. His tax situation meant that he had used up his allotted time in this country and was allowed back only to have a suit fitting in Savile Row. He flew from Cap Ferrat and was whisked from his tailor to Stowe at high speed by Peter Sleigh, the husband of a secretary in the bursar's department, who owned a Jaguar.

In 1967 an exchange was arranged with Wolverstone, one of the few boarding schools which had been launched by local authorities and the L.E.A. It was part of a policy which included co-operation with the Royal Latin School in the social service work, and invitations to local schools to send parties to Stowe's Saturday Morning Lectures and special conferences. The Wolverstone delegation reflected afterwards that individual pursuits and hobbies seemed to be more difficult to pursue at Stowe as so much free time was absorbed by activities. It considered that there was too great a difference between older boys with privileges and those without, a valid point, and despite the sophisticated teaching and the tutorial methods it did not detect a fundamentally different attitude to work. The Stoics noticed the absence of prefectorial roles at Wolverstone and the inadequate facilities for art, music and sport, though there was a good Rugby XV. They also found that religion played a minor part in school life compared with the central role of Stowe Chapel.

In fact it was about this time that Drayson instituted a survey into worship at Stowe and the views of all parties were sought. He, himself, was against the wholly voluntary principle as it had been adopted at Marlborough, Bryanston and elsewhere and thought that the majority would follow the lead of the absentees. The 1960s had furthermore been marked by many experimental services arranged by the students in which guitars and recorded rock music played a part. One chaplain had sought to illustrate Christian humility by putting the boys into the masters' stalls before the service began, with results for the brotherhood of man that can be imagined. There were some like Angus Watson who wished to see the voluntary principle adopted and some such as Brian Stephan who thought that weekday services might go, in line with normal parish practice. Others like D.J. Arnold and Roger Rawcliffe wished to see greater adherence to the Prayer Book and a more traditional and dignified liturgy. One of the most sensible viewpoints was put forward by Anthony Pedder, who reflected that a wholly voluntary regime would lead to 'a small clique of sanctimonious people who attended all the services in a pharisaical manner . . . and as there could be little music there would be a good deal of soul baring which would militate against the appearance of the ordinarily mildly pious kind of person.' In the final printing the appeal for more Cranmer services became by a slip an appeal for more Crammer services, but the whole matter remained one in which enthusiasm and traditionalism came into conflict for many years. In 1967 the entire school travelled in coaches to a special service in Coventry Cathedral which, despite some criticism in the Ephemerals was something of a grand occasion.

In 1969 two Stoics, B. Helweg Larsen and N. Downing, reached the Final of the BBC 'Young Scientist of the Year' Competition with a project on 'Colour Vision in Fish' under the direction of Mr A.J.E. Lloyd and the Biology department. Stowe was the only public school to reach the Final and both contestants were congratulated by the producer on their exposition. The fish had to make an early departure for Television Centre in order to acclimatize and at the producer's request a party of younger Stoics ('They clap louder') attended as supporters. The school was given three tape-recorders to mark the appearance. After Cambridge, Nigel Downing went on to do underwater research on fish and coral in the Persian Gulf and Virgin Islands.

There was another ambitious project in 1966 when Richard Branson, whom Drayson described as 'an enthusiastic seventeen year old', planned a magazine, *Student*, which was to be launched the following year to embrace state schools, public schools and universities. It was to be a platform for those who wished to address students and exchange views between independent and state schools. Edward Heath granted a personal interview, and Drayson assisted with approaches to Colin Welch and other Old Stoics. Articles by Vanessa Redgrave, Yehudi Menuhin and John le Carré were solicited and over 3000 schools contacted.

Publication plans went as far afield as Australia and the United States and a French edition was promised. The venture was not long-lasting but it was the start of Richard Branson's involvement in the record business, from which his future enterprises grew.

The Myles Henry Prize was founded in memory of a Stoic killed at Arnhem. At first intended to be an incentive for outstanding boys to remain at school for a final period, it became an award to assist ambitious expeditions. G.M. Wolfson worked at Dr Albert Schweitzer's leper colony at Lambarene, C.J. English and R.K. Hay travelled 1200 miles by canoe down the Danube from Ulm to Calafat in Rumania, where the canoe finally sank while they were engaged in disputes over immigration with the local police. Other adventurous plans fully upheld this standard.

Major A.J.E. Lloyd and Major R.C. Pinchbeck continued to give to the C.C.F. a more modern and challenging image. After visits to France and Germany, 1966 witnessed a party of twenty Stoics leaving for Denmark to undertake arduous training with the Danish Life Guards. They were the first tourists to be conducted round the Fredensborg Summer Palace at the invitation of King Frederick and they sampled the Embassy hospitality provided by the Old Stoic Ambassador and Lady Henniker-Major. Orienteering exercises were carried out in the Danish forests and escape and evasion encounters with the Danish forces.

Nearer home a group of Chandosians worked on the Upper Styx to establish a duckery, and a trout farm was built on the Oxford Water. In 1968 the Natural History Society marked out a nature reserve to protect species of flora and fauna which were threatened by the inroads of Milton Keynes upon the local environment and the mini-ecology of the region. It was the brainchild of John Dobinson and John Lloyd and situated in the south-west area of the grounds. Reed beds on the Octagon were cut back and concerts held in the Queen's Temple to raise funds to restore adornments such as the Congreve Monument and the Seasons Fountain. The Gothic Temple was refurbished as a private residence that might be hired out at weekends. The restoration of its heraldic ceiling by the Gibbon brothers required much scholarly research as well as skilled craftsmanship. The drain on resources was considerable despite grants from the Historic Buildings Commission and other bodies, for the school had normally to find the balance of costs to qualify for grants and the proceeds of concerts had frequently to be diverted to the Temples when they could have been used for educational amenities. Moreover each project required letters of solicitation for funds from the headmaster. There were few men in his position adding the burdens of running a palatial estate to those of running a school.

By the time that Stowe entered its sixth decade there had been many changes in the Common Room and stalwarts of its formative years had gone. Raymond Walker, senior tutor, died in 1966. Dr Zettl who had taught Modern Languages for many years retired. He had run the Film Society and during the war had managed to search out foreign films with a skill that suggested espionage. He helped with advice on careers and was one of the first to bring down Old Stoics to the school to discuss their businesses and professions. A.A. Dams retired in 1964. So too did Tom Connor who had given riding lessons since 1925. D.I. Brown, who had served for thirty-six years, and W.H. Bradshaw, for twenty-seven, retired in 1969. Alasdair Macdonald had been prevailed upon to remain for an extra year but he had retired in 1968. David Shepherd braved the wind and the rain to paint a view of Chatham House from the lake as one of the school's leaving presents. J.C. Saunders, who had played oboe, bassoon, French horn and percussion in the orchestra as well as contributing to the school's dramatic and literary life, left in 1966. Miss M.E. Johnston, matron of Walpole for thirty years also retired. In 1970 Angus Watson left to become Director of Music at Winchester. R.C. Pinchbeck had become headmaster of Markham College, Lima, Peru, and Bruce Barr had retired to Ireland. The average age of the staff was now under forty. Masters' plays revived and Muir Temple nobly offered himself to play 'the Himmler of the Lower Fifth' in Rattigan's *The Browning Version*. There were a number of younger wives who acted and contributed to the regular play-readings.

In 1973 the school reached its golden jubilee. Its resurgence had been remarkable. There were 611 boys in the school, 160 sons of Old Stoics and 56 grandsons. Thirty-eight per cent of future registrations were from Stowe families. The Royal Visitor on this occasion was Princess Alice, Duchess of Gloucester, who stayed for four hours and saw as many aspects of school life as possible. It was a thoughtful gesture to introduce her to some of the old people who benefited from the community service work and some of the longest-serving school servants such as Dougie, the chef, who had worked at Stowe for thirty-seven years and Sid Jones, head groundsman and a champion of local horticultural shows, who had been at Stowe for forty-seven. The Duchess, who made her visit on 11 May, Jubilee Day itself, arrived by helicopter, opened an Old Stoics art exhibition which included open-air sculpture by David Wynne, paintings by David Shepherd and pottery by Alan Caiger-Smith. Retired masters came back to the Commemoration Dinner, there was a school ball, costumed in the fashions of 1923, an ox roast, a parachute display by the Red Devils and a horse show arranged by Barry Pride O.S., Chief International Steward. For this last event boys worked round the clock in mud and rain to prepare the tents and enclosures. Other festivities included a broadcast of *Songs of Praise* from Chapel and a celebratory cantata 'Templa Quam Dilecta' by Paul Drayton of the Music department. The Duchess planted a hawthorn on her visit and further planting was undertaken to mask the utilitarian outlines of the swimming pool from the North Front. There had been an assault on the grounds prior to the royal visit. Beech stumps, 250 years old, had been attacked with fire, sledge-hammers and axes on the lawns of the North Front and boy foresters almost unaided burnt out nineteen huge stumps from the edges of Chatham Field.

Despite outward buoyancy Drayson was fully aware of the perils that lurked in the path of these great private enterprises called the public schools. 'I am bound to admit', he wrote to the Governors, 'that this terrible problem of money, of inflation, of pressure on parents' pockets, the constant discussion about economies, has taken a lot of the fun out of running a school. It used to be very much a matter of dealing with people and personal relationships.' In his 1969 report, making reference to the 'feverish re-examination of the landmarks of School life', he observed that the increasing momentum 'leaves very little time for those responsible to sit back and think things out quietly'. The endemic risks of an over-populated school continued. Despite the success of the appeals, the expensive building programme and the broadening range of activities had to be financed and, although the pass levels at Common Entrance rose, quite a large number of pupils were admitted with insubstantial credentials. The expression he preferred was 'accepted at owner's risk', but that implied a degree of philosophic detachment which parents did not always have, and much time was consumed in the exercising of pastoral care. After quoting from Christopher Booker's *The Neophiliacs* on the fashionable resistance to authority he added: 'The majority of boys here are polite, considerate, and sensible. They are easy conversationalists and usually tolerant and amenable to reason and I think it is certainly true to say that the Stoic says what he thinks – albeit politely – and I hope and trust that this freedom of speech and openness of relationships through the School will provide the necessary safety valve in these turbulent times.' It is true that Stowe suffered no more than echoes of the turbulent times. Headmaster and housemasters did a great deal to soften the excesses of the old drills and defaulters' parades. Nevertheless in the *Voice*, the *Mole*, *Playfair* and even in *Middle Voice*, an ephemeral established by Roger Potter to thread a course between official and opposition stances, there were some rumblings typical of the times: 'the monotony of the factory assembly line on which most Stoics spend their five years', or 'Term is more than half-way and we have had 23 rustications, one demonitorisation and various beatings and tickings off by RQD and his massed band of Housemasters'. The Coventry Cathedral service came in for heavy criticism and a poll showed 477 opposed to the idea as against 55 in favour. 'Moral implications aside, surely the energy crisis must stand up and argue the point with us.' There were also ripples of the *dolce vita* beyond the vales and woods of Stowe which beckoned from these pages: reviews of rock concerts, pressure for soccer in termtime, and hints for indulgence over exeats. Brian Stephan in one of his senior tutor's reports discussed the questions raised by the breadth of Stowe's intake from 'boys of exceptional ability and dedication [to those] who by general opinion do not work hard enough, especially as some of them are not at all bright academically. Despite the headmaster's repeated reminders of the need to gain a good set of 'O' levels (because many new universities scrutinised form before 'A' levels were taken) many of these boys are too immature and irresponsible either to see the need of this for themselves or take the Headmaster's advice.' He concluded by stressing the inordinate amount of laborious work undertaken by the Common Room as a result, though he himself did not put it by way of complaint: 'A great deal of effort is being put by many people into the ancillary aspects of the School's life, discussions with other schools, relations with parents and a full and expanding careers service for the boys.

I believe that we are certainly doing our best for them and perhaps we are gradually educating them to take a more responsible part in their own development.' One certainly has the impression that the staff at Stowe worked harder than many colleagues elsewhere.

Speaking of a very different but an equally exacting situation from that which had faced Stowe in the mid-sixties, Leonard Cheshire, opening the new Pineapple premises in Harrow Road in 1968 declared: 'What man needs if he is going to do his best is a challenge. This is easy in war. But now the challenge is in those who have less than ourselves and the best way is to fix our minds on some goal outside of our own selves. The more we think of others the better we are. We tend to forget the value of one small act – people tend to say if they cannot solve all of a problem it is no good solving part of it.'

Bob Drayson and his wife Rachel had worked tirelessly to avert the threats of fragmentation and decline that had loomed up ten years earlier and demolished much of Stowe's apartness from other great schools. In the year following the Jubilee they demonstrated Crichton-Miller's definition of a good school as being one from which the Headmaster could absent himself without disaster by taking a sabbatical holiday and making a world tour to meet Old Stoics in faraway places.

Old Stoics continued to shed lustre. Professor P.G.H. Gell became Stowe's first Fellow of the Royal Society; J.F. Nye Professor of Experimental Physics at Bristol; and C.F. Cullis, Professor of Chemistry at the City University. R.G.L. McCrone was awarded a Fellowship in Economics at Brasenose, Oxford; B.R. Arkwright, a Fellowship at King's, Cambridge; and R.B.J. Gadney, a Fellowship in Advanced Visual Studies at the Massachusetts Institute of Technology. M.H. Toovey, who unfortunately died young, received his Doctorate of Music from London University. A.M. Quinton became Radcliffe Fellow in Philosophy at Oxford; M.C. Scrutton, Assistant Professor of Biochemistry at Rutger's Medical School, New Brunswick. O.A.W. Dilke became Professor of Latin at Leeds University; C.W.N. Miles, Professor of Estate Management at Reading; and J.W.R. Kempe headmaster of Gordonstoun. Sir John Henniker-Major was Director-General of the British Council; Sir Colin Crowe United Kingdom representative at the United Nations; P.A.G. Dixey Chairman of Lloyds. A.R. Negus, son of A.A. Negus, who for many years was a member of the

Stowe Music Staff, joined the Music Staff at Bayreuth; David Wynne designed the fifty pence piece which marked Britain's entry into the Common Market; P.A. Willes, who received many awards for TV productions, became Head of Drama at Yorkshire Television. In the Labour Government Lord Taylor was Parliamentary Secretary at the Commonwealth Office and S.T. Swingler Joint Parliamentary Secretary at the Ministry of Transport. Lord Taylor, who led the United Kingdom Delegation to the Commonwealth Conference in Jamaica, found himself next to P. Howson leading the Australian Delegation as Minister for Air. A.J.C. Hamp-Ferguson played for the Cambridge XV and C.A. McIntyre represented the University in the 440 yards hurdles. N.J. Durlacher was Captain of the Cambridge Skiing Team and R.A. Durrant captained a Youth International Golf Team. N.K. Rice recorded the fastest 220 yards in the A.A.A. Championships and took part in international events. J.H.G. Kinahan represented Northern Ireland in the Commonwealth Games. J.W.O. Allerton captained Oxford University squash and gained a Cricket Blue. W. Shand Kydd rode Dorimont in the Grand National. R.B. Matthews, Chief Constable of Warwickshire, received the Queen's Police Medal. Lord Kennet, shortly before his appointment as Parliamentary Secretary to the Minister of Housing and Local Government published *Eros Denied*, which was boldly controversial. Anthony Elliott, while still a student at Keele University, started publishing *Time Out* magazine with capital of £100. By 1972 it had a 32,000 circulation and a strong cult following. R.J. McCay partnered Tommy Steele in a London coffee bar skiffle group. Many Old Stoics inspired by the community service work went on to do Voluntary Service Overseas. Timothy Kinahan undertook a sponsored walk of 544 kilometres over a war-ravaged region in Ethiopia to raise funds for a school of 3000 children where the headmaster was only twenty-six and had survived a number of assassination attempts. Thirty-eight American friends of A.A.J. Baird, who had lost his life together with the crew of the *Windfall* in an Atlantic storm, made a presentation to the World Wildlife Fund to mark 'his effective representation of international understanding in every aspect'.

12

Co-Education

Inflationary times tend to benefit the public schools. Many parents anticipate that their income will go on rising and regard education as an asset that will not diminish as the years go by. The immediate results in the 1970s however, were annual increases in salaries and fees, soaring budgets for food and services and therefore economy drives, second-hand clothes shops and the descent of financial consultants upon the schools to suggest cuts in staff and limits upon the variety of courses offered.

'The whole of our lives are circumscribed by economic problems', wrote Drayson to the Governors in 1974. 'Although all Public Schools are full and most of them have waiting-lists, there is no doubt at all that the next few years are going to be a time of financial crisis for each one of them.' His 1975 report pursued the same theme:

Whereas Headmasters used to deal with masters and boys they are now more and more concerned with making ends meet . . . The emphasis at Governors' Meetings has been on economies and savings and the need to accept more boys into the School in order to keep costs down. In spite of this the fees have escalated by 200% in the last twelve years and now increase term by term instead of annually or even bi-annually as in the past. This constant consideration of the financial viability of a school is a Headmaster's permanent headache when he should be first and foremost concerned with the academic and personal development of his pupils.

His own position was rendered more difficult than that of many other headmasters as time and again funds which might have been used for stimulating educational ideas were sucked into restoration:

> There are many requests for innovations, but these would all require considerable capital outlay. This does not mean that from time to time those whose requests have been blocked are unconvinced that special treatment is offered to those men whose plans have been blessed . . . The constant consideration of salaries has created certain tensions among the masters as men become aware of possible unfairnesses in allowances and charges for some compared with others. For example, the Governors' decision to increase the rents of masters' houses has led to a lot of ill-feeling and the Headmaster has the difficult task of acting as a buffer in any discussions which may take place.

The estate showed no signs of relaxing its grasp upon expenditure. Dutch Elm disease had destroyed sections of the Grand Avenue though the last of the great elms were retained by the Forestry Commission (unavailingly) as subjects for experiments in combating the disease. The Countryside Commission gave a 75 per cent grant to cover planting around the Corinthian Arch, but the balance had to be found. The Historic Buildings Council doubled a grant from the Estates and Sports Club established to raise money for the school, to enable work to be done on repairing the Grotto. The task called for unusual experience and skill. Mr Hearn, the restorer, was over seventy and the architect felt that he should start without delay. Boy foresters cut away undergrowth from the top of the Grotto and undercut three large yews standing above the main chamber in order that they could be winched out and the vaulting repaired. The methods of Mr Wackford Squeers, albeit at a more humane and exalted level, were certainly practised at Stowe. Opportunities for practical land management and engineering were ever-present.

In the spring of 1974, while the Draysons were abroad, the school was successfully conducted and then handed back by Brian Stephan. He himself reached retirement age in 1974 and relinquished his post as second master, but he agreed to stay as senior tutor until George Clarke returned from the Huntington Library in California where he was studying the vast mass of Stowe

Papers. Ronnie Adams, housemaster of Walpole, became second master but Brian Stephan's long association with Stowe was far from over. He continued as Classics tutor and librarian and 'the sempiternal Brian', as Patrick Hunter described him; two more headmasters yet to come would rely upon his experience.

Another theme in Drayson's reports was the difficulty in finding younger masters well qualified in their subjects who could offer games skills and coaching. The admissions tutors at the Oxbridge colleges were happy to import American oarsmen and post-graduates from colleges of physical education to buttress university and college sport, stultifying efforts to raise national standards of amateur accomplishment in games and athletics. The school-master with a good degree and a Blue was becoming an endangered species and, to complicate matters further, each traditional sport as well as several new ones, such as water-polo or archery, had its band of devotees among Old Boys who campaigned for expert coaching in their own sphere of interest. A headmaster could not duplicate staff for, as bursars were quick to observe, each extra man meant not only a salary but housing, food and insurance.

On the maintenance side there were problems as the loyal retainers became less sound in wind and limb and reached retirement. Elsie Jones left after fifty years of service on the domestic staff. Charlie Oakes, after nineteen years as cricket coach and green keeper, retired in 1976. George Hensley, foreman of works, who had overseen much of the restoration, died in April 1974. Fortunately for the school it acquired the services of Mr Redshaw who was adept at replacing ornamental stone and plasterwork in the cornices and pilasters of the state rooms. At a time of grave financial worry fate decreed that the roof should give trouble and the heating system show signs of age. Prospective parents were not likely to be won over by the sight of pails and containers catching drips from stained ceilings and encrusted pipes. 'There are few heavy showers', wrote Drayson, 'when the bursar is not invited to survey and deal with the latest ravages . . . The privations resulting from the cessation of heating draw attention to the fact that this problem will become progressively more pressing in the course of the next decade or two.' In January 1974 there were severe gales and in July the tail of Hurricane 'Betsy' wreaked havoc among newly-planted limes on the Straight Course. There was some consolation in the fact that Stowe won an award in a Tree

Planting Year competition organized by the Department of the Environment.

Necessity gave rise to invention not least by means of plans to turn the grounds into assets instead of liabilities.[1] Chris Atkinson, the Double Oxford Blue whom Drayson had attracted back to Stowe from industry and who became housemaster of Walpole, launched the Stowe Estates and Sports Club to make the golf course, swimming pool and squash courts and other amenities available to a membership, which very soon exceeded 100. The grounds were opened more frequently to the public, a policy long frowned upon as likely to lead to vandalism and litter. Even quite recently lead had been removed from the Temple of Venus and balustrading from the Palladian Bridge. Nevertheless, 2500 people paid for admission in the first year and a profit of £3000 was recorded. Holiday courses were instituted to use the plant in the idle months, one for French schoolchildren and another for musicians. In 1975 there were 5150 visitors to Stowe and a surplus of £5000 was expected. The previous year's profits were used variously for two changing-rooms, four chandeliers and a mirror for the Music Room, a part-purchase of some ducal porcelain, a ladies' powder room and a lawn mower for the Natural History Society. The new ventures meant less holiday tranquillity for masters and families and there was some opposition, especially as the same sum might have been raised with two or three extra pupils. But it was useful to have some funds separated from the general account to subsidize small indulgences that might otherwise have been cut from the estimates year after year. By 1977 the Sports Club was bringing in around £8000 per annum and the summer schools something of the order of £5000–6000. To cater for the holiday visitors as well as the needs of the sixth form a club-room was created out of the dark cellars below Assembly. Walls were demolished and concealed lighting installed to provide a social centre for seniors where, in the fashion of the times, beer and cider could be purchased

---

[1] In the past the bursary had given permission for various pieces of cinema and television filming to be done in the precincts. Permission was innocently granted for what was believed to be an educational film featuring Fiona Richmond, a well-known model of her day. The masters' meeting was informed by an astonished colleague that not far from the Temple of Venus he had seen the dedicatee herself rising naked from the waters.

'in moderate quantities' in surroundings that suggested Soho just enough to prevent them remaining empty.

In 1975 the Governors planned a fresh appeal with the aim of raising money for the sports hall and the all-weather playing surface, both projects very near to the headmaster's heart. Between 1975 and 1977 sixty meetings were held in places as far apart as Edinburgh and Torquay. P.L. Morris O.S. was chairman and a professional expert, Bernard Ashford, was employed to travel with the headmaster. As always the campaign was an excellent public relations exercise and by the end of 1977 £222,000 had been raised, although the target figure was soon made obsolete by inflation and it was estimated that as much again would be needed. Even at the outset Drayson was writing to George Clarke in California: 'As far as I can tell all seems to go well here apart from the terrible business of inflation. Our fees have gone up to £1479 per annum. We seem to talk about nothing but how to save money and I am having weekly meetings with all departments to discuss economy cuts.'

Such comments were made against the background of the general opinion that the birth-rate was on a downward path. Like similar schools Stowe was bemused by the registrations situation and there was little way of knowing which applications were solely for one school. Schools' reputations tended to rise or fall year on year rather than over long periods. In such a volatile situation the seven open awards and organ scholarship to Balliol, won in 1974, provided a useful contribution to the appeal speeches and literature. There were other sources of satisfaction as 'A' level passes reached 86 per cent in 1974 and 89 per cent in 1976, with a 91 per cent pass rate in Science. Many of the grades were not of the highest but there was a welcome increase in the number of Distinctions. Most of the major schools anticipated results at 90 per cent and above but Stowe had a larger proportion of entrants taken 'at owner's risk', and Stoics had a great many distractions from study. Even Drayson at times wondered whether praise-worthy enterprises such as community service were not absorbing too much energy. House plays came and went with relentless frequency and at times housemasters must have sighed for a non-proliferation treaty, bearing in mind the need for audiences as well as players.

One further addition to the list of activities available had been the Duke of Edinburgh Award scheme, with its combination of social service, physical challenge and individual hobbies. Stowe was well placed to provide opportunities for all three aspects and the various bronze, silver and gold stages became alternatives to the C.C.F. thus reducing the number of dissentients in the ranks. G. Klonarides had been the first Stoic to win the gold Duke of Edinburgh award in the late 60s but the scheme absorbed large numbers from the start. Community service reached its apogee in the 1970s and was described in *Understanding* by Jonathan Kreeger, a future housemaster of Temple. Three and a half tons of logs were despatched each week from the school's own mill along with weekly supplies of vegetables from the market garden. Four hundred pensioners were visited as far afield as Winslow on a weekly basis and a daily programme assisted the disabled and lonely. A light music quartet did the rounds of hospitals and old people's homes, there were Christmas expeditions and parties, and boy managers controlled a complex organization which had a turnover of more than £6000 per annum.

Other initiatives sprang from a variety of causes. One result of the economy drives had been to set up a reprographics department to limit the amount of printing work handed over to outside firms. By 1976 it was carrying out 1500 jobs each year and producing house play programmes, invitations, posters and school circulars. The increasing emphasis in Nuffield Science and 'A' Level Biology on project work and individual discovery brought the Stowe grounds into their own. The unrivalled facilities included the Nature Reserve, the trout hatchery and the compilation of Natural History records. Botanical surveys were placed with the county archives and there was more local involvement with enterprises such as the clearing of the old Buckingham Canal. Among new societies, Zymnase, a wine-making group, won first prize at the Buckinghamshire Show with a parsnip confection. Mark Flawn-Thomas, a founder member of the Corkscrew Society, later became a most successful connoisseur and was runner-up in the *Evening Standard*'s 'Wine Taster of the Year' competition. A third factor was the release of space afforded by the new Science Schools. Headquarters were provided for the Duke of Edinburgh's Award projects, for community service, photography and Geology as well as a careers room and an audio-visual centre where a library of films, photographs and videos could be stored for teaching purposes.[2] This last amenity became so popular that masters had to be rationed in their use of time and it was another feature which attracted prospective parents.

Stowe Church was brought more fully into use. Bob Drayson was not a proselytising evangelical and had been known to turn down offers of a speaker from the Oxford Group, but he valued religious sincerity where it appeared and would discuss and encourage it. His own son, Nicholas, was working as a Christian missionary in South America, and to an Old Stoic, who had been prefect of Chapel and a member of the First XV, doing voluntary work in Africa he wrote: 'I am sure you will continue to pray for the School that it may send more Christians into the world each year'. The Reverend H.F. Hodge, priest-in-charge of Dadford and Stowe, was an able scholar known for his stalwart labours with 'O' level laggards. He was also a keen golfer and his regular partnership with the headmaster symbolized the concordat between Church and State. 'It is now a real part of the Stowe scene', wrote Drayson of Stowe Church. 'In the past a good many people apparently did not know there was a Church in the grounds.' New boys were now given a special introductory service in the Church each autumn and there were regular communion services for which it was well suited. Boys assisted as organists and there was a team of bell-ringers. Family Services brought in Stowe children. Laurence Whistler designed a memorial window to the Hon. Mary Close-Smith, a descendant of the Dukes of Buckingham who had always taken a great interest in the school. When Mr Hodge died in 1975 the Revd 'Jos' Nicholl, housemaster of Cobham, who had combined the duties of acting chaplain with command of the most senior commando-style platoon in the C.C.F. took on the parish responsibilities.

A determined effort was made at this time to give Chapel a more prominent role. In *Middle Voice* the 'parliamentary correspondent' from 'Plugminster' reported meetings of 'the Prime Minister' with the 'Church Synod' intended to counter the Laodicean tendencies which had often prevailed at Stowe. At a new boys' tea the religious life of the school was explained and a retreat for Confirmands made confirmation less of a formality. Lenten addresses

---

[2] In 1966 T. Reid won the Gold and Onyx Trophy for Junior Photographer of the Year out of 4000 entries from over 300 schools.

were arranged and small Bible-study circles met in a number of houses. Choir outings made recompense for the time given up to rehearsal on Sundays. An unexpected use of Chapel came in the summer of 1977. The old gymnasium had been dismantled to make way for the sports hall and was not available for examinations. Chapel was the only area of ground space sufficient unto the day, and no doubt witnessed prayers of the utmost sincerity.

Slipped almost imperceptibly into the 1975 report was one statement that foretold the most major change to overtake Stowe since the time of its foundation: 'We have this September accepted five day girls and I am able to report that after three weeks, they all seem to have settled down very well. Two have come from the local Grammar School and three from boarding schools – Masters and boys alike regard them as a real asset to the School.' In previous speeches to the Old Stoics Drayson had deprecated the idea of accepting girls not least on the grounds that the very isolation of Stowe would create pressures. As far back as the mid-1930s the Inspectors had commented on the unrelieved masculinity of the Stowe community, though in more recent years girls had come occasionally from local schools to act in plays and four from Thornton College had sung in the Vivaldi Gloria. A younger Common Room with a majority of masters married made the idea of co-education seem less revolutionary, though when the introduction of female teachers was mooted one senior master was heard to growl: 'It's all very well but it's not like the real thing'. At the Debating Society one brave individualist voted against the prospect of girls at Stowe against sixty-eight of his brethren. Numbers were once again running at over 600 and it was not easy to see where additional accommodation could be found but, as elsewhere, the change sprang from the wishes of parents with sons at the school, masters with daughters who did not wish to pay high boarding fees for something so cheaply available near at hand, and the ambitions of strong-minded girls who had often spent many long years at a girls' school and wanted a change.

The first group of girls came from the vicinity but of the further fourteen admitted in the next year, three were weekly and five were full boarders which meant that the question of accommodation had to be addressed. 'There will, I am sure, be an increase in the number of applications', the headmaster told the Governors, 'and our problem will then be the question of accommodation for those who do not live close enough to come in daily, and we shall be turning away pupils who could be an asset to the School.' A temporary solution was to place girls with married masters or local families who happened to have spare rooms, though this raised questions of transport and attendance at extra-mural appointments in the evenings. By 1977 there were 37 girls. Numbers in the school had risen to 663 and the entry lists were full until 1982. In order to seat everyone, chairs had to be placed in the aisles of the Roxburgh Hall, Chapel overflowed, classes in the Lower School numbered twenty-four and five part-time teachers, mostly women, were required to cope with the sixth-form sets. A girls' house, Stanhope, was created out of part of the sanatorium when the lists of empty rooms in family houses were exhausted.

The competition for girls' places meant that almost everyone accepted had sound academic claims and the presence of purposeful and conscientious girls balanced the groups of adolescent boys relaxing after 'O' levels in the first-year sixth. Some of the staider masters treated the girls with what one has described as 'defensive courtesy' and called them *Miss* Smith or *Miss* Jones. Ronnie Adams had the habit of hurling balls of paper in class to summon back attention. 'The day he threw one at me,' wrote one of the very first girls, 'I knew we had been accepted.' Many joined the Congreve Club and Choral Society and found it an exhilarating experience to sing in full choirs in works such as *The Dream of Gerontius*, and act under the direction of Stowe's strong team of producers in male-dominated dramas by Ibsen which no girls' school could have performed confidently. Socially the presence of girls was preferable to the clumsy necessity of having headmistresses' and parents' consent to any tryst at a local girls' school, a procedure calculated to dampen the most ardent admirer. Some girls found in the absence of the constraints of the larger schools that they had previously attended a path to confrontations with authority; and those who came from small and homely schools had to adjust to stricter rules of punctuality and a more demanding work rate. All were agreed that the tutorial system and the teaching itself were stimulating and demanding. There were few girls' schools which could provide several sixth-form teachers in any given subject among whom one was fairly certain to find a sympathetic helper.

For the average Stoic a life of great variety was available. Notable speakers still came to the Roxburgh Hall: Mrs Mary

Whitehouse, Douglas Hurd (then in Edward Heath's political office) and Reginald Maudling, Deputy Leader of the Conservative Party. It had never been easy to attract left-wing speakers but a member of the Communist Party was persuaded and addressed his audience with great conviction, condemning Britain's entry into the Common Market and the 'Social Contract' between the Labour Party and the Trade Unions. The young English Society heard Michael Holroyd speak on 'Biography' and the existence of the Reprographic Unit led a number of societies into publication of their findings. The Natural History Society, which had almost 200 members, published *Grebe*. It seemed as if all that Montauban and others had hoped for in the use of Stowe's setting was being achieved. The wildfowl collection on the edge of the Octagon boasted seven species. Tufted duck were bred for the first time since the war and widgeon, mallard and bantams reared successfully. The water supply on which this rested was improved by pumping from the lake. Only the trout hatchery suffered a loss of stock owing to strikes and power-cuts, which were a feature of life at the time. Zymnase had risen from its humble experiments with parsnip wine to create a prize-winning variety of champagne from grapes gathered at the Chiltern Hundred Vineyard and donated by a parent. The Young Farmers Club spent Wednesday afternoons sheep dipping, shearing and fence building.

The Spanish Society, another new group, published a magazine, *Il Foque*, and carried off a number of prizes at Canning House, the headquarters of Latin American Studies in London, for verse and prose reading. A school visit was made to Burgos and interviews recorded for future consumption ranging from the accounts of village life by a priest to a talk with – surprisingly – the Chief of the Secret Police. Musical Concerts included a performance of the Tallis forty-part motet in Assembly and quadrilles on themes from *Tristan and Isolde* by Paul Drayton and David Gatehouse, the new Director of Music. A Speech-Day concert included an arrangement of the '1812' Overture which allowed almost everyone who could hold an instrument and play a simple part (about one quarter of the school) to take part. At the Buckingham Festival the choir gained the highest mark of the year, 92 per cent. Paul Drayton had his opera, *Nero*, presented at the Queen Elizabeth Hall. The competitive spirit gripped the drama enthusiasts and in 1976 there were several entries in the Buckingham Drama Festival, which carried off nine first and eight second places. Marc Hope won the Embleton Cup for the best rendering of Shakespeare in any class, just ahead of a Stowe girl, Julie Marler, who was runner-up. The Classical Society performed *Oedipus Rex* at the Queen's Temple. In 1977 there was a Greek Drama week: 'We wallowed in blood,' wrote Drayson to a parent.

In 1976 the Rugby season included a win over Oundle after thirty-five unsuccessful attempts. J.J.L. Bone had come from Loughborough University to assist with the XV. He was a county athlete and swimmer and a coach of the Cheshire Rugby side. The golf team won the Micklem Trophy for the eighth time in twenty years. Drayson had introduced the Stowe Putter, a competition for preparatory schools which attracted over one hundred entries and which was another means of introducing parents and headmasters to the splendours of Stowe. Andrew Vinen was the organizer. The headmaster noted that since the opening of the new golf course 100 matches had been won, 11 drawn and 12 lost. The new swimming pool led to fifteen school records being broken. Stowe supplied more than half of the North Buckinghamshire team. Brian Brinckley, an Olympic Bronze Medallist and O.B.E., came as swimming coach and the team won 23 out of 24 matches. The archery team completed five years of unbroken victory but were beaten in the last match of the season.

In 1977 Stowe won five of the first six Rugby games including those against Radley and the ancient and powerful foe, Bedford. The Junior Colts won all games and there were good results from the Second and Third XVs which indicated a greater degree of depth and a better knowledge of 'games skills', which was the Loughborough message. Over ninety boys played a regular part in athletics and Stowe dominated the county team. By the end of 1977 it was calculated that the junior athletes, undefeated for two seasons, had won 157 out of 166 single events.

The C.C.F. remained steady in strength but had problems with finance and staffing. Official grants for transport and equipment were reduced and fewer masters felt drawn to the Corps as an obligatory duty. The average age of the officers in 1977 was 43. Nevertheless the results of inspections continued to be complimentary and R.S.M. Keown entered his eighteenth year of service supplementing the gaps in the officer ranks in stalwart fashion. 1975 marked the fiftieth anniversary of the founding of the O.T.C.

and a dinner was held at the school attended by one Air Marshal, three Major-Generals, one Brigadier and two Air Commodores. A telegram of loyal greetings was sent to H.M. the Queen. The C.C.F. numbered around 150 and in the anniversary year fourteen Stoics joined the services. R.G.A. Westlake won the Sword of Honour and received the Queen's Medal for the officer 'who has produced the best performance in all aspects of training in the Royal Air Force'. To round off the roll of Service tributes R.C. Clifford O.S. was named as the Royal Navy's 'Man of the Year' in 1972 after parachuting into the Atlantic to deal with a bomb scare on the *Queen Elizabeth II*. The Mountaineering Club had a membership of 40 boys and 5 girls and there were expeditions in Skye, Snowdonia and the Lake District. R.C. Theobald, a master closely identified with community service, cycled 1000 miles from Land's End to John o' Groats raising £2500 which was much needed as many vehicles were suffering from age. It was decided to sell off the most decrepit and use the money to provide a steady income, though this curtailed some of the services provided. A Cycling Club was formed to develop an interest in racing, touring and timed trials.

In the autumn of 1976 there was a total of ten Oxbridge awards, including three exhibitions in Engineering at Cambridge, and Stowe came 23rd in the league table of scholarship results, an honourable position. Fifty-seven out of eighty-one Stoics who applied for other universities gained places. The Gibbon brothers were pressing on with their remarkable work on the Music Room decorations: the school was outbid at auction for the original circular ceiling panel but it seemed possible that Ben Gibbon could execute a copy. The Drayson Hall arose and a number of Old Stoics asked if they could present the plantation of beech trees, guelder rose and laurel around it as a memorial to Norman Barling, Captain of the XV in 1943, a prominent figure both in the City and in Rugby circles, and a founder of the Stowe Templars. Work on the Grotto was interrupted by Mr Hearns' illness but Holmes, the school plumber, continued with the lead work in appalling weather conditions with what the headmaster described as 'loving care'.

In almost every aspect Stowe was achieving its aims and justifying Drayson's claims: 'We are rich in time. Time for activities, time for personal relationships. Time to become a person. And above all, in our Independent Schools, we have the authority and the freedom to acclaim that the school lives by certain standards. We are able to lay emphasis on such things as truthfulness, honesty, loyalty and selflessness.' The 1970s were a rewarding period for the public schools. The imposition of the comprehensive system upon the old and respected grammar schools brought a whole new constituency of applicants, parents who had risen in the world and homes where the work ethic was strong. Competition between the leading schools had added many splendid new buildings and amenities and the standards reached in music, drama, art and craftsmanship were often astonishing. In 1978 the head of school wrote on leaving: 'I can safely say that Stowe under your leadership must be one of the best public schools in the country; it is certainly the nicest place I have ever been to and the past five years have been the happiest of my life.' A distinguished Old Stoic wrote in similar terms: 'I have been happier as a parent during your reign than I ever was as a boy.'

In his valedictory speech to the Draysons on Speech Day 1979, Anthony Quinton, then President of Trinity College, Oxford (and Chairman of the Stowe Governors from 1969 to 1975), made reference to the patience required in dealing with the host of disciplinary lapses that still beset the best regulated of establishments: 'In the Victorian age a properly bearded headmaster simply had to flash his eye and gesture vaguely to the corner of the room where the instruments of execution were kept and order was restored.' Escapades with cars and motorcycles were not new at Stowe. Dr Zettl had on one occasion been summoned by whispers from a thicket to use his mechanical skills and rescue a stranded Stoic on an illicit machine. Not all breaches of the rules could be countered by communication and fairness. The ever-present menace of soft drugs was not the only one presented by modern society. Credit cards, telephone cards and the expensive paraphernalia of sound reproduction added to the housemasters' tasks. The estate might be an admirable laboratory for scientific research but it was also good land for commercial ferreting by enterprising rule breakers. Younger housemasters were less inclined to overlook breaches of the rules than their predecessors and swifter to scent whiffs of tobacco or alcohol in the air. There were still a number of Stoics who found the ambience restrictive and left for crammers or coaching. Because of his apprehensions about inflation and his wish to build up warm relations with the preparatory schools Bob

Drayson had never quite succeeded in excluding the borderline candidates whose reports could find little to say beyond, 'He will be bitterly disappointed if he is refused a place at Stowe'. Niceness and soundness of character which was often a boy's sole recommendation sometimes evaporated with adolescence. This, too, was a hedonistic time in which evidence of youthful unhappiness implied faults and misunderstanding on the part of elders. Parents were frequently as bewildered as the school but took to heart more readily minor injustices over promotion or tutorial reproofs. Correspondence at times ran to such lengths that the reader yearns for the equivalent of the choleric voice of Charles Rowlatt, Vice-Provost and one time housemaster at Eton, who was heard to boom at a complaining mother: 'Madam, take your beastly boy away!'

A younger Common Room meant more changes, particularly among the housemasters. Joe Bain who had presided over a colourful house in Chandos celebrated his greatly improved accommodation by marrying the headmistress of Tudor Hall and later moved to Winchester as Director of Drama. J.S.M. Morris followed in Chandos. At the same time Michael Waldman followed Brian Mead in Bruce and R.C. Theobald succeeded George Clarke in Grenville. After one year Theobald moved north to be headmaster of Ranby Hall. D.J. Arnold left to be headmaster of King George V School, Southport; and Morris to be headmaster of Papplewick School at Ascot. In 1978 Chris Atkinson took over Walpole from Michael Kirk and in 1979 Roger Rawcliffe handed over Chatham to A.G. Meredith. Rawcliffe had helped to found a Business Studies course, and led Stoic teams to great success in business games competitions.

He returned to accountancy. A Classics graduate, he had been able to speak with experience of the value of a Classical training in the world of finance. The spirit of business had made him a prime mover in the founding of the Estates and Sports Club and the commercial use of Stowe's natural assets – and something of a scourge to the bursary. He had audited the accounts of the bookshop and various private funds available to the school. He had founded Side X in Accountancy and Business Studies, served in the C.C.F. for seventeen years and been its commander for three. In the house he had fought a strong campaign against any intrusions by the permissive society. 'Jos' Nicholl retired from Cobham, though not from the Common Room, in 1976 and was followed by Antony

Lloyd. Roger Potter, who had been two years on secondment to Ashbury College, Ottawa followed Theobald in Grenville. C.P. Macdonald had taken over Lyttelton when David Donaldson left to be headmaster of Kimbolton. David Mee succeeded to Muir Temple in Grafton; John Dobinson to Morris in Chandos. These numerous changes coincided with the arrival of a new headmaster, and the ending of a decade.

The death of Michael Edmonds in 1979 after nine years in the Music department was a great loss. One visiting adjudicator had praised the cello players of Stowe as the best he had ever encountered. O.L.Ridge re-joined the Common Room in 1976, bearing valuable experience from his years at Manchester Grammar School, to take over the Physics department. Andrew Rudolf O.S. came from Repton to take charge of History. A.M. Macoun O.S. who had been head of Geography for five years moved to Ashbury College, Ottawa as headmaster. A Fives Blue, he had done a great deal to revive interest in a sport that had been available since Stowe's first weeks.

Old Stoics were constantly mounting the steps of the legal profession and business worlds. The Stoic grip on the world of the art collections was remarkable. Gordon Darling was Chairman of the Council of the Australian Art Gallery; Noel Annan, who had moved from King's, Cambridge to become Provost of University College, London was Chairman of the National Gallery; J.C. Carter Brown was Director of the National Gallery of Washington and Lord Hutchinson Chairman of the Trustees of the Tate Gallery. Sir Nicholas Henderson served as Ambassador in Bonn, Paris and Washington. Sir Peter Hayman retired after four years as High Commissioner in Canada. T.R. Lancaster, Scholar of Corpus Christi, Oxford, scored the highest marks of his year in English Mods and was awarded the Beddington Prize. D.G. Choyce captained the Oxford squash team and two other second-generation Stoics among others gained Blues: R.G.G. Carr for hockey and squash and D.G. Lucas for golf. J.S.B. Henderson, R.J. Maxwell-Hyslop and P.W.I. Rees maintained Stowe representation in Parliament and Karan Tharpar was elected President of the Cambridge Union. The Hon. Sir Peter Vanneck was Lord Mayor of London. Maintaining also the Stowe diversity of enterprise Peter Hinwood starred as 'Rocky' in *The Rocky Horror Show*.

R.W.K. Beckett held the South African altitude record for

free-fall parachuting; J.A. Pearman the world record for black-fin tuna fishing. B.J. Calvert was co-pilot on Concorde's inaugural flight; and C.J. English represented Oxford in the pole vault. Nigel Broackes became *Guardian* Young Businessman of the Year; Colin Welch Granada's Journalist of the Year; and Geoffrey Lewis International Reporter of the Year in the Press Awards. J.V. Doubleday designed the life-size statue of Charlie Chaplin for Leicester Square; and J.S. Furber the games for *It's a Knock-Out*. Michael Deeley won an Oscar as producer of *The Deerhunter*; and R.N. Harding directed television series such as *'Z' Cars, Coronation Street* and *Emergency Ward 10*. H.M. Campbell was the National Police Cadet Champion in judo; David Cowper the first yachtsman to circumnavigate the world single-handed both east–west and west–east. Professor J.F. Tuohy was another Stoic winner of the James Tait Black Memorial Prize; and Professor J.F. Nye a Fellow of the Royal Society, who was to have an Antarctic glacier named after him.

The tempo of Drayson's headmastership was 'allegro con brio'. Good humour allayed many anxieties and calmed many potential sources of unrest. The Governors were kept up to the mark. Anthony Quinton remembered setting out for the meetings: 'I always had to look at my haircut before leaving home and try to stick the hair down a bit so as not to cast distress of any kind'! Much was achieved by persistence, not only in the day-to-day supervision of the manners and obligations of the youthful barbarians but in carrying out the bold extension of facilities. To quote Anthony Quinton once more,

There is nevertheless that terrible minute at the end of a Governors' Meeting when we're just hoping for a little refreshing glass, but the Bursar says, 'HmHmHm just a moment! It has been discovered that Vanbrugh's South Front is entirely high-alumina cement and will all have to be replaced' or 'I regret to announce that Chatham has sunk'. Bursarial disasters always used to cause a thrill of terror and apprehension in the Governors. Bob was always unbroken by these to such an extent that, even when we had pulled ourselves together after them, for many years there was a little refrain that used to come out: 'I think we mustn't lose sight of the desirability of an all-weather hockey pitch'. I don't think I've ever been kept in sight of something quite so regularly and constantly and courteously and insistently and inescapably as I have for the need of an all-weather hockey pitch.

He enjoyed some strong office staff-work in noting the engagements, the weddings and births in the Old Stoic community and followed Roxburgh's practice of issuing invitations to families to visit the school. His appeal tours established firm links with former generations. He took pride in the fact that Stowe retained a national constituency and had not become a regional school. He was, as Anthony Quinton said in his farewell, a 'great getter about . . . I see pulpits have been shivered to fragments all over the English independent educational system network by Bob's constant readiness to offer a sermon and to inform people, by the way, after they've been shown the light, about the particular bit of light that's been gleaming here under his guardianship.'

This was indeed true. But there was also an engaging realism about the limitations of the headmaster's role. In his final report, having extolled the outward-looking mentality of the modern schoolboy and his interest in the wider issues of human rights, social deprivation and political oppression, he added: 'I stop at this point to draw breath . . . and am conscious of being rather pompous and of making sweeping assertions, but I believe there is a good deal of truth in what I have written. It is, of course, virtually impossible for any Headmaster to know the state of his school.'

13

Christopher Turner 1979–83

Governing bodies making appointments are subject to the natural human instinct for change. Long experience of a disciplinarian will incline them to look for a touch of democratic joviality; weaknesses in administration and finance may cause them to look with a friendly eye upon the candidate who has the air of a painstaking auditor. Bob Drayson had successfully transformed Stowe's fortunes, but he would have been the first to admit that he had little experience of teaching those scholars who graced the upper reaches of the older schools or of the traditions in which they were nurtured. The Governors probably felt that a successor who had taught some of the cleverest groups of sixth formers in the land and had personal knowledge of the ways of the older foundations would bring a new perspective to bear.

Christopher Turner could claim these qualifications. He had been a scholar at Winchester and exhibitioner at New College. His family had risen by intellectual resource along varied paths. He described his paternal grandfather as 'an elderly success from the Mile End Road'.[1] His maternal grandfather, Lord Schuster, was Permanent Secretary to the Lord Chancellor. After reading Greats at Oxford, Christopher joined the Classics department at Radley and became head of Classics both there and later at Charterhouse.

[1] He came from a family of rope and brush makers and as a boy sold brushes from a barrow in the streets of East London with his father. Having put together some small capital by working for a bookmaker, he made a fortunate loan to the inventor of Nugget boot polish and prospered thereafter. His son, Christopher Turner's father, was a Q.C.

At both schools he produced Greek plays and published contributions to Classical studies. He was an oarsman and a member of the Oxford crew which memorably sank in the Boat Race of 1951. His wife, Lucia, was the daughter of a Provost of King's College, Cambridge, one of the country's leading Egyptologists, and well qualified to pursue an academic career herself.

In 1967 Christopher Turner was awarded a Schoolmaster Fellowship at Christ Church, Oxford, and in the following year was appointed as headmaster of Dean Close, Cheltenham. Here he introduced and pressed forward with great conviction a policy of co-education. One of the principal needs at Stowe was to systematize the piecemeal arrangements by which girls had come to be accepted and he was admirably versed in the requirements. He had the strong Wykehamist belief in academic rigour (at an early masters' meeting he confessed to the grating irritations of split infinitives and misuse of 'hopefully') and a strong conviction that slipshod attitudes to learning or to life were to be deplored. Clifford, who became a fervent admirer and copious correspondent, was profoundly impressed by Turner's first sermon on 'Truth' declaring that he stood for 'thought taken to a logical conclusion', and remarking that 'he opened fresh ground for training by believing that boys (and girls) should bring to industry and business management the officer and gentleman-like qualities that are needed'. At his first masters' meeting Christopher Turner observed that the two images which filled him most with horror were the barren fig tree and the hungry sheep. He had noticed the paucity of books in certain studies, thought that sixth-form general discussion was often uninformed and the importance of General Paper work underrated. He suggested that *Guardian* leaders might profitably be copied instead of 'Standards', the Stowe equivalent of 'lines'.

One of the first manifestations of the new academic rigour was a move to instal desks in all studies so that private study periods should not be socialized away. The removal of armchairs to make this possible within the narrow confines emphasised the point. Coloured lights were banned by the end of the first term. Reference was made to the heavily draped and cushioned bowers in which Wagner wrote his 'Venusberg' pages. This transformation reached the ears of the gossip columnist of the *Daily Express* who commented, 'Mr Turner has clamped down upon youths lolling about in their studies . . . furnished with soft armchairs. Quite right too. It's bad enough subsidizing the education of other people's brats without paying £2,385 a year for their own to live the life of Riley.' More serious scholars welcomed the opportunity to study without distractions. The editor of the *Stoic* recalled that its pages had often complained about complacency. 'The Headmaster made it plain from the beginning that mediocrity would not be tolerated. The goal of any undertaking from woodwork and athletics to Grade VIII Music Examinations and 'A' levels must be 'nothing less than excellence . . . Sceptics may believe that this will be impossible to achieve, but this is unimportant; it is the pursuit of excellence which has the greatest value.'

His own industry was immense. His reports on pupils were full, analytical and individual. The maintenance of records and reports was thorough. At the same time he was anxious to reward greater pupil dedication with better conditions. He persuaded the governing body to increase the food allowance; dress regulations were relaxed at weekends and improvements to general living conditions were hastened. In Drayson's final terms there had been a major effort to improve bachelor accommodation but this had diverted funds from renovations of the domestic quarters which remained overcrowded and sub-standard. The new headmaster was not disposed to favour cosmetic solutions. He wished to show parents clean and modernized lavatories, and kitchens that came up to the highest standards. He announced that, in the coming summer, there would be a major refurbishment of the 'ill-designed and unhygienic kitchen area which has, for generations, had to put up with patching-up operations or sheer neglect'. The underground heating remained a problem and it seemed as though a cold winter would have to be faced before the necessary explorations could begin.

At the masters' meetings he was always very careful to thank those who had carried out the less pleasurable administrative chores or undertaken special duties on the school's behalf. But he had experience of schools where responsibilities were fully shared and the headmaster was not the all-pervading presence which had come to be accepted at Stowe. He reminded masters that 'if they were sometimes disheartened by inefficient prefects the reverse was sometimes the case.' Study desks of robust design were built by the school carpenters with almost miraculous speed: two hundred in the first year. Studies were henceforth to be cleaned by domestic staff, which not only made them more hygienic but eliminated gradually the drapes and cushions that suggested indolence. A five-year programme of replacing the old horse hair mattresses on sagging metal frames was instituted in dormitories. Wooden bed-boards and proper bedroom units were made by the indefatigable carpenters and spring mattresses purchased. Domestic quarters were carpeted throughout and, where necessary, uniforms pro-vided. Improved working conditions meant that the domestic situation was less subject to change and there was a waiting-list of applicants for jobs. Attention was given to the bursary accounting system, especially to the extras charges, as over 10,000 items had to be entered at the end of each term. 'With the high fees being charged parents expect to be provided within a few days of the end of term with a full and detailed analysis of all charges.'

Turner's arrival coincided with a number of changes in the ranks of the housemasters and for some years he had little room for manoeuvre in this respect. Despite the work of the first space committee the allocation of rooms within the main building still required rationalisation: 'Housemasters at Stowe have greater problems than in almost any other school,' he wrote in an early report. 'Their houses are very large, in some cases widely scattered and composed of sections very hard to supervise. They themselves lead very active lives in School.' This resulted occasionally in groups of boys taking advantage of the difficulties of supervision. Study periods for younger specialists were to be supervised in classrooms. A reading list was compiled to give guidance on general reading and briefings on the Library and its importance were given to new boys at the outset of their careers. There were many calls at masters' meetings for a more lavish setting of prep and attention to punctuality and diligence in class. At the end of his second term there was a discussion on the distinction between informality and familiarity. The practice of having girls boarded with host families had revealed information that too little work was sometimes set and there was particular stress laid upon the need to make the third forms work harder. In speeches and frequently in reports the importance of the first year of 'A' level work was emphasised, together with sterner standards of self-motivation. That this was at times effective is exemplified in a letter from a Canadian pupil who arrived for the sixth form and almost succumbed to the attack: 'I guess I did over-react to the workload I have – but no kidding, it's huge!' There was a stronger intention to have instructions carried out. Like the coloured lights, the privately maintained ferrets were slow to disappear and an order was given that, previous notices having been disregarded, they were to be gone by half-term. There were recommendations on good manners in a more than general form. English masters were asked to explain the role of audiences at plays and the beneficial effects of co-operation. Discourtesy to the new girls was frowned upon particularly when this was aimed at discouraging over-zealous work. An end was put to the tradition whereby incoming study occupants were obliged to pay for built-in furniture and fittings from the leavers. A compensation payment of £1067 put a stop to this archaic commerce. While the headmaster appreciated the warmth and good nature which were characteristic of Stoics – on his first evening a boy arrived at Kinloss with two trout caught in the Oxford Water for his inaugural supper – there was no amusement displayed over pranks with cars or damage to the Worthies and other sections of the fabric.

Fortified by a strong Protestant faith, which soon after retirement was to take him into the ordained ministry, he stood well above the moral turbulence of the times. He welcomed the growth of small and serious discussion groups in houses and more than once suggested to the masters that there should be wider-ranging debates upon philosophical issues in boarding-school education. The old-style public school chapel services, corporate acts identifying the community and now subject to much experimentation, appealed to him less than the voluntary services in Stowe Church where only minor concessions were made to novelty. 'We remain', he declared in one of his first reports, 'a Bastion of Orthodoxy or a Beacon of Tradition in a sea of change.' Yet there was no hauteur or arrogance of manner. He had great sincerity and acts of Christian charity came naturally to both him and Lucia. He had liberal views on the choice of plays and subjects for discussion. Stoics had no reason to presume that they were shielded from the modern world and its issues. On hearing of the social work of an American Old Stoic being carried out in Harlem, New York, he wrote to say, 'The Christian out-reach of so many old Stoics is a great source of inspiration to those still working at the School.' He did not lack a quiet sense of humour and when an American E.S.U. scholar and his family had stayed at Kinloss shortly before the start of term he wrote to explain that a morning cup of tea brought up by the head-master was 'not part of the normal service'.

One of the first areas in which action was taken was in the organization of the girls. The work of housemistresses had at the start been carried out by wives who, while enthusiastic to ensure success, had sometimes young families and commitments of their own. With the help of Julie Nixon, a full-time housemistress of Stanhope, changes were introduced. Weekly boarding, not permit-ted to boys (one parent made a suggestion that if it were, the money paid to local hotels by parents visiting boys could be usefully diverted into the appeals), was eliminated, dress regulations issued and mini-bus transport provided to avoid walking and cycling at night to the remoter destinations. It was planned to have more girl boarders, earlier girl registration and hence greater selection. Dur-ing his first year he was obliged to announce that whereas hitherto it had not seemed necessary to define to sixth formers the limits of relationships, he would now be making these clear, and equally clear that over-stepping them would lead to expulsion. The girls nevertheless were by now valued citizens. Two shared the McElwee travelling prize, and another won a major prize in the Barclay's Bank essay competition. Five girls returned in September 1981 to sit for Oxbridge, a higher number than from any single boys' house. At that time there were 46 girls in the school, 38 boarders and 8 day girls. They enhanced the academic tables and to assist their studies further a Portakabin was lowered by crane into the enclosed sanatorium garden. A part-time physical education mistress put the girls' sports training on to a more regular basis. Several took part in the Himalayan expeditions and many worked for the Duke of Edinburgh's Awards and the community service projects. In 1982 more than one hundred girls were interviewed for the limited number of places available at Stowe.

At first it was planned to build a girls' house north of the swim-ming pool, at the same time as improving the boys' accommoda-tion. The Historic Buildings Council produced objections to the effect of this upon the Grecian Valley panorama; fresh plans were made for one just to the north of the masters' hostel, within the main group of buildings, and a new boys' house beyond Lyttelton. When the costings were finally completed it was decided to close Nugent house as a waiting house for new boys and make it into a resident area for girls. The purchase of Boycott Manor, which lay outside the school grounds, was rejected but the Nugent plan would permit the building of a new house for Bruce and greatly extend the space for better amenities at the heart of things. Such a plan would be dependent upon the response to a further appeal in the Diamond Jubilee Year, 1983.

The liquidation of the Buckingham Carpet Company benefited its near neighbour. Huge lengths of high-quality carpet were purchased and did much to soften the austerity of the older buildings. The campaign to present a more modern image to parents was pressed forward. When all the studies were furnished the carpenters turned their attentions to replacing the well-worn desks, ex-War Department writing bureaux, in the house rooms. At high cost the two-year programme of replacing the decaying underground heating system was completed despite emergencies such as a lightning-strike on the Chapel flue. The bursar, Commander Burley, larded normally prosaic sections of the annual report with graphic references to 'baffling encounters with uncharted subterranean obstructions and the reconciliation of the new system with plumbing imbroglios which snaked Emett-like throughout the labyrinthine recesses of Stowe'. An aged lavatory block at the back of Chatham, where the water had often been known to freeze, was bulldozed away. It was said of the French conservative writer, de Bonald, that had he been present at the Creation he would have cried out: 'Mon Dieu! Let us stick to the Chaos'. As if to prove that no aspect of a school can be changed without complaint even this edifice, an embarrassment from the start, found a champion and a parent wrote to comment upon 'the inexcusable removal of the Egypts so indelibly stamped as they are on the emotions of generations of Chathamites'. Just as Christopher Turner proclaimed that 'the war of attrition' with Stowe's leaking roofs was being slowly won new problems broke out on the North Front, where a series of sharp frosts caused the façade to flake.

Work began on the conversion of dormitories into subdivided units, carpeted and furnished, with accessories such as wardrobes and table lamps. The curtaining of formerly bare windows, the new carpets and spring mattresses, all essentials if the recce patrols of prospective parents were borne in mind, added to the costs of housekeeping. An annual outlay on dry-cleaning, shampooing and the machinery for these tasks had to be found if the improved areas were to remain presentable. The modernized kitchens, too, had major assignments to contend with. The Commemoration Dinners, appeal meetings and various hirings-out of the premises meant a continuous round of additional duties for the chefs. The Pineapple Ball had transferred from Park Lane to Stowe and might bring as many as a thousand patrons. On one occasion it coincided with the Stowe Putter and a luncheon for the Duke of Gloucester given at a business conference. Such a culinary outburst had not been witnessed since the days of the Marquis of Buckingham.

This was not all. The headmaster belonged to a body known as the Rugby Group, formed from seventeen top schools, where matters of common interest could be discussed without minutes and or the intrusion of the press. It took its name, not from the school, but from the railway hotel in Rugby town where a number of headmasters were wont to linger after the Midlands division of the Headmasters' Conference had concluded its deliberations. It spawned many sub-groups – housemasters, heads of departments, Rugby Group chaplains and the like – which moved in orbit from school to school, requiring sustenance and exchanging information which it would be charitable to suppose was focused narrowly on education.

Although Britain's industrial base was eroded during the 1980s the decline was not due to any lack of exhortation directed at the public schools, urged to turn out captains of commerce. The change of government which coincided with Christopher Turner's arrival at Stowe also signified a more competitive world and a utilitarian attitude towards education and career choice. Stowe's careers department developed apace. A headmaster's 'Industry Essay' prize was introduced. It was intended that the best entries would go forward to national competitions such as those sponsored by the *Observer* and Whitbread Breweries. Computer Studies were introduced at 'O' level. Roger Rawcliffe had already begun a Business Studies course in the sixth form. 'Science and Society' became part of a General Studies course for the lower sixth, and brighter fifth forms were given a new subject with the all-embracing title of 'The Future'. Business games became part of the sixth-form curriculum and an optional Monday activity. Lectures were presented on interview techniques by experienced recruiters and in October 1980, the independently run 'Challenge of Industry' conference returned to Stowe after an interval of five years. The

Chairman, Anthony Wood of Metal Box, mindful of his surroundings, began by quoting from Lord Annan: 'Art is manured by money and so, in the end, is a more just and humane society'. There were speakers from management and the unions but interesting contributions came from the floor and set part of the agenda for the future careers programme.

The headmaster spoke at the start of each year to parents of fifth-form boys and lower-sixth girls about the careers advice available. Rodney Exton, Drayson's successor at Reed's School and more recently Director of the Independent Schools' Careers Organization, I.S.C.O., had talks with parents at the close and several offered help from their own professions and businesses. As the Industrial Conference went on its way to other schools, A.J.E. Lloyd who had been seconded to industry for a term, organized a similar event at Stowe without outside assistance. A booklet was compiled from the impressions of Stoics who had done holiday work in various fields and Old Stoics were brought back from universities and polytechnics to relate their findings in a forum. When internal examinations were over, boys and girls were permitted to spend time with local firms. The Stowe business game team reached the semi-finals of a competition sponsored by the Institute of Chartered Accountants.

'Young Enterprise', a scheme which gave pupils some experience of business management, brought masters and pupils into participation with other Buckingham schools. 'Television' and 'the Media' were topics added to the lists at careers conferences. As a result of these initiatives and parental links it was noted that 10 per cent of Stoics were going directly into employment. As part of the Diamond Jubilee celebrations a Science fair was organized by Dr Orger and Dr King. More than fifty Stowe students were joined by contemporaries from local schools in the Science block for an intensive programme of 'workshops' on the general theme of 'Light'. Each group was led by a visiting scientist from industrial research or a university and demonstrations brought to 'A' level candidates knowledge of topics currently in the forefront of scientific research: photochemistry, flash photolysis, holography and optical fibres. Over £30,000 worth of modern instrumentation was loaned by firms and Plessey mounted an exhibition of optical fibre communication and a plenary lecture on holography to larger audiences.

In this respect, as in all others, schools had to be seen to be taking their responsibilities seriously. As the 1980s advanced, changes in the political climate affected the independent schools. When the weakest in many walks of life seemed likely to go to the wall indolence could not be condoned. The strident nature of the tabloid press added to the chances of adolescent misdemeanours becoming public knowledge. Apropos of extreme views promulgated at the Junior Debating Society the headmaster at a masters' meeting reported the collective opinion of the preparatory schools that a wave of right-wing fervour had just passed through their ranks and that careful adjustment and amelioration was called for. Concentration upon the public examinations did not always fit happily with teaching methods, especially of older masters. The love of debate which had characterized the lessons of such as McLaughlin and the impromptu digressions of Roxburgh were not techniques favoured by the young, who were apt to be impatient when reminiscence and surmise intruded irrelevantly upon the syllabus. The headmaster was well aware of the teaching loads which many of the tutors and others carried. He noted that it was unsatisfactory that heads of department might, under the tutorial system, be catering for the needs of more than twenty pupils with too little time left for reading and reflection on their subjects. Moreover, individual attention – the constant monitoring of the progress or the delinquencies of particular pupils, which was seen as an indispensable part of the Stowe tradition – consumed great quantities of time. The pleasant and relaxed atmosphere could sometimes militate against the most stringent and effective criticisms. The headmaster noted that masters and prefects found it hard to be unpleasant but added, 'the situation is improving'.

By 1983 there was a great deal happening from which encouragement could be drawn. Although traditional forms of leadership were currently out of favour, adventure training in its various forms and the theatre had elicited new capacities for enthusing and directing others. Certificate candidates, hemmed in by their desks, were thought to be working harder than before. The hours during which recorded music might be played had been limited. A special meeting with new parents had been called to re-kindle reading habits at home. The Common Room, less remote than its predecessors, was playing a wider role in the educational world generally, serving on local committees, on examining boards and as representatives on professional bodies. The fact that the head-master's annual report, which in Roxburgh's time had been two sides of a foolscap sheet, now ran to over thirty pages, was in some respects an indication of the diversity and richness of the fare on offer.

The societies and lectures which drew the greatest support were often those which gave some reinforcement to the syllabus, but this was not universally true. When Brian Stephan, now the most senior member of the teaching staff, gave a long-awaited talk on 'Myth and Vision in Classical and Modern Times' the audience overflowed into the aisles. An Art Appreciation Society engineered the first colour photograph in the *Stoic*, Rossetti's *Francesca da Rimini*. The Classical Society, as well as listening to David Champion O.S. on 'Tiberius', providing 'valuable information for those members who were studying Tacitus as part of their 'A' level syllabus', produced a magazine, *Cyclops*, and assisted with a production in English of *Hippolytus* before the Queen's Temple. Three members of the Classical Society carried out research on Michael Ventris and his elucidation of Linear B. The Spanish Society went to see Paco Pena and his Flamenco dancers. Geographers attended a conference in Milton Keynes on 'Inner City Planning Problems'. The Natural History Society worked on a project for a Peter Scott conservation award. Debates, after some years of frivolity, returned to more serious subjects. The average attendance numbered around 120, though more controversial topics could attract as many as 200. Stowe 'had confidence in Her Majesty's Government', 'declined to break the school rules', 'thought Man superior to Woman', 'did not believe that public-school education was a waste of time and money' and (by a majority of one) 'did not think that God was Man's most dangerous invention'. The Political Club's reappearance was a sign of the times and with some boldness it invited Martin Webster of the National Front and Bruce Kent of C.N.D. to speak. Christopher Turner himself was heard in contest with the headmaster of a local secondary school on the subject of the Assisted Places Scheme. The Stowe Amnesty International group was host to a sixth-form conference and half a dozen boys took part regularly in Amnesty's 'Prisoner of the Month' campaign. Merlyn Rees, former Home Secretary, gave to the Political Club what was in the memory of listeners their most memorable address, on the problems of Northern Ireland. The Club also screened *The War Game* which the BBC had rejected. As the *Stoic* reported: 'The BBC by banning the showing of this film have to accept responsibility for a queue that stretched from the Audio-Visual Room to the South Front and for the not inappropriate outbreak of hostilities at the door-ways.' In fact the film had to be shown three times to accommodate the throng. A 'Thursday Society' was founded by Dr King to increase awareness of environmental issues. A McDonough Essay Prize was instituted for studies on political topics.

Among guest speakers were Dave Sexton, of Coventry Football Club, who debated the motion: 'This House regrets the Passing of the Amateur', with Dorian Williams, equestrian champion. Mrs Mary Whitehouse drew an audience of 273 to a debate on television sex and violence. Her opponent, Victor Lownes of the Playboy Club, who had taken part in similar debates at the Oxford and Cambridge Unions, commended the supporting speeches as more thoughtful than those which had surfaced in the University debates. John Gummer, then Chairman of the Conservative Party, came to debate for the opposition the motion: 'The public schools have outlived their usefulness', with the headmaster as his seconder. Down on the waters of the Styx the ducks responded nobly to the challenge of the 1983 Jubilee Year despite having been rained on by shot and pellets in a recent game fair. Some twenty mallard were hatched, Carolina Duck and mandarins were bred. Justin Coleman, an enthusiast for the duckery, presented a pair of pintail before he left; rats and poachers were kept at bay and the season was regarded as one of the best ever.

This was a time when a number of schools were appointing a composer-in-residence to their Music departments. Stowe had no need to explore the field. Paul Drayton, already a member of the department, composed 'God's Anvil', a song cycle for chorus and orchestra, a setting of poems by Blake and others on the theme of 'Creation'. He was given an Arts Council grant and sabbatical leave to write a further major score. Verdi's Requiem was given by the Choral Society, a work on which Warrington would not have smiled – better the sensualities of the 'Rio Grande' than the eschatology of Rome. The Marble Hall was the setting for Schönberg's 'Verklärte Nacht' and the Monteverdi Vespers. There was further evidence of Stowe's much closer involvement in local life when Britten's 'Noyes Fludde' was performed in Buckingham

Parish Church by an ensemble drawn from many of the town's schools. Mr and Mrs Noye were played and sung by the housemaster of Chandos and the wife of the History tutor. Many of the string players, all the percussionists and the conductor came from Stowe. In a concert at the school Louise Wilson, violinist, performed Vaughan Williams' 'Lark Ascending' which the composer had once declared at Charterhouse to be beyond the capabilities of young instrumentalists. Jonathan Bayntun, who won a choral scholarship to Christ Church, Oxford, had a remarkable 'gap' year. He left Stowe ostensibly to work in Australia as a tennis coach. While there he played a role in *Peter Grimes* with the Canberra Opera Company and sang on the stage of the Sydney Opera House in the Sailors' Chorus in *Tristan and Isolde*. This was combined with coaching at the Champions' Tennis School in Sydney and some Rugby coaching in Walroonga.

There was a 'Grand Tchaikovsky Concert' which comprised the *Romeo and Juliet* overture, the Fourth Symphony and First Piano Concerto played by Paul Drayton. On another occasion David Arkell, a pupil, played the Third Beethoven Piano Concerto and Richard Lloyd Morgan O.S. was bass soloist in the 'Choral' Symphony. Past and present orchestral players gathered at the Jubilee to give a concert which included Saint-Saëns' 'Carnival of the Animals' and the '1812' Overture. Concessions were made to popular taste with performances by Georgie Fame and the rock group Marillion ('after Tolkien's rather forbidding book', observed Turner) who had a hit in the Top Ten at the time. Humphrey Lyttelton's trumpet arabesques, like the verbal skills of Oliver Lyttelton on Stowe's Speech Day platforms, soothed away any lingering doubts concerning the family's objections to Stowe.

Following a visit from H.M's Inspectors to advise on the Art department, Mr Guy St John Scott came in the summer of 1982. A former head of Art at the Royal Latin School, he had spent some years in industry specializing in the development of media for artists and designers. The Art School was by now providing a full timetable of lessons rather than a centre for leisure hour activity. External examinations were taken by large groups and art appreciation was included in the Upper School General Studies curriculum. The results of all this were that the two masters were teaching on average twenty-nine lessons per week each as well as the large voluntary groups. There were demands for a

Junior Art School and a Sculpture Studio for the use of plaster and resins.

The Design and Technology Centre had already acquired extra space, and was moving into the curriculum. A course for third forms was introduced, one of many initiatives aimed at the Lower School. There was a Junior Electronics Society and Wednesday activities were organized to prevent the slide into boredom which could occur when the excitement of being a newcomer in a large institution had worn off. The Design and Technology Centre was soon one of the showpieces, not the least of its designs being to impress the outside visitor. Other amenities grew and formed part of a determined plan to slough off the image of the secluded country club which had prevailed earlier. Geography, Science, Music and Art were given their own video recorders. A closed-circuit television system proved of value in Games, Drama and Corps instruction. The school acquired a cottage on the Duke of Atholl's estate at Cuilltemhue for a nominal rent and this proved a useful base for mountaineering and geographical expeditions.

Some years previously Sir Ralph Verney had made his house on Anglesey available for Stowe reading parties and it became customary for parts of the holiday period to be absorbed in 'A' level field-work projects. The old-style special holiday trains, leaving the country terminus amid scenes of mild disorder, and drawing into Euston with cheering youths at the windows, had passed into history. During the holidays the modern schoolboy might be found orienteering in the Highlands for a Duke of Edinburgh Award or counting the traffic flow at the roundabouts of Milton Keynes as part of a Geography study.

Computer news became a regular feature of the headmaster's reports. 'It is difficult to imagine that only two years ago the School had only one computer', he wrote in 1982. Even with the rapid spread of the new technology the demand for instruction often outran the extended facilities. Michael Manisty was allotted a special timetable to enable him to guide the computer enthusiasts and assistance came from the Micro-Electronics Centre at Oxford which the public schools had provided and financed to give training and advice. A Stowe slide-making service was introduced and the reprographics section completed £13,000 worth of work which would otherwise have gone to outside contracts. As its labours were all too often interrupted by masters, the need for a Common

Room copier was recognized. As students moved from room to room with ever bulkier files of photocopied notes the days of Socratic cut-and-thrust in the average lesson became more remote and some teachers must have felt that they were falling into the category of 'research assistants'. But the librarian reported (with an annual *cri de coeur* on the temperature of his domain in winter) that the Library was being well used. The total of titles was over 8000 and more than 4000 volumes were borrowed during the academic year, a considerable increase over former times. A Medieval History section had been vastly augmented and Britain's relationship with the European Community was reflected in the addition of a large number of books on its workings. A grateful parent provided equipment and materials for the Economics department. Computers spread to the school administration. Inflation had raised the size of the annual budget to over £2,000,000 and modern technology was essential. Old Stoic records had rested on the files and the encyclopaedic knowledge of the registrar and the appeal managers. All this information had now to be computerized as had future registrations and personal records. Wilson Knight had once likened Stowe to a great ocean liner moving over the waters. The headmaster's offices strike the modern visitor rather as would the operations deck of an aircraft carrier with its flashing screens preparing for a series of engagements.

Out of doors the Duke of Edinburgh's Awards were pursued with commitment. By 1980, eleven Gold Awards had been approved and eighteen more were nearing completion. By 1983, over 100 Stoics were participating: 58 Gold and Silver candidates camped in Skye and 48, without a single absentee, began on the Bronze course at a camp in Wales. The Mountaineering Club went to the Alps and a party, which included one of the matrons, completed six challenging ascents. It acquired a partner in the new Caving and Potholing Club which went on subterranean explorations. Most importantly came the first of the Stowe Himalayan Expeditions, planned by Roger Potter and his assistants Andrew Wild and Dr Hornby. The first was undertaken by a mixed party of Stoics, Old Stoics, parents, staff and a sister. Jim Edwards of Tiger Tops, a nature reserve, who provided help and information, was a future parent. Even by the ambitious standards of the time this was a brave venture and H.R.H. the Prince of Wales wrote a Foreword to the published account. Back at home £1551 was raised at the school for a Nepalese village project and Jim Edwards offered a scholarship to any Stoic interested in conservation and wildlife. The 1983 party to the Himalayas was designed to go further and explore part of the Great Tibetan Plateau. For younger boys a newly re-constituted Venture Wing catered for fourth formers and provided experience in fell-walking, abseiling, and riding. The Myles Henry Prize winner J.F. Derry travelled to the interior of Ghana where he worked at a hospital for the rehabilitation of the blind. His successor in 1983 went to Belize where he had the satisfaction of helping in the arrest of a local mugger.

Although the C.C.F. was now voluntary the contingent numbered around 150. The Falklands War brought a renewed interest in regimental training. The school had the benefit of the local knowlege of the Falklands provided by the bursar, Commander Burley, who had patrolled the region and made expeditions across South Georgia in the 1960s. The Diamond Jubilee attracted many Old Stoics from the forces to an open day and the guard of honour was inspected by General Sir Frank Kitson G.B.E., K.C.B. and Admiral Sir James Kennon K.C.B, C.B.E., soon to be Chairman of the Governors. Twenty cadets spent a week of the summer holidays in 1983 with regular army units at Minden in West Germany experiencing the life of a fusilier. There was morning P.E., inspections, simulated attacks through operating computers and a thirty-six-hour tour of the Allied battlefields in Germany and Holland. For the rest of the contingent a more traditional kind of camp was held at Longmoor. On three successive days the temperature soared to over ninety degrees, hot weather for tactical exercises, one of which ran for fifteen hours. Jusifiable pride was taken in the fact that Stowe had no candidates fall out because of the heat and their fitness was commended by the commanding officer. A change of plan took the next Himalayan Expedition, a party of twenty, trekking through Ladakh, Zamskar and Kashmir amid some of the wildest and least populated regions of the globe. The late melting of the snows and swollen rivers added to the hazards and many different types of terrain had to be covered.

These examples of physical fitness have been cited since the Jubilee Year also produced an unfortunate disciplinary crisis which allowed the press to spread abroad the sophisticated image of the Stoic, lingering on deposit in the memory-banks of Fleet Street. The housemaster of Grenville became suspicious of nocturnal adventures and another master believed that his car had been taken and used without permission. A group of Stoics were caught at night with the vehicle and subsequent investigations disclosed that they had been bound for a party in South Buckinghamshire. Tales of the smoking of cannabis emerged and the subsequent expulsion of fifteen pupils provided the newspapers with one of the most dramatic public-school headlines in the long-running saga of public schools and drugs. It was impossible to foretell at which school such an incident might explode. 'Public School Headmasters these days live on the edge of volcanoes', Bob Drayson had written over fifteen years before and the craters still smouldered. A school's attitude to drugs was a question which bubbled to the surface with a touch of drama in all interviews with prospective parents. Even the most worldly and flamboyant would put on expressions of the deepest gravity and descend to hushed tones when making enquiries. As a result many schools, not necessarily Stowe, had painted themselves into a corner by giving assurances that, even should such an unimaginable example of turpitude be uncovered, the most extreme measures would be brought to bear as punishment.

The expulsion of fifteen Stoics and the suspension of others, some of whom left voluntarily, certainly extirpated the problem. Charlie Macdonald, present second master, recalls one head of house saying to him that he did not think drugs would cross the threshold for many years. Parents in general approved. One Harley Street psychiatrist who specialized in drug abuse was persuaded to register his son for Stowe because of the stern action taken. Taking cannabis did not appear to the young as more serious than the consumption of alcohol and the temptation to experiment and brag is always strong in an enclosed community. On the school's behalf it could be argued that these situations are never static and grow out of control if unchecked; that public schools are places where relative affluence attracts the professional 'pusher'; and that a great deal of instruction and warning had been given. Unfairly, the resultant publicity undid some of the good work laboriously carried out over the years to win the confidence of the preparatory schools and seemed to diminish the value of the links with neighbouring communities and the services rendered to them, which were less newsworthy.

An excellent example of good works unlikely to capture the

headlines is afforded by the Physically Handicapped Able Bodied (P.H.A.B.) courses held at Stowe in the 1980s. The 'International Year of the Disabled' had been one of the themes chosen for the experimental chapel services and inspired the P.H.A.B. enterprises which brought together young people, those with handicaps and others fully active, for shared holidays. Thirty-two teenagers gathered, half Stowe fifth formers and half disabled youngsters from all parts of country. They were housed for part of the holiday period in the Chandos dormitories and meals were taken in the dining halls. There were many activities arranged including a voluntary service in the Chapel and a buffet-disco in the Marble Hall. Links with the disabled continued with weekly swimming sessions for local disabled children in the indoor pool on Saturdays. A second P.H.A.B. course, also based on Chandos, offered Art, Cookery and Photography classes, visits to the Aston Martin works, backstage tours of the National Theatre, a trip to Harrods, a barbecue by the Temple of Venus and an evening excursion on the River Thames. Stowe was not unique in holding such courses but its programmes were unusually imaginative.

Another striking scheme was Intermediate Care, a project to help deal with young people either on the edge of trouble with the law or slightly over it. The near-offenders were involved in waterpolo, canoeing, sports in the Drayson Hall, and other worthwhile leisure pursuits. The community service section began to build up an oral archive of Buckingham history. Stoics organized shopping expeditions for elderly citizens to Milton Keynes, and brought mentally handicapped patients from Bletchley to the school fireworks display. Christmas hamper appeals to parents and Governors raised thousands of pounds and about 200 hampers were annually delivered.

Christopher Turner's first year was marked by success in games. Lionel Weston had brought Loughborough methods to bear on the Rugby training and in one of his first seasons eight out of eleven matches were won including a game against a Rugby School side which had not been defeated for two years. A Close-Smith great-grandson of Lady Kinloss was the individual winner in seven out of nine cross-country races and, had he been born two centuries earlier, might have had a column erected to honour his achievements somewhere on the estate. The Drayson Hall was in constant use as was the all-weather playing surface which, said the *Stoic,* 'has seen the robust activity of the Girls' hockey and lacrosse let loose upon it'. The tennis team retained the Youll Cup and V. St G. de la Rue won the British Schools Small Bore Rifle Association junior championship. The Hockey XI, for once favoured by the climate, won eleven games out of twelve and the Cricket XI lost only once. It was noted that in golf eight Stoics had single-figure handicaps and the Micklem Trophy was won, in what was yet again a succession of victories. Jeremy Robinson at sixteen represented England against Scotland in a Boys' International and won both his matches. Squash, for many years under the direction of Peter Longhurst, enjoyed more rewarding seasons. The VI won 24 out of 25 matches in 1992, the sole defeat being at the hands of Aylesbury Grammar School, national champions. At the Felsted Squash Festival Stowe were the victors and all younger teams had an unbeaten record. Life-saving became part of the P.E. curriculum and Stowe entered the London Schools Water-Polo League, a highly competitive arena.

In the world of field sports the Stowe Beagles were renowned. 'The fact that the pack continues to be welcomed almost everywhere in the neighbourhood (including some places from which the local fox-hounds are banned) speaks well for the impression which the boys and huntsman have made over the years', wrote the headmaster. At the Great Yorkshire Show they had the Champion Dog and a number of Firsts. At a smaller meeting at Honiton Stowe emerged with both Champions and seven other Firsts. Like the Dukes of old the Peterborough Hound Show Champions from Stowe were immortalized in oils, a gift of the Houghton Brown family. In the 1982/3 season the Rugby XV attack was affected by a serious injury sustained by a player at Rugby but the Yearlings went through the season without defeat and the Colts almost did the same. The Hockey XI was unbeaten, the first record of total success for twelve years, including a victory over Canford at Lord's, despite the fact that no old Colours were available from previous seasons. The Stowe cricketers went on a pre-season tour of Australia but this ambitious form of training appeared to have benefited the bowling rather than the batting. The Jublilee cricket match with Canford ended in a draw. During the Easter holidays the Hockey XI won the tournament in Amsterdam. Cross-country runners were successful in every age group and M.B. Walley, Captain, won every race save one. The intermediate team was unbeaten and J.S.R. Nicholl broke the existing record for the Junior Course. On a Saturday in March 1983 a team of twenty-two Old Stoics, ages ranging from 17 to over 50, ran a Jubilee Race against the school and won it. Jeremy Robinson, before leaving for an American University, had played golf on the amateur circuit for eighteen months and reached the semi-finals of the English Amateur Championship.

Golf continued to attract many talented players and the course, tended by Mr David King, was a tremendous asset. Maintenance was paid for by the outside members and a small clubhouse was planned as a further neighbourly gesture. The squash team once more in 1983 won all but one of its matches and these included a victory over Warwick School, which fielded one nationally ranked player and two county juniors. J.M. Bewes, the Captain, was a member of the Buckinghamshire Under 19 Team. The Sailing Club had nine boats on the lake and the headmaster's own interests encouraged sculling. The Northampton Rowing Club generously agreed to build an extension to its own premises in order that Stowe boats might be housed and, as the rowing improved, competition at regattas became possible. Rowers entered for the Reading Long Distance Sculls and regattas at Weybridge and Pangbourne.

The beagles won both championships at the South of England Show. Unfortunately as the result of a fracas with a group of hunt saboteurs two hounds were killed. There was also press criticism of a meet held at the country home of Mr Michael Heseltine whose daughter was a Stowe pupil, though the text was aimed at Mr Heseltine (now Baron Heseltine) rather than Stowe. In view of the publicity and other encounters with the anti-hunting fraternity it was decided to discontinue advertising the meets in local newspapers. A dinner to celebrate the twenty-first anniversary of the pack was attended by 140 guests including several former Masters of the Beagles. Donald Crichton-Miller recalled the early days of the pack and the work of his secretary, Rosemary Hill, who had been a prime mover, and the many achievements of John Thornton who had been an outstanding breeder of show-ring champions.

Interest in drama continued to envelop ever increasing numbers. In Turner's first year there were eighteen productions ranging from *The Merchant of Venice* to pantomime and including a staff production of *The Pirates of Penzance*. The presence and possibly the pertinacity of the girls led to some tampering with Shakespeare's sex discrimination in the matter of cast lists. In *The Merchant* girlfriends were provided for Solanio and Solarino with stolen lines to speak, a frolic with the text which incurred the disapproval of the *Stoic* critic. A resurrected Junior Congreve gave *A Penny for a Song* beside the Temple of Venus. This romantic comedy by John Whiting about a threatened Napoleonic invasion was ideally suited to outdoor treatment. Look-outs climbed on to genuine rooftops, genuine cannon-balls rolled over the grass while fireworks and explosions broke out unconfined. Whether Roxburgh would have approved of so much greasepaint is open to question. In 1944 he wrote to an ex-member of Bruce in the R.A.F., 'There has been an epidemic of House Plays and I think it is one of the distinctions of Bruce that it has never (if I remember rightly) staged a Play.' Forty years on, the theatrical tide was irresistible. House plays were often serious and ambitious. A production by Walpole of the relatively recent *Whose Life is it Anyway?* is an example. What was originally conceived as a lower-sixth play drew such enthusiasm that it became a full weekend festival in three venues: *Rosencrantz and Guildenstern are Dead* before the Queen's Temple, Feydeau's *Flea in her Ear* in the Roxburgh Hall and *Look Back in Anger* in the Rehearsal Room.

In an effort to concentrate and confine activity into the shortest time a 1981 Festival of Drama was planned. The Common Room discussed a proposal for representative ties to be awarded for outstanding performances in the arts, as in the major sports. The Drama Festival when it arrived was attended by professionals such as the actor Christopher Villiers O.S. and Michael Langdon O.S., stage manager for the complex production of *Nicholas Nickleby* by the Royal Shakespeare Company. In 1982 all new boys took part in a Festival of Drama arranged by Tony Meredith. In addition to breaking down some initial shyness and providing an opportunity for bringing parents to the school, the use of sixth-form directors in different versions of the same play illustrated the importance of the director's role and the diversity of interpretations. Chatham House unaided presented *The Tempest*. The Congreve performed Peter Barnes' *The Ruling Class* and a dramatized version of *Billy Budd* which required the construction of a man o' war on the Roxburgh stage. The headmaster released funds to improve the sound system and a team called Theatre Workshop toiled in the brief intervals when the stage was not in use to repair and maintain equipment.

The public schools had found in drama an apparently inexhaustible repository of house spirit to replace the camaraderie once created by sport. House prefects and lofty seniors seemed happy to have minor roles while humbler juniors attained unaccustomed prominence. The *Stoic* in many pages of play reviews gave to the nuances of direction the same attention that had once been devoted to the amazing try in Rugby or the spectacular stroke in a house cricket final. Age gaps were submerged and the interdependence of actors and stage crew engendered solidarity. In 1982 a production of *Peer Gynt* tested to the full the resources of the Art and Design departments as well as much carefully trained acting talent. James Price gave a highly praised performance in the title role. The Common Room gave Britten's *The Little Sweep* and *H.M.S. Pinafore*. Spontaneously formed casts produced *The Comedy of Errors*, *Equus*, and *The Odd Couple*. Ian Small, who also compiled a revue, *Withering Depths*, wrote: 'Over the past few years Drama at Stowe has become one of the jewels in the School's crown and all Stoics can be proud of the School's achievements in the past year. The Philistines are gradually being routed and support from the pupils has been outstanding, both as participants and audiences.' It would certainly be fair to say that over his five years a modern Stoic encountered a range of theatrical experiences that would have been unobtainable in the West End, at least in the range of the productions.

The staff, being younger, was more mobile. Stowe, like other schools, was destined to have fewer long-established characters happy to spend their entire lives in one place. Andrew Wild, who had come from Trinity College, Cambridge, in 1973, left to take over the Physics department at Markham College, Peru. In drama he had been both performer and technical advisor. He was responsible for the growth of the Duke of Edinburgh's Award Scheme which involved not only organization but willingness to take great responsibilities for participants' safety. He left behind a thriving Mountaineering Club. A replacement was found for September but a temporary substitute was required. Mr G.L. Platt 'dropped from heaven' as the headmaster put it (the arrival of physicists really did call for prayer as well as advertising), and was earmarked for a future vacancy. Chris Deacon retired. He had succeeded David Brown as president of the games committee and coached the First XI under suspicion by the elderly Clifford for delaying declarations. He was also that indispensable asset, a viola player, and had a fine record library. Maurice Acton had come to Stowe in 1952 when the workshops had a Cinderella air, housed in the Stone Yard and ruled by the Science department. He was a strong believer in the therapeutic value of craftsmanship for the scholarly as well as those better with hand than brain and he encouraged ambitious projects which increased the prestige of the Speech Day exhibitions. He had himself designed some of the carvings in Chapel and his skill as a boat repairer had been used often by the Sailing Club. 'Jos' Nicholl, whose connection with Stowe went back to 1934, ('It's Jos isn't it?' Roxburgh had enquired at their second meeting) left at the end of 1981 to become rector of Angmering in Sussex. As a schoolboy he had been a prefect and member of the First XV. During the war he served first with the Royal Artillery but was attached to No. 2 Commando Unit and Tito's partisans and was awarded the M.C. in 1945. From Sutton Valence School, where he served as chaplain after ordination, he came to Stowe. He was noted for his pastiche sermons which were parables of Stowe life dressed in a Biblical idiom. He had been local secretary of the Old Stoic Society (and on one occasion had, in his words, 'to publish and be damned' when the bulletin printed details of an Old Stoic in the Births and Marriages Sections with dates too close for propriety) and a tireless priest-in-charge of Dadford and Stowe. Christopher Turner ignored his request that his departure should be untrumpeted. A repository of school lore, one of his final duties was to compose the obituary of Humphrey Playford.

Andrew Vinen also left to join the staff of Maidwell Hall Preparatory School. He had been housemaster of Temple and organizer-in-chief of the Stowe Putter which had been a powerful influence in drawing the preparatory schools and their best golfers to Stowe. As secretary of one space committee and chairman of another he had solved many of the problems of allocation within the main building. Martin Burke, who had retired just before Turner's arrival, died at this time. He had been the first house-master of Nugent and one of Stowe's most interesting personalities. A Medal Winner at the Royal Academy he had studied conducting under Sir Henry Wood and had been due to proceed to Salzburg for lessons under Furtwangler when war intervened. He carried on with his music while serving with the R.A.F. and at the Military Headquarters in Italy. It was his proud boast that he had once conducted at La Scala. Much music had poured out of the French windows of Nugent punctuated by iconoclastic comments on the recordings and dashes to the piano to prove a point.

Michael Fox left in the Jubilee Year. He also had commanded the C.C.F. and done a great deal for the Old Stoic Society. His good living made him a frequent feature of the Ephemerals and there were several stories of clashes at Common Room breakfasts when the occasional fried egg had been known to cross the room. Among the new arrivals was Peter Farquhar who came from Manchester Grammar School to be senior English master. He was instrumental in building up a department of specialists in a subject that had often been reliant upon the Classics and other disciplines for its teaching. Dr B.H. Orger, a scientist, had university experience in South Africa and, with a Bursary from the Royal Society, attended an international conference on Chemistry education in the United States.

The Chapel choir had given an early performance of the 'African Sanctus', a religious cantata by David Fanshawe O.S. which brought together the music of Muslim and tribal Africa. It had been received with acclaim at the Three Choirs' Festival in 1978 and had the rare distinction of being repeated two years later. He himself began a new work based on the musical heritage of the Pacific islands, 'Pacific Odyssey'. Other Stoic composers included H.L. Goodall who wrote for a Rowan Atkinson Revue at the Globe Theatre; K. Emrys Roberts who provided the incidental score for the television adaptation of the Delderfield novel *To Serve Them All My Days*; and A. Miall, who did the same for a radio adaptation of Anthony Powell's *Dance to the Music of Time*. Colin Graham produced *La Traviata* for the Metropolitan Opera. In journalism Robert Kee was awarded the Richard Dimbleby Award and Peregrine Worsthorne the 'Columnist of the Year' Granada Award. Of Stoic artists, Robert Wraith studied under Annigoni and was commissioned to paint the portrait of Dr Robert Runcie, Archbishop of Canterbury. David Wynne completed a bust of Earl Mountbatten and there were exhibitions of the work of David Williams-Ellis in London, Europe and America. Algy Cluff became Proprietor of the *Spectator*; P.B. Lucas published *The Sport of Princes: Reflections of a Golfer*; J.A.P. Methuen-Campbell *Chopin Playing*; C.M.V. Nicholl a study of alchemical themes in Shakespeare; S.J.L. Spicer *The Motor Cars We Owned*; and the Hon. T.F.C. Prittie *Whose Jerusalem?* and *The Velvet Chancellors*. C.R. Bingham and A.R. Bird were in the winning Oxford Pentathlon Team. J.H.G. Carr and C.D. Forbes-Adam cycled from Cairo to Nairobi and Catarina Cowan won the Ladies Cup for Oxford in the first University Womens' Ski Race. Most honoured of all, Leonard Cheshire V.C. became Stowe's first recipient of the Order of Merit.

To celebrate the Diamond Jubilee a year rather than a month of special events was planned by a committee under John Boyd-Carpenter. Survivors of the first ninety-nine were invited to a service of thanksgiving in Chapel and a lunch in the State Music Room. The Archbishop of Canterbury, after having had what he described as 'a somewhat bumpy descent by helicopter into your beautiful grounds', preached on the theme of freedom:

> Freedom from mass opinion, from fashionable theories and from lazy over-simplifications . . . To learn to be loyal members of a community at the same time as we learn freedom should be the strength of a school like yours. Loyalty to a school can easily be laughed at, and when it is narrow or pompous or stuffy it should certainly be mocked: but at its best it can be a nursery for our affections which need to be deepened as well as to expand in scope through service to a wider community.

The occasion also saw the launching of an appeal for the Roxburgh Trust which would give an endowment not only for radical improvements to the buildings but for the foundation of scholarships. The Thatcher government seemed likely to be in power for many years, the Labour Party was in disarray and speculation over the dissolution of the public schools no longer intruded into conversation. Stowe itself had witnessed major changes. The interiors of houses accepted by previous generations without complaint had been brought up to modern standards and made more comfortable. The unique inheritance of temples and pavilions had been cared for to the uttermost farthing available. The variety of enterprises, the willingness to pick up the challenge of external competition, remained, and so did the desire, a more recent tradition, for active participation in the life of town and county. Herculean efforts had been made to provide an education of the kind demanded by modern industry and business and to increase careers advice.

Inflation brought one unexpected boon. By 1980 the loans from Legal and General, which had rescued the Allied Schools in 1934, had shrunk to a smaller proportion of the budgets and rapidly been paid off. In theory by the original terms of agreement, the Martyrs' Memorial Trust, now subsumed in the Church Pastoral Aid Society, could have resumed full control, dissolved Allied Schools and steered Stowe into the swirling waters of evangelical Protestantism. Sensibly it was agreed that the governing body represented a level of distinction and expertise which it would be foolish to cast aside. Two years earlier Boyd Carpenter had proposed a degree of severance from Allied Schools in whose councils the Martyrs' Memorial Trust was more strongly placed than at Stowe. This had been opposed and Bob Drayson had made the surprising comment that Stowe's Protestant affiliations, while not offending High Church parents, brought to the school at least fifteen entrants per annum or a total of around eighty in all at a given time. So the Allied Schools remained in being though the schools had greater freedom to use their incomes autonomously and Old Boys could be represented on the governing bodies in larger numbers.

The Martyrs' Memorial Trust did in fact have a turn of the chairmanship under the Reverend John Eddison from 1981–7. In public schools the lot of the governed is at one with that of pots and statues in museums and art galleries, in so far as the boards of directors are selected for public merit and have no financial dependence upon the institution or more than an episodic knowledge of its workings. In such circumstances the interest and capabilities of a Chairman are vital. Christopher Turner praised highly the expertise of John Taylor, an architect who gave close attention to all the plans for building, and was a loyal attender at Speech Days and public occasions. John Eddison was able to give warm support throughout the mid-80s and his successor, Vice-Admiral Sir James Kennon, Chairman during these last years, drove himself relentlessly to achieve a satisfactory agreement with the National Trust over the buildings on the estate. John Taylor went on to be Chairman of Allied Schools and Kennon supported the policy of retaining the services of the Allied Schools agency based in Banbury. It is worth recalling that James Kennon as a boy at Stowe had taken issue with the London County Council which had scorned the proposals that local authorities might co-operate with the public schools and take up places, and published a defence of the system in the *Stoic*:

> To live tolerantly and successfully broadmindedness is essential in a boy. He is unable to develop his views or learn much from others if he only lives within his own family circle whose views may be far from ideal . . . A Boarding School comprises Life and all the problems and difficulties of Life in miniature which the boy will later meet; he learns to take orders and later to give them, he learns the meaning of responsibility and initiative, he finds out what it is to start at the bottom and work up to the top . . . in short he is trained for Life itself . . . The Public Schools much resent the ignorant attitude of the L.C.C. towards their system and deeply regret that the L.C.C. should so curtly refuse to collaborate with them for the good of national education . . . Co-operation between the State system and the Public Schools is essential to produce the best educational equality of opportunity vital to the working of an efficient democracy.

That was in 1943, and there must be many who regret that in fifty years the two highways in education have remained so widely separated.

14

Christopher Turner 1983-9

In the late 1980s changes in British society became ever more apparent. The tasks of the Welfare State were becoming increasingly onerous and the problems of Europe, 'developing countries' and the environment had to be faced in a world of banner slogans and demonstrations, with much vulgarization and strident sentiment interfused. Britain was very different from the country out of which the public schools had arisen. The gaps between Oxford and Cambridge and all but a few of the schools widened. The cavalier recommendations which Roxburgh sent to the colleges make strange and comical reading today: 'His cricket atones for the deficiencies of his brains', 'He rides very well to hounds', 'He ran two splendid races against Eton', or 'The name of — 's Housemaster is I.M. Cross. It is characteristic of the father to have forgotten it'. High-fliers were still successful. In 1983, when Stowe gained five open awards, M.R. Downing of Grafton was reported to have submitted five 'perfect' answers out of seven on the Advanced Papers for Maths and Physics. But for the good all-rounder the competition was fiercer, colleges had taken to having seminars to stimulate interest among the head teachers of comprehensive schools which had not considered the oldest universities in the past. Though this was sometimes infuriating to heads of independent schools when public-spirited boys were rejected, there was some truth in the belief that their students, well grounded, obliged to do long hours of supervised work from an early age and taught by some of the best teachers in the land, would wilt in less structured systems. By contrast the bright pupil, brought up with less

ambitious classmates and overcoming possibly difficult conditions
for study at home, found the resources of universities inspiring.
Other factors hampered public-school candidates: gifted sportsmen put in hours of training, evenings were interrupted by prefectorial duties, house prayers and the ever-growing fashion for
consultation between prefects and housemasters. Fortunately the
situation was partially remedied by the increased popularity of
universities such as Durham, St. Andrew's and Edinburgh where
sport and social life were strengthened by public-school contingents. In schools where the intake was not academically exclusive
much attention had to be paid to extracting larger measures of
work from weaker candidates.

In 1984 the senior tutor reported that the 'A' level passes had been
86.8 per cent for the second year in succession, a figure within 0.1
per cent of the highest total in recent years. As this group of candidates had always been reckoned to contain some weaker brethren
there was some room for congratulation. In several subjects there
had been improvement without any rise in the quality of entrants.
Masters' meetings devoted much time to the subject of literacy and
improving standards in the years before public examinations
loomed over the horizon. Modern times did not bring many allies
to the battlefield. 'The habit of reading with earphones plugged
into Radio One and the insidious influence of television on the
under-tens must share some blame', the headmaster told the Governors, adding, 'It is scholarship only that wins high grades and that
is not yet in plentiful enough supply on the Arts Sides.' A sign that
was marginally depressing for the future was the fall in the
I.Q. standards of new boys entering at thirteen plus. The yearly
averages were as follows:

76/7	77/8	78/9	79/80	80/1	81/2	82/3	83/4	84/5
119.4	117.7	117.8	118.0	117.6	115.2	115.2	115.6	114.7

Indications were that many professional people and especially
teachers, professors and parsons were unable to pay the ever-rising
fees. The monied classes, while keen to obtain the best education
for their children, came from different backgrounds. Moreover,
the upheavals of the 1960s and the dismal records of some pupils
in the 1970s had alienated quite large numbers from the public
school system, those who should have been the next generation of
fee-paying parents. There was another factor which should not be

overlooked. Under the Provostship of Lord Caccia, Eton College had disbanded the Choir School and made available large funds for Music Scholarships. At the same time a larger proportion of college funds had been released to support the general expenditure and the provision of bursaries and supplementary grants was greatly increased. By changing the modes of entry at the same time and abolishing the old tradition of registering at birth, opportunities for entry were afforded to bright pupils from the ages of seven or eight. The exclusion of many long-established Eton families opened the doors to others and few preparatory schools could resist the lure of announcing a clutch of Eton places. The result was to disrupt established affiliations between families, prep schools and other public schools, and candidates for Eton who were withdrawn as having little likelihood of passing its exacting standards were not always the best substitutes for the entries which were lost.

At Stowe all these changes meant greater pressures in the form-room and in the provision of advice on higher education and careers. There was some discussion on the wisdom of removing less able candidates from 'O' level courses and entering them for the less academic C.S.E. examinations, although this decision was over-taken by events as the new G.C.S.E. exam, something of a panto-mime horse embracing both 'O' levels and C.S.Es, was decreed nationally for 1988, which meant that third formers coming to Stowe in 1985 would be required to take it. In the meanwhile there was a search for new subjects in which enterprise might add to the number of 'O' levels gained. Photography fared well, all ten candidates being successful at the first venture. Psychology, undertaken by a bold group of seven, yielded only one pass. The increasingly cosmopolitan nature of Stowe was demonstrated by a 100 per cent pass rate at 'O' level in Modern Greek, Chinese, Hindi, Norwegian, Portugese and Persian. Roxburgh, who had once regretted that an undoubtedly English boy had an Italian name, would have been bemused. The ever-widening spectrum of ability was displayed by the results in 1984 when the number of Grades A and B at 'O' level was the highest ever and the entire top set in Physics gained 'A' grades, but a further fall in the I.Q. rate showed that some in the lowest third form to arrive registered below 100 and would experience difficulties with 'O' level courses. The start of G.C.S.E. was, as expected, an untidy one. In some subjects the syllabus arrived only days before the start of the Autumn Term 1986, which impeded the ordering of books and materials. The examination boards found their tasks more complex than before and the burden of paperwork increased. As a feature of the G.C.S.E. was continuous assessment during termtime there was even less scope for the stimulating digression or the prolonged argument in class. It was a time of uncertainty for the National Curriculum, towards which some gesture had to be made by independent schools, as it set its hounds upon the G.C.S.E.'s traces. It was not known whether the wish to include Technology might exclude German or Greek, and this at a time when over two hundred copies of *Michael Ventris Remembered*, researched by the Classical Side, had been distributed to preparatory schools. The future of 'A' levels was in doubt. The likelihood of teacher appraisal becoming part of the career pattern was something of a spectre in the common rooms of boarding schools where staff both lived and worked together out of school and in. In his 1985 report and elsewhere the headmaster praised the degree of commitment which the teaching body displayed in the face of current demands. He had some misgivings about the breadth of activity and the wide dispersion of energies by staff and pupils, but concluded that they were good training for initiative in a world 'which needs industrial leadership more than it needs academic distinction'.

An example of ever-increasing expansion and adaptation was to be found in the careers department which James Larcombe had run for eight years before taking over Grafton House. Four members of staff went on a special course at Warwick University to assess the new Morrisby Careers Test progamme. Sixteen Stoics who had been put through the Birkbeck Tests already in use were assessed by Morrisby procedures. In nearly every case it was found that the Morrisby testing gave additional information and it was decided to adopt the new methods from 1985. Career profiles and recommendations had to be fed back to housemasters and tutors, all of which added to the burdens of administrative work demanded. The parents of fifth formers received the analyses of the tests with the Easter reports and fact sheets to encourage research into areas of special interest. The Royal Latin School shared interview practices with Stowe in conjunction with the newly established University College of Buckingham. Interview techniques were demonstrated with videos, slides and practical examples. Among Old Stoics who helped at a two-day careers conference was Michael Grade who, said the headmaster, 'fielded questions on all aspects of the BBC brilliantly'. At the Higher Education Conference in May 1988, the student guidance counsellor from Oxford Polytechnic was particularly persuasive on the subject of the good degree courses at polytechnics. New parents were brought into the occupation survey. The Old Stoic Committee, and in particular Bryan Toye O.S. who had an extensive knowledge of the City, compiled a register of Old Stoics prepared to help in various ways. The McAlpine family endowed an annual lecture on the theme of 'Technology and Society', the first three speakers being Lord Joseph, Sir Reay Geddes and Bill Sirs. The visit of Bill Sirs coincided with the miner's strike and his analysis of the relevance of Trade Unions in the modern industrial framework was followed by lively discussion and some surprise that a major Union leader could have views that were by no means extreme. Other lectures on 'Understanding Industry' were given by visiting experts in the Spring Term section of the General Studies course. Twelve members of the lower sixth took part in an 'Insight into Management' forum for local schools at Milton Keynes and British Alcan sent a team of six managers to spend an evening at Stowe and explain how the company worked. During the summer holidays of 1986 senior members of the Careers department manned the telephones to give advice following the publication of 'A' level results.

'The keys on the Career Master's home computer are wearing out', wrote the headmaster. In a design and build competition sponsored by British Aerospace twelve teams competed to fly an egg across a given space without breaking it. Stowe won the event, for which the prize was a day's flight to the company's headquarters at Chester. The 'Young Enterprise' company of lower sixth formers made a profit of £200 marketing boxes of luxury chocolates in specially designed wrappers and gave the proceeds to charity.

To accompany the growth in Business Studies, Computing swept along on its upward path. Christopher Turner thought that recognition should he given to Stowe's pioneering work in this area. 'The completion of Bruce has, undoubtedly, been the focus of attention for the start of the academic year', he wrote in 1986. 'But perhaps some thought could be given to an "official" opening of the Computer Centre by a prominent industrialist next year.' All new members of the sixth form were given a policy document summarizing the computer facilities available. While the Centre was in action during half of the teaching timetable it was almost always occupied out of school hours and the early zest for computer games gradually gave way to more productive uses. Importance was attached to integrating computing with other disciplines. Stowe was taking a lead in Graphic Design. Modern Linguists were experimenting with word-processing in foreign languages and the Music department installed an electronic music studio. Sir Edwin Nixon, Chairman of I.B.M., formally opened the full Computer Centre. One hundred and twenty students were awarded Cambridge Information Technology Certificates and sixty entered for the R.S.A. Examination were all successful. The Audio-Visual department obtained a licence to record Open University programmes and it is interesting to note that the cost of these, at under £5 per programme, compared favourably with the rising costs of books. The three millionth sheet passed through the photocopier in the Common Room towards the close of 1986.

In the summer of 1988 'A' level passes reached 90 per cent for the first time. Anthony Pedder, who had succeeded as senior tutor, commented that the statistics had been boosted by the shedding of weaker candidates after 'O' level, but as tables of results became matters of national interest and concern all schools were inclined to dissuade doubtful starters from embarking upon examination courses. Of the ten boys and girls who gained Oxbridge places (awards having been discontinued) half had entered the school at fifth form level, illustrating that the third form intake still needed to be more competitive. In G.C.S.E. the English department had opted for 100 per cent coursework and been faced with mountainous piles of marking. 'Few members of staff looked greyer with fatigue in the middle of last term', said the senior tutor. Like many older colleagues Anthony Pedder found the numbing effects upon individuality of new methods and new examinations tiresome. He had been wont to slip scholarship level questions into the 'O' level syllabus and set prodigiously testing Chemistry preps. He had specially large test tubes made for his lessons so that various bubblings and colourful reactions were made the more striking and his lessons were renowned for the explosions and smells which lent an appeal to early learning.

A more ominous threat from the State came in the form of the encouragement of competition between maintained schools. The intention to fund schools which opted out of local authority control from central funds, coupled with plans to set up technology colleges with avowed dedication to excellence in large cities, resurrected some of the old grammar-school ideals. The virtual annihilation of grammar-school places in previous decades had served to fill the public schools with the children of families prepared to make the sacrifices involved. The chances were that grant-aided schools would elevate themselves to become selective, especially in middle-class areas, and so significantly reduce the ranks from which fee-paying pupils might be expected.

There was no indication that the severe measures taken against the drug taking in 1983 had been harmful to recruiting. Many parents endorsed Draconian methods. Most other schools had suffered and weathered similar crises or felt unusually blessed in avoiding them. In 1984, however, there was an incident at Stowe which seized the headlines in both the tabloids and the serious press and had a uniquely horrific quality which even those most versed in public school pranks and escapades would not have dreamed up. The Airey Neave Trust had been founded in memory of the Member of Parliament murdered by an IRA bomb within the precincts of the Palace of Westminster. Under the presidency of Lady Airey, as his widow became, the Trust planned a Vietnam Refugees' Art Exhibition to which Stowe agreed to act as host. It was to be opened by H.R.H. the Duchess of Gloucester and, in accordance with customary practice, the police mounted an intensive security operation. Three boys, including an American E.S.U. scholar, planted a hoax bomb which was discovered and treated momentarily as genuine. Adolescents sometimes miscalculate tremendously over practical jokes. The headmaster was of the opinion that the intention was to try and outwit a rather intrusive and heavy-handed police search. There was no wish to signal support for the IRA, the culprits to their credit readily confessed, were subsequently prosecuted in a Crown Court and given short detention sentences.

In reality it was far from being the most culpable offence in the annals of Stowe. In the high noon of Roxburgh's reign three Old Stoics (one in his O.S. tie) had appeared in the dock pleading guilty to a string of somewhat drunken car-thefts. The cars had been used eventually to come to Stowe where there were some larcenies from house and armoury. The illicit car-racing at Silverstone had been potentially more lethal. The school had a good record in the work of reconciliation and one Old Stoic had recently been involved in community projects in the Ardoyne district of Belfast.[1] However, it was not hard to portray the hoax as flippant and callous. The response of the school was admirable. The Summer Ball was cancelled and instead, on a June day, large numbers took part in a sponsored walk which raised a considerable sum for the Airey Neave Trust. It was an imaginative solution to a highly unpleasant situation and the cheque was presented to Lady Airey in the Autumn.

To overcome the effects of bad publicity, in addition to battling with the general needs of recruitment in a shrinking market, ever more energetic drives were needed. More parental requests for visits were acceded to: 367 in the year 1986/7 as against 288 in 1983. By the autumn of 1987, when more than 156 sets of parents were destined for interview, the headmaster's diary had reached saturation point. The Milton Keynes Development Corporation showed some interest in independent education as part of its package of attractions for industrial investors. Members of staff, principally housemasters, visited thirty-six preparatory schools in the year 1987/8. Fifty-two headmasters of prep schools and their wives visited Stowe over a period of eighteen months so that what Christopher Turner termed the 'real' Stowe could be witnessed in contrast with the press image. It was reported that eleven couples had 'attended a most enjoyable discussion on the theme of moral education'. Roger Potter prepared a paper for the Governors on overseas recruitment and co-ordinated articles and news items in the local press. An exhibition of preparatory school art was arranged and a new prospectus distributed. As a result entries for the future recovered and it was noted in 1986 that the 1084 registrations included a girl for the year 2001! By contrast the group most likely to react to unfavourable publicity, the Old Stoics, had shrunk and now provided around 19 per cent of the student population as against 30 per cent in the 1970s.

In his early days Christopher Turner had noted that visiting parents had been impressed by the friendliness and spontaneity of the students but critical of the living conditions. Much had been

[1] J.M. Earle O.S. was for a time Director of the Corrymeela Project in Northern Ireland.

done to improve the latter. The sprung mattresses were advancing dormitory by dormitory. 'We are now in the position of having a depressed, albeit diminishing, minority of boys having to sleep on these terrible mattresses', commented the bursar in reference to the horsehair variety. The holiday lettings and courses demanded that chefs and domestic workers would be in residence permanently and their accommodation was accordingly up-graded. The eventual completion of the new Bruce House enabled the finishing touches to be made to the interior improvements. The initial plans for a girls' house, which Turner had felt was indispensable if the admission of girls was to continue, were drawn up by architects suggested by Lord Carrington, who had re-modelled his local village. They were imaginative plans aimed at a building on the North Front and were finalized after long consultations. Lord Esher, a member of the Landscape Committee, and Sherban Cantacusino of the Royal Fine Arts Commission were impressed but John Taylor, Vice-Chairman of the Governors, and other Governors were appalled at the costs, while the Historic Monuments and Buildings Commission disagreed with Fine Arts.

The scheme was abandoned and, while the experts had debated, the headmaster had become convinced that conditions in the main block were responsible for many of the problems of supervision and behaviour. Bruce, whose housemaster had to go out of doors to visit any part of the house, was still split into thirteen fragments, not all salubrious. The decrease in pupil numbers had rendered Nugent superfluous and the proposal was made to fuse it into the Bruce housemaster's residence and refurbish it for girls. If an entire house could be moved from the central building further developments would flow, such as the move of the bookshop to a more heavily used trade route and, by chain reaction, a more commodious Common Room. The new Bruce, which the architects Barnsley, Hewett and Mallinson fitted with some dexterity into the existing cluster of buildings west of Chapel, was opened in 1985 by Lord Boyd Carpenter. The following summer Admiral Sir James Kennon opened Grenville's wider domains within the main block. The resident girls were accommodated in the extended Nugent and there were no longer girl pupils scattered among staff residences in the grounds. Stanhope continued in the old sanatorium, taking all the day girls, although the school authorities occasionally had problems allocating places between the two. The new Common

Room was spacious and could at last match the standards elsewhere, the new bookshop housed on a prime site became one of the
most impressive in any school. Work could now concentrate on
studies in Grafton, Stanhope and Chatham and four more dormitories in Chandos and Chatham were fitted with the new furniture. The more notorious leaking roofs in Grafton and over the
swimming pool were sealed and few areas were left which could
invite adverse criticism.

The Ghosts of the Past, however, were not to be easily laid.
Inquiries into the structure of the West Pavilion revealed that the
core of the wall had a number of voids and deposits of rubble
where solid materials should have been. The cost of repairs was
estimated at £120,000 of which English Heritage was expected to
contribute 40 per cent. The discovery emphasised once more the
need to transfer the responsibility for preserving Stowe's architectural inheritance on to more broadly based institutions. A new
Reservoirs Act came into force in 1987 and remedial work to the
Octagon and Eleven-Acre lakes was advised by the Department of
the Environment. Once again the Oxford Lake had to be drained
and the dam repaired. Stoics still laboured for four or five afternoons a week and the Mathematics department assisted with tasks
of surveying. Profiles of the tree population were computerized;
planting was carried out around the Roxburgh Hall with a view to
providing a vivid range of autumnal tints. Several thousand
visitors were now admitted to the grounds annually. The proceeds
went towards furnishing houses with snooker tables though Temple opted for six dozen bedspreads!

The much-desired 'A' level course in Art History began in
the autumn of 1987. Ken Melber joined the department from
Framlingham College to conduct it, and became director when Guy
Scott took over from Charlie Macdonald as housemaster of Lyttelton. An innovative feature was the appointment of an artist-in-
residence, a post which required the holder to teach for half the
timetable, leaving the remainder for creative work. There was a
large response to the advertisement and fourteen candidates were
invited to submit portfolios. The final choice was Julia Estdale, a
postgraduate of the Slade; specialists in ceramics and sculpture
followed. A mezzanine floor was constructed in the Art School
which greatly increased the display area. Even so the demand for
tuition exceeded the space available and some aspiring artists had

to be turned away from the 'O' level classes. Derek Barlow came to the Design department as workshop technician. An experienced craftsman and model-maker he helped to found a Model-Making Junior Society. There were many Stoics who went on to Art, Design, Architecture and Art History courses in Further Education. Under Michael Carpenter, who had come to Stowe as a craftsman and headed the department of Design, better storage space was created to facilitate ambitious projects and to house timber and metal stocks.

Audiences for concerts were numerically stronger, not surprising for guest artists such as Johnny Dankworth and Cleo Laine, but gratifying for recitalists such as David Arkell O.S. and 'Janiculum', a chamber ensemble organized by the wife of Stephen Dodgson O.S., composer and teacher at the Royal College of Music. The aid which the sixth-form girls brought to school music was acknowledged in a frank report from the Director of Music, David Gatehouse, on the shortage of trebles. Music scholars from prestigious cathedral or college choirs seemed to lose their quality and range and sometimes even their voices between audition and arrival. Humbler members of junior school choirs often proved less able than glowing reports had portrayed: ' These reports can range from enthusiastic exaggeration to downright untruths regarding a boy's musical interest and experience'. The girls on the other hand had new opportunities to develop their talents. Fiona Swadling played a piano concerto in one concert and a violin concerto in the next. A Mozart horn concerto was performed by a girl, Annabel Grey-Edwards. For the boys Giles Munt was highly praised for negotiating the perils of the Hummel Trumpet Concerto. 'Carols by Candlelight' were introduced at Christmas and choral groups gave concerts in local churches under boy conductors. The Electronic Music Studio was established in the Roxburgh Hall, a room packed from floor to ceiling with synthesizers, recording machines, a music computer and ancillary devices. As the new G.C.S.E. syllabus demanded compositions and performances recorded by candidates this nest of exotic machinery was a basic requirement.

Art department and workshops also joined in preparing the sets for a major Congreve production of Anouilh's *Ring Round The Moon* directed by Tony Meredith. The set was designed by Guy Scott and lit by James Ewens. In 1986 a record number of ten houses took part in the Drama Festival. Temple and Walpole converted their house rooms into auditoria, Cobham annexed the cricket pavilion, others used the Rehearsal Room or the Roxburgh. In the summer of 1986 Lionel Weston directed the staff in *The Gondoliers*. Student producers spurned such light-hearted fare and mobilized the lower sixth into the more sombre worlds of Miller (*All My Sons*), Albee (*The Zoo Story*) and Camus (*Les Justes*). Another artist-in-residence, Mark Hancock, not only helped with theatre design but exceeded his brief by acting in the staff play and coaching Rugby.

One idea mooted during the course of the year was a small theatre named after David Niven. His son had given approval and an architect father prepared plans. The double use of the Roxburgh Hall for music and drama put a strain on management and storage. A great deal of effort went into the creation of scenery and costumes and this was wasted when items could not be preserved. In 1988, Paul Dobinson, son of the housemaster of Chandos, had been tragically killed in an accident while on an English Speaking Union scholarship in America. At Stowe he had been Captain of Swimming, an enterprising play producer and one of a new generation to take an interest in the Pineapple. Many friends among pupils and staff raised over £20,000 by sponsored walks and other means to provide a workshop theatre named the Paul Dobinson Theatre which would allow greater flexibility and experiment than the Roxburgh Hall. As the Spring Festival of 1989 witnessed eleven plays by eleven houses the need was amply demonstrated.

As in the West End, musical productions enjoyed a wave of popularity. The Congreve performed *The Boy Friend* and it was reported that even the critics old enough to know what they were talking about were loud in praise of the final Charleston, choreographed by Lionel Weston taking time out from training the heavier steps of the First XV. The Common Room countered with *My Fair Lady* and *Guys and Dolls*. Serious drama was not totally neglected and Grenville, in particular, earned plaudits for tackling the hazards of *Dr Faustus* against a simple house-room set.

The 'A' level examiners shaped some but not all the programmes of societies. The Modern Linguists organized a week of language teaching in Brittany, but also an extensive exhibition of French, German and Russian culture which occupied all the ground floor of the new classroom block on Speech Day. George Clarke whose retirement, as the headmaster said, 'left a large gap in the cultural life of Stowe', gave his farewell talk to the Literary Society on 'The Lady with the Squint' inspired by a sly allusion to John Wilkes in the pediment statuary of Stowe. English Society meetings sometimes proved controversial. The persuasive powers of Mr J.C. Venning, head of English at Malvern College, were tested in trying to win sympathy for Goneril and Regan, and an attempt by Dr Wakelin of Royal Holloway and Bedford College to deny Chaucer's 'Merchant's Tale' any symbolic quality caused 'polite outrage' and called for the diplomatic intervention of an Old Stoic from Brasenose who presented 'a *via media* amongst the potentially warring factions on the staff'. Rachel Trickett, Principal of St Hugh's College, Oxford, gave a much admired lecture on *Tess of the d'Urbervilles* relating scholarship to the excitement of a first reading. Peter Farquhar contrasted the savagery of Cyprus with the ordered morality of Venice as a theme in *Othello*. Further spirited discussion broke out when Dr Fleeman of Pembroke College, Oxford ventured into the subject of 'Goodness' as displayed by Hamlet and the Ghost. Dr Richards of Brasenose College was able to illuminate his talk on 'Jane Austen and the Picturesque' with references to the Classical and Gothic landscapes immediately beyond the Lecture Hall.

All Stoics taking 'A' level Biology were expected to attend a field trip. Bardsey Island had first been selected, but bad sailing weather and some memorably hazardous crossings led to the search for a new centre on the Lleyn Peninsula, where two cottages were rented. Twenty-seven Geographers attended a residential course in Snowdonia and twenty-three in Cumbria. Geography studies now stretched from field work on fluvial, glacial and marine geomorphology in North Wales to topics such as urban morphology, consumer allegiance, environmental abuses and 'recreational diffusion' in Milton Keynes. The number of leisure days sliced from the holidays continued to grow.

Further afield successive Himalayan expeditions rafted down Nepalese rivers, crossed the Tiru Danda Ridge waist-deep in snow while carrying heavy baggage loads, and came upon unmapped valleys. The 1985 Expedition met a Nepalese boy, Shaligram Ghimire, then aged sixteen and acting headmaster of his village school. As a result of the encounter Stowe raised funds to help him through university at Kathmandu for the six years required to gain an Engineering BSc. Support was also given to a Save the Children hospital at Baglung for which sponsored walks raised several thousands of pounds and at which a Stoic worked for three months. In its enthusiasm for field work the Biology department outdid the visions of Elizabethan imperialists. Twenty pupils and staff under Dr James crossed South America overland from Rio de Janeiro to Lima, a venture shared with Rugby School and a triumph of organization.

Similarly in search of new worlds to conquer, the winners of the Myles Henry Prizes produced plans that to an older generation must have seemed realizable only in the adventure stories of Rider Haggard. J.R. Hazell and S.C. Todd went in search of pygmy tribes in Zaire, travelling the Congo by steamer and meeting Africans who had never seen a white man before. G.C. Hooper and W.W.M. Chambre ranged Ecuador from its volcanic spine to the rain forests and followed a tributary of the Amazon by canoe. W.T. Fraser-Allen and A.J.H. Diamond travelled in the footsteps of Livingston, and lectures were given by them and other travellers returned from the interior of Iceland and oases west of the Nile. David Part O.S. raised funds to provide more McElwee Travel Awards and these inspired studies in Viennese history, the development of early Italian fresco and sites associated with the astronomers Brahe and Galileo. Fiona Lockton, housemistress, who had sailed with Operation Raleigh to New Zealand, came back to speak on the geographical and biological work carried out.

The Cuilltemhue bothy on the Atholl Estate was a base for the fifty-mile expeditions demanded from Duke of Edinburgh Gold candidates. Although its original earth floor had been covered and, for £25 per annum, fallen timber from the estate could be collected for fuel, it was no luxury chalet. During one New Year visit the school transport was snowed in for several days many miles from the main road and on a mountain track. Torrential Scottish rain was frequent but boys and girls returned for a variety of challenging pursuits. In the Shropshire Hills, during a March camp, members of the youthful Venture Wing had to be ordered into buildings after a valiant attempt to weather temperatures of minus 8°C. As part of the process of creating local support and goodwill the C.C.F. offered a place on its adventure training camps to an Army cadet from the Buckingham district. This proved worthwhile and became an annual gesture. The C.C.F. programme included commando training, mountain exercises in Bavaria and 'the ever popular parachute courses'. At an inspection carried out by Brigadier C. Dunphie M.C. the contingent was granted the distinction of wearing the green beret of the Royal Green Jackets, enhancing links with the military history of the local area, recruiting ground for the Oxfordshire and Buckinghamshire Light Infantry. Even Roxburgh had recalled memories of keeping in step with the rapid march of the Green Jackets at the Winchester depot. Shortage of officers still handicapped the effectiveness of the training and the signals and pioneers sections had to be discontinued. Captain C.D. Mullineux was awarded the C.C.F. Medal with double clasp for thirty years of service but his record did not appear likely to be equalled. Help came from Old Stoics. One brought a troop from the Queen's Own Mercian Yeomanry to train with cadets and take part in a night exercise. Another arranged a summer camp with the Grenadier Guards in West Germany. The Royal Signals provided full programmes for recruits from Stowe on more than one occasion. R.S.M. Brannam was worth several pressed men and looked after the Shooting Teams in addition to C.C.F. training. The contingent numbered just under 150, about 80 Stoics were at the various stages of the Duke of Edinburgh's Awards and the Venture Wing occupied some 40 fourth formers, 12 sixth formers and 3 masters. The Corps relied heavily upon the N.C.O.s and, while the older prefectorial style was out of fashion, modern times called for more realistic qualities of leadership in genuine situations whether on the crags of the Cairngorms or suspended between naval vessels in mid-Channel.

Compulsory attendance at school matches had ended in Bob Drayson's time and the major sports were played for personal pleasure rather than school prestige, an issue long outflanked by World Cups and Test Series on television. Mike Harris came from Nottinghamshire County Cricket Club as professional, ran regular nets throughout the winter and assisted public relations by coaching groups from preparatory schools at Easter courses. In one season R.S.M. Morris scored four centuries and became the first Stoic to reach 1000 runs in a single season. He was selected as Captain of The Rest at the Public Schools XI Trial at Oxford and subsequently toured the West Indies with a British Universities XI and played for Worcester Second XI. Another record was established by C. Whitmore who took 121 wickets in a season. Northamptonshire brought a team which contained players with first-class experience and were so impressed with recent improvements in the pitch and the attitudes to play that the county sought a regular fixture. A scrummaging machine gave a mechanized dimension to Rugby training and the 1986 season was one of the best for over twenty years. In Athletics the 4 × 100 metres team defeated twenty-six other schools to win the Achilles Relay for the first time since 1967. It was in the 1920s that Dr Vaughan, headmaster of Rugby, had objected to the Achilles Relays at Oxford on the grounds that they would involve additional expense for parents and that public schoolboys were sufficiently spoiled by press attention already! At the same Oxford Meeting in 1987, Stowe intermediate team came second but in virtually the same time as Millfield, a school which had long had a policy of recruiting outstanding athletes. The Buckinghamshire Schools cross-country championships were held at Stowe for the first time in the 1987/8 season. There were 400 competitors and the Stowe VIII won the senior trophy. In the school cross-country competition both Nugent and Stanhope entered girls' teams. In the Under 17 event Simon Montford broke the existing record by three seconds exactly. Golf began to experience more competition as more schools built courses or made arrangements with clubs for mid-week use but the Micklem Trophy came back to Stowe after six annual contests out of seven. The 1985 tournament witnessed three conclusive victories: 4–1, $4\frac{1}{2}$–$\frac{1}{2}$ and 5–0 against Bradfield, Winchester and Eton respectively. This was achieved without the help of the Captain, Charles Rotheroe, who was playing for the Swifts' touring team in the United States. Jeremy Robinson, a very recent member of the school golf team, represented Great Britain in the Walker Cup side at Sunningdale and was top amateur in the order of merit before turning professional. The instinct to go for outside competition remained strong. Croquet had been established as a summer sport and Stowe was one of the first fifteen schools to enter the national championships organized by the Croquet Association. The team reached one final in the mid-80s and lost 2–1 but had beaten Merchant Taylors', Dulwich, St John's Leatherhead, and Oundle *en route.*

As in most other rugger schools the old-style prejudices against soccer relented and there were house and even inter-school matches. On one occasion there was even a soccer match against the Common Room which had dubiously recruited a father who had been a professional player. One could continue to detail the long series without defeat in squash, successful seasons in hockey both in home games and against Dutch clubs, a revival in shooting which brought some good totals at Bisley and the development of 'new' sports such as badminton in the Drayson Hall. Enough has been said to illustrate the headmaster's contention that there was a 'real' Stowe which eluded the press or journalists who descended for single day forays into the public schools. When problems arose they stemmed from the spread of G.C.S.E. and its time-consuming assessments across the summer terms, which hampered sports such as sculling and sailing where travelling and maintenance took up much time, and from the necessity of providing contestants in such a multiplicity of events. The struggles waged by masters to produce teams is exemplified by the story of a Cadet Shooting VIII having to withdraw from a meeting as thirteen Rugby XVs were playing at Radley on the same day. However, these large-scale deployments and the fact that in certain sports substitutes had to be found for those drawn off to the major sports teams gave wider opportunities to represent the school and gain experience of competition. For certain new activities such as clay-pigeon shooting, developed by a parent, Mr Colin Walker, in what had been a derelict area around the Bourbon Tower, there was a waiting list for places on the courses conducted by a local marksman.

It would be difficult and invidious to appraise the contributions made by those presently teaching at Stowe. Losses to the Common Room in the 1980s included Peter Longhurst who left to teach at Papplewick School. As head of Economics he had accepted many students with doubtful qualifications into Side IX and turned them into university entrants. He had represented counties in three different sports – lawn tennis, hockey and table tennis – and played a large part in the successes of Stowe squash and tennis teams. He had been in charge of swimming in the days when training required the clearing of the lake. An oft-quoted achievement had been to take a party of 120 Stoics on a school trip to Brighton and return with 121. Frank Hudson, physicist, had been appointed at short notice from Hawker Siddeley but had established himself as one of the most adept of professional teachers. He had campaigned for the indoor swimming pool and done much to ensure the prowess of the teams which rapidly followed its opening. He possessed a cherished collection of ancient firearms which some Stoics were able to replicate with much skill in the Technology Centre and he succeeded George Clarke as guardian of Stowe's archives. Roger Potter, head of English and housemaster of Grenville, left to become Principal of a London tutorial college. His interest in the Indian sub-continent had first been awakened by Voluntary Service Overseas in Bangladesh. He had initiated the Himalayan Expeditions and been influential in turning the attention of Stoics to humanitarian projects overseas. In the difficult years of the mid-80s his previous training in public relations was employed in presenting a balanced picture of the school and he had played a very full part in maintaining the surge in Stowe drama. His final production was *Julius Caesar* before the Queen's Temple.

Ian Small progressed to Bootham School, York. He and his wife, Alison, had jointly supervised the launch and the initial years of Nugent as a girls' house and both, as actors and vocalists, had taken part in the staff musicals. Ian had helped to found the Venture Wing and the Occasionals cricket team which played the local villages. Alison Small's departure was a loss both to the house and to the History department. Julie Nixon had been the first full-time housemistress of Stanhope. She had done much to formalize and enhance the role of the girls not only by advice but by example, assisting with the Himalayan Expeditions, the Stowe Putter and many other interests in which the girls were prevailed upon to take part. She left to be a housemistress at Headington Girls' School in Oxford having been one of Stowe's most forceful pioneers. Michael Manisty was another master who had come to teaching from a different career, as a submariner in the Royal Navy. Within a short time he had become commander of the C.C.F. but his principal contribution had been in the development of the Computer Centre together with Oliver Ridge, head of Physics. In addition to initiating many into the mysteries of computing, he had used his expertise to reform the Blue Book, the examination entries and the Headmaster's office. To landlocked Stowe he had brought enthusiasm for canoeing, sailing, and canal voyages. Another who led by example, he had joined in the challenging S.A.S. assault course at Cwrt-Gollen. He left to go into the Shell company.

Muir Temple, housemaster of Grafton, head of Modern Languages and to date Stowe's longest-serving second master, generously retired from this last post two terms early in order that the changes of headmaster and second master would not be simultaneous and his successor, Charlie Macdonald, should have time to settle into the work before a new headmaster arrived. A brilliant teacher, musical, and an actor of distinction, he was noted along with Michael Waldman, housemaster of Bruce, for enlivening comments at masters' meetings, and he had a healthy scepticism about the extent to which Governors' experiences in their own lofty spheres were relevant to the subtle workings of a public school. Margaret Temple had been a zealous wardrobe mistress for many of Stowe's increasingly lavish stage productions.

The Common Room was extremely stable in Christopher Turner's final years. Chris Atkinson had given up the housemastership of Walpole in 1987 in order to concentrate on the appeal direction and the further strengthening of links with the Old Stoic constituency. Mike Smith took over Grenville from Roger Potter in 1988 and Guy Scott, Lyttelton in 1987. Other appointments awaited the arrival of a new headmaster.

The years were not without those incidents which make the fabric of public-school life rich and varied. In 1985 a loyal Old Stoic in Canada went to see the film of E.M. Forster's *Passage to India* and noticed that the District Commissioner, 'a thoroughly unpleasant man whose behaviour would bring no credit to Stowe', was wearing an O.S. tie. He was of the opinion that this monstrous slur should be repudiated. Muir Temple suggested that 'a gently reproving letter with a light touch suitable for the bottom right-hand corner of *The Times* letterpage might meet the case, as the headmaster felt that he could not rush into print to suggest that no Old Stoic was ever unpleasant. When it was learned that the film was to have a royal première, however, minds were concentrated wonderfully. It was discovered that celluloid often distorted colours and Stowe might unfairly have to shoulder this burden of guilt. The headmaster finally wrote to his correspondent to affirm that Mr Turton was 'as unlike a Stoic as anyone could possibly be . . . Stoics hardly ever err from being too conventional and cautious. Arrogance and pomposity can always be found among public schoolboys but we have less than our share of these vices.' It was decided that a school founded in 1923 could hardly have furnished India with a District Commissioner at the date in question.

One of the last and most important events of Christopher Turner's time did have the most improbably romantic origins.

Early in 1988 a young man who appears to have had no previous knowledge of Stowe arrived with his family to picnic in the grounds and used the occasion to take a stroll round the temples and gardens. Moved by influences which almost cause one to believe in Wilson Knight's supernatural exhalations from the landscape, he subsequently called upon Dame Jennifer Jenkins, Chairman of the National Trust, and promised a gift of £2,000,000 if the task of restoration could be undertaken on the gigantic scale it deserved. His identity, like that of the Man in the Iron Mask, remains a mystery and a subject of much conjecture. There were already portents in the air of greater involvement with the Trust. In October 1985, H.R.H. the Duke of Gloucester had paid the first royal visit to Stowe that was not purely ceremonial. An architect by profession, he discussed together with representatives of English Heritage the conditions under which grants could be made to carry out the plans of the Landscape Committee already begun with the help of outside agencies. A principal stipulation was that the public should be allowed access to the gardens and house on at least sixty days a year. At about the same time the Water Stratford Avenue, another fine approach to the school, was purchased from the Close-Smith family by the National Trust and leased at a nominal rent to the school.

The unknown benefactor now pressed forward a comprehensive agreement with urgency. The Chairman of the Stowe Governors, Sir James Kennon, the headmaster and the bursar, Brigadier Pulverman, had to ensure freedom for the school to plan future additions and total control over vital school amenities. Complicated leases and sub-leases had to be drawn up and legal costs were high. The need for some kind of regulated subsidy was obvious even if ownership were partly forfeited. The speed of educational changes and the competition between major schools in harsh economic times demanded that the school's income should be concentrated upon teaching needs and equipment. The last appeal on behalf of the park buildings had barely raised sufficient to re-roof the Temple of Concord though appeals for the school itself had gone remarkably well. Along with the agreements signed with the National Trust came a fifteen-year plan of which the second phase would begin in the year AD 2005. Although at the time too little credit was accorded to the labours of schoolboy foresters and gardeners in the past the arrival of professional workers, experts and youth employees launched a major rejuvenation of the estate. A nursery of over 80,000 trees was created and clearing began on the four miles of leaf-mould four feet deep which had silted up the ha-ha. Detective work located some items which had gone missing since the sales of former times. From the original Saxon deities the Goddess of Friday had been taken by Clough Williams-Ellis to Portmeirion and renamed Venus. Tuesday had been re-christened 'Old Father Time' and placed in Anglesey Abbey. Statues of Hercules and Antaeus were traced to the Quadrangle at Middlesex Polytechnic. Sadly, Euphoria and her acolytes were not found and are still being sought. The total cost of the plans came to £10,000,000 and it was anticipated that grants from English Heritage and the Landmark Trust would be forthcoming. Under the auspices of the National Trust Dr John Martin Robinson, Maltravers Herald Extraordinary, published an illustrated volume, *Temples of Delight*, royalties to be used for a gardens appeal.

15

Present and Future

The watershed year 1988/9 rightly marks the concluding point of this history. The Autumn Term contained the centenary of Roxburgh's birth, the Summer Term Christopher Turner's final Speech Day. As the barrage of reminiscence died away the buzz of conjecture could be heard in the land. The advent of the National Trust had cleared away many besetting problems. The G.C.S.E. results were digested and the outlines of the future curriculum were clearer.

In the long-discarded school song dear old Bishop Burroughs of Ripon had referred to 'Temples and Grenvilles, Lords of Stowe'. They were no longer unique. Lord Sainsbury was Chairman of Covent Garden; Lord Quinton Chairman of the British Library; Lord Chorley soon to be Chairman of the National Trust; and Lord Stevens Chairman of Express Newspapers. In diverse fields, A.R. Barrowclough was the Ombudsman; Sir Nicholas Lyell, Solicitor-General; Sir David Croom-Johnson a Lord of Appeal; Sir Nicholas Henderson the Romanes Lecturer at Oxford; C.S. Churcher had world-wide recognition as a geologist. M.A.S.G. Stewart, diver and bomb disposer, held the world record for deep-sea bullion recovery; while A.R. Whitty was a South African wind-surfing champion and came fourth in the International Championships in Australia; Richard Branson was a veritable symbol of youthful entrepreneurial enterprise in the 1980s and held the world record for an Atlantic crossing by balloon. M. Kitto had produced *The Importance of Being Earnest* in Chinese on national television from Peking; R.F. Wraith had fashioned the icon of Thomas Becket which the Archbishop of Canterbury had presented to the Pope; C.B.H. Woolley had won the Sword of Honour at Sandhurst; and C.M. Gayford an International conducting competition in Besançon, to name just a few of Stowe's offspring.

The Roxburgh Centenary Dinner was attended by the Duke of Gloucester. The headmaster aptly recalled the words of Mrs Croom-Johnson to *The Times* of 18 January 1922, when the realization of Montauban's hopes hung in the balance: 'Every school has had to make a beginning and in general it is just those who are pioneers of an educational movement who are most distinguished in after-life.' He was able to cite Stoics who had indeed been pioneers, in aeronautics, surgery, eye surgery, exploration, air traffic safety, care for the incurable and a host of other fields. The horizons of Stowe were broader than ever. The Stoics of 1923 were aware still of many countries from whose bourn not every traveller returned. Now the 16 year old who had arrived with two trout from the Oxford Water on the Turners' first night in Stowe was working at great risk among threatened tribes in New Guinea; David Scott Cowper had just lectured on his solo voyages round the world. The Rugby XV had extended its fixture list to Northern Spain. David Shepherd was employing his talents as an artist on behalf of endangered species in Africa and Lord Cheshire V.C. had spoken as President at the O.S. Dinner of his dreams of a fund to commemorate the war dead and to bring immediate disaster relief across the globe.

The 150 guests and senior staff were addressed by Lord Boyd-Carpenter and Lord Annan both of whom had imbibed more than a little of their headmaster's style. Lord Annan referred to Roxburgh's humour, personal generosity and the warm relations which he enjoyed with parents, as distinct from an older generation of heads who 'regarded parents as an inevitable evil redeemed only by their ability to propagate more boys'. Lord Boyd-Carpenter concluded with a peroration which must have touched even the hardest Establishment heart:

I do not know, none of us know, whether in the mysterious way in which our universe works, there is any way in which somehow, somewhere, some time, he may know that we have assembled tonight to express our gratitude, admiration and affection for him. Those of us who are Christians can think that in some way the system, in a way that we do not understand, may none-theless enable him to know this and to know that, headed by a distinguished member of our Royal House, a large assembly of those whom he served desire to acknowledge his greatness and to say a deep and warm thank-you to him for all he did for Stowe.

The humane qualities which Stowe had embraced during the years of its foundation had never expired. There must have been individual cases of unhappiness and times when more selfish ruling cliques had taken over houses. But Stowe had never suffered from long bouts of institutional harshness and repression which older foundations had endured at certain periods in their history, leaving behind legacies of unchallenged regulations. Nor had it ever been a dull place. Its intake had always been broadly based, occasion-ally even eccentric, and there had throughout been the benefit of the goodnatured companionship which slower and more stolid souls provide for the more mercurial. The civilizing spirit derived from sources wider than the graciousness of its setting. The estate was a product of the Age of Enlightenment when it seemed con-ceivable that reason would drive back superstition and error. But enlightenment has other meanings. Education may be enlightened by being made less burdensome and fusty; light may be brought into the lives of the sick and aged and handicapped; in the darker areas of social disintegration beacons are needed to lighten the paths. The message of the Stowe landscape was not just the graciousness of eighteenth-century life but the countless hours of unpaid toil put in by masters and boys over the years to reverse the processes of decay. The stately pile at its centre, if outwardly domi-nating, also implied leadership and accountability for the welfare of others, a concept which had grown from small beginnings into the many imaginative enterprises of the most recent decades. The clos-ing words of Christopher Turner's last Speech Day address show how far the school had moved from its early reliance on its grace-ful environment to establish the necessary ethos and inspiration for a successful school. 'Those whose fortune is to live here owe to Stowe School a spirit which has mysteriously taken root, a spirit unknown to the rationalists who planned the park and not acknow-ledged by all even now . . . I acknowledge the beauty, but without the School, which has indeed preserved it, without the School which has made this a 'People-place', I would want no part of it.'

This ultimate source of moral support was to be called upon in the last weeks of the Summer Term when, tragically, the Turners' elder and married daughter, Rosalie, was killed in a car accident. A classical education has often been observed to breed the classical virtues and, although the news came as the headmaster was about to address a gathering of preparatory school masters, he finished the evening and spoke to the guests before retiring. Lucia, by her public testimony to the nature of her Christian beliefs in a Chapel service, added to the high regard in which she was held by the Stowe community. Masters such as Charlie Macdonald, who sensed public opinion, were already aware of a strong tide of affection for the Turners and their unwavering adherence to spiritual values in tempestuous times. Many Stoics had come to know the headmaster well not just in the conventional exchanges but in sculling training on the lakes, in shooting practice, in the informal worship at the parish church and in the orchestra. At the final Speech Day concert he was allotted the role of the solitary last violinist in Haydn's 'Farewell Symphony'. This inspired tribute, one feels, must have outweighed many valedictory toasts.

The year 1989 also proved to be the threshold of a deep economic recession. The onus of prophecy is not laid upon the historian but few can doubt that the public schools face times of competition and difficulty which recall the anxieties and retrenchments of the 1930s. There are certain general assets enjoyed by all. Just as the railways brought about the growth of the boarding schools in the nineteenth century so the modern airlines provide the means of attracting clients from the prosperous and ambitious overseas. Public sector education, despite much activity at a bureaucratic level, continues to suffer from all the evils that afflict an overburdened state and a culturally cheapened society. Stowe, itself, has certain assets which are not universally shared. It is a school that has never been able to rest on its name or traditions and it has had experience of going into battle to change circumstances from the days of the Warrington collapse onwards. Its Common Room has long been aware of the importance of public perception and the need to go far beyond the normal calls of duty in the many different sorts of service which the reputation of the school demands. Its administrative machinery provides information for Old Stoics and keeps in touch with a thoroughness that other schools are only beginning to emulate. The processes of modernization in living conditions and amenities have been accomplished during the two previous headmasterships. It is a school which from the start has crossed frontiers and sensed the benefits of exploration.

One of the principal annual events of pre-war Stowe was the triangular athletics match with Lancing and Eton. Stowe's new headmaster, Jeremy Nichols, embodies the triple alliance as a student at Lancing and housemaster at Eton. An accomplished sportsman and coach at both schools and at Cambridge he has brought to Kinloss not only a young and lively family but a vintage Bentley only one year younger than the school. That his zest and energies will do much for Stowe is indubitable and his wide interests cover many of the most enterprising areas of Stowe life. His appointment recalls the early link established when the Old Etonians made the gift of the Grand Avenue as a kind of baptismal offering to the new foundation.

The Grand Avenue itself is something of an allegory of a public school. It rises and falls; it gives an impression of timeless calm but requires constant re-planting and nurture. It directs the gaze to the distant prospect, but firmly rules out any notions of the short-cut. For Stowe it has always been a great corridor witnessing arrivals and departures, a listener to many different sounds: the hooting of the buses which brought the first 'ninety-nine'; the tramping feet of cadets marching to wartime parades in Buckingham; the smooth growls of limousines arriving in fleets for Speech Days and, no doubt, the nervous footfalls of the unpunctual and otherwise punishable hurrying back to 'Stance'. Its perspective conveys the impression that Stowe rests on a lofty eminence. In its first aristocratic incarnation this illusion was to prove a cruel deception; in its second it has been an inspiration. The Avenue also leads outwards into a world where many peaks have been scaled and broad uplands crossed by those who have set out upon it.

INDEX